005.12 Su56o
Sullo, Gary, 1953-
Object engineering :
designing large-scale,
object-oriented systems

WITHDRAWN

DATE DUE

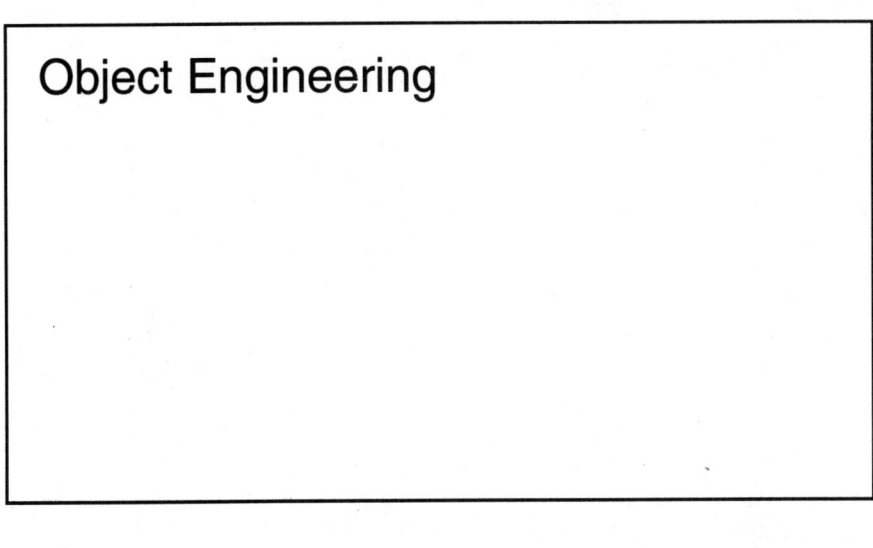
Object Engineering

Object Engineering

Designing Large-Scale, Object-Oriented Systems

Gary C. Sullo

A Wiley–QED Publication

WILEY

JOHN WILEY & SONS, INC.
New York • Chichester • Brisbande • Toronto • Singapore

Designations used by companies to distinguish their products are often claimed as trademarks. In all instances where John Wiley & Sons, Inc. is aware of a claim, the product names appear in initial capital or all capital letters. Readers, however, should contact the appropriate companies for more complete information regarding trademarks and registration.

This text is printed on acid-free paper.

Copyright © 1994   by John Wiley & Sons, Inc.

All rights reserved. Published simultaneously in Canada.

This publication is designed to provide accurate and authoritative information in regard to the subject matter covered. It is sold with the understanding that the publisher is not engaged in rendering legal, accounting, or other professional service. If legal advice or other assistance is required, the services of a competent professional person should be sought.

Reproduction or translation of any part of this work beyond that permitted by sections 107 or 108 of the 1976 United States Copyright Act without the permission of the copyright owner is unlawful. Requests for permission or further information should be addressed to the Permission Department, John Wiley & Sons, Inc.

Library of Congress Cataloging-in-Publication Data:

Sullo, Gary, 1953-
   Object engineering: designing large-scale, object-oriented systems/Gary Sullo.
      p.   cm.
   Includes index.
   ISBN 0-471-62369-5
   1. Object-oriented programming (Computer science)
   2. System design.   I.   Title.
QA76.64.S83   1994
005.1'2—dc20   94-1968
                                                       CIP

Printed in the United States of America

10 9 8 7 6 5 4 3 2 1

Contents

Preface   xix

1   Introduction   1

1.1	The Purpose of the Book		1
	Making Sense of Objects		1
1.2	The Object-Oriented World		2
	1.2.1	What Is Object Engineering?	2
		A Methodology for Object-Oriented Design	2
	1.2.2	What Is Object-Oriented Design?	2
		Looking at Data and Processes	2
	1.2.3	When Do You Need Object Engineering?	3
		Developing Client/Server Systems	3
	1.2.4	What Is a Client/Server System?	3
		Distributed Modules	3
		Large-Scale Systems	4
	1.2.5	What Is the Payoff?	4
		Reusable Software Objects	4
1.3	Software Design as a Discipline		5
	Large-Scale Software Design		5
1.4	The Object-Oriented Design Model		5
	Object-Oriented Terminology		5

v

	1.5	The Object-Engineering Methodology	6
		Object-Oriented Methodology	6

PART I LARGE-SCALE SOFTWARE DESIGN 7

2 Software Engineering 8

	2.1	The Software Engineering Model	8
	2.1.1	The Concepts of Software Engineering	8
	2.2	Development Approaches	10
	2.2.1	What Is Life-Cycle Development?	10
		Software-Engineering Principles	10
		Conventional Models	13
		A Framework for Development	14
	2.2.2	Why Are Life-Cycle Phases Used?	15
		The Transformation of Requirements	15
	2.2.3	How Does This Apply to Objects?	16
		A Similar Framework	16
		Similarities in Approach	17
		Similarities in Techniques	17
	2.3	Design Techniques	18
	2.3.1	What Is Process-Driven Design?	18
		The Concept of Processes	18
		Designing a Program around Processes	19
	2.3.2	What Is Data-Driven Design?	20
		The Concept of Entities	20
		Designing a Program around Entities	21
	2.3.3	What Is Object-Oriented Design?	22
		The Concept of Objects	22
		Designing a Program around Objects	26
		Using Processes and Entities	26

3 Conventional Design 29

	3.1	Conventional Models	29
	3.1.1	What Is the Process-Driven Approach?	29
		The Concept of Process Requirements	29
	3.1.2	What Is the Data-Driven Approach?	30
		The Concept of Data Requirements	30
	3.1.3	When Is Conventional Design Useful?	32
		Process-Intensive Applications	32
		Data-Intensive Applications	32

3.2	A Process-Driven Approach		33
	3.2.1	How Do You Develop a Process-Driven Design?	33
		The Original Approach	33
		The Revised Approach	34
		Process Decomposition	35
	3.2.2	How Do You Decompose Processes?	36
		Identifying Process Functions	36
		Allocating the Processes into Groups	38
		Implementing the Process Groups	39
	3.2.3	When Is an Object Design Process Driven?	40
		The Concept of Encapsulated Objects	40
		The Concept of Operation Decomposition	41
3.3	A Data-Driven Approach		41
	3.3.1	How Do You Develop a Data-Driven Design?	41
		The Business Enterprise	41
		Entity Analysis	43
	3.3.2	How Do You Analyze Data Entities?	44
		Identifying Data Entities	44
		Allocating the Entities into Groups	46
		Implementing the Entity Groups	48
	3.3.3	When Is an Object Design Data Driven?	50
		The Concept of Classified Object	50
		The Concept of Attribute Analysis	50

4 Object-Oriented Design 54

4.1	Object Requirements		54
	The Concept of Object Requirements		54
4.2	The Client/Server Model		57
	4.2.1	What Is a Client/Server Domain?	57
		The Concept of Client Objects	57
		The Concept of Server Objects	59
		The Concept of a Domain	60
	4.2.2	What Are Reusable Components?	61
		A Matter of Perspective	61
		The Concept of Abstraction	62
		The Concept of Inheritance	64
		The Concept of Collaboration	67
4.3	Distributed Applications		69
	4.3.1	What Is Context-Sensitive Referencing?	69

		The Concept of Polymorphism	69
		The Concept of Visibility	70
		Implied Function Calling	71
		Implied Data Referencing	71
	4.3.2	What Is Event-Driven Operation?	72
		The Concept of an Event	72
		Triggering Object Operations	73
		Accessing Object Attributes	74
		Programmed Events	74
		User Events	75
	4.3.3	When Is an Application Distributed?	75
		Client/Server Applications	75
		The Concept of Extensibility	76

5 Object Engineering — 81

| 5.1 | An Object-Oriented Model | 81 |
| | Context-Sensitive Referencing | 81 |

5.2	An Object-Oriented Approach	82
	5.2.1 How Do You Develop an Object-Oriented Design?	82
	The Transformation of Requirements	82
	Objects as Operations and Attributes	84
	5.2.2 When is Object-Oriented Design Recursive?	84
	The Object-Engineering Approach	84
	Reusing Classes in a Domain	85
	Redesigning Objects in a Class	86

5.3	Object-Oriented Techniques	86
	5.3.1 How Do You Identify Object Requirements?	86
	The Class Hierarchies of a Domain	86
	Identifying Inheritance Hierarchies	88
	Identifying Collaboration Hierarchies	88
	5.3.2 How Do You Allocate Object Requirements?	89
	Objects Associated with Classes	89
	Allocating Requirements by Classification	91
	Allocating Requirements by Encapsulation	91
	5.3.3 How Do You Implement Object Requirements?	92
	Individual Object Design	92

			Implementing Object Operations	93
			Implementing Object Attributes	93

PART II OBJECT-ORIENTED TERMINOLOGY 95

6 The Definition of an Object 96

6.1	Objects and Instances			96
	6.1.1	What Is an Object?		96
		A Standardized Representation		96
		A Component of a System		97
		Modularity and Reusability		98
		Packaged Requirements		100
		Operation Characteristics		101
		Attribute Characteristics		101
	6.1.2	What Do Operations Represent?		102
		Process Requirements		102
		Data-Flow Diagrams		102
	6.1.3	What Do Attributes Represent?		103
		Data Requirements		103
		Entity Relationships		103
	6.1.4	What Is an Instance of an Object?		106
		An Array of Identical Objects		106
		The State of an Object		107
6.2	Object Classification			108
	6.2.1	What Is Object Classification?		108
		Common Requirements		108
		Separate Internal Designs		108
	6.2.2	How Is Classification Used?		109
		Similar to Entity Analysis		109
		The Intersection of Requirements		110
		Inheritance Characteristics		111
6.3	Object Encapsulation			112
	6.3.1	What Is Object Encapsulation?		112
		Subordinate Requirements		112
		Well-Defined Interfaces		112
	6.3.2	How Is Encapsulation Used?		113
		Similar to Process Decomposition		113
		The Union of Requirements		114
		Collaboration Characteristics		117

7 The Definition of a Class 119

7.1	Classes and Instances		119
	7.1.1	What Is a Class?	119

		Objects Linked to Hierarchies	119
		A Group of Related Objects	119
		Abstract Classes of Objects	122
		Concrete Classes of Objects	123
	7.1.2	What Is an Instance of a Class?	123
		A Composite Instance of an Object	123
	7.1.3	What Is a Member of a Class?	124
		Subclasses of an Abstract Class	124
		Instances of a Concrete Class	124
7.2	Abstract Classes		124
	7.2.1	What Is an Abstract Class?	124
		The Result of Classification	124
		A Catalog of Common Parts	125
	7.2.2	How Are Abstract Classes Used?	127
		Object-Oriented Representation	127
		The Inheritance Hierarchy	127
7.3	Concrete Classes		128
	7.3.1	What Is a Concrete Class?	128
		The Result of Classification	128
		The Result of Encapsulation	128
		Modules of the Operational Design	129
	7.3.2	How Are Concrete Classes Used?	131
		Conventional Representation	131
		The Collaboration Hierarchy	132

8 The Definition of Inheritance 134

8.1	The Inheritance Hierarchy		134
	8.1.1	What Is Class Inheritance?	134
		An Object-Oriented Hierarchy	134
		Diagrammed Classification	135
		Abstract-Class Interaction	136
		Factoring and Prototyping	137
		Single-Inheritance Hierarchies	138
	8.1.2	What Is Multiple Inheritance?	138
		Multiple-Inheritance Hierarchies	138
		Metaclass Inheritance Hierarchies	140
	8.1.3	What Does Inheritance Represent?	141
		An *Is-a-Kind-of* Relationship	141
		A Pattern of Common Objects	142
		Class Categories in a Domain	144
8.2	Object Visibility		145
	8.2.1	What Is Object Visibility?	145

			Access to Characteristics	145
			Public Characteristics	146
			Private Characteristics	148
		8.2.2	How Is Visibility Used?	148
			The Scope of a Member	148
	8.3	Object Types		149
		8.3.1	What Is Object Typing?	149
			Class Consistency	149
			Data-Attribute Types	150
			Process-Operation Types	150
		8.3.2	How Is Typing Used?	151
			Language Extensions	151
			Strong and Weak Typing	152
			Early and Late Binding	152

9 The Definition of Collaboration   155

	9.1	The Collaboration Hierarchy		155
		9.1.1	What Is Class Collaboration?	155
			A Conventional Hierarchy	155
			Diagrammed Encapsulation	156
			Concrete Class Interaction	157
		9.1.2	What Does Collaboration Represent?	158
			A *Makes-Use-of* Relationship	158
			A Pattern of Object Operation	159
			Module Assemblies in a Domain	160
			Schema Assemblies in a Domain	161
	9.2	Object Requests		162
		9.2.1	What Is a Collaboration Contract?	162
			A Package of Requests	162
			Interobject Relationship	164
		9.2.2	What Is a Collaboration Request?	166
			Interobject Communication	166
			The Request Stimulus	167
			The Request Response	168
		9.2.3	How Are Requests Used?	168
			Hierarchical Encapsulation	168
			Lateral Encapsulation	170

10 The Definition of a Domain   173

	10.1	Object Hierarchies		173
		10.1.1	What Is a Domain?	173

		A Large-Scale Design	173
		Organized Requirements	174
		Inheritance and Collaboration	175
		Classes and Objects	176
		Operations and Attributes	176
	10.1.2	What Is Class Aggregation?	178
		Organization of a Large Domain	178
		An *Is-a-Part-of* Relationship	178
	10.1.3	How Are the Hierarchies Used?	179
		Coding the Inheritance Hierarchy	179
		Coding the Collaboration Hierarchy	181
		Coding the Object Internal Designs	181
		Operational Logic of the Program	182
10.2		The Application Program	182
	10.2.1	How Are Operations Triggered?	182
		Common Subroutine Inheritance	182
		Local Subroutine Collaboration	183
		The Concept of Concurrency	184
	10.2.2	How Are Attributes Accessed?	186
		Common Data Inheritance	186
		Local Data Collaboration	187
		The Concept of Persistence	188

PART III OBJECT-ORIENTED METHODOLOGY 193

11 The Object-Engineering Model 194

11.1		The Model Composition	194
		An Object-Oriented Approach	194
11.2		The Domain Model	196
	11.2.1	What Is a Domain Model?	196
		A Domain Perspective	196
		The Inheritance Diagram	198
		The Collaboration Diagram	198
	11.2.2	How Do You Design a Domain?	199
		Identify Objects in a Domain	199
		The Domain Provides Polymorphism	201
	11.2.3	How Do You Use the Domain?	201
		Inheritance Polymorphism	201
		Collaboration Polymorphism	202
11.3		The Interface Model	202
	11.3.1	What Is an Interface Model?	202

		A Class Perspective	202
		The Class Descriptions	203
		The Object Descriptions	203
		The Request Descriptions	204
	11.3.2	How Do You Design Classes?	205
		Allocate Object Requirements	205
		The Classes Provide Extensibility	206
	11.3.3	How Do You Use the Classses?	207
		Static Source Libraries	207
		Dynamic Link Libraries	208
11.4	The Implementation Model		208
	11.4.1	What Is an Implementation Model?	208
		An Object Perspective	208
		The Operation Descriptions	209
		The Attribute Descriptions	210
	11.4.2	How Do You Design Objects?	210
		Implement Individual Objects	210
		The Objects Provide Source Code	213
	11.4.3	How Do You Use the Objects?	213
		An Object's Range Is Determined by Its Type	213
		An Object's Scope Is Called Its Visibility	214
		An Object's Extent Is Called Its Persistence	214
		Object Instances Depend on Concurrency	215

12 Design at the Domain Layer 217

12.1	Identifying Objects in a Domain		217
	12.1.1	What Does a Design Represent?	217
		The Domain Model	217
	12.1.2	How Do You Start Your Design?	219
		Designing a New Domain	219
		Modifying an Existing Domain	220
12.2	The Inheritance Diagram		221
	12.2.1	How Do You Determine Inheritance?	221
		A Hierarchy of Common Requirements	221
		The Classification of Requirements	223
		Diagram the Inheritance Relationships	224
	12.2.2	How Do You Diagram Inheritance?	225
		Draw the Abstract Classes	225

		Draw the Concrete Classes	226
		Draw the Inheritance Lines	226
	12.2.3	How Do You Organize the Diagrams?	227
		Define Class Categories	227
		Define Utility Classes	227
		Define Metaclasses	228
12.3		The Collaboration Diagram	228
	12.3.1	How Do You Determine Collaboration?	228
		A Hierarchy of Operational Requirements	228
		The Encapsulation of Requirements	230
		Diagram the Collaboration Relationships	232
	12.3.2	How Do You Diagram Collaboration?	233
		Draw the Concrete Classes	233
		Draw the Collaboration Lines	234
	12.3.3	How Do You Nest the Diagrams?	235
		Draw Separate Hardware Diagrams	235
		Draw Separate Software Diagrams	235

13 Design at the Class Layer 237

13.1		Allocating Object Requirements	237
		The Interface Model	237
13.2		The Class Descriptions	239
	13.2.1	How Do You Determine Classes?	239
		The Interaction between Objects	239
		Inheritance Defines Abstract Classes	241
		Encapsulation Defines Collaboration	243
	13.2.2	How Do You Define Classes?	243
		Name the Classes	243
		Identify the Superior Classes	244
		Identify the Contracts	245
		Signify the Concurrency	246
		Signify the Persistence	247
13.3		The Object Descriptions	248
	13.3.1	How Do You Determine Objects?	248
		The Requirements of Objects	248
	13.3.2	How Do You Define Objects?	249
		Name the Objects	249
		Identify the Operations	251
		Identify the Attributes	252
13.4		The Request Descriptions	252

	13.4.1	How Do You Determine Requests?	252
		The Interface of an Object	252
		Request Documentation	254
	13.4.2	How Do You Define a Request?	255
		Name the Requests	255
		List the Stimulus Parameters	256
		List the Response Parameters	257
		Define Request Handling	257

14 Design at the Object Layer   259

14.1		Implementing Individual Objects	259
		The Implementation Model	259
14.2		The Operation Descriptions	262
	14.2.1	How Do You Design Operations?	262
		Examine Process Requirements	262
		Design Public Operations	263
		Describe Private Operations	264
	14.2.2	When Do You Use State-Transition Diagrams?	265
		Complex Public Operations	265
	14.2.3	When Do You Use Data-Flow Diagrams?	266
		Simple Public Operations	266
14.3		The Attribute Descriptions	266
	14.3.1	How Do You Design Attributes?	266
		Examine Data Requirements	266
		Design Public Attributes	267
		Describe Private Attributes	269
	14.3.2	When Do You Use Entity Relationship Diagrams?	269
		Complex Public Attributes	269
	14.3.3	When Do You Use Normalized Data Diagrams?	270
		Simple Public Attributes	270

15 Designing Object Operations   272

15.1		The Operations of an Object	272
		Structured Design of Operations	272
15.2		Process-Driven Design	274
	15.2.1	When Do You Use Process-Driven Design?	274

		Object Operations Are Processes	274
		Designing the Major Operations	275
	15.2.2	How Do You Program the Design?	277
		Object-Oriented Programming Languages	277
		Application Development Environments	278
		Using the Implementation Model	278
		Using the Interface Model	279
		Using the Domain Model	280
15.3	Process-Driven Techniques		280
	15.3.1	How Do You Identify Process Requirements?	280
		The Essential Model	280
	15.3.2	How Do You Allocate Process Requirements?	281
		The Environmental Model	281
		Data-Flow Diagrams	283
		State-Transition Diagrams	284
	15.3.3	How Do You Implement Process Requirements?	285
		The Implementation Model	285
		Process-Structure Charts	287

16 Designing Object Attributes — 289

16.1	The Attributes in an Object		289
16.2	Data-Driven Design		291
	16.2.1	When Do You Use Data-Driven Design?	291
		Object Attributes Are Entities	291
		Designing the Major Attributes	291
	16.2.2	How Do You Design an Object Base?	293
		The Persistence of Objects	293
		Object-Base Management Systems	294
		Passive Object-Base Design	294
		Active Object-Base Design	295
16.3	Data-Driven Techniques		296
	16.3.1	How Do You Identify Data Requirements?	296
		The Information Strategy Plan	296
	16.3.2	How Do You Allocate Data Requirements?	297
		The Business-Area Analysis	297

			Entity-Relationship Diagrams	299
			Process-Sequence Diagrams	300
		16.3.3	How Do You Implement Data Requirements?	300
			The Business-System Design	300
			Data-Structure Diagrams	302

17 Conclusion 304

17.1 Summary 304
17.1.1 How Do You Perform Object Engineering? 304
  Identify Objects in Your Domain 304
  Allocate Requirements to Objects 305
  Implement Individual Object Designs 305
17.1.2 How Is It Different from Conventional Design? 306
  A Model-Based Development Approach 306
  Considering Both Processes and Data 307
17.1.3 How Is It Similar to Conventional Design? 307
  A Life-Cycle Development Framework 307
  Process-Driven Design Techniques 307
  Data-Driven Design Techniques 308

17.2 Future Trends 308
17.2.1 How Will Programming Change? 308
  More Flexible Computer Programs 308
  More Reusable Design Components 309
17.2.2 How Will the Design Process Improve? 310
  A Repository for Object-Oriented Designs 310
  A Formal-Based Model Representation 311
  Support for the Object-Engineering Model 312

Bibliography 313

Index 317

Preface

As a software engineer on real-world projects, like many of you, it seems that I am continually faced with learning new ways of looking at my craft and new ways of applying my skills to build systems and to advise others in doing the same. Structured design was good, and it helped to build better systems (sometimes). Then information engineering was introduced, and it was sometimes better for building other kinds of systems. A lot to learn, but it seemed like this covered it all, and in many ways, it did. What, then, is object-oriented design all about? An object is just another way of looking at a component of a system, like the process modules in structured design or the data entities in information engineering. This is good news. It means that your prior knowledge is useful after all.

Object-oriented programs are said to be easy to use. Very easy. Why then, must their design be so complicated? The answer, of course, is that it doesn't have to be. Surely, something as popular as object-oriented design can be explained without requiring that we totally retrain our professional work force. And that is the purpose of this book—to explain object-oriented design in the context of the things that you already know (which is how we all learn it, anyway) and, as a result, to help you to upgrade your skills with the least amount of pain this time. This shouldn't be the only book that you read on object-oriented design, but it should be one of them.

This book is for those professionals and students of computer science who are familiar with software engineering methodologies and who have been exposed to objects, object languages, and object tools, but who need to have the smoke cleared away. This will include software engineers, programmers, analysts, and systems integrators. The software engineers and systems integrators who will benefit from reading this book are those who are charged with designing, managing, or integrating large scale industrial strength systems using object-oriented technology. The programmers and analysts who will benefit are those charged with carrying out those projects.

Object engineering doesn't rely on any one particular technology, but rather gives you the understanding of how that technology fits into your project. If you are interested in keeping your skills up to date and need to have all of the new terminology put into a more meaningful perspective, then this book is for you. It will :

- Define the terms used in object-oriented design in a clear and concise manner, so as to bring them together in a meaningful way.

- Relate object-oriented design to concepts borrowed from conventional design, which are more familiar to you anyway.

- Lay out an organized model and a corresponding methodology for object-oriented design which is both comprehensive and yet flexible.

- Provide cross references to the many other object-oriented notations, diagrams, and techniques commonly used in the industry.

Object engineering is a methodology for designing large-scale, object-oriented systems. This book explains *the methodology* in a way that eases your transition into the object-oriented world. The book builds on what you already know about system development. Part I reviews the principles of conventional software design as the context for designing objects. Part II then defines the specific components of an object-oriented design within that context. Finally, Part III provides a layered model for developing that design. The book tells a building story from front to back, but you can also skip around from topic to topic without any loss of continuity. It is, therefore, both a training guide and a reference book.

By approaching the topic in this way, the book helps you to understand that object-oriented design is an evolution, rather than a revolution, in software engineering. This is a unique approach to teaching object-oriented design techniques, and yet, results in a model which is still consistent with the many other diagram notations and design methods that you may encounter elsewhere. Whether you are using Booch, Coad/Yourdon, or some other specific set of diagrams and techniques, and whether you favor CORBA, IEEE, Microsoft, or some other set of object standards, the principles of object engineering should help you to move more quickly and to be more effective in the new world of object-oriented design.

Gary C. Sullo

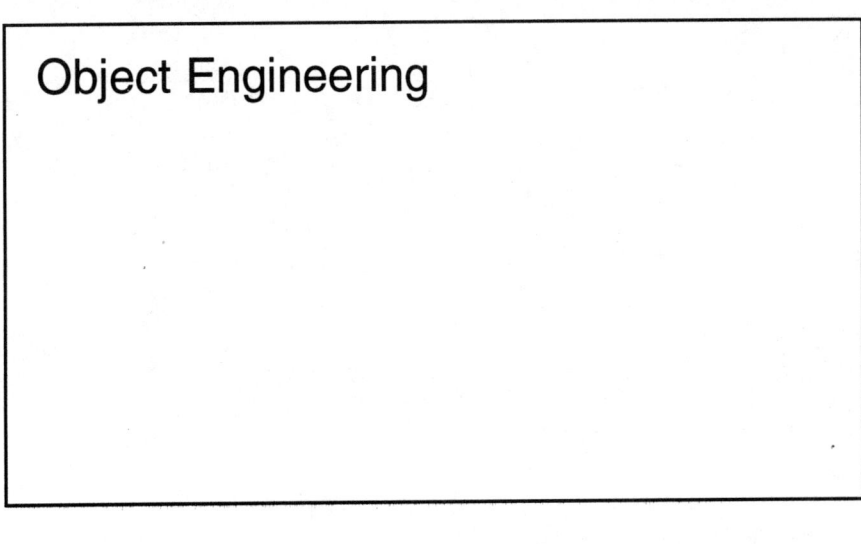

1

Introduction

1.1 THE PURPOSE OF THE BOOK

Making Sense of Objects

The purpose of this book is to introduce and explain object engineering in a way that eases your transition into the object-oriented world by relating it to its predecessors, structured design and information engineering. Object engineering—and the object-oriented design techniques on which it is based—adds value to the process of software development but is not an entirely new and foreign universe. It builds on and makes use of some of the techniques that you already know.

If you compare object-oriented techniques to some of the more conventional techniques which preceded them, you will find that object-oriented design is easier to understand than you may have thought. You will find that many of the "new" techniques are directly related to earlier techniques. This is the foundation of science and engineering: to build on what has gone before. You will find that while object-oriented design is indeed different from the conventional design that you may have done in the past, it is still similar in many respects and relies on some of the same concepts.

1.2 THE OBJECT-ORIENTED WORLD

1.2.1 What Is Object Engineering?

A Methodology for Object-Oriented Design

Object engineering is a methodology for object-oriented design. It is particularly useful in the design of large distributed systems. It is an approach to software development that allows you to determine the application functions required of a system when programming in the object-oriented world. Object-oriented programming is a back-end process in software development. Object-oriented design is the front-end or more conceptual process of design organization that preceeds programing.

Object-oriented techniques are gaining acceptance in the design and programming of software systems. New software languages, complete with compilers and graphically oriented application development environments, have been taking hold of the software industry in the last few years. These languages, and the design techniques that go with them, are more than just a passing novelty—they are becoming the basis for cost-effective programming in the 1990s.

Object engineering is the process in the object-oriented world that corresponds to structured design and information engineering in the procedure-oriented world. Object engineering is the methodology by which object-oriented design techniques are used. Data-flow diagrams and structure charts are the primary tools used in structured design. Cluster matrices and entity relationship diagrams are the primary tools used in information engineering. Similarly, inheritance diagrams and collaboration diagrams are the primary tools used in object engineering. The process of using these tools in object engineering leads to the development of an object-oriented program.

1.2.2 What Is Object-Oriented Design?

Looking at Data and Processes

Object-oriented design and programming is a way of developing a computer program by packaging data variables and process functions into common groups called *objects*. There are computer languages and compilers that are specifically designed for object-oriented programming. Object-oriented design enables the effective use of these languages to develop and maintain object-oriented programs. Object engineering is the organized process of designing an object-oriented program.

As object-oriented programming environments become more powerful and the cost of hardware shifts our attention to distribute platforms, object-oriented programming is becoming the common ground for software development. Object-oriented programming started as a controlled means of designing hard-wired programs for microprocessors called firmware. It then grew into the most popular technique for application programming on personal computers. Now object-oriented programming is becoming the leading contender for the design of complex applications on distributed platforms.

Early uses of object-oriented languages have flourished on personal-computer platforms, on workstations for performing local functions, and on networked platforms for very specific and well-contained applications. For most of these purposes, small object-oriented designs have been sufficient to stand alone without an organized design methodology. An object-oriented design is a physical model of the program you are developing. It corresponds almost directly to the program structure. Indeed, the shorter and less costly development cycle is one of the chief benefits of object-oriented languages.

1.2.3 When Do You Need Object Engineering?
Developing Client/Server Systems

Major systems are moving to distributed platforms and the object-oriented languages used to develop them are becoming more sophisticated. As this continues, the process of designing those systems is changing. Programmers who have moved from COBOL to an object-oriented language such as C++ or ADA will remember their first encounters all too well. Although the process of programming is easier and quicker because the language is more powerful, successful use of the language presumes an additional level of understanding on the programmer's part.

Object-oriented languages are more powerful than procedural languages because they (or rather, their compilers) perform much of what used to be called *variable referencing* and *function calling*. This is performed in a manner transparent to the programmer based on a particular framework inherent in the program's design. However, the programmer needs to understand the framework in order to use it effectively. This framework is called an *object-oriented design*.

To develop a standalone program using an object-oriented language, you need to use the framework of object-oriented design. Object-oriented design then leads you to an object-oriented program. Similarly, to successfully develop large client/server systems in an object-oriented environment, you need to uses a more complete framework. That is where object engineering comes in. Object engineering leads you to an object-oriented design for multiple programs in a client/server system.

1.2.4 What Is a Client/Server System?
Distributed Modules

The *client/server model* of a system is a way of looking at a set of related modules which must interact with each other. In its simplest form, the client/server model is a client module calling upon a server module to perform a function or determine a value. The server then operates parallel to the normal operation of the client and other servers. Any particular module can be a client, a server, or both with respect to its relationship to other modules. A module can be a set of programs, a single program, or a routine within a program.

A client/server model is often used to describe object-oriented programs. In a client/server system, the interfaces and internal features of client and server programs must be well defined, which is the primary focus of an object-oriented design. Therefore, object-oriented programs are particularly well suited to the client/server model and the two concepts are sometimes used interchangeably. However, a client/server system is best thought of as the physical implementation of programs developed from an object-oriented design.

Large-Scale Systems

Object-oriented design is the framework by which a programmer can develop an object-oriented program. In a similar way, object engineering is the framework by which a programmer can use object-oriented design to develop larger, more complex systems. Object engineering leads to and includes the object-oriented design of the programs in a client/server system. The extent to which you use object engineering will be governed by the nature of the application program you are developing, the platform on which it will run, and the timetable under which it is developed.

Object engineering is not always required or appropriate every time you use an object-oriented language to develop a program. Certainly, many well-contained programs have been successfully developed in the object-oriented world without object engineering. Object engineering becomes more important, however, as object-oriented applications become larger and more complex. Object engineering is appropriate in the design of large-scale business and scientific systems, in the design of systems that will run on distributed platforms, and in the design of object-oriented systems that will be developed in phases over time.

1.2.5 What Is the Payoff?

Reusable Software Objects

Object engineering is a controlled process of software development. While it is always beneficial to control software development, the amount of control should be appropriate to its cost. Object engineering reduces the speed which characterizes individual program development in the object-oriented world. This is the cost of control. However, complex client/server systems cannot be developed without some form of object engineering.

Although object engineering takes some preparatory time, the primary benefits of object-oriented development are still retained. The features of context-sensitive variable referencing and context-sensitive function calling are still embedded in the program as standard overhead, thanks to the object-oriented language and its compiler. This makes it easier to reuse modules that have been designed and programmed as objects. Furthermore, object engineering is a compressed form of software development in comparison to the more conventional methodologies of information engineering or structured design. This makes object engineering a more cost-effective approach for developing client/server systems using object-oriented design.

1.3 SOFTWARE DESIGN AS A DISCIPLINE

Large-Scale Software Design

The first part of this book (Chapters 2, 3, 4, and 5) reviews the principles of large-scale software design as the context for object engineering. *Software engineering* is the discipline of developing computer programs and systems by an organized approach. The evolution of software engineering is important, not just as an historical note, but to prepare you to make the transition to the object-oriented world.

The principles of software engineering are the same whether applied to process-driven design, data-driven design, or object-oriented design. The transition into object-oriented design will be made easier when you relate it to the things that you already know. Structure charts and entity relationship diagrams address many of the same concepts that appear in the object-oriented world under different names.

If you are already an expert in the field of software development methodologies you may want to skim these four chapters; but if you are a software engineer or programmer whose exposure to methodologies has always been in support of your other primary duties, you will find these chapters interesting. It's light reading and sets the stage for a detailed discussion of object engineering. It will help you to make some old concepts click and give you an advantage in putting the new concepts into perspective.

1.4 THE OBJECT-ORIENTED DESIGN MODEL

Object-Oriented Terminology

The second part of this book (Chapters 6, 7, 8, 9, and 10) uses the context of software engineering introduced in the prior chapters to define the components of large-scale object-oriented systems. These components demonstrate the terminology used in object-oriented design. The software-engineering context serves as a basis for conveying the principles of object-oriented design and relating it to some of the software design techniques that you already understand.

The terminology of object-oriented design provides you with the complete vocabulary for describing an object-oriented approach to the development of client/server systems. The approach used to develop a system is called its *methodology*. Object engineering is one particular methodology for developing large and complex object-oriented systems.

If you are new to the object-oriented world, or even if you have been working with objects, classes, attributes, and operations for some time, you will want to read these five chapters to see how all these things fit together. It's helpful to have all the terms and concepts defined in one place and in relation to one another. The lack of a cohesive explanation has been the most frustrating part of learning the jargon of the object-oriented world.

1.5 THE OBJECT-ENGINEERING METHODOLOGY

Object-Oriented Methodology

The third and final part of this book (Chapters 11, 12, 13, 14, 15, and 16) uses the terms and principles that were introduced in the previous two parts of the book to define object engineering as a layered approach for software development and a methodology for object-oriented design. These chapters contain the same type of object-oriented discussions and diagrams that you are accustomed to seeing elsewhere, but presented in a context that should be more familiar to you.

The methodology of object-oriented design provides you with an explanation of the process of developing object-oriented systems. This detailed view is consistent with the bulk of the current literature in object-oriented design, but should be more meaningful to you because of the groundwork covered in the prior two parts of the book. You will see that object engineering is flexible. The design of large and complex systems will use the entire model. The design of small individual programs might involve only the detailed portions.

If you are new to the world of object-oriented design and programming, or are frustrated in using object-oriented design and want some guidelines to follow, or even if you have already mastered object-oriented design for individual programs and just want to apply your skills to developing complete client/server systems, these six chapters are for you. With the first two parts of this book as your foundation, you will find that these techniques are neither earth-shattering nor revolutionary but straightforward and understandable.

Part I
LARGE-SCALE SOFTWARE DESIGN

In the next four chapters of this book, the stage is set for understanding object-oriented design by reviewing the context in which it evolved from the more conventional forms of software engineering.

Chapter 2 discusses software engineering as the context for developing large-scale object-oriented systems. Software engineering is the discipline of developing computer programs, and systems. If you understand the goals of software engineering in a general sense, you can easily apply that discipline to any particular type of design process. Object engineering is one particular type of software engineering—one that concentrates of developing object-oriented programs and systems.

Chapter 3 covers conventional design in order to refamiliarize you with the family of software engineering approaches known as structured design and information engineering. A review of the process-driven design techniques of structured design helps to set the state for understanding the concept of operations in object engineering. A review of data-driven design techniques of information engineering helps to set the stage for understanding the concept of attributes in object engineering.

Chapter 4 discusses object-oriented design in terms of the client/server model and the distributed applications in which you are most likely to first encounter it. The concepts of object-oriented design may be new to you, but you will find that operations are based on processes from process-driven design and attributes are based on data entities from data-driven design. Object-oriented design concentrates on the grouping of operations and attributes into classes of objects.

Chapter 5 introduces object engineering as an approach for developing an object-oriented design and relates it to the process-driven and data-driven techniques that are more familiar to you. Object-oriented techniques are, in one sense, the resolution of the competing techniques of process-driven and data-driven design. Operations and attributes are both important to the design of a software system. They are both used to drive an object-oriented design.

2

Software Engineering

2.1 THE SOFTWARE ENGINEERING MODEL

2.1.1 The Concepts of Software Engineering

Object engineering is a form of software engineering that makes use of object-oriented analysis and design techniques to develop programs. Before we get into the detailed process of designing object-oriented programs, there are a few underlying concepts to define. These concepts will be used in later chapters to explain the details of object engineering and to relate those new techniques to some of the techniques you already know.

> **CONCEPT 1**
>
> Software engineering is the discipline of transforming a set of data-processing requirements into a computer program.

Software engineering is the discipline of developing computer programs and systems. A *system* is a collection of programs that work together. The goal of software engineering is to provide a mechanism by which to transform the statement of a requirement into a working system of computer programs. As described in the *Software Methodology*

Catalog of the U.S. Army Center for Software Engineering, this transformation process is usually characterized by a high-level development approach and a detailed set of design techniques.

A *development approach* is a way of managing an effort to develop software: a way of analyzing, planning, or directing a project and conducting operations. An approach suggests ways to identify goals initially and/or suggests, at an abstract level, ways to proceed toward goals. This is a high-level view of software engineering.

A *design technique* is a definite, established, logical, or systematic way to design software where the steps and purposes have been thought out in detail beforehand. A technique guides the user to a predictable result given an appropriate set of starting conditions through the use of a set of notations and a set of techniques. This is a detailed view of software engineering.

This is a two-tiered view of software engineering. An *approach* is concerned with the development of software, including the execution of specific techniques. A *technique* is concerned with the design of software and with the tools to accomplish that design. Therefore, an approach is characterized by the steps and procedures to apply a particular set of techniques and a technique is characterized by the analytical tools used to represent the design through its evolution.

The fundamental difference between approaches and techniques are shown in Figure 2-1. An approach for developing software will contain various techniques for identifying, allocating, and implementing a set of requirements as an organized design. All approaches follow this basic formula, although the specific techniques will vary. Some approaches use process-driven techniques, some use data-driven techniques, and still others use object-oriented techniques.

An approach provides the framework for software engineering. Various authors, such as James Martin, Ed Yourdon, Peter Chen, Chris Gane and Trish Sarson, Tom DeMarco, and Larry Constantine, have each defined specific approaches to software development. Structured design is one approach to software engineering. Information engineering is another approach. We will refer to these as conventional approaches. Object engineering is the development approach presented in this book.

A technique is subordinate to the approach that it supports. However, individual techniques are usually not unique to particular approaches and there is considerable overlap in the applicability of techniques to approaches. Techniques, such as data flow diagramming and entity relationship analysis, are used in similar ways within various different approaches. Each system development approach defines how to develop computer programs by using these and other specific techniques for software design. Object-oriented design is the design technique presented in this book.

Object engineering is an approach for developing object-oriented programs and systems. A development approach provides the framework for

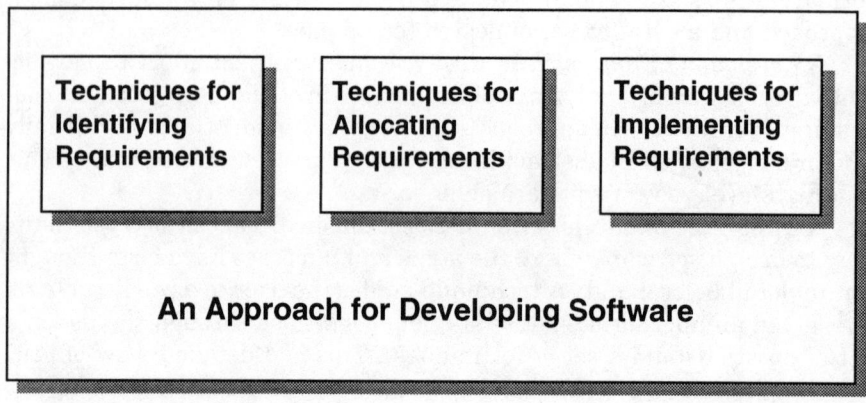

Figure 2-1. Approaches and techniques.

designing the system and is sometimes called a life-cycle approach. This is the context for explaining object engineering. A life-cycle approach is used to show you how to apply object-oriented techniques for the design of large-scale systems.

2.2 DEVELOPMENT APPROACHES
2.2.1 What Is Life-Cycle Development?
Software Engineering Principles

Conventional software development approaches make use of the concept of a software-development life cycle. The development of a large-scale software system, like the development of any complex system, is best performed within an organized and predetermined framework. This framework is usually referred to as its life cycle, and has been represented in a number of different ways. Understanding the life-cycle framework will help you to grasp the process of object engineering in the object-oriented world.

The basic principle of a software life cycle is portrayed in Figure 2-2. In this life cycle, four mutually exclusive phases of the life of a software system are identified. Each phase leads directly to another phase. Since our interest is in the design activities, three design phases and only one operational phase are shown.

In academic discussions, the software life cycle is generally explained in terms of the design of a new software system. You enter the cycle for a new system at the functional design phase, taking the design through its physical and program phases and finally into operation. Eventually, the operational software will need new or modified functionality and this

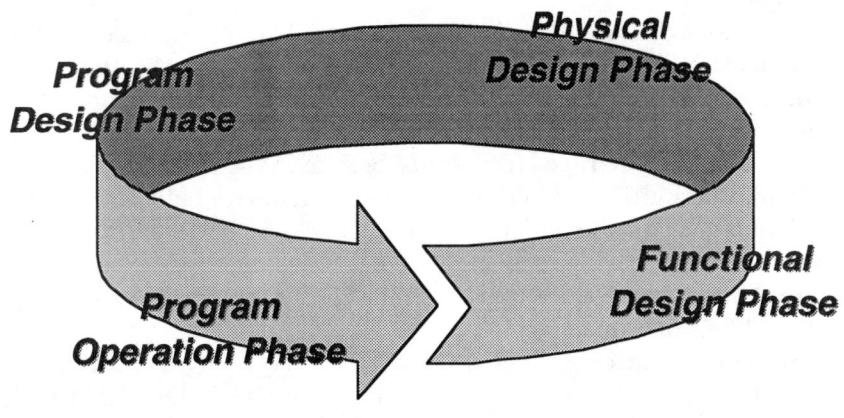

Figure 2-2. The software life cycle.

cycle is then repeated. More often, however, you will encounter the life cycle of a particular software system some time later in this cycle.

In practical usage, you will most often encounter a software life cycle by entering it somewhere other than at the functional design phase. In the pure maintenance mode, you will enter the cycle at the operation phase and move quickly through the functional and physical design phases. In redevelopment projects, you will have some preexisting programs which form the basis for a sightly modified physical design to be programmed and put into operation. You can, therefore, enter the software life cycle at any point.

A specific approach to software development is usually characterized by its life cycle. In the same way that you can enter the software life cycle at any point, you can artificially break the cycle at any point and portray the phases as a series of activities from phase to phase. This is the way in which most software life cycles are portrayed. You can represent all or part of the life cycle in this way, and you can represent the phases in any number of ways.

The development portion of a life cycle is most often represented in one of two ways: as a bar divided into a series of sequential phases from left to right, or as a pyramid of increasing levels of detail from top to bottom. Structured design approaches tend to be based on the bar life cycle, while information engineering approaches tend to be based on the pyramid life cycle. For all practical purposes, however, the pyramid is just a vertical form of the bar life cycle.

Figure 2-3 is an example of the bar form of the software life cycle. The design phases are portrayed from left to right in the diagram. The design steps which guide the activities associated with each phase are listed below them. At the right end of the bar (the end of the design phases) it is implied that the design is complete. In actuality, a completed program design leads into the operation phase, which is not shown on the bar.

In a similar way, Figure 2-4 shows an example of the pyramid form of the software life cycle. The same design phases that were shown in the bar form are now portrayed from top to bottom in the diagram. The pyramid implies a multifaceted design and a detailed base built down from a less detailed peak. For all intents and purposes, however, it still addresses the same fundamental series of activities required to transform a set of requirements from a functional design into a physical design and finally into a program design.

The same principles of the software life cycle apply to both the bar form and the pyramid form. The important aspects of a life cycle are the recursive nature of its cycle and the framework it provides for software development. The differences between the structured design approach, the information engineering approach, and the object engineering approach are only the amount of emphasis which is placed on the recursive nature of the life cycle and the detailed techniques which are used within the life cycle framework.

The life cycle for the development and operation of a software system is analogous to a biological life cycle. It is defined as the full set of activities applicable to the development of the system from initiation (birth), through operation (life), until it reaches obsolescence (death). Both the bar representation and the pyramid representation of the software life cycle, however, can mask its most important feature—its recursive nature. By definition, a cycle is a repetitive process. It folds back on itself, triggering subsequent cycles (reproduction).

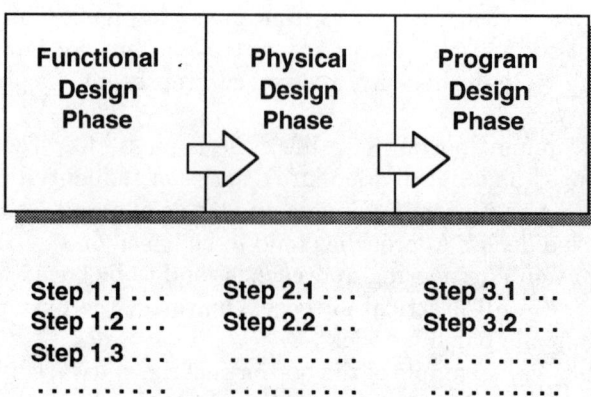

Figure 2-3. The bar form of life cycle.

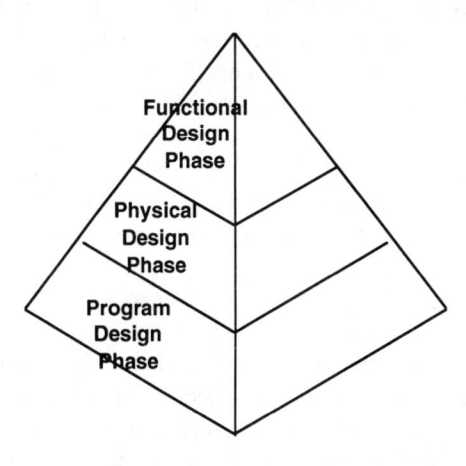

Figure 2-4. The pyramid form of life cycle.

Conventional Models

The *waterfall model*, which usually consists of four or five phases in sequence, is the best example of the bar life cycle. Its recursive nature is not readily apparent, but it does exist. At each phase of the life cycle, you may decide to return to an earlier phase to add more detail or to modify requirements. You might use these new requirements to refine the system, to define subsystems, or to specify entirely new systems that you then design in subsequent cycles of the development process. However, more emphasis is usually placed on the development sequence of the waterfall life cycle rather than on its recursive nature.

The *prototyping model* described by Barry Boehm is a portrayal of a software development life cycle which emphasizes its recursive nature. Rather than a simple bar form of phases, the phases spiral outward to represent the repeated development stages of an ever more complete software system. This concept of repeated cycles can also be applied to the waterfall model, but is often obscured by its portrayal in bar form. The bar form, however, helps to highlight the framework that a life cycle provides.

The framework for a software development life cycle typically includes phases, steps, check points, and deliverables. Each phase is composed of steps which lead to a deliverable. The *deliverable* is a document which serves as the checkpoint upon which the next phase is based. Any life cycle can be either procedural based or model based, depending on where the emphasis is placed by its approach.

In a *procedural-based approach*, the emphasis is placed on the steps to derive the design. Most conventional approaches are procedural based. They focus your attention on the means to arrive at the end design. The means are represented by a rigid set of steps and procedures intended to lead to the design document. This provides a limited view of your requirements and is not always a successful way to design software.

In a *model-based approach*, the emphasis is placed on the documentation of the design. Most object-oriented approaches are model based. They focus your attention on the model itself (the design documents) which can be supported by various alternative steps and procedures as each particular case may warrant. Therefore, many conventional techniques can still be used as a means to support an object-oriented approach.

The development sequence of a software life cycle is usually composed of phases, check points, and design documentation. The phases of the life cycle represent distinct sequential developments of system design. The check points in the life cycle occur at the juncture of the phases. The design documentation is the tangible representation of the program or system at each check point. Just like any other software development approach, object engineering can be portrayed as a life cycle of phases, check points, and design documentation.

A Framework for Development

The phases of a specific software life cycle characterize a particular software development approach. The names of the phases depend on the nature of the software being designed, on the software engineering techniques being used, and on the relative size of the system. Each phase represents a complete specification of one aspect of a system's design, such as its intended functioning, its physical organization, and the program code structure.

The checkpoints are where measures of design quality can be taken. You can measure design quality by examining the appropriate design documentation in comparison to standards and expectations, which is done by surveying the content of the design documentation for internal consistency (*verification*) and by surveying the satisfaction of the users that the system portrayed in the design documentation meets their intent (*validation*).

The design documents are the result of the software development phases. They represent the program design during a particular phase of development. They are the basis for verification, validation, revision, and eventual refinement in subsequent phases. You can use any number or type of design documents for this purpose, so long as they form an interrelated set of specifications corresponding to the life-cycle phases. Design documents can include such things as policy statements, specifications, diagrams, prototypes, and finished programs.

A new cycle of development can be triggered in order to meet the needs reflected in the design documents at any one of the checkpoints. In a structured-design approach, this can occur as the start of a parallel life cycle to develop a subsystem. In an information-engineering approach, this can occur as the subdivision of a business area into multiple business areas. In an object-engineering approach, this can occur in the design of subordinate operations and attributes as entirely new and complete objects.

It is easier to understand object engineering as the approach for object-oriented design when you think of it in terms of previous approaches that you may have used. Much of this book addresses how object engineering differs from other approaches, but for now, let's concentrate on the similarities. Object engineering is still concerned with the transformation of requirements into a working computer program; it still provides you with a framework for designing software; and it still can be thought of in terms of life-cycle development.

2.2.2 Why Are Life-Cycle Phases Used?

The Transformation of Requirements

The life-cycle phases of a conventional approach focus your attention on transforming a set of requirements into a working system of computer programs. The detailed techniques may vary, but the framework for each approach is remarkably similar. Object engineering can also be viewed within a life-cycle framework.

A software development approach is usually represented by its life cycle. The life cycle lays out the framework to transform any set of requirements into a working system of programs: You identify the requirements transform them into an organized physical model, and then transform them into a specific model of the computer program.

As shown in Figure 2-5, the progression between phases in a software life cycle corresponds to the transformation of the requirements for your system. The life cycles for all development approaches serve this same purpose. The names of the phases may vary from approach to approach, but they always satisfy the same development goals:

Development Goals	Development Phases
Identify Requirements	Functional Design
Allocate Requirements	Physical Design
Implement Requirements	Program Design

Functional design identifies the requirements that the program must meet. Various names have been used to describe this phase of development. It may be called *concept development, functional analysis, logical design, essential modeling,* or *strategy planning.* However, the common purpose for developing a functional design by any approach is to focus your attention on the identification of the requirements that your program must satisfy.

Physical design allocates the requirements from the functional design into physical groups as a rough-cut design of the program. Various names

```
┌─────────────┐    ┌─────────────┐    ┌─────────────┐
│ Functional  │ ➡  │  Physical   │ ➡  │   Program   │
│   Design    │    │   Design    │    │   Design    │
│   Phase     │    │   Phase     │    │   Phase     │
└─────────────┘    └─────────────┘    └─────────────┘

  Identified         Allocated         Implemented
 Requirements      Requirements       Requirements
```

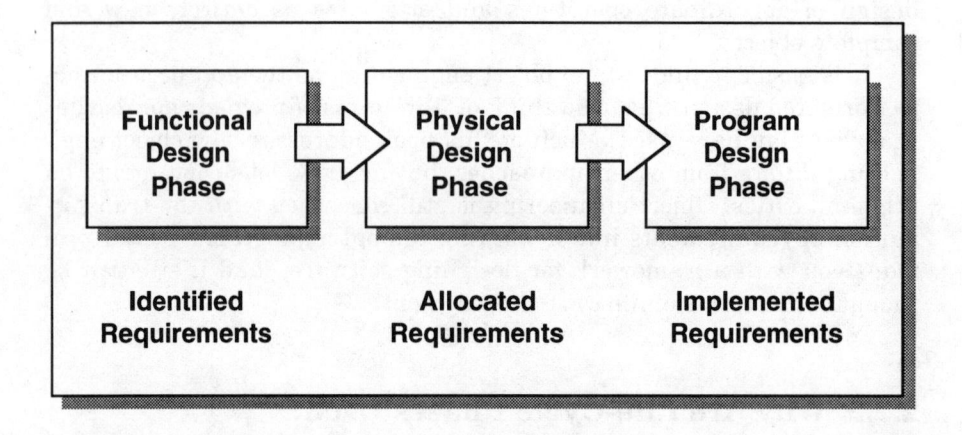

Figure 2-5. Transforming requirements.

have been used to describe this phase of development. It may be called *general design, environmental modeling,* or *business area analysis.* However, the common purpose for developing a physical design using any approach is to focus your attention on allocating the known requirements into some manageable organizational structure such as subroutines or data base schemas.

Program design is the result of transforming the physical design to accommodate characteristics of the implementation environment. Various names have been used to describe this phase of development. It may be called *detailed design, implementation modeling,* or *business system design.* However, the common purpose for developing a program design by any approach is to focus your attention on resolving the technical issues associated with the hardware, the system software, and the programming language.

2.2.3 How Does This Apply to Objects?

A Similar Framework

Object engineering is one particular approach to software development, based on the use of object-oriented design techniques. Object-oriented design is quite different from design using structured design or information engineering. However, it can be approached using the same framework. The goals are the same: to transform a set of requirements into a working computer program.

In object engineering, the transformation of requirements into a program can be viewed using a life-cycle approach, as in structured design or information engineering. The steps to develop an object-oriented design using object engineering correspond to the same generic phases of any life-cycle approach: functional design, physical design, and program design. Of course, object-oriented design has its own set of terms and notation. The names are different, but the concepts are the same.

Similarities in the Approach

In addition to the framework of a life-cycle approach, many of the principles that you use in object engineering are borrowed directly from structured design and information engineering. In particular, object-oriented design is concerned with the identification, allocation, and implementation of operations and attributes. *Operations* bear a remarkable resemblance to *processes* in structured design. Similarly, *attributes* bear a remarkable resemblance to *entities* in information engineering.

Structured design was developed in the 1970s by Ed Yourdon, Tom DeMarco, and Larry Constantine, among others. In addition to the approach called Yourdon Structured Analysis and Design, there are a number of variations still widely used today. These include Gane/Sarson techniques, Ward/Mellor techniques, and even the old HIPO techniques. If you are familiar with some of these approaches, you will see many similarities in the part of object engineering concerned with operation decomposition.

Information engineering was developed in the 1980s by James Martin, among others. In addition to the James Martin model, there are a number of variations used both with manual techniques and within CASE tools. These include the Clive Finklestein model, Jackson techniques, and Chen techniques. If you are familiar with some of these approaches, then you will see a lot of similarities in the part of object engineering concerned with attribute analysis.

Similarities in the Techniques

Each variation of either structured design or information engineering has its own particular detailed techniques and symbology, but they all share a common thread. All approaches within the structured design family rely on process-driven design as their philosophy for transforming a set of requirements into a working computer program. Similarly, the information engineering family relies on data-driven design.

In process-driven design, your attention is focused on transforming a set of process requirements into a program design. The program's requirements are revealed by expanding the process hierarchy. This is called *process decomposition*. Process decomposition reappears in object-oriented design as *object encapsulation*. Process-driven design concepts, therefore, are also useful in object-oriented design.

In data-driven design, your attention is on transforming a set of data requirements into a program design. The program's requirements are revealed by expanding the relationships between data entities. This is called *entity analysis*. Entity analysis reappears in object-oriented design as *object classification*. Data-driven design concepts, therefore, are also useful in object-oriented design.

There are many such similarities between the concepts of object-oriented design and the concepts of either process-driven or data-driven design. The detailed techniques that you use in each type of design overlap quite a bit. This should be no surprise when you realize that object-oriented design is, in many ways, just a more tightly defined combination of the other two design techniques. A look at some of the techniques used in conventional approaches will reveal this.

2.3 DESIGN TECHNIQUES

2.3.1 What Is Process-Driven Design?

The Concept of Processes

Process-driven design is a particular technique for designing software in a top–down manner. You identify the program's processes in order to derive its design. The program's data is identified only as to how it relates to those processes and as a means for identifying more processes. Process-driven design is usually associated with the structured-design approach to software development, but some of the same concepts can be applied to object-oriented design.

As shown in Figure 2-6, a process-driven approach is the transformation of requirements based on a particular set of design techniques at each phase in sequence. The design techniques are process oriented, that is, they focus on process requirements. In particular, the functional design is represented as logical data-flow diagrams, the physical design is represented as physical data flow diagrams, and the program design is represented as physical structure charts.

Process-driven design relies on the decomposition of processes to transform requirements into programs. Process decomposition is the mechanism by which the design is expanded until it is sufficiently detailed for programming. In this way, the set of process requirements becomes a working computer program. You can think of process requirements as the program's operations. A process in a design diagram is an operation in the executable program.

CONCEPT 2

Process requirements represent the eventual operations of the computer program.

CHAPTER 2: SOFTWARE ENGINEERING **19**

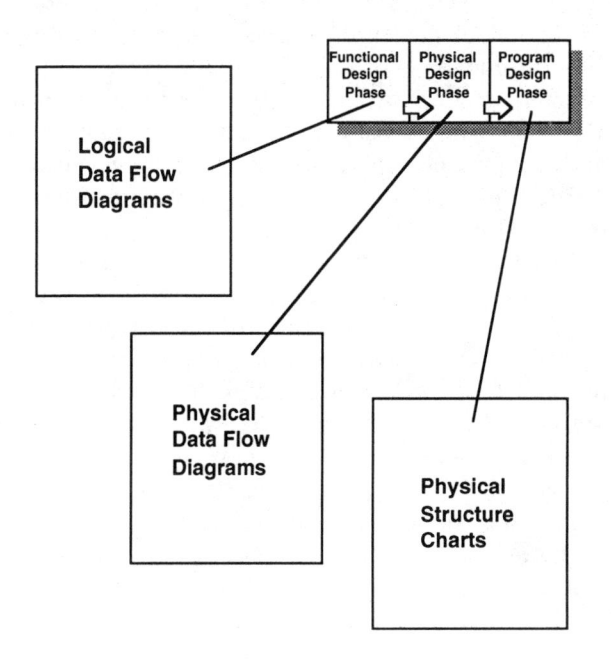

Figure 2-6.   Process-driven design.

The process perspective provides a particular way to determine the requirements of a program and to drive its design. Process-driven design focuses on the decomposition of processes. You decompose each process into ever lower-level processes, while transforming their representation from a functional design (by identifying operations), to a physical design (by allocating operations), and finally to a program design (for implementing operations).

Designing a Program around Processes

You identify the operations in a process-driven design by listing major process functions and then decomposing them hierarchically. The most typical type of functional process hierarchy is a leveled set of data flow diagrams. It is a functional design representing the known requirements as processes on the data-flow diagrams. This results in a complete identification of the required operations, which must then be allocated with in a physical design and implemented by means of a program design.

You allocate operations to process groups by revising the functional design represented in the data-flow diagrams. You move processes into new groups, add new processes, and combine others. The new groupings are determined based on common characteristics of processes such as access to data bases, user screens, or other programs. This results in a revised set of leveled data-flow diagrams, structured along these more physical groupings. It is now a physical design, representing the physical grouping of operations.

You implement the operations by transforming the physical design represented in the revised data-flow diagrams one more time. You move processes into new groups again, this time based on platform considerations such as the capabilities of the computer language in which you will be programming. This revised grouping can be represented using structure charts, state transition diagrams, process-design language, or some combination of these. It is now a program design, representing the revised physical groupings of operations in the way that they need to be organized on a particular hardware/software platform.

The concepts of process-driven design are just as valid in object-oriented design when you are trying to determine the operations required of your objects (functional design), and how to allocate those operations to different classes of objects (physical design). This similarity can be useful in developing an object-oriented design. However, program operations in an object-oriented programming language are implemented differently from a procedural language, and the program design must reflect this.

2.3.2 What Is Data-Driven Design?

The Concept of Entities

Data-driven design is a particular technique for designing software in an outside–in manner. You identify a program's data in order to derive its design. The program's processes are identified only as to how they form relationships among data and as a mechanism for identifying more data. Data-driven design is usually associated with the information engineering approach to software development, but some of the same concepts can be applied to object-oriented design.

As shown in Figure 2-7, a data-driven approach is the transformation of requirements based on a particular set of design techniques at each phase in sequence. The design techniques are data oriented, that is, they focus on data requirements. In particular, the functional design is represented as entity relationship diagrams, the physical design is represented as process sequence diagrams, and the program design is represented as physical structure charts.

CONCEPT 3

Data requirements represent the eventual attributes of the computer program.

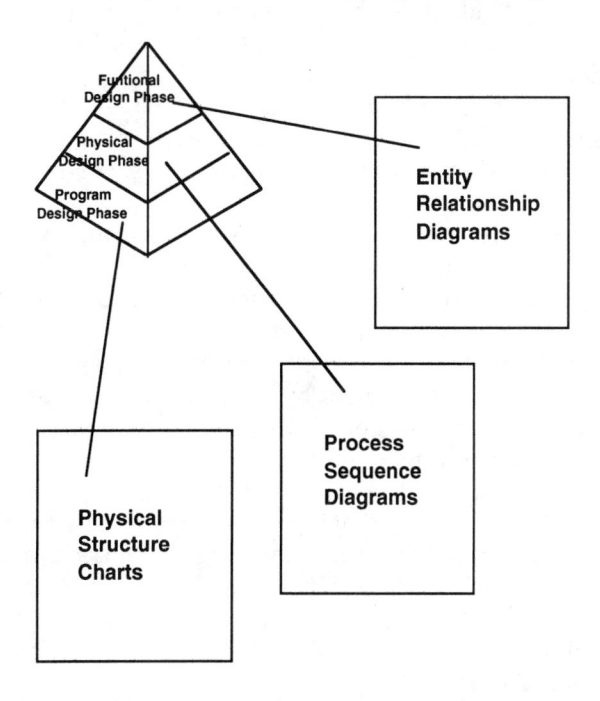

Figure 2-7. Data-driven design.

Data-driven design relies on the expansion of the relationships among data to transform requirements into programs. The data is represented as entities. Entity analysis is the mechanism by which you expand your design until it is sufficiently detailed for programming. In this way, the set of data requirements becomes a working computer program. You can think of data requirements as the program's attributes. An entity in a design diagram is an attribute in the executable program.

The data perspective provides a particular way to determine the requirements of a program and to drive its design. Data-driven design focuses on the expansion of data. You expand data entities by defining ever wider sets of relationships, while also transforming their representation from a functional design (by identifying attributes), to a physical design (by allocating attributes), and, finally, to a program design (for implementing attributes).

Designing a Program around Entities

You identify the attributes in a data-driven design by constructing a comprehensive model of major entities and then elaborating on them. The most typical representation of this model is a complete set of entity-relationship diagrams. It is a functional design, representing the known requirements as the entities on the entity-relationship diagrams. This results in a complete identification of the required attributes, which must then be allocated within a physical design and implemented by means of a program design.

You allocate attributes into process groups by transforming the etity-relationship diagrams into a leveled set of process-sequence diagrams. You identify processes in order to physically accomplish the physical movement of data between data entities. These processes are determined based on additional information regarding the movement of data between entities and the required sequence of this movement. This results in a set of leveled diagrams, structured along the physical movement of data. It is now a physical design, representing attributes in terms of the processes required to sustain them.

You implement the attributes by transforming the physical design represented in the process-sequence diagrams into a more specific form. You move processes into new groups based on platform considerations such as the capabilities of the computer language in which you will be programming. This revised grouping can be represented using process-structure diagrams, data-structure diagrams, state-transition diagrams, or some combination of these. It is now a program design, representing the physical groupings of attributes and their attendant processes in the way that they need to be organized on a particular hardware/software platform.

The concepts of data-driven design are just as valid in object-oriented design when you are trying to determine the attributes required of your objects (functional design), and how to allocate those attributes to different classes of objects (physical design). This similarity can be useful in developing an object-oriented design. However, program attributes in an object-oriented programming language are implemented differently from a procedural language, and the program design must reflect this.

2.3.3 What Is Object-Oriented Design?

The Concept of Objects

Object-oriented design is literally the design of a computer program as an object. An *object* is a meaningful group of operations and attributes. You can think of operations as the processes in a process-driven design. Similarly, you can think of attributes as the entities in a data-driven design. You can think of object-oriented design, then, as the concept of

---

CONCEPT 4

An object is a meaningful group of processes and data.

---

grouping operations (*process modules*) and attributes (*data entities*) to take advantage of the capabilities of object-oriented language compilers.

Object-oriented design has a life-cycle framework which is similar to both process-driven design and data-driven design. As shown in Figure 2-8, you can also view an object-oriented approach as the transformation of requirements through a series of phases. Each phase is a more detailed component of the prior phase. This is, therefore, more a layered approach than a phased approach, but it makes use of many of the same principles of process-driven and data-driven design.

The steps for designing software using either process-driven or data-driven techniques are remarkably similar, particularly in the later phases of design. In each technique, you transform a set of requirements into a working computer program by first identifying those requirements in a functional design, then by allocating them to physical groups in a physical design, and finally, by reorganizing them for implementation in a program design.

Both process-driven and data-driven techniques arrive at program designs which are represented almost identically. In process-driven

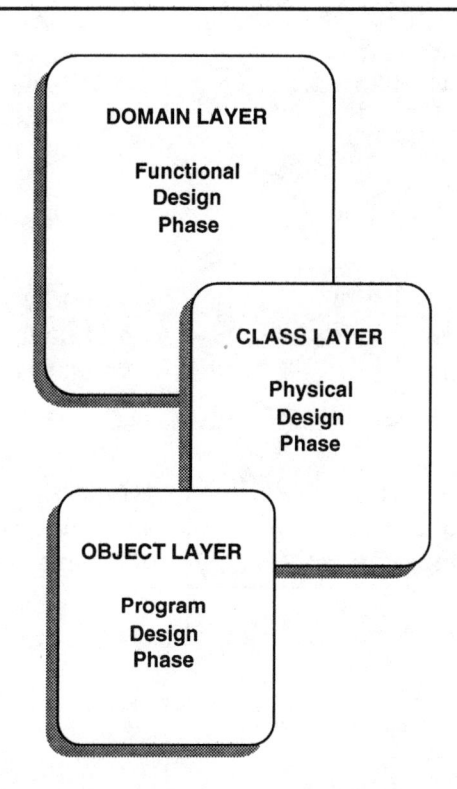

Figure 2-8.   Object-oriented design.

design, you transform functional data-flow diagrams into physical data-flow diagrams, then into structure charts. In data-driven design, you transform entity relationship diagrams into process sequence diagrams, then into structure charts. These techniques converge as you move from functional design to physical design to program design.

Many of the same concepts that you've used to identify, allocate, and

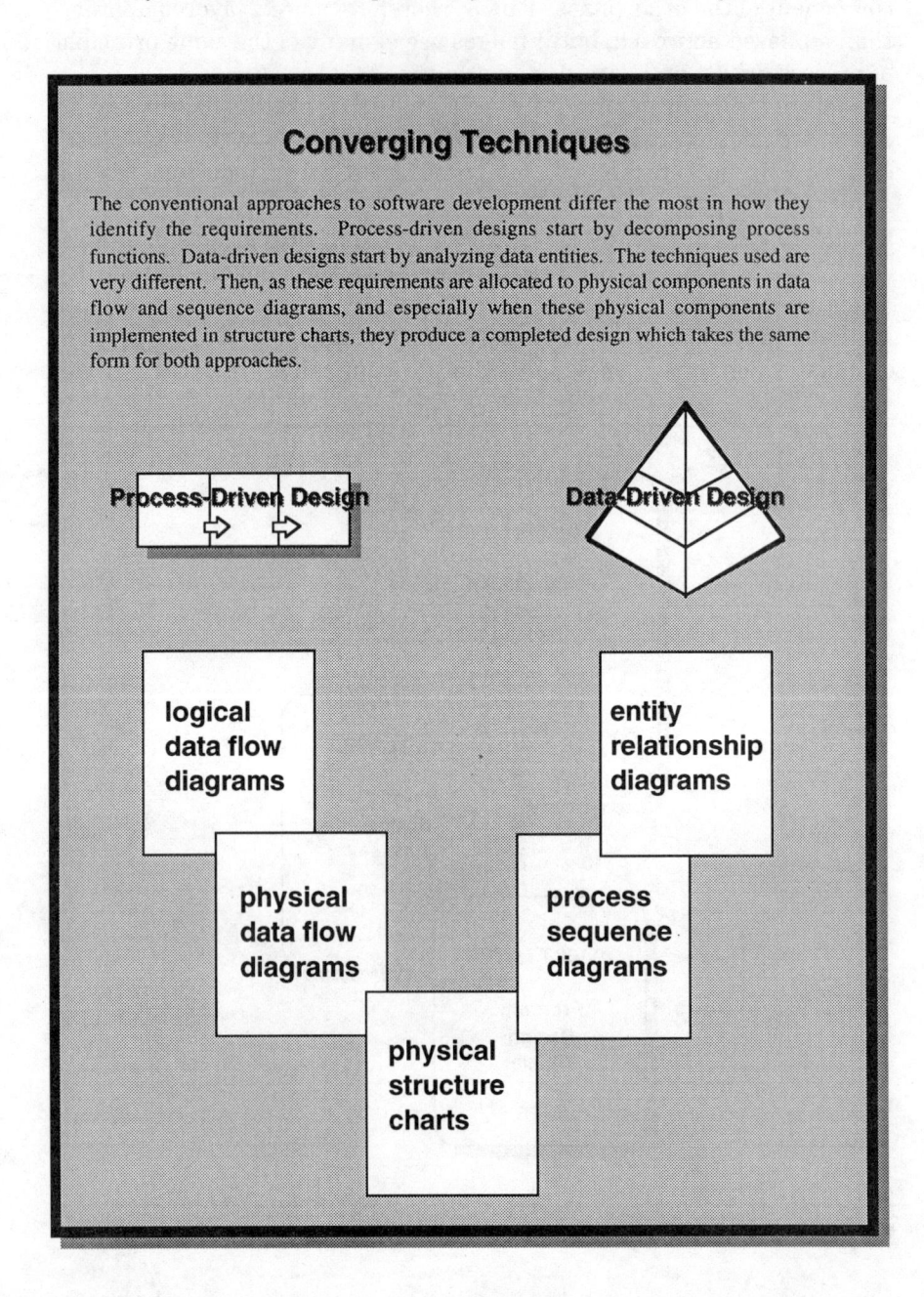

Converging Techniques

The conventional approaches to software development differ the most in how they identify the requirements. Process-driven designs start by decomposing process functions. Data-driven designs start by analyzing data entities. The techniques used are very different. Then, as these requirements are allocated to physical components in data flow and sequence diagrams, and especially when these physical components are implemented in structure charts, they produce a completed design which takes the same form for both approaches.

Process-Driven Design   Data-Driven Design

- logical data flow diagrams
- entity relationship diagrams
- physical data flow diagrams
- process sequence diagrams
- physical structure charts

implement your program's process and data requirements are used again in object-oriented design. Your program design must always have the same two components: processing operations and data attributes. It is only the manner in which you derive operations and attributes, and the amount of overhead burden assumed by the compiler, that differs.

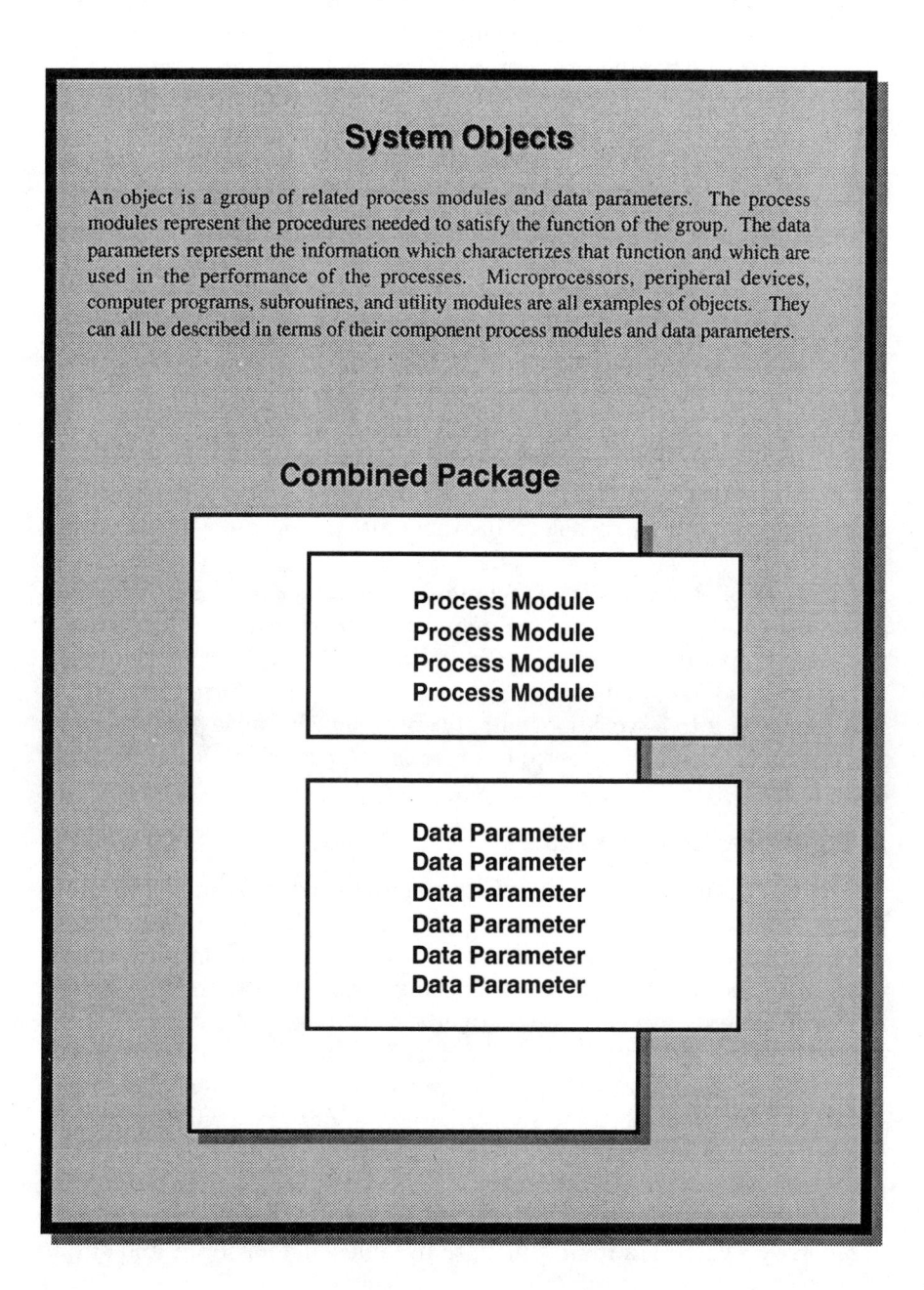

System Objects

An object is a group of related process modules and data parameters. The process modules represent the procedures needed to satisfy the function of the group. The data parameters represent the information which characterizes that function and which are used in the performance of the processes. Microprocessors, peripheral devices, computer programs, subroutines, and utility modules are all examples of objects. They can all be described in terms of their component process modules and data parameters.

Combined Package

Process Module
Process Module
Process Module
Process Module

Data Parameter
Data Parameter
Data Parameter
Data Parameter
Data Parameter
Data Parameter

Designing a Program around Objects

Object-oriented programming languages resolve much of the process referencing and data referencing for you as overhead when your program is compiled. They do this based on a predefined hierarchy of object classes and on the explicitly defined collaborations between objects. Because the referencing logic is absorbed into the program overhead, your source program is simpler and its development is easier.

In an object-oriented programming language, you must define object inheritance and object collaborations as part of your program design. However, once defined, you can reference process operations and data attributes more easily than you would be able to in procedural languages. The compiler will resolve these references based on the program design. This requires more emphasis on defining operations and attributes early in the design cycle. Your design is therefore more physical from the start and its development time is shorter.

Object-oriented design places more emphasis on the physical representation of operations and attributes, but the generic framework to develop the design is still the same. You still start by identifying the functional requirements, which is called *domain design*. You then allocate those requirements by transforming them into physical requirements, which is called *class design*. Finally, you implement those requirements by transforming them into a program, which is called *object design*.

The use of object-oriented techniques produces the same type of program design as conventional techniques: a structural representation of the process operations and the data attributes of the program. Similarly, object-oriented techniques are concerned with transforming a set of requirements into a working computer program. Because your design is more physical from the start, however, the object-oriented development cycle is shorter.

Using Processes and Entities

The only fundamental difference between process-driven and data-driven design is in how requirements are represented. In process-driven design, the requirements are represented by processes, and the data considerations are subordinate to these processing needs. In data-driven design, the requirements are represented by data entities, and the process considerations are subordinate to these data manipulation needs.

Conventional data-driven and process-driven design techniques result in the same representation of program design (structure charts), but with different performance characteristics. By focusing attention on process decomposition during design, a program that is built using process-driven techniques will be efficient in operation, but may be cumbersome when manipulating data in tables and for input and output

(I/O). Similarly, by focusing attention on entity relationships, data-driven techniques may result in a program with efficient I/O but sluggish processing operation.

Both process-driven and data-driven design techniques eventually provide a program design that includes both process requirements and data requirements, but from different perspectives. In object-oriented design, however, you use both a process-based perspective and a data-based perspective to develop your design. Object-oriented design combines the single focus (either process or data) used in conventional

CONCEPT SUMMARY - The Fundamentals

CONCEPT 1. *Software Engineering* is the discipline of transforming a set of data-processing requirements into a computer program.

CONCEPT 2. *Process requirements* represent the eventual operations of the computer program.

CONCEPT 3. *Data requirements* represent the eventual attributes of the computer program.

CONCEPT 4. An *object* is a meaningful group of process requirements and data requirements.

techniques into a single technique with a double focus (process and data).

The detailed techniques for designing a large-scale object-oriented system are presented in the later chapters of this book. You will decompose operations using a concept called encapsulation which is similar to some aspects of process-driven techniques. You will expand and regroup attributes using a concept called classification which is similar to some aspects of data-driven techniques. Object-oriented concepts are just a more tightly defined and combined form of process-driven and data-driven concepts.

CHAPTER REVIEW

Software Engineering

What is life-cycle development? An organized framework to transform requirements into a working computer program.

Why are life-cycle phases used? To describe a series of sequential steps to develop a computer program.

How does this apply to objects? They can also be designed using the framework of life-cycle development.

What is process-driven design? A life-cycle development approach based on discovering and then satisfying the process requirements for a computer program.

What is data-driven design? A life-cycle development approach based on discovering and then satisfying the data requirements for a computer program.

What is object-oriented design? A life-cycle development approach that simulateously considers both process and data requirements by concentrating on the design products in the life cycle rather than the life cycle phases.

3

Conventional Design

3.1 CONVENTIONAL MODELS

3.1.1 What Is the Process-Driven Approach?

The Concept of Process Requirements

Process-driven design is a conventional technique used for software development. It focuses on deriving the process requirements for a program. Process-driven design is particularly suitable for designing scientific application software that will be implemented using procedural programming languages. Scientific applications are process intensive and, therefore, can most easily be represented by a process-driven model.

The concepts of process-driven design provide insight into the design of object-oriented systems. Objects are composed of operations and attributes. Operations can be derived using process-driven design concepts. Structured design is the specific family of approaches for developing computer programs and systems using process-driven design. Structured design was widely used in the 1970s based on the techniques described primarily by Yourdon, DeMarco, and Constantine.

The structured-design model is usually portrayed as a bar form of life-cycle development and a top-down technique of design. The bar form of the life cycle is used as the framework for transforming process requirements into a working computer program through a series of design phases. The specific top-down technique used to transform requirements is called *process decomposition*. Process decomposition is used within each phase of the life cycle to design your program.

> **CONCEPT 5**
>
> Process decomposition is used to determine a program's process requirements as the basis to drive its design. The conventional life cycle framework for applying process decomposition is called structured design.

The phases of structured design provide you with a framework for transforming a set of process requirements into a working computer program. You use process operations to represent the requirements of your program and to drive its design. This approach focuses on the decomposition of process requirements. Within the life-cycle phases, these process requirements are transformed from a functional design to a physical design and, finally, to a program design.

There are many variations of the structured-design approach. Each variation provides you with a slightly different set of design techniques that shifts your attention to a particular aspect of your design. For example, some approaches emphasize the use of state transition diagrams to focus your attention on the discrete events important in a real-time system design. However, structured design uses the same framework for development and the same basic set of process-driven techniques for design.

The structured-design model has a direct bearing on object-oriented design. In particular, the use of processes to represent a program's requirements reappears in object-oriented design. The representation of an object's operations in an object-oriented design is based on the same concept of process decomposition used in the process-driven approach. If you already understand the role of processes in process-driven design, then you will understand the role of operations in an object-oriented design.

3.1.2 What Is the Data-Driven Approach?

The Concept of Data Requirements

Data-driven design is a conventional technique for software development. It focuses on deriving the data requirements for your program. Data-driven design is particularly suited for designing business software applications that will be implemented using procedural programming languages. Business applications are data intensive and, therefore, can most easily be represented by a data-driven model.

The concepts of data-driven design provide insight into the design of object-oriented systems. Objects are composed of attributes and operations. Attributes can be derived using data-driven design concepts. Information engineering is the specific discipline of developing computer programs and systems using data-driven design techniques. Information engineering was widely used in the 1980s based on the techniques described primarily by James Martin.

The information-engineering model is usually shown as a pyramid form of life-cycle development and an outside-in design technique. The pyramid form of the life cycle is used as the framework for transforming your data requirements into a working computer program through a series of design phases. The specific outside-in technique used to

---

CONCEPT 6

Entity analysis is used to determine a program's data requirements as the basis to drive its design. The conventional life cycle framework for applying entity analysis is called information engineering.

---

transform requirements is called *entity analysis*. Entity analysis is used during the early phases of the life cycle to express the data requirements of your program.

The phases of information engineering provide you with a framework for transforming a set of data requirements into a working computer program. You use data attributes to represent the requirements of your program and to drive its design. This approach focuses your attention on the expansion of data entities and their relationships to one another as your program's data requirements. Within the life-cycle phases, you transform these data requirements from a functional design to a physical design, and, finally, to a program design.

During the transformation of requirements into a working computer program, you slowly shift your attention from the data attributes required of your program to the processes required to support them. Information engineering relies very heavily on data representations of your program's requirements during the first two phases of design. This approach differs from structured design, which uses input and output requirements only to start the design cycle.

The information-engineering model has a direct bearing on object-oriented design in the use of data entities to represent a program's requirements. The representation of an object's attributes in an object-oriented design is based on the same concept of entity analysis used in the data-driven design approach. If you understand the role of entities in a data-driven design, you will understand the role of attributes in an object-oriented design.

3.1.3 When Is Conventional Design Useful?

Process-Intensive Applications

Process-driven design is useful when the program or system you are developing is process intensive. All computer programs perform some processes and manipulate some data. However, the characteristics of a particular application usually require more of one than the other. When an application requires more processing than data manipulation, it is said to be *processing intensive*. These are sometimes called *scientific applications*.

The development of scientific software involves the modeling of program processes. Process representations, such as process-design language and flowcharts, are useful in the design of a system's timing and sequence requirements. These types of systems are often programmed in FORTRAN, C, or PASCAL. They include such applications as real-time embedded systems, systems software, device drivers, simulations, military systems, the user-interface portions of terminal-based and personal-computer programs, inventory systems, and statistical programs.

Object-oriented design is different from process-driven design. You complete the details of your design in a manner that is more specific to object-oriented programming languages and define the specific interface requirements of objects as requests and request protocols. However, you define the internal structure of an object with procedural source code. As a result, many scientific applications can be developed as embedded components of an object-oriented design.

Many application programs are both process intensive and data intensive. Their development requires both process-driven and data-driven design. Object-oriented design is suitable for these mixed types of systems. It makes use of both process-driven and data-driven concepts to transform requirements into a working computer program. Operations in object-oriented design have certain process-driven characteristics.

Data-Intensive Applications

Data-driven design is useful when the program or system you are developing is data intensive. All computer programs manipulate some data and perform some processes. However, the characteristics of a particular application usually require more of one than the other. When an application requires more data manipulation than processing, it is said to be *data intensive*. These are sometimes called *business applications*.

The development of business software involves the modeling of its data manipulation needs. Data representations, such as entity relationship diagrams, are useful in the design of the system's data manipulation requirements. These types of systems are often programmed in COBOL and 4th generation languages and often oriented toward data bases. They include such applications as payroll systems, personnel systems, accounting systems, general ledgers, transaction processors, and text editors.

Object-oriented design is different from data-driven design. You complete the details of your design in a manner that is more specific to oject-oriented programming languages. You define the specific interface requirements of objects as requests and request protocols. However, you define the internal state of an object as a set of attributes. As a result, many business applications can be developed as embedded components of an object-oriented design.

Many application programs are both data intensive and process intensive. Their development requires both data-driven as well as process-driven design. Object-oriented design is suitable for these mixed types of systems. It makes use of both data-driven and process-driven concepts to transform requirements into a working computer program. Attributes in object-oriented design have certain data-driven characteristics.

3.2 A PROCESS-DRIVEN APPROACH

3.2.1 How Do You Develop a Process-Driven Design?

The Original Approach

A process-driven approach to software development is one in which you use a program's process requirements to drive its design. You develop software using this approach by identifying process functions, allocating them to physical groups, and then reorganizing the groups for efficient program implementation. You may be familiar with two slightly different approaches to process-driven design, both of which are called structured design.

The early structured-design approach, as explained by Yourdon and DeMarco, lays out the development approach you use to transform your program's requirements through a sequential series of five phases to develop: a current physical model, a current logical model, a new logical model, a new physical model, and a detailed design model. The last three of these models correspond to the phases for identifying, allocating, and implementing requirements:

Development Goals	*Early Structured Design*
Identify Requirements	The New Logical Model
Allocate Requirements	The New Physical Model
Implement Requirements	The Detailed Design Model

When using the early structured-design model, you start by developing two preliminary design representations called a current physical model and a current logical model. You derive the current physical model from descriptions of preexisting automated or manual systems, and then derive the current logical model by transforming the physical model into a more general representation. Finally, you add new requirements to transform the current logical model into the new logical model.

The current physical and current logical models are mechanisms used to identify the requirements which are then represented in the new logical model. For the purposes of our discussion, they can be viewed as part of the new logical model development process. In fact, the burden of developing all of these models just to identify your program's requirements led the proponents of structured design to combine them into a single equivalent called the essential model.

The Revised Approach

The later structured-design approach, as explained by Yourdon and Constantine, lays out the development approach you use to transform your program's requirements through a sequential series of three phases, to develop: an essential model, an environmental model, and an implementation model. These models also correspond to the phases for identifying, allocating, and implementing requirements:

Development Goals	*Later Structured Design*
Identify Requirements	The Essential Model
Allocate Requirements	The Environmental Model
Implement Requirements	The Implementation Model

The primary difference in the later structured-design model from the early model is the manner in which requirements are first identified. Rather than building several transitional forms of the new logical model, the revised approach provides for the development of the essential model. This revised approach makes use of some data-driven design techniques to identify the initial requirements, but it is primarily just a variation of the earlier process-driven model.

The structured design approach to software development is shown in Figure 3-1. As you progress from one design phase to another in this approach, you identify, allocate, and implement your system requirements in a series of models. These models progress from a functional representation (the essential model) to a physical representation (the environmental model) and, finally, to a program representation (the implementation model). For the most part, each model is a further decomposed representation of the processes of the prior model.

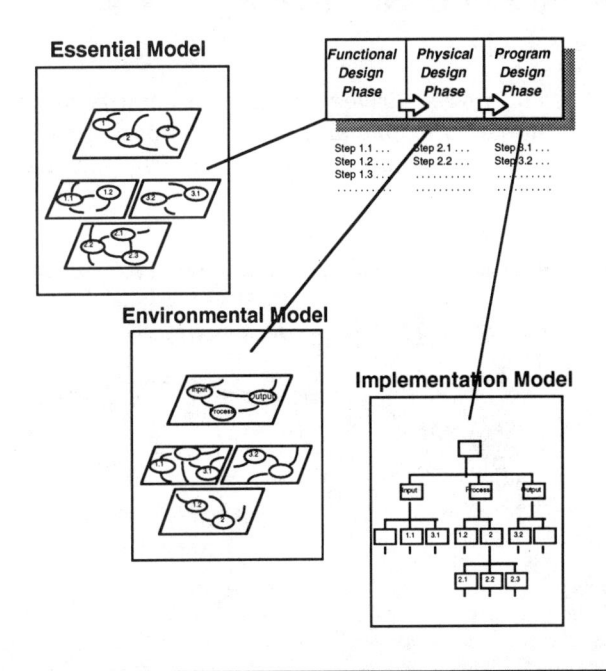

Figure 3-1. The structured design approach.

Process Decomposition

The differences between the early and later structured designs are not significant for our purposes. Both models still provide the same insight into the use of process operations as a means to represent requirements. All process-driven approaches rely on process decomposition as the mechanism you use to identify, allocate, and implement your program's requirements. In object-oriented design, you decompose a program's operations in the same way.

Process decomposition plays an important role in determining the required operation of a program. In process-driven design, the requirements are determined by process decomposition in each phase of the life cycle. In object-oriented design, the requirements are determined by examining the operations and attributes of objects. An operation is very similar to a process. Understanding how to decompose processes will help you to use operations in object-oriented design.

You decompose each process into ever lower-level processes, while also transforming their representation from a functional design (the essential model) to a physical design (the environmental model) and, finally, to a program design (the implementation model). By repeating process decomposition during each phase, you transform program requirements into a working computer program.

3.2.2 How Do You Decompose Processes?

Identifying Process Functions

In the first phase of process-driven design, you identify process requirements by listing major functions and then decomposing them hierarchically. Using the early structured-design approach, you determine the

---

Process Requirements

In process-driven design, you focus your attention on the decomposition of the functions of a system in order to derive its design. Process modules are used to represent the functions which belong to the system. After identifying the set of functions for a system at one level, you then examine each function in turn, and decompose it into the lower set of functions of which it is composed (until you can decompose it no further).

The process modules at any one level interact with one another to accomplish their function. The interactions, called data flows, represent an abstract composite of the data parameters which are needed to support the process modules. However, the design of the data parameters is addressed only after the process modules are fully decomposed.

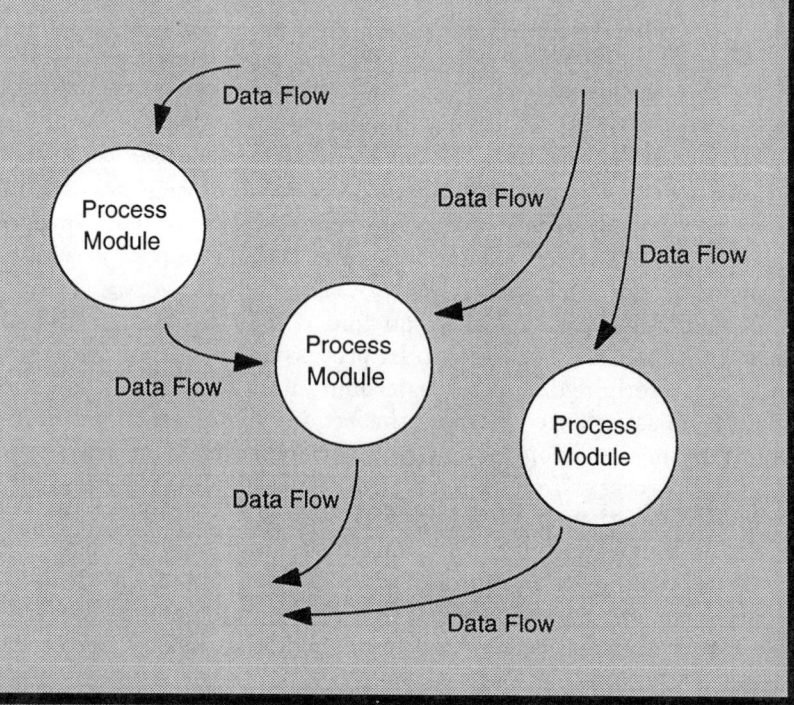

major process functions based on the functions of preexisting programs, systems, and manual procedures. Using the later structured-design approach, you determine the major functions by looking at each input and/or output requirement and then listing the respective process required to support it. In both cases, however, you eventually decompose and represent the process operations in a hierarchical form.

As shown in Figure 3-2, the functional design phase of a process-driven approach identifies process requirements as a leveled set of logical data-flow diagrams called the *essential model*. In the essential model, you decompose each logical process on a high-level diagram into its constituent parts on a lower-level diagram. The process-numbering scheme reflects this decomposition and documents the relationships between processes on different levels.

Individual functional requirements are represented as process bubbles on the data-flow diagrams. The functions of preexisting programs, systems, or manual procedures are easily represented in data-flow diagrams. Similarly, even if you use the input/output requirements as your starting point to determine the functions, they are still portrayed in data-flow diagrams.

The essential model is the functional design. The leveled set of data-flow diagrams represents the known requirements as processes on the

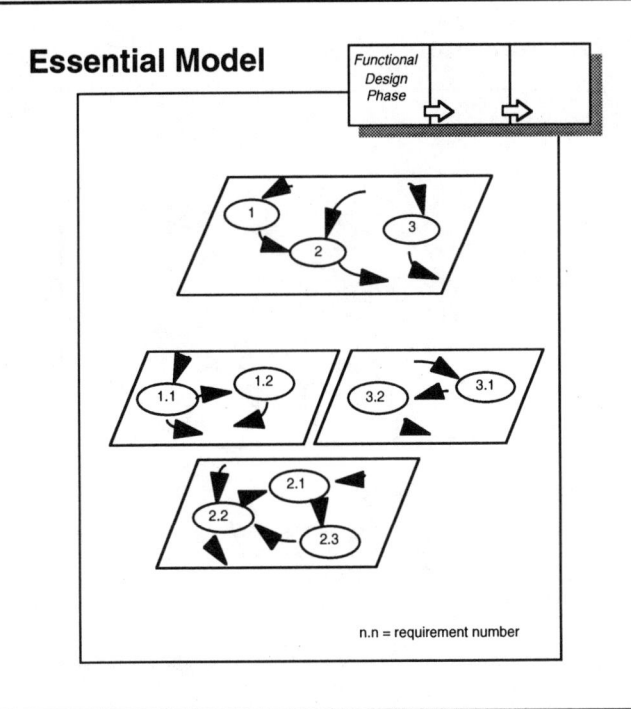

Figure 3-2.   Identified process requirements.

data-flow diagrams. The assembled set of data-flow diagrams at any one level represents one complete picture of all the required functions. These functions are decomposed to clarify their meanings, and the decomposition is repeated until you have sufficient detail. You use process decomposition during this phase to fully identify your program's requirements.

Allocating the Processes into Groups

In the second phase of process-driven design, you allocate the process requirements to groups by revising the functional design represented in the data-flow diagrams. This is primarily an exercise in reorganization. You create new process groups from pieces of the original process groups, although you still represent them in the same diagram form (data-flow diagrams). You move processes into new groups, add new processes, and combine others.

As shown in Figure 3-3, the physical design phase of a process-driven approach allocates process requirements as a leveled set of physical data-flow diagrams called the *environmental model*. In the environmental model, you retain many of the same lower-level processes, but rearrange them into different, more physical, groups. In this example, we have regrouped some of the processes (numbered 1.1 and 3.1) as

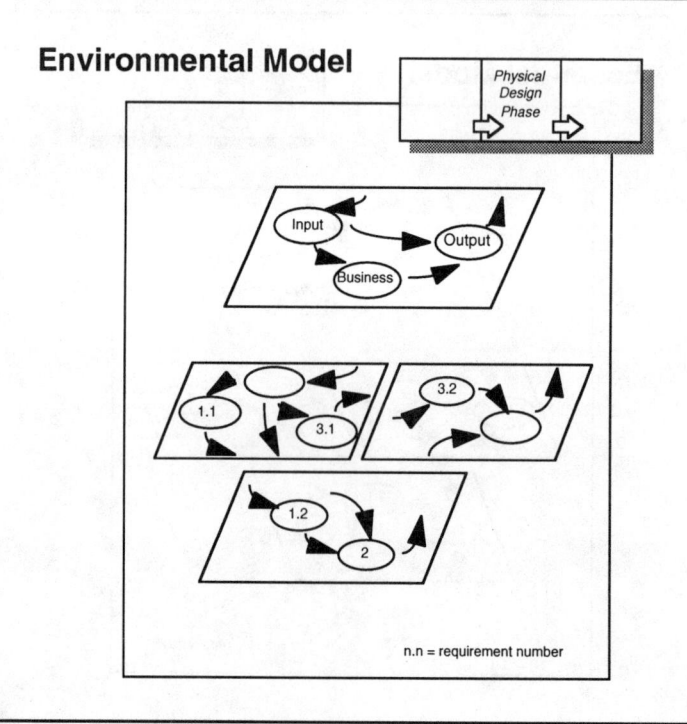

Figure 3-3. Allocated process requirements.

input functions, some (numbered 1.2 and 2) as standard process functions, and some (numbered 3.2) as output functions to show one typical type of regrouping.

You determine the new groupings based on common characteristics of processes such as access to data bases, user screens, or other programs. Often, you regroup processes both within a single level as well as from several different levels. However, the lower-level processes that are subordinate to the processes you group together will remain subordinate and will be carried along into the new group.

The environmental model is the physical design. You transform your requirements by regrouping the functional data-flow diagrams into physical groupings. Think of this transformation as merely pulling apart the functional design and reassembling it as a physical design. You use process decomposition during this phase of design to fully represent the physical allocation of your program's requirements.

Implementing the Process Groups

In the third phase of process-driven design, you define how to implement the process groups in your program by transforming the physical design one more time—a more difficult transformation. The physical design is represented in one form (usually data-flow diagrams), while the program design will be represented in another (usually structure charts). The structure charts start out as a side view of the data flow diagrams, but can evolve into a completely different structure.

As shown in Figure 3-4, the program design phase of a process-driven approach implements process requirements as a physical structure chart called the *implementation model*. In the implementation model, you draw a side view of your physical data-flow diagrams. Note that in this example, the same numbered lower-level processes are grouped under the input functions, business functions, and output functions. This model is then used to further decompose your processes and to further regroup them into your final design.

You move processes into new groups based on platform considerations such as the capabilities of the computer language in which you will be programming. You can use various techniques, such as transaction analysis or transformation analysis, to determine these new groups. The objective of these techniques is to identify the commonalty between otherwise separate processes as the criteria for new groups.

The implementation model is the program design. It can be represented using structure charts, state transition diagrams, process-design language, or some combination of these. These charts often bear little resemblance to the previous set of data-flow diagrams, partially because the processes have been regrouped, but primarily because so many new and detailed processes have been added. You use process decomposition during this phase of design to group requirements into a program design organized for implementation on a particular hardware/software platform.

Implementation Model

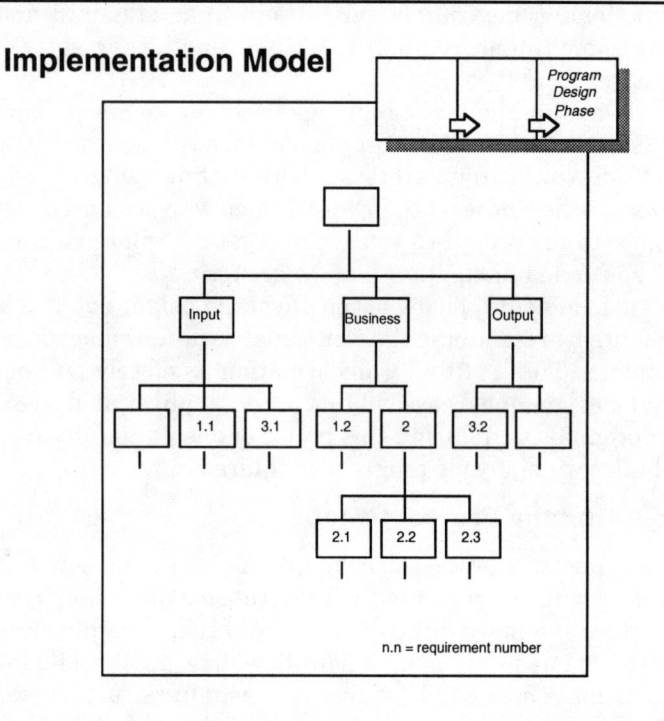

[Diagram showing hierarchical tree with Input, Business, Output branches, containing nodes 1.1, 3.1, 1.2, 2, 3.2, and sub-nodes 2.1, 2.2, 2.3; labeled with "Program Design Phase" and "n.n = requirement number"]

Figure 3-4. Implemented process requirements.

3.2.3 When Is an Object Design Process Driven?
The Concept of Encapsulated Objects

The concepts of process-driven design are just as valid in object-oriented design when you determine the operations required of your objects, and when you allocate those operations to different classes of objects. You identify object operations by decomposing known functions into a complete set. You then allocate them into physical groups called objects, which can be made up of other objects, particularly, other objects with which they collaborate. This concept is called *encapsulation*, and is very similar to process decomposition.

CONCEPT 7

An object contained within another object is said to be encapsulated.

In encapsulation, you define lower-level object operations as encapsulated subroutines with well-defined interfaces. You then design these subroutines as additional independent objects, and/or design the internal workings of an object's operations using structure charts. Many object-oriented design concepts are borrowed from process-driven design. Object-oriented design, however, places more emphasis on the concept of encapsulation and its representation as object collaborations.

The Concept of Operation Decomposition

Object-oriented design is process driven in the derivation of operations, but not in their representation. You conceptually decompose object operations to further define their function. In doing so, you identify more individual lower-level operations. However, rather than representing the operations in data-flow diagrams, an object-oriented model of functions is presented as lists of operations and attributes.

CONCEPT 8

Operation decomposition is the distribution of a list of subordinate operations across a set of encapsulated objects.

Object-oriented design is also process driven in the organization of operations. You group operations as subordinate structures within objects. You represent the subordinate relationships between objects in collaboration diagrams, which are not as complex as data-flow diagrams, but still represent the same type of physical design that is required to allocate the original process operations into groups.

This similarity can be useful in the early steps of object-oriented design. You follow a specific set of steps to identify requirements. The requirements are partially expressed as operations, which are similar to processes. You then allocate them into physical groups called objects. You use collaboration diagrams to represent the same type of physical design as a leveled set of data-flow diagrams represents but in a much more readable and understandable form.

3.3 A DATA-DRIVEN APPROACH

3.3.1 How Do You Develop a Data-Driven Design?

The Business Enterprise

A data-driven approach to software development is one in which you use a program's data requirements to drive its design. You develop software using this approach by identifying the data entities used in a business enterprise, allocating those entities into physical groups, and then reorganizing those groups for efficient programming implementation.

Information engineering, as explained by James Martin, lays out the development approach used to transform your program's requirements through a sequential series of four phases, specifically: planning,

Process Modules

Process-driven design leads you to an organized set of process modules. Each of the modules performs its function, in part, by calling other process modules as lower level functions. This results in a process structure that characterizes the system design. The data aspects in a process-driven design are then derived to support this process structure.

Process Package

analsis, design, and construction. The first three of these phases correspond to the phases for identifying, allocating, and implementing requirements.

Development Goals	Information Engineering
Identify Requirements	The Information Strategy Plan
Allocate Requirements	The Business Area Analysis
Implement Requirements	The Business System Design

In information engineering, you start by examining business information needs in terms of organizations, goals, business functions, and data subjects. In particular, you list and compare business functions and data subjects to model your requirements. This gives you an enterprisewide perspective on the systems (business functions) and entities (data subjects) needed, and a way to represent this in a comprehensive information model which can be transformed into a complete program design.

The information engineering approach to software development is shown in Figure 3-5. As you progress from one design phase to another in this approach, you identify, allocate, and implement system requirements in a series of models. These models progress from a functional representation (the information strategy plan) to a physical representation (the business area analysis) and, finally, to a program representation (the business system design). For the most part, each model is a further analysis of the entities represented in the prior model.

Entity Analysis

The information-engineering model provides insight into the use of data attributes as a means to represent requirements. Entity analysis is the primary way in which you derive and represent data attributes. Data-driven approaches rely on entity analysis as the mechanism used to identify, allocate, and implement your program's requirements. In object-oriented design, you expand on a program's attributes in the same way.

Entity analysis plays an important role in determining the required attributes of a program. In data-driven design, the requirements are determined by entity analysis in each phase of the life cycle. In object-oriented design, the requirements are determined by examining the attributes and operations of objects. An attribute is very similar to an entity. Understanding how to analyze entities in a data-driven design will help you to use attributes in object-oriented design.

You analyze entities by examining the data needs of your program during each phase of its design. You identify requirements by listing data entities and process functions in your business enterprise, and then allocating those requirements by grouping them according to their read/write relationships to each other. Finally, you implement the requirements by deriving the detailed processing needed to manipulate the data entities within those groups.

44   OBJECT ENGINEERING

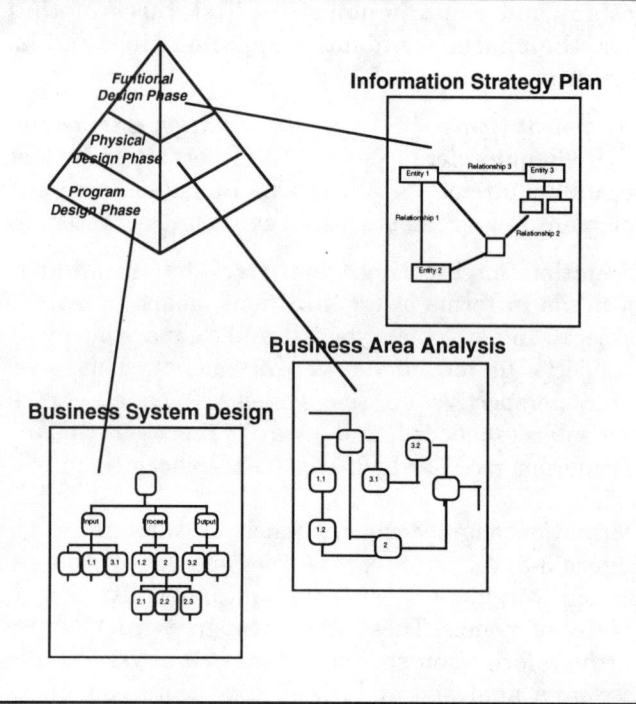

Figure 3-5.   The information engineering approach.

3.3.2   How Do You Analyze Data Entities?

Identifying Data Entities

In the first phase of data-driven design, you identify data entities in a comprehensive model of the major information needs of your enterprise by preparing lists of business functions and data subjects. You decompose business functions by further listing the processes needed to support them, and decompose data subjects by further listing the data entities which they need to contain. You then determine business areas by relating processes to data entities in matrices and by clustering the matrices' rows and columns

Eventually, you derive a complete set of entity relationship diagrams from the lists of requirements and the matrices. The matrices show the business processes and the data entities in clustered groups. Each such group of entities represents a business area of your enterprise. You use the entities in a business area to draw a complete set of entity relationship diagrams. These diagrams and the supporting matrices form the starting point of a data-driven approach.

As shown in Figure 3-6, the functional design phase of a data-driven approach identifies data requirements in terms of the entity relationship diagram, of an *information strategy plan*. In the information strategy plan, you assess the needs of your system as the data entities which characterize it, and as the relationships between these entities. You use this model to explore the data requirements of your system by analyzing the entities on the diagram.

The information strategy plan is the functional design. The entity relationship diagrams represent the known requirements as entities on the

---

Data Requirements

In data-driven design, you focus your attention on the entities which characterize a system in order to derive its design. Data parameters are represented as entities that belong to the system. After identifying a set of entities for one aspect of a system, you then expand the design by examining the relationships between entities in order to identify additional entities needed to support those relationships (until you can expand it no further).

The data parameters, called entities, have various relationships with one another which amplify the requirements of the system. The relationships represent an abstract composite of the process modules which are needed to support the data parameters. Some relationships show how one entity uses another. Other relationships show how an entity is composed of several others. The processes of the system will support these relationships. However, the design of the process modules is addressed only after the set of data parameters is fully expanded.

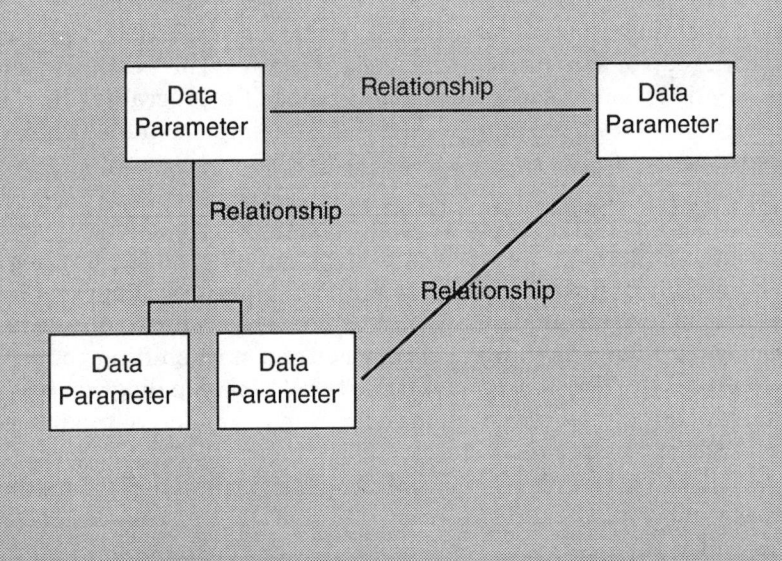

```
    ┌──────────┐   Relationship   ┌──────────┐
    │   Data   │──────────────────│   Data   │
    │ Parameter│                  │ Parameter│
    └────┬─────┘                  └──────────┘
         │                           ╱
    Relationship                    ╱
         │                    Relationship
    ┌────┴────┬──────────┐       ╱
    │  Data   │   Data   │      ╱
    │Parameter│ Parameter│     ╱
    └─────────┴──────────┘
```

46 OBJECT ENGINEERING

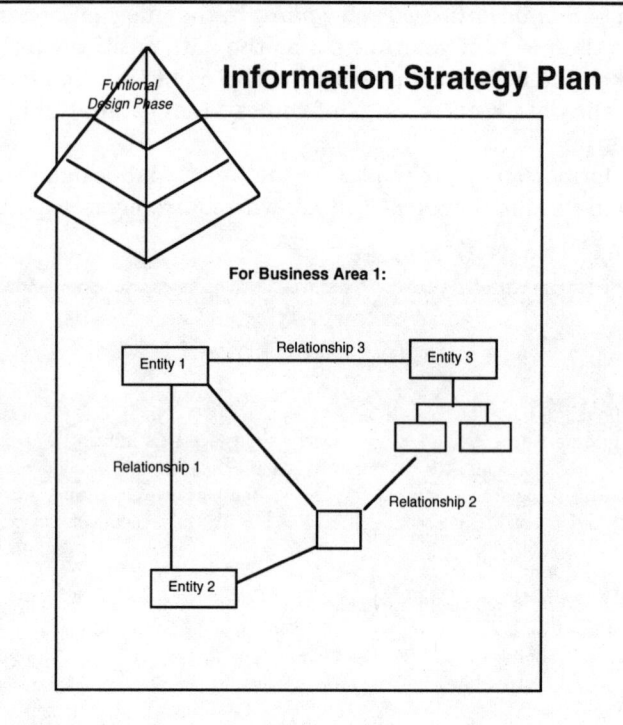

Figure 3-6. Identified data requirements.

entity relationship diagrams. Entity analysis is the process of subdividing and grouping data in order to arrive at this diagram. You redraw portions of the diagrams to show all the relationships around a particular entity or group of entities, called its *neighborhood*. This results in a complete identification of the required attributes of a program, which then must be allocated within a physical design and implemented by means of a program design.

Allocating the Entities into Groups

In the second phase of data-driven design, you allocate the entities into process groups by transforming the entity relationship diagrams into a leveled set of process-sequence diagrams. Process-sequence diagrams are primarily data-flow diagrams. This is when you start shifting your attention to processes. Each entity on an entity relationship diagram becomes a data store on the process-sequence diagrams. You derive the processes in order to support the data stores.

As shown in Figure 3-7, the physical design phase of a data-driven approach allocates data requirements as a set of process-sequence diagrams called the *business area analysis*. In the business area analysis, you use the entities from the prior model to examine and then draw

Business Area Analysis

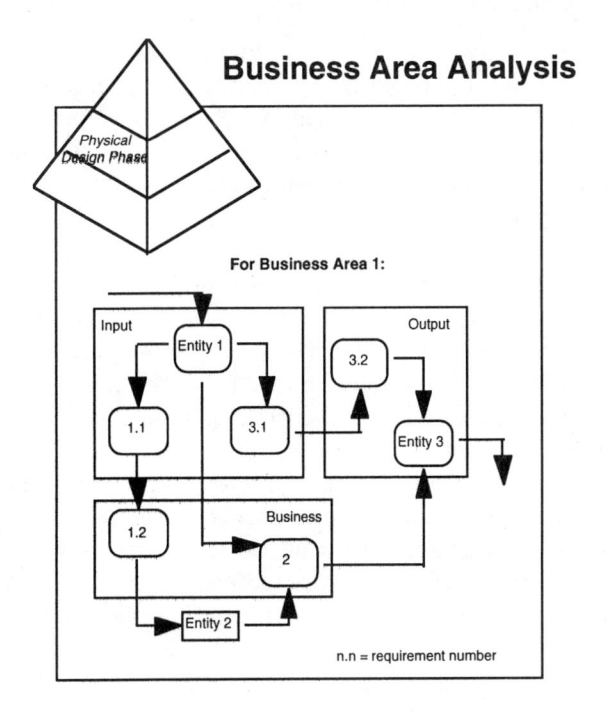

[Diagram: Pyramid showing Physical Design Phase at top, with business area analysis below showing For Business Area 1: Input box containing Entity 1, 1.1, 3.1; Output box containing 3.2, Entity 3; Business box containing 1.2, 2, Entity 2. n.n = requirement number]

Figure 3-7. Allocated data requirements.

the process sequences needed to support them. The process sequences are often derived by looking at the relationships among the entities. In this example, the entities and their supporting processes are grouped as input, business, and output functions to show that this representation is somewhat similar to a physical data-flow diagram from process-driven design.

You identify process sequences in order to physically accomplish the actual movement of data among data entities. You determine these processes based on additional information regarding the movement of data between entities and the required sequence of this movement. The process-sequence diagrams for each business area look quite similar to a leveled set of data-flow diagrams in the environmental model of structured design.

The business area analysis is the physical design. In the same way that data stores represent entities, groups of processes among entities represent relationships. This leveled set of diagrams is structured along the physical movement of data. Groups of processes correspond to neighborhoods in a set of entity relationship diagrams. The process-sequence diagrams still represent the required attributes of a program, but now in terms of the processes required to sustain them.

Implementing the Entity Groups

In the third phase of data-driven design, you define how you will implement the entity groups in your program by transforming the physical design represented in the process-sequence diagrams into process-structure diagrams. Process-structure diagrams look like, and serve the same purpose as, structure charts in the implementation model of process-driven design. Your data-driven design now looks exactly like its equivalent process-driven design.

As shown in Figure 3-8, the program design phase of a data-driven approach implements data requirements as a physical-structure chart called the *business system design*. The business system design servers the same purpose as the implementation model in a process-driven design, and looks remarkably similar. It is primarily a side view of the hierarchy implied on a process-sequence diagram.

You derive process structure diagrams in a similar manner to structure charts. You move processes into new groups based on platform considerations such as the capabilities of the computer language in which you will be programming. Supporting information can be represented using data-structure diagrams or state-transition diagrams.

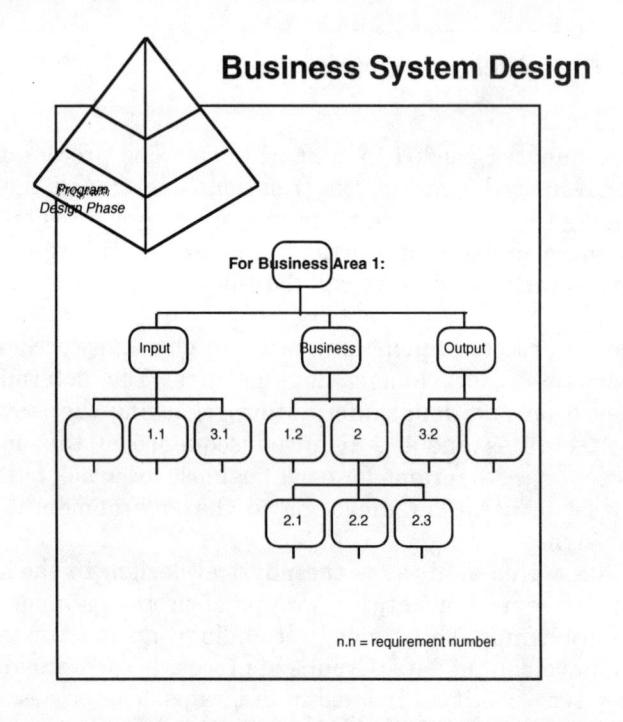

Figure 3-8. Implemented data requirements.

The business system design is the program design. It represents the physical groupings of attributes and their attendant processes in the way that they should be organized on a particular hardware/software platform. Although it looks just like the implementation model of a process-driven design, it is more conducive to the manipulation of data due to the manner in which it was derived. In data-driven design, you rely heavily on entity analysis in all phases.

Data Parameters

Data-driven design leads you to an organized set of data parameters. Each of the parameters characterizes one part of the function of the system, in part, by making use of other data parameters as lower level characteristics. This results in a data structure which characterizes the system design. The process aspects in a data-driven design are then derived to support this data structure.

Data Package

```
Data Parameter
    ├── Data Parameter
    │       ├── Data Parameter
    │       └── Data Parameter
    ├── Data Parameter
    ├── Data Parameter
    │       ├── Data Parameter
    │       └── Data Parameter
    ├── Data Parameter
    └── Data Parameter
```

3.3.3 When Is an Object Design Data Driven?

The Concept of Classified Object

The concepts of data-driven design are just as valid in object-oriented design when you determine the attributes required of your objects, and when you allocate those attributes to different classes of objects. You identify object attributes by elaborating on the characteristics of known entities and then allocating those characteristics into physical groups called objects, in particular, to classes of objects in a hierarchy. This concept is called *classification*, and is very similar to separating entities into neighborhoods during entity analysis.

CONCEPT 9

Objects which use the same group of operations and attributes are said to be of the same class.

In classification, you set up a hierarchy of object classes as an inverted tree of common attributes called the *inheritance diagram*. Eventually, you design your program in terms of objects which are each of a specific class. Because of the concept of classification, however, you do not need to list all of the shared attributes within each object. An object is of a particular type (its class) which, by inference, includes all of the operations and attributes of that class. The representation of classes of objects in the inheritance diagram is an extension of entity analysis in data-driven design.

The Concept of Attribute Analysis

Object-oriented design is data driven in the derivation of attributes, but not in their representation. You conceptually expand your list of attributes by considering the relationships among them and the additional attributes needed to support their relationships. However, rather than representing the attributes in entity relationship diagrams, an object-oriented model of functions is just presented as a list of attributes and operations.

CONCEPT 10

Attribute analysis is the distribution of a list of distinct attributes across the objects in a class.

Object-oriented design is also data driven in the organization of attributes. You group attributes into an inheritance diagram that conveys a hierarchy of objects. Objects belong to classes, and classes belong to other classes. The inheritance diagrams are not as complex as entity relationship diagrams, but still represent the same type of physical design that is required to allocate the original data attributes into groups.

This similarity can be useful in the early steps of object-oriented design. You follow a specific set of steps to identify requirements. The requirements are partially expressed as attributes, which are similar to entities. You then allocate them into physical groups called objects. You use inheritance diagrams to represent the same type of physical design as a comprehensive entity relationship diagram represents but in a much more readable and understandable form.

CONCEPT SUMMARY - Conventional Analysis

> **CONCEPT 5.** Process decomposition is used to determine a program's process requirements as the basis to drive its design. The conventional life-cycle framework for applying process decomposition is called structured design.

> **CONCEPT 6.** Entity analysis is used to determine a program's data requirements as the basis to drive its design. The conventional life cycle framework for applying entity analysis is called information engineering.

CONCEPT SUMMARY - Analyzing Objects

CONCEPT 7. An object contained within another object is said to be encapsulated.

CONCEPT 8. Operation decomposition is the distribution of a list of subordinate operations across a set of encapsulated objects.

CONCEPT 9. Objects which use the same group of operations and attributes are said to be of the same class.

CONCEPT 10. Attribute analysis is the distribution of a list of distinct attributes across the objects in a class.

CHAPTER REVIEW

Conventional Design

When is conventional design useful? To design a system which is either highly process oriented or highly data oriented.

How do you develop a process-driven design? Decompose the processes of a system to discover its requirements.

How do you decompose processes? Identify individual process operations and then break them into their constituent smaller (lower-level) operations.

When is an object design process driven? As you encapsulate some objects within others, and as you later decompose individual operations within those objects.

How do you develop a data-driven design? Analyze the data entities of a system to discover its requirements.

How do you analyze data entities? Identify individual data attributes and then examine their relationships with one another to identify additional attributes.

When is an object design data driven? As you classify some objects into groups with others, and later analyze the individual attributes within those objects.

4

Object–Oriented Design

4.1 OBJECT REQUIREMENTS

The Concept of Object Requirements

Object-oriented design is a technique for software development that is quite different from conventional techniques. It focuses your attention on deriving both the process requirements and the data requirements for your program at the same time. Object-oriented design is particularly well suited to designing distributed software that will be implemented using object-oriented programming languages. Distributed software may be either process intensive or data intensive, and therefore, object-oriented design can be applied to either scientific or business applications.

The concepts of object-oriented design are often applied to the design of client/server programs for midrange distributed platforms. Object-oriented design and programming has been popularized by authors like Booch, and has been implemented for programmers in application development environments and for users in graphical user interfaces. Object engineering is a specific discipline for developing client/server systems using object-oriented design techniques.

The object engineering model relies on a combined top-down and outside-in technique of design, similar to both process decomposition and entity analysis, respectively. The decomposition aspects of object-oriented design are called *encapsulation*. Encapsulation shows up as collaborations between objects. The entity analysis aspects are called *classification*. Classification shows up as inheritance of object characteristics.

CHAPTER 4: OBJECT-ORIENTED DESIGN

Similar to either structured design or information engineering, object engineering can also be portrayed as either a bar form or a pyramid form of life cycle. Different from those conventional approaches, however, the object-engineering approach places much more emphasis on the recursive nature of its life cycle. As a result, object engineering provides for a higher degree of reusability of software modules.

The object-engineering life cycle is used in the same way as any life cycle—as a framework to transform a set of requirements into a working computer program. Those requirements are usually expressed in terms of either processes or data. However, in object engineering, you constantly consider both the process requirements (*operations*) and the data requirements (*attributes*) of your program.

The phases of object engineering provide you with a framework for transforming a set of object requirements into a working computer program. You use the concept of an object to represent the requirements of your program and to drive its design. An object is composed of operations and attributes. This approach focuses your attention on the decomposition and expansion of process operations and data attributes as your program's requirements. Within the life-cycle phases, you transform these requirements from a functional design to a physical design and, finally, to a program design.

CONCEPT 11

Object engineering is the transformation of a set of requirements into an organized collection of interacting client and server objects.

The object-engineering life cycle is the development sequence for object-oriented design. However, the recursive nature of the life cycle is emphasized more than in conventional design. An object-oriented computer program is characterized by the interfaces between independent objects (called *clients* and *servers*). These objects are separate and distinct from one another, and may be implemented on different hardware and/or software platforms (called *distributed modules*). Their well defined interfaces enable you to reuse them.

Rather than repeating the entire life cycle for new object-oriented designs, you often reuse existing software objects. You can reuse existing inheritance to create new objects in new programs and reuse existing collaborations as new programs by substituting new designs for encapsulated objects. You can even reuse compiled objects as parts of new systems.

The object-engineering model borrows many concepts from both structured design and information engineering. In particular, you apply the concepts of process decomposition to encapsulate sets of operations and attributes within an object, and apply the concepts of entity analysis to distribute operations and attributes across related object classes. The

Objects as Requirements

Objects are packages of operations and attributes. The operations represent the processess which belong to that object. The attributes represent the data used in the performance of those processes. You identify objects by the names of things in your domain, and by the groups of operations and attributes of which they are composed. You identify operations and attributes by the description of the things needed to be done (process operations) and the information needed to do them (data attributes).

The process of identifying objects, operations, and attributes is recursive. Objects suggest operations and attributes. Operations suggest other attributes. Attributes suggest other operations. Together, these new attributes and operations suggest other objects. Each object represents one requirement of your system. A robust set of objects, therefore, represents the total requirements of your system.

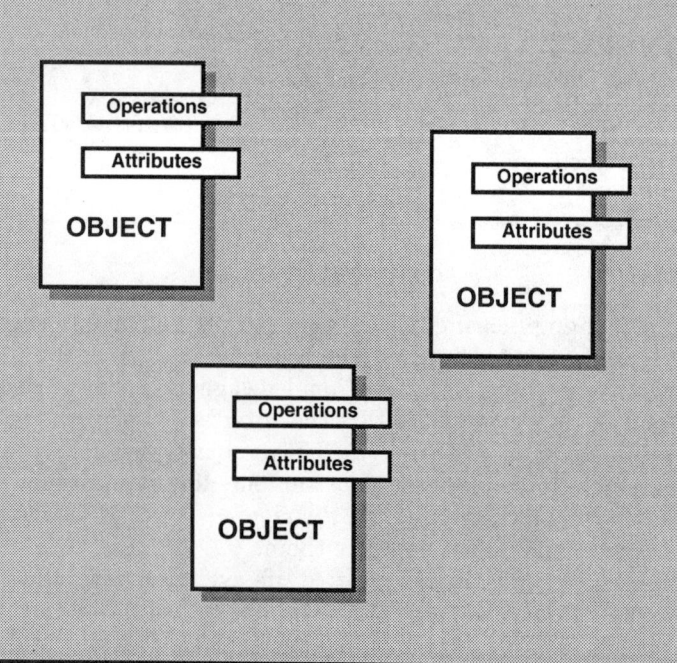

value added by object engineering is the coupling of these two different concepts into a single more powerful approach to software development.

The domain of an object-oriented system consists of a collection of client and server objects with well-defined interfaces and separately maintained internal structures. This provides each object with a level of autonomy unmatched in conventional designs. The internal design of a server object can be modified in many respects at a later time without causing changes to its interfaces of to its client objects. New client objects can be constructed using old servers without any concern for the internal design of the servers themselves.

4.2 THE CLIENT/SERVER MODEL

4.2.1 What Is a Client/Server Domain?

The Concept of Client Objects

Clients are physical objects that require that one or more process be performed, or that one or more data values be determined, by some other object. A client may represent either a piece of hardware or a piece of software. Furthermore, it may represent either a complete system, a program within a system, or a module within a program. However, for the sake of discussion, it is easier to think of a client object as a software module.

By definition, a client is an object which makes a request of another object, called the *server*. You can think of this as one module calling another. The request is directional and consists of a set of calling parameters (the *stimulus*) and/or a set of return parameters (the *response*). It is the direction of the request, not the number of stimulus and response parameters, that determines which object is the client and which object is the server.

CONCEPT 12

A client object is one that makes a request of another object to trigger one of its operations or to access one of its attributes.

A client's server module can be contained in the same program or in a different program from the client module. It can be in the same or a different system, and it can be on the same or a different hardware platform. In addition, client modules may themselves be servers to other clients. It all depends on the particular request with which you are concerned. Client modules represent a point of control from the server's perspective, in particular, the point where the control originates.

In hardware environments, the controlling devices are the clients. They typically include the CPU, the network controller (from the perspective of the cable), the cable (from the perspective of a node), and even a terminal (from the perspective of either its keyboard or its display

---

The Client/Server Relationship

Objects are packages of related operations and attributes. They represent the processes (the operations) and the data (the attributes) that will characterize the finished computer program(s). The manner in which operations and/or attributes of different objects relate to one another helps to determine these characteristics.

The internal design of any one object shows how its internal operations and attributes interact with one another. Some of these operations and attributes, however, may need to trigger operations or to access attributes in other objects. This is accomplished by making requests of one object from within another.

Part of the design of a domain shows the request relationships between objects (actually between the operations and/or the attributes within those objects). Objects which make requests are called clients, since they call upon other objects to perform some service for them. Objects which receive and respond to requests are called servers, since they perform the services required by other objects.

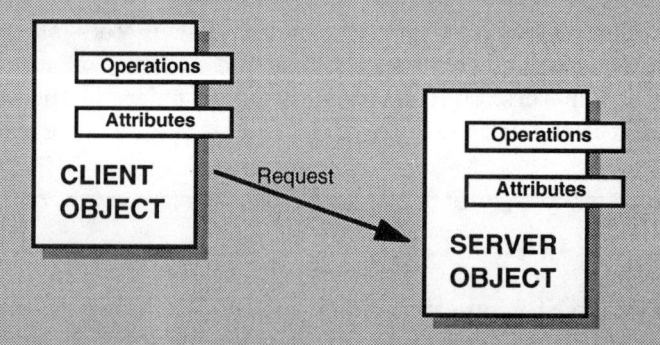

```
    ┌─────────────┐
    │ Operations  │
  ┌─┴─────────────┴─┐
  │ │ Attributes  │ │              ┌─────────────┐
  │ └─────────────┘ │              │ Operations  │
  │                 │            ┌─┴─────────────┴─┐
  │    CLIENT       │  Request   │ │ Attributes  │ │
  │    OBJECT       │──────────▶ │ └─────────────┘ │
  │                 │            │                 │
  └─────────────────┘            │    SERVER       │
                                 │    OBJECT       │
                                 └─────────────────┘
```

A domain is just a complete collection of requirements. In object-oriented design, a domain is a complete collection of objects which satisfy the design requirement for a particular system. A client/server domain is a complete collection of objects designed around the client and server relationships between the objects in the domain. The client/server relationships portray the collaborations between object classes. The object classes are also related to one another by another mechanism called *inheritance*.

monitor). Some of these relationships, of course, may be reversed if the hardware or systems software is designed differently. It all depends on which device makes the request.

In software environments, the controlling modules are the clients. They typically include such things as operating systems (from the perspective of application programs) and the main routine in an application program (from the perspective its of subroutines). There is considerable flexibility in defining which modules are clients and which are servers within an application program since the programmer can decide which way a request flows. However, the rule is constant. The calling module is the client.

The Concept of Server Objects

Servers are physical objects that perform one or more processes, or that determine one or more data values, at the request of some other object. Similar to client objects, a server may represent either hardware or software and either a system, a program, or a module. Servers are defined by the receipt of requests, and can best be thought of as a called module in a software program.

CONCEPT 13

A server object is one that responds to a request from another object by triggering one of its operations or by accessing one of its attributes.

The requests received by a server may or may not contain calling parameters (stimuli) or return parameters (responses), but they are always directional. The calling parameters are usually present in a request when a client needs to trigger a server operation (that is, to perform a process). The return parameters are usually present in a request when a client needs to access a server attribute (that is, to determine a data value). In either case, however, the server receives a request from the client.

In hardware environments, the individual devices controlled by other platform components are the servers. They include such things as dumb terminals, file servers, workstations at network nodes (from the perspective of remote applications), and peripheral devices such as printers, plotters, and graphical displays. The important factor is that the control of these devices originates elsewhere. Conversely, if control originates within the device, it is a client rather than a server. For example, peripheral devices act as clients when they can be operated directly by users and when they poll their ports for input.

In software environments, the dormant modules controlled by other main modules are the servers. They include such things as subroutines, common modules, screen windows, device drivers, embedded firmware, and the basic input/output system (BIOS) in a desktop microcomputer. The ability of a server to perform its functions and to derive its data values independent of the client enables client and server objects to be reused in multiple domains.

The Concept of a Domain

The concept of a domain in object-oriented design is no different from the concept of a domain using any other technique of design. A domain is a complete application area (a *vertical domain*) or a set of related functions (a *horizontal domain*). In structured design, domains are represented by context diagrams. In information engineering, domains are represented by business areas. A *domain* is an abstract area of business and usually represented as one self-contained data processing situation.

In object-oriented design, a domain is the collection of objects which address some self-contained data-processing situation. A domain is just a high-level aggregation of a particular set of objects. Domains can be composed of subdomains, but ultimately are always composed of objects. Domains can overlap one another, and are usually described as either vertical domains or horizontal domains.

CONCEPT 14

A domain is an organized collection of interacting objects which address a self-contained situation.

Vertical domains usually represent cohesive business application areas. By an application area, we mean such things employee payrolls, personnel records, inventory records, sales and purchasing activity, simulations, or statistical reports. The objects which you may design to satisfy these applications could be viewed as assets which you can then reuse in various systems within the domain.

Horizontal domains usually represent cohesive sets of analytical functions. By analytical functions, we mean such things as user interfaces, database management systems, arithmetic operations, matrix operations, or memory managers. The objects which you may design to satisfy these functions could be viewed as assets which you can then reuse in various systems within the domain.

The purpose of collecting objects within domains is to provide some organized means of cataloging a closely related set of objects. As the number of objects that you develop grows, cataloging them becomes very important if you wish to reuse some of them in new systems. After all, that is one of the chief benefits of object-oriented design. Objects can be treated as reusable components. They are assets of your business.

4.2.2 What Are Reusable Components?

A Matter of Perspective

A domain is composed of objects, and objects are composed of other objects. Within the domain, objects are eventually implemented as systems, or as programs within a system, or as modules within a program. The design of an object, therefore, can describe either a system, a program, a module, or some part of a module. The point at which you define an object as a physically reusable component is just a matter of perspective based on the specific requirements you need to meet for any new application.

The objects in a domain address a self-contained data-processing situation. They share a common application area or a related set of functions. It is likely, therefore, that some of these objects could be used in multiple systems within the domain. Many of the same object operations (print a report, record a sale, etc.) may be required in many different systems. Similarly, many of the same object attributes (employee name, item price, average value, etc.) may be used as well.

A domain is just an aggregation of objects. The objects are components of the domain. If many of an object's process operations and data attributes are useful in more than one case, then it stands to reason that a standardized design for the object may prove useful more than once. All that is required is that the component interfaces be well defined and that their internal structures be independently maintained. Therefore, objects are the reusable components of a domain.

Objects themselves are composed of other lower-level objects. You may also view some of these lower-level objects as reusable components. In inheritance hierarchies, related types of objects are organized into classes. In collaboration hierarchies, subordinate objects are encapsulated within the internal structure of some objects. In either case, the lower-level objects could be viewed as reusable components if their operations and attributes were needed in several systems, programs, or modules.

Domains can overlap, and the objects in the overlapping area are candidates for reuse. Two vertical domains may have subapplications which they share. For example, you would certainly like a payroll domain and a personnel domain to share a common employee database. Similarly, a vertical domain and a horizontal domain often overlap. For example, an inventory domain would certainly benefit from the use of preexisting modules from a statistical domain to calculate averages and mean values of inventory cost and turnover in the warehouse.

The reuse of components is one of the chief benefits of object-oriented design. Objects can be treated as assets of your business. They merely need to be designed with well-defined interfaces and documented in a way which makes their similarity to other situations readily apparent. Their design needs to be abstract yet precise. The purpose of object-oriented design is to represent the operations and attributes of your systems, programs, and modules in such a manner.

The Concept of Abstraction

The concept of *abstraction* comes up many times in object-oriented design. Classes, objects, operations, and attributes are the primary abstractions used in object-oriented design. Classes are abstract representations of objects. Objects are abstract representations of operations and attributes. Operations are abstract representations of processes. Attributes are abstract representations of data.

Abstraction is the principle of focusing your attention at a level of detail appropriate to your interest. One type of abstraction is *aggregation*. You aggregate representative characteristics of your design to present higher-level views of its purpose. In object-oriented design, the characteristics that you use to represent your design are objects. The purpose of an object is conveyed by its operations and its attributes.

CONCEPT 15

Abstraction is the process of focusing your attention on the level of detail appropriate to your interest.

The important abstractions used throughout object-oriented design involve representations of inheritance, collaboration, classes, objects, operations, attributes, processes, and data. The manner in which those abstractions are related to one another is shown in Figure 4-1. Abstraction is the key to understanding object-oriented design. The question to ask yourself at any stage in your design is "at what level of abstraction are we working now?" When you answer that question, everything else should fall into place.

Classes are abstract representations of objects. They represent either a type of object (a *concrete class*) or a type of another class (an *abstract class*). An object of a particular class is called an *instance* of that class. A class of another particular class is called a *subclass* in the inheritance hierarchy. Objects and subclasses are both said to inherit all of the characteristics of their class. In addition, objects of a particular class can also be defined to collaborate with the objects of other classes.

CHAPTER 4: OBJECT-ORIENTED DESIGN   **63**

```
         Inheritance           Collaboration
             ⬆                      ⬆
       Abstract Classes       Concrete Classes

                         ⬆
                       Objects

                ⬆                ⬆
            Operations       Attributes

                ⬆                ⬆
             Processes         Data
```

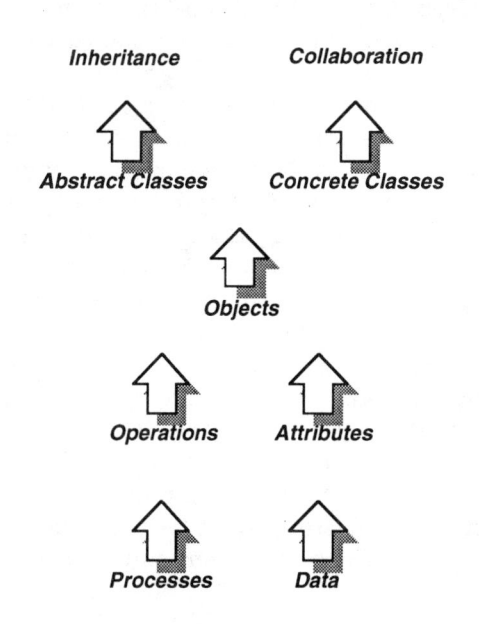

Figure 4-1.   Making use of abstraction.

Classes are primarily represented in two ways to show two different abstractions of objects: inheritance and collaboration. *Inheritance* is one type of abstraction of object classes. The analytical process of abstracting objects into inheritance hierarchies is called *classification*. *Collaborations* are another type of abstraction of object classes. The analytical process of abstracting objects into collaboration hierarchies is called *encapsulation*.

Objects are abstract representations of operations and attributes. They are the single most important abstraction in object-oriented design. Objects represent a meaningful group of characteristics. By characteristics, we mean the object's operations and attributes which represent both the processing and data needs of your program. The operations and attributes of an object are usually, but not necessarily, related to one another.

Operations are abstract representations of processes. They portray what a process does rather than how it does it. In object-oriented design, you identify, allocate, and implement operations in ways very similar to process-driven design. When you finally implement the operations of an object, they are no different from named process routines in a conventional design.

Attributes are abstract representations of data. They portray what the data represents rather than how it is stored. In object-oriented design, you identify, allocate, and implement attributes in ways very similar to data-driven design. When you finally implement the attributes of an object, they are no different from named data variables in a conventional design.

The concept of abstraction is the same in object-oriented design as in conventional process-driven and data-driven design. In process-driven design, abstraction is the fundamental principle in process decomposition. Leveled sets of data-flow diagrams portray the decomposition of process requirements. In data-driven design, abstraction is just as important. The "is-a-part-of" relationships on an entity relationship diagram are abstract representations of data structures, and the "uses" relationships are abstract representations of process requirements.

In object-oriented design, abstract representations are important for the reusability of object components. Rather than designing entirely new systems, you can often reuse existing software objects as parts of a new design. You use an abstract view of operations and attributes to determine the suitability of an existing object for a new design. You may use inheritance hierarchies, collaboration hierarchies, or both, as an abstract view of your design.

The Concept of Inheritance

As you refine the definitions of the objects in your domain, you reorganize their contents (their operations and attributes). Objects are divided into smaller groups of operations and attributes. As a result, you have more objects each of which are composed of fewer operations and fewer attributes. These smaller objects represent more cohesive and meaningful packages of operations and attributes, such as are shown in Figure 4-2.

The new smaller objects now have relationships with each other due to the manner in which the original large objects were divided. They are better organized sets of operations and attributes, characterized also by their particular hierarchical relationships with the operations and attributes in other objects. Organized objects are, therefore, also referred to as *classes of operations and attributes* (or *classes* for short). Classes are just smaller, well-defined, well-organized objects. Object classes are represented in terms of their relationships with one another, in particular in two types of relationships.

The nonconventional type of relationship between object classes is the inheritance relationship. Inheritance is characterized by the nesting of object classes according to the operations and the attributes which they must share, as shown in Figure 4-3. For all practical purposes, inheritance simply shows the internal operation hierarchy (utility routines) and the internal attribute hierarchy (common block data) in a system design.

The inheritance relationships between objects (objects are the software modules) is the characteristic feature of object-oriented software design. Inheritance is used in object-oriented programming languages to

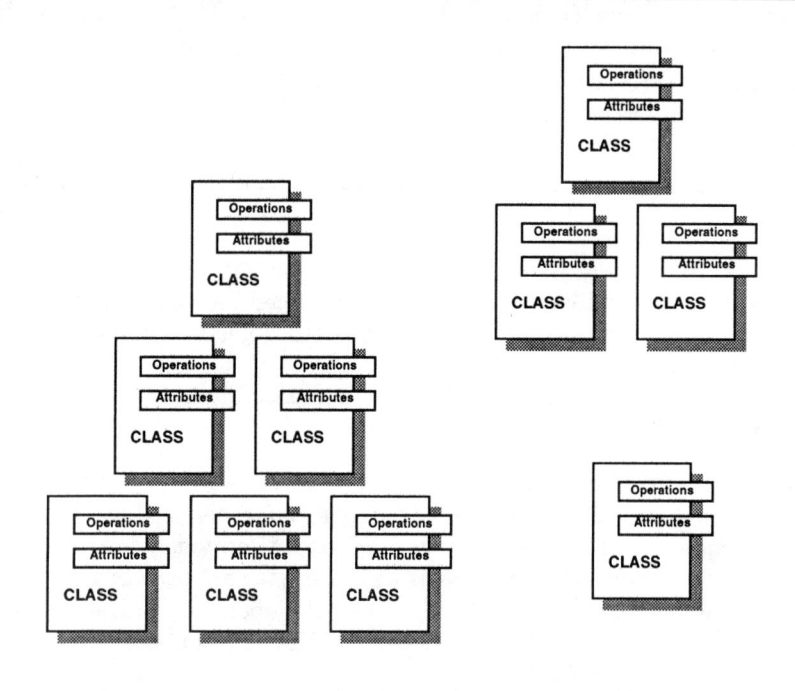

Figure 4-2. Classes of objects.

catalog the availability of common operations and common attributes. This leads to more readily reusable modular designs and more easily expandable programs. Inheritance diagrams simply show the relationships of the programmable modules (at the lower levels of the diagram) to the packages of common operations and attributes (at the higher levels of the diagram).

Inheritance hierarchies are a means of classifying objects. They are inverted trees of common subroutines. We use the term *inverted* to convey the sense that the commonalty of objects is portrayed upwardly in the tree as compared to the downward representation of common modules in a structure chart. Each higher object represents a set of operations and attributes common to all levels to which it is connected below.

Each object in the tree is called the class of the objects below it. The concept of an inheritance hierarchy is the distinguishing feature of object-oriented programming languages. Object-oriented compilers use the inheritance hierarchy to resolve data and process referencing as part of their standard overhead. The inheritance hierarchy is the feature most often used to describe the nature of object-oriented programming.

Inheritance hierarchies are also the primary mechanism by which you reuse object classes as templates for new designs. You can think of an inheritance hierarchy as a hidden catalog of common routines and common data for each object class in the hierarchy. The common routines and common data of a class are its object's operations and attributes, respectively. You create templates of objects by abstracting their requirements into a hierarchy of classes.

> ## CONCEPT 16
> An inheritance hierarchy is a catalog of common processes and common data which helps to organize the objects in a domain.

An object will inherit operations and attributes as common characteristics from the class to which it belongs. This means that you do not need to redesign these characteristics every time you use them in an object, yet can reference them as if they were a part of your object. You can program the object to perform any public operation of its class or to access any public attribute of its class, or of any class above the object in its inheritance hierarchy.

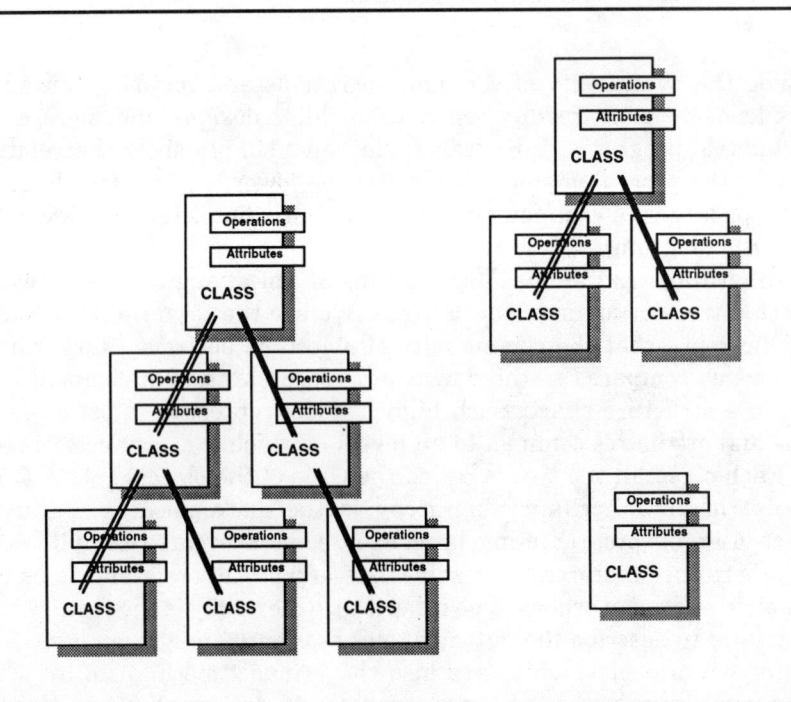

Figure 4-3.   Inheritance relationships.

Inheritance hierarchies enable you to define your objects as abstract classes of operations and attributes. You can reuse the characteristics of an existing object as a template for a new object by creating a new subclass in the hierarchy. In this way, you are extending the depth of your inheritance hierarchy without disturbing the objects that you have already designed and programmed.

The structure of an inheritance hierarchy determines how you trigger internal operations and how you access internal attributes. By *internal*, we mean operations and attributes within an object or within higher level objects in its hierarchy. Inheritance hierarchies represent an abstract view of the common processes that you would represent in structure charts in a process-driven design, and the common data that you would represent in data structure diagrams in a data-driven design.

The Concept of Collaboration

The more conventional type of relationship between object classes is the *collaboration relationship*. Collaborations are characterized by a client object sending a request to a server object to trigger one of its operations or to access one of its attributes, as shown in Figure 4-4. Collaborations simply show subroutine calls (triggering an external operation) or data value retrieval (accessing an external attribute).

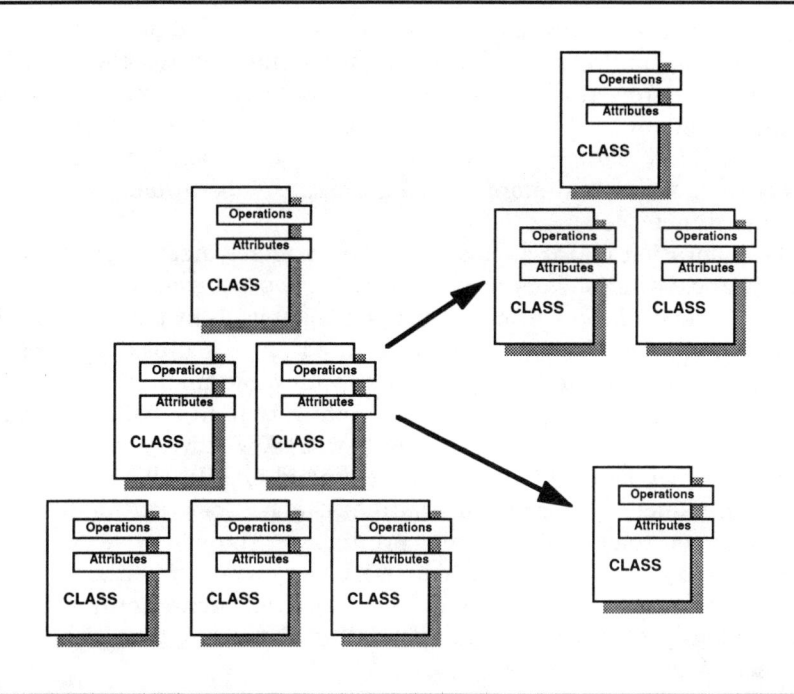

Figure 4-4. Collaboration relationships.

Collaboration relationships between software modules are addressed quite well by the conventional methods of software design with which you may already be familiar (data-flow diagrams and structure charts). The only difference between collaboration diagrams and conventional module diagrams is in the level of abstraction used to portray the calling relationships. Collaborations are shown in terms of the relationships between object classes, rather than between the individual process operations and data attributes within those objects.

Collaboration hierarchies are a means of portraying program operation. They represent the calling connections between objects when they are implemented as clients and servers. We use the term *calling* to convey the passing of requests from client to server. Collaborations represent the same type of design abstraction as the data flows in a data flow diagram and as the data couples on a structure chart.

CONCEPT 17

A collaboration hierarchy is a means of portraying program operation as the interaction between objects in a domain.

Collaboration hierarchies enable you to view your objects as abstract sets of clients and servers. This completes the picture of your design started by the inheritance hierarchy. Collaboration hierarchies, however, are more fundamental to the design of your program than the inheritance hierarchy. They show the operation of your objects as systems, programs, or modules. You spend more time designing collaborations than designing inheritance.

Collaboration hierarchies are also the primary mechanism by which you reuse existing objects in new designs. You can reuse client objects with new servers, or you can reuse server objects in new clients. The client and server objects are encapsulated or "black-box" components which are each compiled and linked into your program. You may later be able to reuse these components in their entirety in new collaborations.

You can reuse existing client objects with new servers by simply substituting a new or modified server for the old one. In this way, specific operations (such as a printing routine) can be designed for a specific printer. If you then use a different printer, you simply revise that server object (a software module) without worrying about any effects it might have on the rest of your program. The internal structure of the server is independently maintained, thus the influence of that type of change is confined to the one module.

You can also reuse existing server objects as parts of new systems by sending them requests from new clients. In this way, the characteristics of an existing server (such as a printing routine) can be applied to new situations (that is, called by many programs). You simply send a valid request to the server module without worrying how it will accomplish its duties. The interface of the server is well defined, so any number of new clients can use it.

The structure of collaboration hierarchies determines how you trigger external operations and how you access external attributes. By *external*, we mean operations and attributes that are internal to objects within other inheritance hierarchies. Collaboration hierarchies represent an abstract view of the subroutine processes you would represent as data flow diagrams or structure charts in a process-driven design, or as entity relationship diagrams and process structure diagrams in a data-driven design.

4.3 DISTRIBUTED APPLICATIONS

4.3.1 What Is Context-Sensitive Referencing?

The Concept of Polymorphism

Distributed applications can be developed in any computer-programming language. To distribute an application across different hardware platforms or different system software environments, you need a program design which is rigidly modular. The design must have modules that are self contained (that is, separately maintained internal designs) and that are controlled with very specific calling parameters (that is, a well-defined interface). The design of a program, not the language in which it is programmed, determines whether it can be implemented in a distributed manner.

Some languages, however, are more suitable for designing distributed applications than others. Object-oriented languages, in particular, have specific internal constructs to design distributed applications. Object-oriented design provides the corresponding mechanisms to make use of these constructs. Furthermore, these object-oriented constructs also provide for design flexibility and program reusability.

The primary constructs for designing distributed applications are the *object specifications*. Object specifications provide the internal design of objects as standalone modules, and the well defined interfaces for using those modules. An object's internal design is represented through *operation descriptions* and *attribute descriptions*. An object's well-defined interfaces are represented through *request descriptions*.

The primary construct for achieving design flexibility and program reusability is the class architecture. The hierarchy diagrams of the class architecture provide for module design in a flexible and reusable manner. Many objects can contain operations and attributes with the same names as in other objects. The resolution of references to these redundant names is known as *context-sensitive referencing*.

Context-sensitive referencing is the feature which differentiates object-oriented languages from procedural languages. Object-oriented languages use inheritance to substitute global operations and attributes for local ones. They use collaboration to identify an object as a reference point for that substitution. The substitution capability of context-sensitive referencing is called *polymorphism*.

Polymorphism is the ability to select between redundant names for operations and/or attributes based on the context in which they are used. An object-oriented programming language (or, rather, its compiler) uses the context of each reference to a redundant operation or attribute name to select one. It uses the inheritance hierarchy to resolve references to redundant names. The inheritance hierarchy is part of your object-oriented design.

CONCEPT 18

Polymorphism is the selection between redundant operation or attribute names based on the context in which they are used.

The naming redundancy of polymorphism is not merely allowed but encouraged. A distributed system must be designed with separately maintained modules, each with well-defined interfaces. The only way that such a rigid design structure can retain its flexibility for later modifications is to also provide a mechanism for context-sensitive referencing. That mechanism is polymorphism.

You can use polymorphism (substitutable operation and attribute names) in your design either within an object's own class inheritance hierarchy, or by using some other class's inheritance hierarchy. The resolution of a polymorphic reference is usually contained to a particular inheritance hierarchy. However, the selection of which inheritance hierarchy to use may be determined by a collaboration.

The Concept of Visibility

Visibility is the availability of operations and attributes to be used outside their own classes. In order to resolve a polymorphic reference, you need information about the availability of the operations and attributes from other objects. Operations and attributes are candidates for usage in

---

CONCEPT 19

Visibility is the capability to trigger operations or to access attributes in an object from within the other objects in the domain.

---

polymorphic references based on their visibility. The visibility of an object's operations and attributes may be either public or private.

Public operations and public attributes are visible to any other object. They can be used in polymorphic substitutions. A public operation can be triggered externally (from within another object) based on the context of the reference as an implied function call. A public attribute can also be accessed externally in a similar manner as an implied data reference.

Private operations and private attributes are not visible to any other object. Private operations cannot be used in polymorphic substitutions, nor in explicit references from outside their own object. Similarly, private attributes cannot be used in polymorphic substitutions or in explicit external references.

Implied Function Calling

The substitution of the names of redundant functions (that is, *operation polymorphism*) results in a form of context-sensitive referencing which we have called *implied function calling*. You can think of implied function calling as the use of a process structure chart to guide a search for module names. In object-oriented programming languages, the compiler takes the burden of finding the appropriate subordinate module.

When you write a reference to a common module in the program statements (source code) for an object, the compiler searches down the structure of common modules until it finds a matching subordinate module name. However, there is no structure chart to search in an object-oriented design. Instead, there is an inheritance hierarchy. The compiler searches up the inheritance hierarchy to resolve an implied call to function.

Implied function calling is usually described in terms of an object's own inheritance hierarchy. However, you can also trigger polymorphic operations in other object's inheritance hierarchies—that is, across channels in the collaboration hierarchy. This occurs when you use a collaboration to explicitly trigger an operation in another object that doesn't exist in that object. Once the target object is identified by the collaboration, an implied function call is made by the compiler within that target object's inheritance hierarchy.

Implied Data Referencing

Since the operational design of an operation usually depends on the use of associated attributes, an implied function call often causes *implied data referencing* as well. The data needed is similar to the parameter list for a function call in a conventional design. In the same way that operation polymorphism is used to identify the operation which is appropriate to the context of a reference, *attribute polymorphism* is used to identify the appropriate attribute.

The substitution of the names of redundant data items (that is, attribute polymorphism) results in a form of context-sensitive referencing which we have called implied data referencing. You can think of implied data referencing as the use of a data-structure chart to guide the search for data-item names. In object-oriented programming languages, however, the compiler takes the burden of finding the appropriate subordinate data item name.

Similar to the case of an implied function call, the compiler searches down the structure of common data items until it finds a matching data item name. The inheritance hierarchy is used again to resolve the reference conflict, this time to find the appropriate attribute. As with operations, you can also access polymorphic attributes in other inheritance hierarchies by starting with a collaboration into your starting point.

4.3.2 What Is Event-Driven Operation?

The Concept of an Event

Distributed applications tend to be event-driven in their operation. In a procedural computer program, process modules are activated by subroutine calls in the program statements (source code). You design these calls to occur in a particular sequence when the program is run. In an object-oriented computer program, you trigger operations using the capabilities of context sensitive referencing and polymorphism. These capabilities enable a more flexible form of operation based on events.

Event-driven applications are object oriented by their nature. Operations can be triggered in a context-sensitive manner. Therefore, a subroutine call need not be specifically predefined in the design. Instead, external events drive the sequence of triggering operations and accessing attributes. In effect, events are specific subroutine calls which are determined at runtime from among all the possible calls identified as collaborations.

An event is anything which triggers an operation or which accesses an attribute. The requests sent from a client to a serve are events. In a windowing environment, loading one program from within a window in another program is also an event. As a context-sensitive event, the loaded program inherits some attributes (for example, screen size and location) from the originally running program. Other examples of events are user input, such as mouse clicks, mouse movements, depressing a key on a keyboard, and selecting an image area on a screen.

CONCEPT 20

An event is any action directed against one object by another object to trigger an operation or to access an attribute.

Collaborations enable event-driven operation in the same way that inheritance enables context-sensitive referencing. Any object which performs some operation and which is the target of a collaboration can respond to an event. Your collaboration hierarchy defines which objects can trigger which operations in other objects. An event is just the triggering of one of these operations (or, similarly, the accessing of an attribute) by a reference to it at runtime.

Event-driven operation builds on the concept of context-sensitive referencing. An event is an operation which is triggered at runtime or an attribute which is accessed at runtime. Events occur because of context-sensitive referencing. The context of the object in which the event takes place is used to find the appropriate operations and attributes referenced by the event.

A procedural subroutine call in a conventional design is a predetermined collaboration. The data couples on a conventional structure chart show the parameters needed to trigger operations in subordinate objects. These data couples are, in effect, the events which drive the lower-level modules at runtime. The same holds true for data flows between processes on a data-flow diagram. They are the events which drive those processes.

An event in an object-oriented design is a runtime collaboration. Because of context-sensitive referencing, event sequences do not need to be predetermined before the program is compiled. Runtime events can be used to control the sequence of operation. The pathways exist for directing the events (*collaborations*) and the context is defined for resolving related references (*inheritance*).

Triggering Object Operations

There are usually stimulus parameters present in the request protocol when a client object triggers an operation in a server object. This makes sense since the purpose of triggering an operation is to cause something to happen—to perform some function based on some set of control values. Therefore, you can usually identify events used to trigger operations by the nature of the protocol of the associated request.

You can think of an event which triggers a particular operation in an object as the object-oriented equivalent of a subroutine call. The calling parameters for a subroutine call are the input data couples drawn on the corresponding structure chart. The calling parameters for triggering an operation correspond to the stimulus portion of the request associated with that operation. The return parameters (if any) correspond to output data couples and are part of the response portion of the request.

Events which trigger operations most often correspond to the type of collaboration derived by hierarchical encapsulation. When you derive your collaboration hierarchy, the hierarchical collaborations represent parent/child relationships between objects similar to hierarchical modules on a structure chart. Hierarchical encapsulation is the most common type of collaboration, so triggering operations in this way is the most common type of event.

Accessing Object Attributes

There are usually response parameters present in the request protocol when a client object accesses an attribute in a server object. This makes sense since the purpose of accessing an attribute is to obtain something, that is, to determine a data value. You can usually identify events used to access attributes by the nature of the protocol of the associated request.

You can think of an event which accesses a particular attribute in an object as the object-oriented equivalent of reading a record from a data file or from an external program. There are usually no calling parameters to get such a record, therefore, the protocol for that event usually contains no stimulus parameters. The return parameters correspond to the items of data which are read, and so the request protocol for accessing an attribute usually contains response parameters.

Events which access attributes most often correspond to the type of collaboration derived by lateral encapsulation. When you derive your collaboration hierarchy, the lateral collaborations represent sibling relationships between objects similar to off-page data flows between modules on different data-flow diagrams. *Lateral encapsulation* is a secondary type of collaboration, and accessing attributes in this way is not as common as triggering operations.

Programmed Events

Some events are created by programmers. You can think of these as *designed-in* events. They are hard-wired into the source code of your program. It is easier to understand events using the analogy of conventional intermodule calling logic. The sequencing of programmer-generated events generally follows the program structure reflected in a structure chart.

Most events go undetected by the user. Operations are triggered and attributes are accessed in various objects at runtime. One module (an object in your design) calls another module (another object) based on a designed relationship (defined by collaborations). These are program-generated events. As the programmer, you set up the object-oriented constructs for these events when you design your system.

Program-generated events are similar to the intermodule calling logic in a conventional design. Object-oriented design, however, allows for context-sensitive referencing. Therefore, the full scope of the intermodule calling logic is never drawn out beforehand. There are too many possible combinations of object-to-object communication (collaboration) and possible alternative operations and attributes (polymorphism) to consider in combination with one another.

The manner in which you define interobject communications (collaborations) in your program depends on the capabilities of the source language you use. Different object-oriented programming languages, such as ADA and C++, handle collaborations in various ways. The manner in which you create events will be different depending on the language you use. However, you will always need a collaboration diagram and request descriptions, regardless of which language you use.

User Events

Some events are created by users. You can think of events created by users as *on-demand* events. They are not hard-wired into the source code of your program. Microcomputer-based GUI environments provide the best example of user-generated events. User-generated events demonstrate the principles of event-driven operation more easily than programmer-generated events.

The most important events—those which most often characterize an object-oriented program—are events created by users. As the user, you trigger operations by clicking buttons or by pointing to the screen. Each input action is an event from the perspective of the object (the module) which receives it. In the case of input events, however, the user creates the event rather than another program module.

The primary difference between event-driven programs and conventional programs is the logic needed to interpret input. In a procedural program, you need comprehensive case logic to handle all possible combinations of user input ("if this device, then do this, else ..."). In an event-driven program, you don't need any specific program logic at all! Your collaboration hierarchy sets up the requesting capability for all possible events, and the inheritance hierarchy handles any case required during runtime.

4.3.3 When Is an Application Distributed?

Client/Server Applications

An application which is implemented as a collection of client/server modules is called a *distributed application*. The modules can be distributed across hardware components or across software environment components. They may be separate programs of a system or just separately compiled and cataloged subroutines within a program. They may be implemented all on one hardware platform or they may be individual programs implemented on different computers.

Process-driven design evolved around the functional requirements of scientific applications. By scientific applications, we mean process-intensive programs such as simulations. Process-driven design can be used to develop scientific applications that are physically implemented in a distributed manner.

Data-driven design evolved around the functional requirements of business applications. By business applications, we mean data-intensive programs such as financial systems. Data-driven design can be used to develop business applications that are physically implemented in a distributed manner.

Object-oriented design is based on the physical design requirements of any application which is to be implemented in a distributed manner. This shift from functional to physical considerations follows the shift from mainframe platforms to networked platforms. Object-oriented design can be used just as well for scientific or business applications that are also distributed.

The Concept of Extensibility

Object-oriented design is particularly well suited for distributed applications. The modules of a distributed application are independent from one another, yet interconnected as clients and servers. The design constructs of object-oriented programming languages focus your attention on the internal design of a module (an object) and on its interface with other modules (its requests).

Each object extends the capabilities of other objects in its domain. They become part of the corporate memory of the domain. The operations, the attributes, and requests of an object characterize its internal operation and its interface. They can be reused by later designs within the domain as if they were a part of the programming language. They extend the programming environment within the domain.

Extensibility is the reuse of flexible objects in a client/server domain. The primary benefits of an object-oriented design are its flexibility and reusability. It is flexible at the general level of the design of a domain. It is reusable at the detailed level.

CONCEPT 21

Extensibility is the regular use of operation names or attribute names in a domain as if they were a part of the programming language.

Object-oriented design is flexible at the general level of the design of a domain. New concrete classes can replace parts of other classes as new encapsulated objects in the collaboration hierarchy. New abstract classes can be added as new classified objects in the inheritance hierarchy. Classes provide you with a tool to extend the functions of a domain as if they were a part of the programming language.

Object-oriented design is reusable at the detailed level of the design of a domain. You can add new requests to the collaboration hierarchy. You can use an operation or an attribute without knowing exactly where it is located in the design. The object designs within classes also provide you with a tool to extend the functions of a domain.

CONCEPT SUMMARY - An Object-Based Model

CONCEPT 11. Object engineering is the transformation of a set of requirements into an organized collection of interacting client and server objects.

CONCEPT 12. A client object is one that makes a request of another object to trigger one of its operations or to access one of its attributes.

CONCEPT 13. A server object is one that responds to a request from another object by triggering one of its operations or by accessing one of its attributes.

CONCEPT SUMMARY - Designing Objects

CONCEPT 14. A domain is an organized collection of interacting objects which address a self-contained situation.

CONCEPT 15. Abstraction is the principle of focusing your attention on the level of detail appropriate to your interest.

CONCEPT 16. An inheritance hierarchy is a catalog of common processes and common data which helps to organize the objects in a domain.

CONCEPT 17. A collaboration hierarchy is a means of portraying program operation as the interaction between the objects in a domain.

CONCEPT SUMMARY - Programming Objects

CONCEPT 18. Polymorphism is the selection between redundant operation or attribute names based on the context in which they are used.

CONCEPT 19. Visibility is the capability to trigger operations or to access attributes in an object from within the other objects in a domain.

CONCEPT 20. An event is any action directed against one object by another object to trigger an operation or to access an attribute.

CONCEPT 21. Extensibility is the regular use of operation names or attribute names in a domain as if they were a part of the programming language.

CHAPTER REVIEW

Object-Oriented Design

What is a client/server domain? An environment composed of interacting objects that communicate with one another by making requests to trigger each other's process operations and/or to access each other's data attributes.

What are reusable components? Parts of an object-oriented design that can be used to satisfy requirements at different periods of time, either because they contain the same common operations and common attributes used by other objects in the domain or because they are used as servers by client objects in another system in the domain.

What is context sensative referencing? The ability of an environment to resolve a reference to a redundantly named operation or attribute based on the object in which it is used and the relationships between the objects in the domain.

What is event driven operation? Any action directed against an object by another object, such as a call from another program module or an external input from a user.

When is an application distributed? Any time that its components need to be treated individually, such as when they are developed at different times, are parts of different systems, or are implemented on different physical platforms.

5

Object Engineering

5.1 AN OBJECT-ORIENTED MODEL

Context-Sensitive Referencing

Object engineering is one particular approach for developing designs using an object-oriented model. Object-oriented designs are more flexible and more reusable than conventional designs, primarily due to a feature known as context-sensitive referencing. They are usually implemented in a distributed manner. The objects in such a design are often implemented on different platforms from one another and at different times.

Distributed applications that are designed using an object-oriented model are flexible. You construct the design in a way which maintains each object as a module separate from the others. Therefore, you can more easily modify the internal design of any one module within a program without disturbing the designs of other modules in that program. This is primarily due to context-sensitive referencing.

Program modules which are designed using an object-oriented model can often be reused by other modules and in different combinations than originally designed. The interface of an object becomes its window for other objects to make use of. The interface is represented by the requests to which the object can respond. They represent the operations and attributes of the object which can be reused by other objects in the domain. This is also primarily due to context-sensitive referencing.

Context-sensitive referencing eliminates the need to resolve naming conflicts during design. Names of modules need not be unique, since the manner in which they interact will help to determine which copy of a named object should be used. You can build or purchase libraries of object modules to meet the growing functional needs of your domain through time. Context-sensitive referencing provides the flexibility which makes an object truly modular and, therefore, reusable.

The framework for context-sensitive referencing is established by the manner in which objects are represented in the model. Objects are represented as independent modules which interact with one another in two ways (by inheritance and by collaboration). Objects in an inheritance hierarchy are often programmed as source libraries which you can reuse by including in programs before you compile them. Objects in a collaboration hierarchy are often programmed and complied as dynamic link libraries (DLLs) which you can reuse by calling them from your program.

5.2 AN OBJECT–ORIENTED APPROACH

5.2.1 How Do You Develop an Object–Oriented Design?

The Transformation of Requirements

An object-oriented approach to software development is one in which you use packages of related processes and data to represent a program's requirements and to drive its design. These packages are called *objects*. You develop software using this approach by identifying the objects of your application domain, allocating specific requirements to those objects, and then designing their internal workings to fulfill those requirements.

Object engineering is a particular object-oriented development approach which you can use to transform your program's requirements through a layered series of three models which correspond to the phases for identifying, allocating, and implementing requirements:

Development Goals	*Object Engineering*
Identify Requirements	The Domain Model
Allocate Requirements	The Interface Model
Implement Requirements	The Implementation Model

As shown in Figure 5-1, object engineering is a layered approach to developing software systems. The *domain model* is composed of two hierarchies, showing the inheritance and the collaboration relationships between classes. The *interface model* is composed of the descriptions of the classes, objects, and requests which characterize those hierarchies. Finally, the *implementation model* is composed of the designs for the operations and attributes which characterize each request.

CHAPTER 5:   OBJECT ENGINEERING   **83**

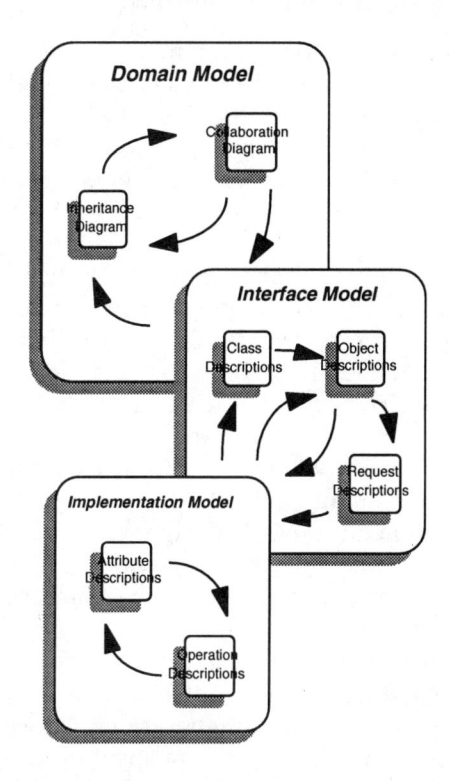

Figure 5-1.   The object-engineering approach.

There are various popular techniques, such as those explained by Booch, which you can use to develop an object-oriented design. These techniques are similar in many respects and can be used within an object-engineering development approach. They all deal with the integrated design of objects. Objects are packages of processes and data, called operations and attributes, respectively. There are many similarities between object-oriented design and both process-driven and data-driven design, but the manner in which objects are represented makes object-oriented design different.

Objects are organized into inheritance hierarchies which maintain the individual object designs separate from one another, and into collaboration hierarchies which establish the interfaces between those objects. The inheritance hierarchy organizes the object designs as separate classes. This is somewhat similar to entity analysis in data-driven design. The collaboration hierarchy provides the well-defined object interfaces as encapsulated components. This is somewhat similar to process decomposition in process-driven design.

Objects as Operations and Attributes

In object-oriented design, you constantly consider both the process requirements and the data requirements of your program. The process requirements are called operations. The data requirements are called attributes. Object-oriented design, therefore, draws on the concepts of both data-driven design and process-driven design. It adds value to the software engineering process by combining both into a single and more complete technique.

Data-driven design is characterized by entity analysis. The entity analysis aspect of object-oriented design is called *classification*. Classification shows up as the development of inheritance hierarchies. Unlike entity analysis, however, classification is applied to both processes and data. You can use the inheritance of object characteristics both to trigger internal operations and to access internal attributes.

You apply the concept of entity analysis to classify sets of operations and attributes across many objects in object-oriented design. This concept is borrowed from data-driven design, but is applied to entire objects rather than just data. Objects are packages of data and processes. Classification is one way in which object-oriented design improves upon conventional design.

Process-driven design is characterized by process decomposition. The decomposition aspect of object-oriented design is called *encapsulation*. Encapsulation shows up as collaborations between objects. Unlike process decomposition, however, encapsulation is applied to both processes and data. You can use the collaboration between objects both to trigger external operations and to access external attributes.

You apply the concept of process decomposition to encapsulate sets of operations and attributes within an object in object-oriented design. This concept is borrowed from process-driven design, but is applied to entire objects rather than just to processes. Objects are packages of processes and data. Encapsulation is another way in which object-oriented design improves upon conventional design.

5.2.2 When Is Object-Oriented Design Recursive?

The Object-Engineering Approach

Object engineering is characterized by a much more recursive life cycle than that of conventional approaches. It makes use of the separately maintained object designs and the well-defined object interfaces to maximize design reusability. Object-oriented systems lend themselves more readily to parallel program development. They more often can be composed of reusable modules, and more easily be developed over time as the controlled expansion of inheritance and collaboration hierarchies.

The recursive nature of the object-engineering life cycle is central to the theme of object-oriented design, and it is characterized by the reuse of existing program designs. The domain of an object-oriented system is a collection of client and server programs with well-defined interfaces and separately maintained internal designs. Well-defined interfaces allow existing server programs to be reused in new clients. Separately maintained internal designs allow existing client programs to be reused with new servers.

The object-oriented design of a system provides a level of autonomy unmatched in conventional designs. Inheritance hierarchies maintain templates of utility functions and common records used within a client. Collaboration hierarchies maintain maps of subroutines and local variables used as server objects to other client objects. Each server and each client in a system is a separate program module, which has its own internal design and may be used to construct many systems. You can, therefore, reuse the modules designed in this way either at the class level or at the object level.

At the class level, you can construct new systems using old modules without any concern for the internal design of the modules themselves. This is an important aspect of parallel program development. It may be needed to implement distributed programs within a system or to design individual modules of a program in a distributed manner. The entire development life cycle can then be repeated to design each such server module, but the effort is shorter and contained to the one new module.

At the object level, you can modify the internal design of a server module in many respects without causing changes to the client modules that use it. In large-scale software systems, this is often necessary, as when different teams may be developing different parts of the system; different time frames may apply to the completion of each program; or different hardware platforms may be used for the programs.

Reusing Classes in a Domain

The recursive nature of object engineering can be applied to classes using the interface model, which is characterized by the reuse of object hierarchies. The development of new client/server programs can often cannabalize old ones. A program consists of objects with well-defined interfaces and separately maintained internal structures. By cannabalizing, we mean that you construct new classes of objects in your interface model from existing classes in the inheritance and/or collaboration hierarchies in your domain model.

The development of new client/server programs can often take shape very quickly within an existing domain model. An object-oriented program consists of a collection of client and server modules (a collaboration hierarchy) with specific common characteristics (an inheritance hierarchy). The design of a new program is similar to the design of an entire system, but is usually accomplished by working only with the interface model and the implementation model.

Each module within the program has a well-defined interface and a separately maintained internal design. You can construct new programs using old modules without changing the internal design of the modules themselves. This is an important aspect of module reusability. The modules are rearrangable black boxes as far as the programs are concerned. This is one of the chief values of the interface model in object engineering.

Redesigning Objects in a Class

The recursive nature of object engineering can be applied to objects using the implementation model. You can redesign individual modules to include new requirements in programs which were quickly designed to provide only partial functionality (sometimes called a *prototype*). You can also redesign modules as parts of fully operational programs which are intended to evolve (sometimes called a *pilot system*). Development using prototypes and pilot systems in object engineering is a straightforward process.

You can easily modify object-oriented prototypes and object-oriented pilot systems within the structure of an existing domain model and interface model by working only with selected parts of the corresponding implementation model. You can modify the internal design of a server module within a program in many respects without causing changes to its client modules. You can also make use of different modules with the same interfaces but from other included source code modules or other dynamic link libraries (DLLs) of compiled modules. The modules are substitutable black boxes as far as the programs are concerned.

The ability to easily modify the design of an object is an important aspect of object reusability. Within the program source code, you can add new subclasses, expand collaborations, or substitute new server objects for old ones without changing the requests they receive. You can make your modules more sophisticated without disrupting the existing functions or data of the module (its operations or attributes). This is one of the chief values of the implementation model in object engineering.

5.3 OBJECT-ORIENTED TECHNIQUES

5.3.1 How Do You Identify Object Requirements?

The Class Hierarchies of a Domain

The first goal of object-oriented design is to identify the relationship requirements of the classes of objects which will comprise your domain—this is called *domain design*. Domain design is the top layer of object engineering. You identify classes of objects by focusing on their hierarchical relationships, represent these hierarchies in diagram form, and use them to identify more classes of objects. The result is called the *domain model*.

As shown in Figure 5-2, the domain model identifies the requirements of your system through the use of inheritance and collaboration diagrams, which in turn define the interaction used to specify the interfaces and internal designs of your objects. The domain model represents the same stage of design as the essential model of a process-driven approach and the information strategy plan of a data-driven approach, but is expressed in terms of the objects in a domain.

Objects are physical packages of operations and attributes. You may start either by listing a preliminary set of objects or by listing a preliminary set of operations and attributes. If you start with objects, you then look for the operations and attributes that help to define each object. If you start with operations and attributes, you then look for natural physical groupings, called objects, which would contain those operations and attributes.

You can look for nouns in descriptions of a system to determine a preliminary set of objects. Objects are the things a system serves (nouns) such as people, places, things, or documents. Similarly, you can look for verbs and adjectives in descriptions of a system to determine its operations and attributes, respectively. Operations are the process functions of a system, that is, the actions it takes (verbs). Attributes are its data entities, that is, its descriptive characteristics (adjectives).

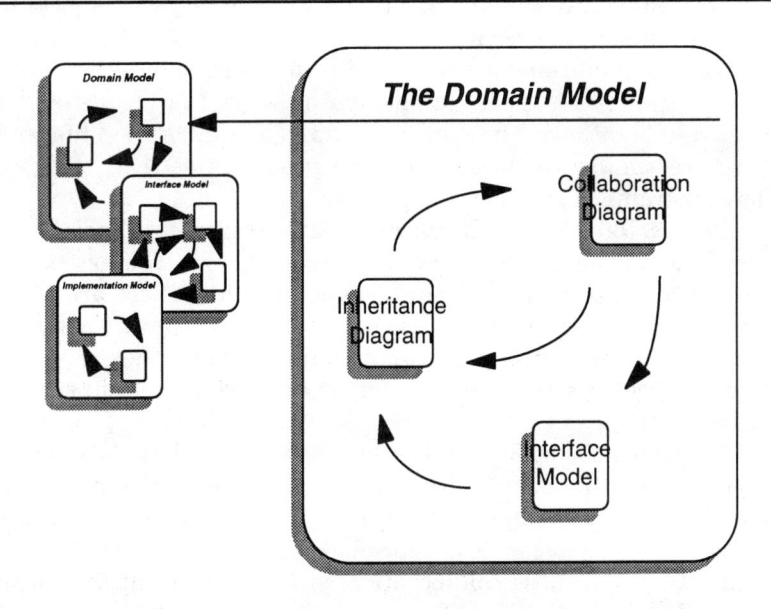

Figure 5-2.   Identified object requirements.

Identifying Inheritance Hierarchies

Apply data-driven concepts to identify the classes of objects in an inheritance hierarchy. You identify classes by considering the operations and attributes which are common to more than one object, and then represent the common operations and attributes as a common class above those objects in an inheritance hierarchy. Classes in an inheritance hierarchy are similar to subentities in entity relationship diagrams.

Building inheritance hierarchies is similar to identifying entities using cluster matrices in data-driven design. You cross-reference the usage of each object by the other objects in your domain. You then gather objects together which are all connected to the same object or to the same small set of other objects, and represent the group by another object. These groups of related objects become tree structures in the inheritance hierarchy, with the common groups (that is, the class of those objects) above the objects from which they were originally derived.

The inheritance diagrams are the object-oriented part of the domain model. You can think of an inheritance diagram as an enhanced entity relationship diagram. It shows the relationships of objects to object classes, that is, to those new objects derived to represent the common characteristics of other objects.

Identifying Collaboration Hierarchies

Apply process-driven concepts to identify the interactions between the objects in your domain in terms of collaboration hierarchies. You identify new objects by decomposing other objects into subordinate sets of strongly related operations and/or attributes. The original objects that you may have identified become the clients in your domain. The new subordinate sets of requirements extracted from these clients become the servers. You represent the relationships between the clients and the servers as collaborations. The server objects in a collaboration hierarchy, therefore, are similar to the decomposed processes on a leveled set of data-flow diagrams.

Building collaboration hierarchies is similar to decomposing processes into smaller groups in process-driven design. You examine the operations and attributes of an object to determine if there are natural subgroups. You may group several operations because they transform the same attribute, or may group several attributes because they serve as alternative transactions to the same operation. The new groups become new server objects.

You determine the collaborations between most objects based on the need of one object (the client) either to trigger an operation or to access an attribute in another object (the server). This is called a *hierarchical collaboration*. As you decompose your objects by regrouping their operations and attributes, these collaborations become apparent. An entirely encapsulated object becomes an external server to a client object in a hierarchical collaboration.

You determine another kind of collaboration between objects based on the need of one object (the client) to access a known attribute in a separate but related object (the server). By related, we mean another object that had not been encapsulated from the original object, but that contains a lone attribute that two have in common. This is called a *lateral collaboration*. A lone attribute would not justify the creation of an encapsulated lower-level object. Instead, you would simply establish a lateral collaboration between the two otherwise unrelated objects.

The collaboration diagrams are the conventional part of the domain model. You can think of a collaboration diagram as an enhanced structure chart. It shows both hierarchical and lateral collaborations as requests between objects. Hierarchical collaborations are analogous to the data couples flowing between connected modules on a structure chart. Lateral collaborations are analogous to off-page data flows in a leveled set of data-flow diagrams.

5.3.2 How do You Allocate Object Requirements?

Objects Associated with Classes

The second goal of object-oriented design is to allocate the object requirements of your domain. This is called *class design,* which is the middle layer of object engineering. You allocate object requirements by listing the operations and attributes that will comprise each object in your domain and by describing the requests which form the interface for triggering those operations and accessing those attributes. This represents the general design of your system, but it is derived in a very physical manner. It results in what we call the *interface model*.

As shown in Figure 5-3, the interface model identifies the requirements of your system in terms of the objects of your domain, the classes associated with them, and the specifications for those objects. The interface model represents the same stage of design as the environmental model of a process-driven approach and the business area analysis of a data-driven approach, but expressed in terms of the classified and encapsulated objects in your domain hierarchies.

Many authors present inheritance and collaboration in a single hierarchical representation of both abstract and concrete classes. We prefer to use two separate hierarchies to depict the inheritance relationships between abstract classes, and the collaboration relationships between concrete classes, respectively. This helps you to better understand the distinction between abstract and concrete classes of objects and how they are derived.

As you allocate specific operations and attributes to objects, you tend to classify and encapsulate more objects, which helps you to refine the hierarchical relationships between objects. The classification of

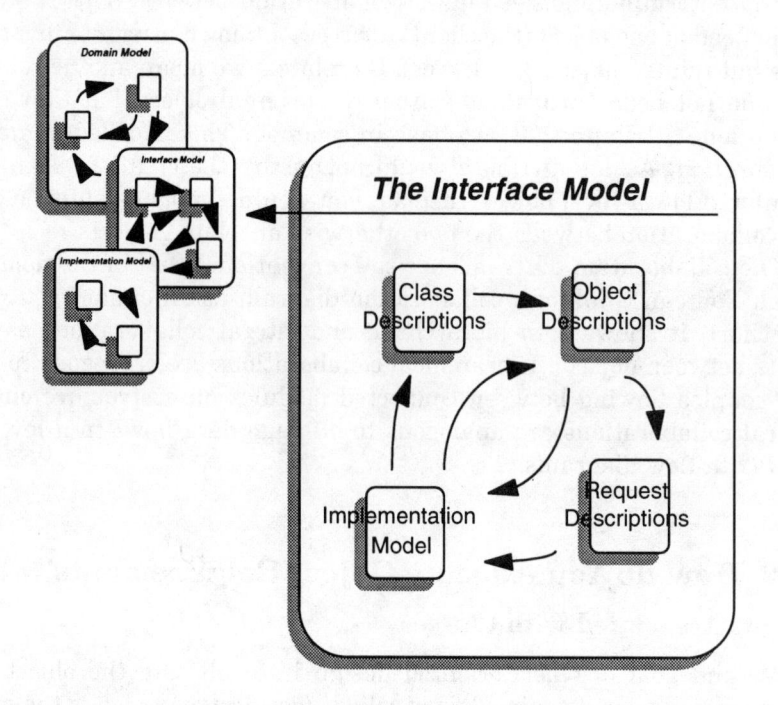

Figure 5-3.   Allocated object requirements.

new objects is, in effect, the modification of the inheritance hierarchy of your domain (adding new abstract classes). Similarly, the encapsulation of objects helps you to refine the collaboration hierarchy (adding new concrete classes).

Expand the lists of operations and attributes within each object to represent as complete a set as you can determine. You then look for common sets of operations and attributes across different objects and look for subordinate sets of operations and attributes within individual objects. The common sets will eventually be used to classify additional objects in the inheritance hierarchy. The subordinate sets will eventually be used to encapsulate additional objects in the collaboration hierarchy.

Your interface model is complete when you have defined all of the objects that you will need to represent all of your system's requirements. Your model may be large or small, depending on the size of your domain. If you have a small domain of one or two programs, there will be a relatively small number of objects (several dozen or so). If you have a large domain for a complex system, there will be a relatively large number of objects (many dozens or even hundreds).

Allocating Requirements by Classification

The inheritance hierarchy represents the common requirements for your program. Allocate these requirements among your objects by listing the common operations and attributes associated with each object class in your inheritance hierarchy. Similar to data-driven design, analyze the objects as related sets of entities. The difference in this case is that the objects contain both process operations and data attributes, whereas in a data-driven design, you are only analyzing data entities.

The allocation of inheritance requirements often uncovers new objects. Determine new object classes by expanding the set of operations or attributes within all objects, grouping the sets to show the sharing of common operations and common attributes, and then considering each group as a potential new class. The classes will eventually be represented hierarchically to convey the inheritance characteristics of the objects that they represent.

Classifying objects into inheritance hierarchies is similar to allocating entities into neighborhood groups in data-driven design, but is applied to both processes and data. You classify objects by extracting common sets of operations and attributes between objects. These new objects are abstract classes in an inheritance hierarchy. In this way, each abstract class becomes the basis for a separately maintained design of the operations (processes) and attributes (data) of a common object.

Allocating Requirements by Encapsulation

The collabration hierarchy represents the standard requirements of your program. Allocate those requirements among your objects by listing the unique operations and attributes that characterize each object class in your collaboration hierarchy. Similar to process-driven design, you decompose the objects in a hierarchical manner. The difference in this case is that the objects contain both process operations and data attributes, whereas in a process-driven design, you are only decomposing processes.

The allocation of collaborative requirements often uncovers new objects. Decompose objects by expanding the lists of operations or attributes within an object, grouping them into sets of related operations and attributes, then considering each group as a new object. Any new objects are said to be encapsulated within the original object and will eventually be represented as a collaboration between the two objects.

Encapsulating objects into collaboration hierarchies is similar to allocating processes into groups in process-driven design, but is applied to both processes and data. You encapsulate objects by extracting subordinate sets of operations and attributes within an object. These new objects are concrete classes in a collaboration hierarchy. In this way, each concrete class becomes the basis for a well-defined interface to trigger the operations (processes) and to access the attributes (data) of a subordinate object.

92 OBJECT ENGINEERING

5.3.3 How Do You Implement Object Requirements?

Individual Object Designs

The third goal of object-oriented design is to implement the requirements of your interface model as the design of a computer program. This is called *object design*. Object design is the bottom layer of object engineering. You implement the design of each object associated with each class in your domain and provide structural designs for the operations and the attributes within each object. The result is called the *implementation model*.

As shown in Figure 5-4, the implementation model implements the requirements of your system by providing the internal designs for the operations and the attributes of your objects. The implementation model of an object-oriented design corresponds to the implementation model of a process-driven approach and the business area design of a data-driven

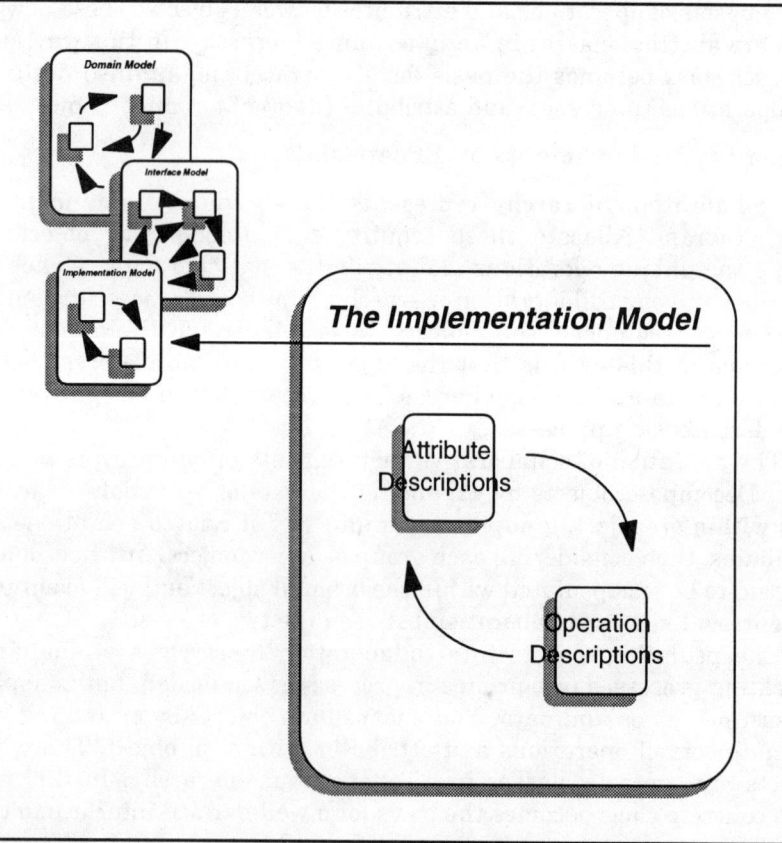

Figure 5-4.   Implemented object requirements.

approach. Parts of the model may even be expressed using some of the same diagram forms as in a conventional design, but now within the standardized context of an object-oriented model. This provides both a reusable and a flexible design representation.

The reusability of an object module is achieved by representing concrete classes of objects as clients and servers that interact in collaborations. Each collaboration is characterized by a well-defined interface (requests). Each operation associated with a request is characterized by its own design separate from other operations. Each attribute associated with a request can also be characterized by a structural design relating it to other attributes.

The flexibility of an object-oriented design is achieved by representing abstract classes of objects as related objects which inherit operations and attributes from one another. The inheritance hierarchy allows the compiler to resolve implied references to common operations and attributes based on the class of the object to which they belong. This results in a context-sensitive programming structure. Redundant names for operations and attributes are resolved based on where they are used.

Implementing Object Operations

In designing individual objects, you may choose to apply process-driven techniques directly to the design of its operations. Requests are used to represent the collaborations between objects. Requests trigger external operations from any remote object; collaborations also access external attributes. However, you still need to design the structure of each object operation and the structure of each object attribute. Operation design is no different than conventional process design.

Objects collaborate with one another by external references within the object's program statements. These usually involve function calls from an operation in one object to another operation in a different object. You may choose to design the internal operation of a fully decomposed and classified object using conventional techniques. The best way to represent the operations of an object is often through the use of data-flow diagrams and structure charts.

Implementing Object Attributes

In designing individual objects, you may choose to apply data-driven techniques directly to the design of its attribute structures. Inheritance classes represent the internal operations that can be triggered from within any object of that class, and similarly, the internal attributes that can be accessed. However, you still need to design each object operation and the structure of each object attribute. Attribute design is no different from conventional data base design.

Objects which contain more than a few attributes may need a separate design to define the structure of those attributes in addition to the operation designs. You may choose to design the internal structure of an object using conventional techniques. The best way to represent the attributes of a fully decomposed and classified object is often through the use of entity relationship diagrams and normalized data structure diagrams.

CHAPTER REVIEW

Object Engineering

How do you develop an object-oriented design? By transforming a combined set of process requirements and data requirements into a design for a working computer program.

When is object-oriented design recursive? When you use object-oriented design techniques to develop individual systems in a domain, or individual objects within your inheritance and collaboration hierarchies, or individual operation modules or attribute schemas within objects.

How do you identify object requirements? By organizing the individual objects of your domain into collaboration diagrams and inheritance diagrams.

How do you allocate object requirements? By listing the individual operations and the individual attributes which characterize the objects in your domain.

How do you implement object requirements? By designing the operations of each object in your domain as sets of process requirements, and by designing the attributes of each object as sets of data requirements.

Part II
OBJECT-ORIENTED TERMINOLOGY

In the next five chapters of this book, the terminology of object engineering is presented. By *terminology*, we mean the jargon and the concepts used both here and elsewhere to describe the components of an object-oriented design. The jargon of object-oriented design can be related to a few basic underlying concepts.

Chapter 6 defines *objects* as the basis for the design of large-scale client/server systems. Objects can be any physical or abstract thing you wish to represent in a computer program. However, there are distinct features which characterize an object in an object-oriented design.

Chapter 7 defines *classes* as the primary building block used in the development of an object-oriented design. Classes are often confused with objects since there is such a close relationship between a class and its object. We differentiate a class from an object so that you can understand and decipher the many other things which you may have read about object-oriented design and programming.

Chapter 8 defines *inheritance* as the fundamental difference between object-oriented design and conventional design. Object-oriented design is more than a new way of looking at the same old thing. An object-oriented software development environment (this is, a compiler, its source language, and related editing tools) provides a distinct advantage over the more conventional procedural techniques because of the concept of inheritance.

Chapter 9 defines *collaboration* as the fundamental similarity between object-oriented design and conventional design. Object-oriented design, although a significant improvement over conventional design, still uses many of the same underlying principles. There are still process requirements and there are still data requirements. These requirements are conveyed by the concept of collaboration.

Chapter 10 defines a *domain* as the culmination of objects, classes, inheritance, and collaboration to represent a complete object-oriented design. A large and complex system, whether expressed in a conventional design or in an object-oriented design, requires that you employ an organized model to control the development of all of the components of your system and to manage their implementation after they are designed. In object-oriented design, the organized model is called the domain.

6
The Definition of an Object

6.1 OBJECTS AND INSTANCES

6.1.1 What Is an Object?

A Standardized Representation

Objects are a different way of looking at the requirements for a system design. However, before you jump into the details of an object's composition and its usage in the design process, it is important to understand that an object is just a way to represent the requirements for a system. An object is a standardized set of components which, taken together with all other objects, describes the requirements for a system. Objects, therefore, are just the design unit for representing a system in a particular way (called object-oriented design).

The use of objects in the design of a computer program is a standardized way to represent the requirements for a system during its development. In particular, an object is a standardized way to represent a package of process requirements and data requirements. This enables you to drive your design based on the combination of its process and data requirements, rather than solely from one perspective or the other. This is the major way in which an object-oriented design improves upon either a conventional process-driven or data-driven design. It combines them by providing a way to represent both processes and data.

The use of standardized objects results in a design composed of programmable black-box modules. Black-box modules can be used in a computer program based on their known interface characteristics.

Furthermore, those same black-box modules can continue to be used independent of any future changes to their internal design. These are the major benefits of using an object-oriented approach. Your design is flexible and reusable because it is standardized.

A Component of a System

An object is a tangible or conceptual entity which is represented in a particular way. An object can be a person, place, or thing (tangible objects), or can be an organization, role, incident, or interaction (conceptual objects). The criteria which establishes something as an object is not so much what it is, but rather, whether actions can be directed against it and whether it can be distinguished from other objects.

In engineering terms, an object is a component of a system. A system is a collection of components which act as whole, that is, their individual functions culminate in the accomplishment of the function of the system. The system may be a software system (a computer program), a hardware system (a computer platform), or any other collection of components which interact to accomplish a single major function (for example, an automobile manufacturing system, an insurance office claims procedural system, or an agricultural system of crop rotation). We will concentrate our discussion on software systems.

In a software system, an object is a component of the software. These components may be programs, subroutines, or modules, and may be either primary components of the system or nested within other components. An object, however, is not so much any one particular kind of component but a particular means of describing any component. An object, therefore, can be defined in terms of how it is represented:

1. An object is an identifiable item that represents something in the real world, either tangible or conceptual, to which attention can be directed and to which characteristics can be ascribed.
2. An object is a component of a system that performs some individual function as its contribution toward the function of the system as a whole.
3. An object is characterized by a specific set of process operations and data attributes that are needed to perform its function.
4. An object has an unambiguous boundary, that is, it is clearly understood what is internal and what is external to the object.
5. An object has an internal design structure that is independent of everything external to the object.

The first two points in this list help you to understand what an object is, while the last three points provide the insight into how to use objects to design software systems. An object is a group of related processes and data, has a well-defined interface, and has a separately maintained internal design. It is this part of the definition of an object which is most useful in object-oriented design.

An object is a group of related process operations and data attributes. As a group, the operations and attributes must be related to each other in some manner. The operations will act upon the attributes and the attributes will describe the state of the operations. This is the first test as to whether something is properly represented as an object: Do the operations and attributes which comprise the object naturally belong together?

An object has a well-defined interface. The group of related operations and attributes that are internal to an object interact with other objects in specific and definable ways. Any one object, therefore, is known in the system by the set of parameters needed to direct actions against it. This is the second test as to whether something is properly represented as an object: Does it have a well-defined set of parameters by which other objects can interact with it?

An object has a separately maintained internal design. As a component of a system, an object must serve a specific purpose in the system. The purpose of an object is satisfied by the function it performs, which is accomplished by its internal operations and attributes. Because of the well-defined interface, however, the internal interaction of its operations and attributes is of no consequence to other objects in the system. This is the third test as to whether something is properly represented as an object: Is its internal design independent of the rest of the system design?

A client object takes action on a server object only in terms of the parameters of the server object's interface. These actions will cause the server object, as one component of the system, to perform its individual function by triggering its operations and/or by accessing its attributes, which are parts of its internal design. The components (objects) of an object-oriented system are truly modular. They are much more likely to be reusable than if developed in a conventional approach.

Modularity and Reusability

In our definition of an object, the implied benefits of using objects as the basis to develop a computer program are modularity and reusability. However, these are the same claims made by proponents of process-driven design and then later by the proponents of data-driven design. Those conventional approaches, although adding value to the field of software development, never quite delivered on modularity and reusability. What, then, makes us think that object-oriented design succeeds where conventional design does not?

Conventional design techniques provide us with an organized and systematic means to transform a set of requirements into a working computer program. Some conventional techniques are process driven, while others are data driven, but they all lead to a working computer program.

The final program, however, is usually not modular enough to be reusable on other projects in any manner which is cost effective.

Object-oriented design techniques provide us with a mechanism to use both the process requirements and the data requirements to derive a working computer program. This, however, is not the reason that the final computer program will be modular and reusable. An object-oriented design is a standardized way of representing process and data requirements. Standardization provides modularity and reusability.

The requirements of an object are packaged as a set of operations and attributes with a well-defined interface and a separately maintained internal design. An object-oriented design, therefore, is a standardized and very specific way of representing the components of a system. This is why an object-oriented computer program is modular and reusable.

Although an object has a well understood and consistent meaning, the terminology used to describe an object varies from author to author and from technique to technique. For example, an object is generally accepted as a package of process operations and data attributes. However, different terms are used to identify what we have been calling the operations and attributes of an object. Sometimes, different terms are used to describe minor shades of difference at various points in their design techniques.

The most common terms that you will encounter when reading other material on object-oriented design are listed below. There are many good books by these and other authors that provide added detail beyond what is covered in this book. The concepts presented in the literature are fundamentally consistent with one another, but the terminology sometimes varies, especially when discussing operations. The following translation table should help you to decipher each author's discussion of object operations and object attributes:

Operations	*Attributes*	*As referred to by*
Methods	Attributes	Andleigh/Gretzinger
Operations	Fields	Booch
Services	Attributes	Coad/Yourdon
Actions	Attributes	Embley/Kurtz/Woodfield
Actions	Attributes	Shlaer/Mellor
Responsibilities	Parameters	Wirfs-Brock/Wilkerson/Wiener

Despite these terminology differences, an object has a very specific and consistent representation in all object-oriented design approaches. Different labels may be used by different authors, but objects are always composed of operations and attributes, objects are always represented to other objects in terms of their interface characteristics, and objects always maintain their internal design separate from one another. An object is a consistent representation of a software-system component across methodologies, across diagram types, across development environments, and across compilers in the object-oriented world.

Packaged Requirements

An object is a group of related processes and data. Therefore, it is convenient to think of an object as a package. The package contains process operations, in particular those operations needed to perform the functions that satisfy the overall function of the object. The package also contains data attributes, in particular those attributes needed to support the functions of the object. Together, a group of related operations and attributes constitute one object.

Figure 6-1 shows an object as a package of operations and attributes—the most fundamental description of an object. There are a finite number of operations and attributes that comprise any one object. Each operation represents a process requirement of the object and each attribute represents a data requirement of the object. Therefore, the composition of an object depends directly on the requirements of the system, or more specifically, on the requirements allocated to it as one component of the system.

OBJECT

Operation 1	Operation 5
Operation 2	Operation 6
Operation 3	Operation 7
Operation 4	

Attribute 1	Attribute 7
Attribute 2	Attribute 8
Attribute 3	Attribute 9
Attribute 4	Attribute 10
Attribute 5	Attribute 11
Attribute 6	

⇧ **Operations**   ⇧ **Attributes**

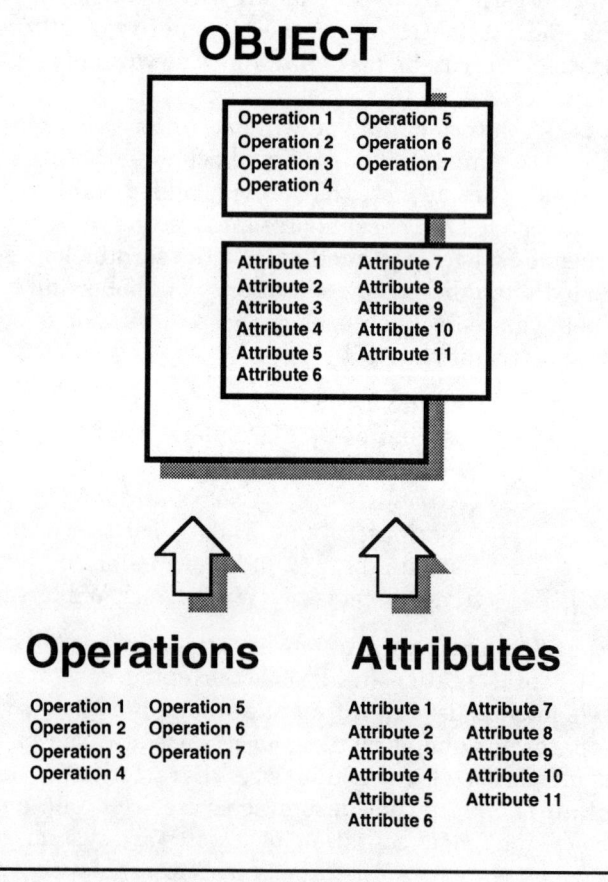

Operation 1	Operation 5		Attribute 1	Attribute 7
Operation 2	Operation 6		Attribute 2	Attribute 8
Operation 3	Operation 7		Attribute 3	Attribute 9
Operation 4			Attribute 4	Attribute 10
			Attribute 5	Attribute 11
			Attribute 6	

Figure 6-1. Object composition.

Most of the operations and attributes which constitute an object are part of its internal design and are said to be encapsulated within the object and inaccessible from the outside world. The information about the internal design of an object is hidden from other objects. Some of the operations and attributes which constitute an object are part of its interface and are accessible from the outside world, in fact, they are the only way in which other objects can communicate with the object they represent.

There are many ways to describe an object in object-oriented design. It can be described in terms of its function, its place in the system, or what it represents. This can sometimes lead to confusion. However, if you translate the description of any object into the set of process operations and data attributes it contains, you will always be able to deduce everything else about that object.

Operation Characteristics

The *operations* of an object are the characteristics that represent how an object reacts to actions directed towards it. Many different terms are used to refer to the operations of objects. They can be called *functions*, *operations*, *methods*, *responsibilities*, or *services*. However, it is generally agreed that they all represent something which responds either directly or indirectly to the actions directed at one object by other objects. In practical terms, operations are the processes that can be triggered in an object.

For example, a file object would be composed of operations which perform all of the file-related functions that might be needed for input and output in an application program. These might include such operations as printing an individual record, listing all records, deleting a record, replacing a record, duplicating a record, copying the file, moving the file, etc. These are the operations that characterize a file. They will eventually be programmed as the processes that can be triggered with respect to any file.

Attribute Characteristics

The *attributes* of an object are the characteristics that represent the properties that give it a distinct identity. They may be called *attributes*, *properties*, *fields*, or *parameters*, but they always represent the same thing. Attributes represent the set of properties to which values can be assigned to describe the object, and thus, to establish its identity. In practical terms, attributes are the data elements which can be accessed in an object.

For example, a file object would be composed of attributes that describe all of the file-related aspects as might be needed for input and output in an application program. These might include such attributes as the name of the file, its size in bytes, its size in characters, the number of records it contains, the directory in which it is stored, the date it was created, the date a record was last updated, the password needed to access it, the maximum number of records allowed, etc. These are the attributes that characterize a file. They will eventually be programmed as the data that can be accessed with respect to any file.

6.1.2 What Do Operations Represent?

Process Requirements

The process requirements of an object are represented by the list of operations that belong to the object. Each operation represents one process requirement. In this way, object-oriented design is no different from process-driven design. The process operations are used to represent the requirements of a system and the design approach is to transform those requirements into a working computer program. The manner in which you represent those requirements as a design, however, affects the nature of your design.

In process-driven design, you spend a significant amount of your time designing the interaction between the processes. Minor changes to some of these interactions often affect large portions of the design. As a result, your design may be a valid and correct implementation of your original requirements, but it is not very flexible. Systems and system designs need to change if they are to be reused as requirements change and as new requirements become known.

In object-oriented design, you are only concerned with the identity of the processes needed to fulfill the object's purpose in the system. Each object has a well-defined interface by which its operations can be triggered. It can be used by any other object that knows its interface characteristics. Similarly, the internal design of the operations of an object is maintained separately from all other objects. It is, therefore, truly modular within the overall design of the system.

Data-Flow Diagrams

Although it need not be designed in any particular manner, there will be some type of internal design for each operation within each object. The representation of an object to the other objects in the system doesn't require that its internal design be known. As the designer, though, you must address an object's internal design and you might find it easier to think of it in terms already familiar to you, such as data-flow diagrams.

You can think of the operations in an object as process bubbles on a data flow diagram. Each operation represents one process requirement, and these process requirements can be decomposed by listing their subordinate processes. Operations, therefore, can be decomposed in the same manner as processes on a data-flow diagram. This is a convenient way to make use of your understanding of process-driven design in an object-oriented representation.

Eventually, you may represent the internal design of the operations of an object using any of several techniques. Sometimes, operation design can be accomplished by procedural programming (just writing a sequence of lines of code). Other times, you will use flow charts, structure charts, or data-flow diagrams. The existence of an object does not depend on any one particular means of internal operation design. The only thing important about the process requirements of an object is that the full list of process operations be known.

6.1.3 What Do Attributes Represent?
Data Requirements

The data requirements of an object are represented by the list of attributes that belong to the object. Each attribute represents one data requirement. In this way, object-oriented design is no different from data-driven design. Data attributes are used to represent the requirements of a system, and the design approach is to transform those requirements into a working computer program. The manner in which you represent those requirements as a design, however, affects the nature of your design.

In data-driven design, you spend a significant amount of your time designing the relationships among data entities. Minor changes to some of these relationships often affect large portions of the design. As a result, your design may be a valid and correct implementation of your original requirements, but it is not very flexible. Systems and system designs need to change if they are to be reused as requirements change and as new requirements become known.

In object-oriented design, you are only concerned with the identity of the data entities needed to fulfill the object's purpose in the system. Each object has a well-defined interface by which its attributes can be accessed. It can be used by any other object which knows its interface characteristics. Similarly, the internal design of the attributes of an object is maintained separately from all other objects. It is, therefore, truly modular within the overall design of the system.

Entity Relationships

Although the attributes in an object need not be designed in any particular manner, there will be some type of internal design for each attribute within each object. The representation of an object to the other objects in the system doesn't require that its internal design be known. As the designer, however, you may find it easier to think of the attributes of an object in terms already familiar to you such as entity relationship diagrams.

You can think of the attributes in an object as entities on an entity relationship diagram. Each attribute represents one data requirement, and these data requirements can be analyzed by examining their relationships to other attributes. Attributes, therefore, can be analyzed in the same manner as entities on an entity relationship diagram. This is a convenient way to make use of your understanding of data-driven design in an object-oriented representation.

You may represent the internal design of the attributes of an object using any of several techniques. Sometimes, attribute design can be accomplished as a flat file design (just listing a sequence of data elements). Other times, you will use normalization diagrams or entity rela-

---

The Members of an Object

The operations and attributes that comprise an object are called the members of that object. There is always an internal interrelationship between the operations and the attributes that are packaged together as an object. For example, the object in Figure 6-1 lists seven operations and eleven attributes in no particular arrangement. Upon closer examination, however, you may find that certain dependencies exist between the members. After all, the operations and attributes were originally grouped together as a package of related processes and data.

You will usually find that only a few of the members of an object are major operations or attributes. By major, we mean that the other operations and attributes are subordinate to (called or accessed by) these major members. For example, the relationhips depicted below show that there are four major members of the object, each composed of some combination of the remaining members:

```
        Operation 5 *              Operation 6 *
          Operation 2                Operation 3 *         Major Members
            Operation 1                Operation 1         Operation 5
            Attribute 1                Attribute 1         Operation 6
            Attribute 2                Operation 4 *       Operation 7
          Attribute 3                  Attribute 7         Attribute 9
          Attribute 4                Attribute 6 *
          Attribute 5                Attribute 8           Entry Points (*)
          Attribute 11 *                                   Operation 3
                                   Operation 7 *           Operation 4
        Attribute 9 *                Operation 3 *         Operation 5
          Attribute 3                  Operation 1         Operation 6
          Attribute 4                  Attribute 1         Operation 7
          Attribute 5                  Attribute 2         Attribute 6
          Attribute 10 *               Attribute 6 *       Attribute 9
                                       Attribute 7         Attribute 10
                                                           Attribute 11
```

As you consider the interrelationships of the members of an object, you will notice several characteristics that will later play an important role in the transformation of an object into a set of related classes. Some of an object's members will need to be accessed from outside of the object (they will be entry points to the encapsulated module), and some of its members will be subordinate to more than one other member (they are the classified common operations and attributes used repeatedly from within this object).

tionship diagrams. The existence of an object, however, does not depend on any one particular means of internal attribute design. The only thing important about the data requirements of an object is that the full list of data attributes be known.

Equivalent Structure Charts

The interrelationships among the members of an object represent the process hierarchy of the operations and the data hierarchy of the attributes. In conventional design, these hierarchical relationships would be represented as process and data structure charts. In object-oriented design, these hierarchical relationships will be used to derive the inheritance and collaboration hierarchies.

The process structure charts shown below depict the hierarchical relationship between the operations of the object from Figure 6-1. Notice that the major members (Operations 5, 6, and 7) all appear at the top of the structure charts, and that the remaining operations are all subordinate in some manner to the major members. Notice also that there are common modules (Operations 1 and 3) whose entire branches are repeated in the structure charts. The purpose of classification in object-oriented design is to extract these common modules and catalog them as separate objects in an inheritance hierarchy. This principle applies equally well to the attributes in a data structure chart as well as to the operations in a process structure chart as we have shown here.

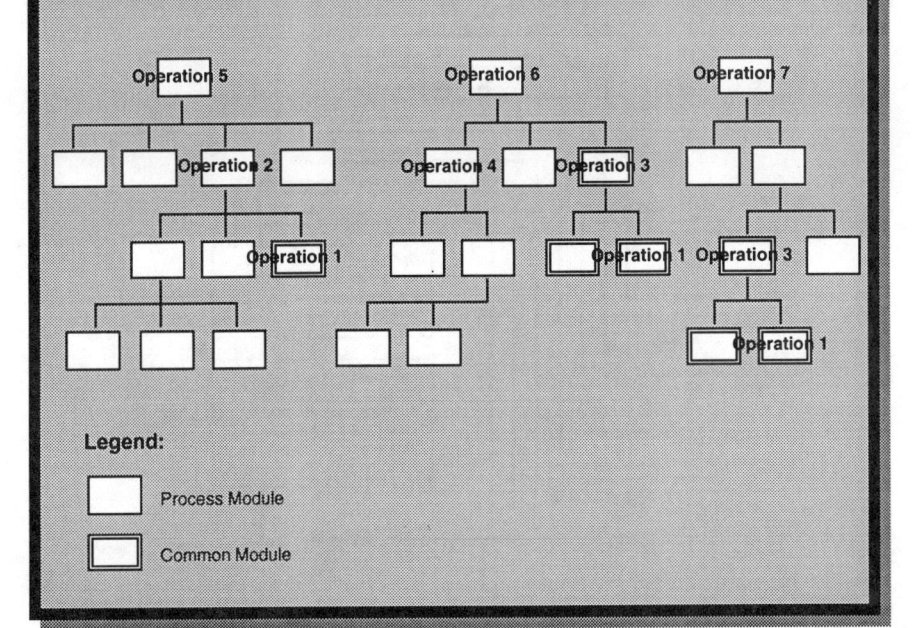

Legend:

- Process Module
- Common Module

6.1.4 What Is an Instance of an Object?
An Array of Identical Objects

An instance of an object is one of several identical copies of that object. By identical, we mean that each instance is composed of the same set of operations and attributes that characterize that object. An object is the abstract representation of a set of operations and attributes; an instance is the physical implementation of an object in a computer program. This subtle distinction is important because you may have many instances (copies) of the same object within the same computer program.

Figure 6-2 shows a conceptual representation of a set of "n" instances of an object (the object from Figure 6-1). You can think of an instance of an object as an array of parallel identical objects. They have the same operations and the same attributes as each other, although their corresponding attributes will most likely contain different values. You can direct actions against each instance and it will behave in the same manner as all instances of that object, but it will have its own identity.

One way to think of the instances of objects is in terms of the computer memory required to sustain them. Each instance will require its own memory area in order to sustain its unique set of values for the

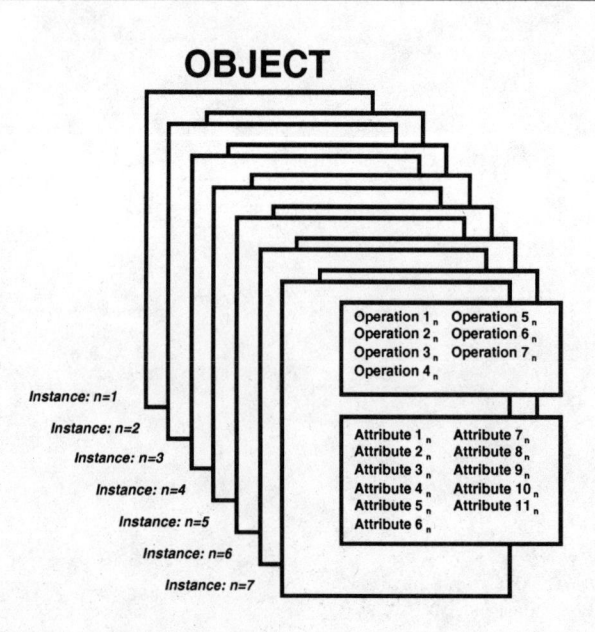

OBJECT

Operation 1$_n$ Operation 5$_n$
Operation 2$_n$ Operation 6$_n$
Operation 3$_n$ Operation 7$_n$
Operation 4$_n$

Instance: n=1
Instance: n=2
Instance: n=3
Instance: n=4
Instance: n=5
Instance: n=6
Instance: n=7

Attribute 1$_n$ Attribute 7$_n$
Attribute 2$_n$ Attribute 8$_n$
Attribute 3$_n$ Attribute 9$_n$
Attribute 4$_n$ Attribute 10$_n$
Attribute 5$_n$ Attribute 11$_n$
Attribute 6$_n$

Figure 6-2.   Object instances.

object attributes. Some compilers may also assign separate runtime memory areas for the executable code associated with the operations for each instance of an object, however, this is not necessarily required. The difference between one instance of an object and another is primarily concerned with the values of their attributes.

For example, you may have a file object as part of an application program. The file object would contain various functions as its operations and various properties as its attributes. As you call (collaborate with) that module (the file object) from various places (other objects) in your application program, you may use parallel instances of the same object, each instance capable of triggering the same operations (such as listing records) but assigning different values to some of the same attributes (such as a file name). In this way, you can use the same object to perform similar parallel functions each time without waiting for it to finish a prior task (it will not be process bound).

Many authors and texts on object-oriented programming equate the concept of an object with its instance. Most times when object-oriented programmers refer to an object, they really mean an instance of an object. It is important to understand the distinction between objects and their instances, however, when discussing object-oriented design. An object is a conceptual package of operations and attributes; an instance is a particular physical implementation of a particular object.

The State of an Object

A concept that is closely related to an instance of an object is its state. Each attribute of an object can have a value, which can be static or dynamic. A *static* value is constant throughout the operation of the program. A *dynamic* value can change as operations are triggered or as the attribute is accessed by other objects. Furthermore, the value of an attribute can be numeric and discrete, it can be numeric and continuous (or so represented), or it can be descriptive (textual). The state of an object depends on the values of its attributes.

The state of an object (or rather, the state of an instance of an object) is one combination of a particular set of values for its attributes. This should not be confused with the concept of an instance of an object. An instance of an object is the capability to differentiate between multiple identical copies of an object. The state of that instance is the particular combination of the values assigned to its attributes at any point in time.

In theory, there can be an astronomical number of states for any one instance of an object. In reality, you will often be concerned with only a very specific and finite number of states. These states will represent a set of very particular conditions around which you will develop the internal design of the operations and attributes in your objects. Just remember that while an object can have n distinct instances during the operation of the program, each of the n instances can have m distinct states.

6.2 OBJECT CLASSIFICATION

6.2.1 What Is Object Classification?

Common Requirements

An object is a package of operations and attributes. The operations and attributes represent process requirements and data requirements, respectively. They are grouped together because they are related to one another. But often, the relationships are not so clear-cut as to entirely distinguish one object from another. Some of the operations and attributes in one object may be similar to operations and attributes in another object. They represent common requirements.

In the same way that related operations and attributes can be grouped as objects, related objects can be grouped as classes of objects. In this context, the relationships among objects is the commonalty of some of the operations and attributes within each object. By common, we mean that some operations and attributes are known to be used many times by other operations and attributes.

The relationships among individual operations and attributes involve the concept of *cohesion*, taken from conventional design. There is a strong measure of cohesion between the operations and attributes within an object. During classification, groups of operations and attributes that are known to be common to several objects can be extracted to form a single new object. Multiple common groups can be extracted to form multiple new objects. However, there is still a strong measure of cohesion among the operations and attributes in these new objects and those remaining in the objects from which they were extracted.

Shown in Figure 6-3 is the original set of operations and attributes (from Figure 6-1) now distributed among several new objects. The new objects were determined based on the commonalty of their operations and attributes. The original set of operations and attributes is now said to be classified. The single original object has been transformed into a set of six related objects. The set of six objects are related to one another because of the strong measure of cohesion which still exists between their operations and attributes.

Separate Internal Designs

An organized set of objects is said to be a *classified* set of operations and attributes. Each of the objects in the class, however, still meets the criteria of an object: It is composed of operations and attributes, it has a well-defined interface, and it has a separately maintained internal design. Object classification merely superimposes an organization scheme in conjunction with these criteria.

Figure 6-4 shows a conceptual representation of the internal structure of a set of classified objects (those from Figure 6-3). Each of the six objects has its own internal relationship between the operations and the attributes of which it is comprised, although they have been physically separated from those of the other five objects. Each of these internal designs is independent of all others.

Some of the objects, however, will use some of the operations and attributes from the other objects. After all, some of these objects were defined as containing operations and attributes that are common to other objects. However, by making them separate objects, the lower-level program design of their operations and attributes can now be derived and maintained independent of the other objects.

6.2.2 How Is Classification Used?

Similar to Entity Analysis

Object classification is similar in concept to entity analysis in data-driven design. In entity analysis, you display the relationships between a known set of highly cohesive entities and then examine the relationships to discover additional entities that may be needed to support your original entities. In object classification, you list a known set of highly cohesive objects and then examine their interaction to discover additional objects. Object classification, like entity analysis, is a process of organizing and then outwardly expanding your list of requirements.

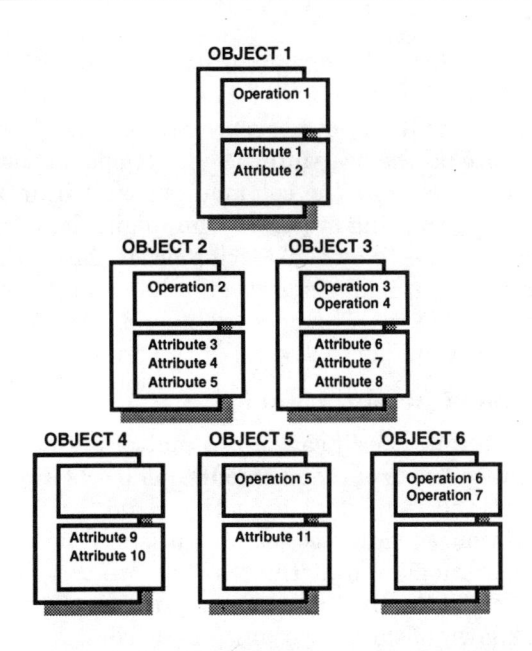

Figure 6-3. Classified objects.

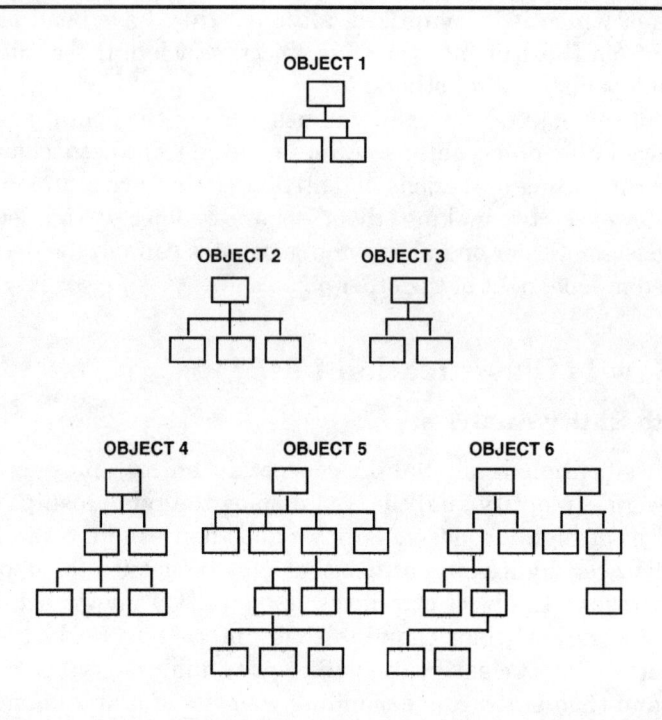

Figure 6-4. Classified object structures.

At first, you consider the commonalty among and within an original set of objects to derive new objects. Later, you consider the cohesion among the new objects to discover even more objects. For example, you might first separate all the user-interface functions (keyboard object, file object, mouse object, etc.) as the common objects within an application object (such as an accounting system). You might then expand your list of attributes and/or objects by considering other things that are needed (character object, screen image object, etc.) to support the relationships among these other objects. The operations and attributes of these new objects will often be common to several of the original objects.

The Intersection of Requirements

In mathematical terms, classification is a matter of finding the intersection between multiple sets of requirements. The sets are the objects; the requirements are the individual operations and attributes within the objects. By definition, the intersection of two sets is the overlapping area, that is, those operations and attributes that are common to both sets. You can easily determine the intersection of requirements by examining a detailed breakdown of the operations and attributes of an object.

The operations and attributes which comprise an object are called the *members* of that object. There is always an internal interrelationship among the individual operations and attributes that are packaged together as an object. If you organize the operations and attributes in some manner to show the relationships among them, you will see that some of them are subordinate to more than one other member. These are the common operations and attributes which will become new objects during object classification.

The internal relationships between the operations and the attributes of an object represent the process and data hierarchies, respectively. In conventional design, these hierarchical relationships would be represented as process and data structure charts. In object-oriented design, these hierarchical relationships are used to derive the collaboration and the inheritance hierarchies. A *collaboration* hierarchy is just an object-oriented representation of the noncommon process modules on a structure chart. Similarly, an *inheritance* hierarchy is just an object-oriented representation of the common modules.

Classification is a matter of finding the intersection of two sets of operations and attributes to derive the inheritance hierarchy. The intersection contains the operations and attributes that would have been shown as common processes and common data on a structure chart of an object. After you find and extract one group of common operations and attributes (along with their own subordinate operations and attributes), you can repeat the process for other groups. This is how you transform a large unorganized object into a classified set of smaller objects.

Inheritance Characteristics

The classification of objects eventually results in the inheritance hierarchy of your domain. The operations and attributes of the objects are organized as related classes of objects, and the relationships between classes of common operations and attributes are known as the inheritance hierarchy. The compiler then uses the documented inheritance hierarchy to make use of the common operations and attributes based on the context in which they are later used.

For example, the source code in an input/output module in an accounting system may refer to a print or a list command (operations) or a file name or the file size (attributes) without having defined or declared them as part of the module, so long as a common file object has been declared as a parent of the input/output module from which it can inherit those operations and attributes.

The inheritance characteristics of an object, therefore, enable common operations and common attributes to be used by all objects that are declared to inherit them, without explicitly designing them into every object. The compiler will find an appropriate operation or attribute which is referenced in an object module at runtime, based on the documented inheritance hierarchy. This is the value added by object-oriented design, or more specifically, by an object-oriented language compiler.

6.3 OBJECT ENCAPSULATION

6.3.1 What Is Object Encapsulation?

Subordinate Requirements

Object encapsulation is similar to object classification. Operations and attributes are originally grouped together because they are related to one another. In classification, the common operations and attributes represent common requirements which are extracted to form new objects. In encapsulation, additional groups of operations and attributes are also extracted to form still more new objects. Encapsulation is a concept which is often used in both object-oriented and conventional software development. You can think of encapsulation as conventional modularity.

The operations and attributes of any object represent an encapsulated set of requirements of a system. Similarly, groups of operations and attributes within an object can be further encapsulated to add more organization by defining more objects which are related to one another. In this context, the relationship among objects is determined by the subordinate relationship among some of the operations and attributes within those objects. By subordinate, we mean that some operations and attributes are known to be more cohesive with each other than with the other operations and attributes in that object. They form an identifiable lower-level unit.

The relationship among different sets of encapsulated operations and attributes within an object involves the concept of *coupling* from conventional design. There is often a stronger measure of cohesion among certain operations and attributes within an object than among them and the other operations and attributes. During encapsulation, these groups of operations and attributes can be extracted to form a new subordinate object. Multiple subordinate groups can be extracted to form multiple new objects. However, there is still some cohesion between the operations and attributes in the different subordinate objects. The subordinate objects are said to be coupled with the original object from which they were derived.

Figure 6-5 shows the operations and attributes of a classified object (from Figure 6-3) now further distributed among two new subordinate objects. The new objects are said to be encapsulated within the original object. The single original object has been transformed into a set of three related objects. The set of three objects are related to one another because of the coupling which exists between their operations and attributes.

Well-Defined Interfaces

An object that is subordinate to another object is said to represent an encapsulated set of operations and attributes. In a sense, encapsulation is the essence of any form of software engineering. It is usually called *modular design*. Classification and encapsulation are both forms of modular

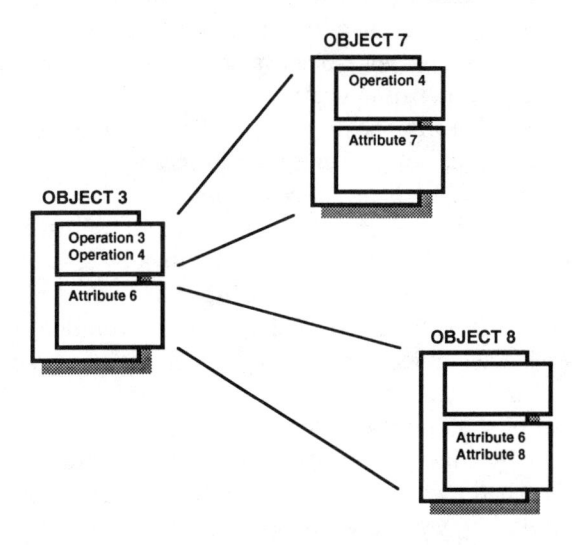

Figure 6-5. Encapsulated objects.

design. Encapsulation is different from classification only in the criteria used to divide an object. Classification extracts only the common groups of operations and attributes. Encapsulation extracts other remaining cohesive groups of operations and attributes.

Figure 6-6 shows a conceptual representation of the internal structure of a set of encapsulated objects (those from Figure 6-5). Notice that the internal structure of each encapsulated object is simply one portion of the internal structure of the original object (as was shown in Figure 6-4). Encapsulation is just the decomposition of a large object into a set of smaller objects which will behave as individual modules at run time.

Similar to classified objects, encapsulated objects will have their own separately maintained internal design. Different from classified objects, however, encapsulated objects will make explicit use of their interface parameters to maintain the coupling relationships which they have with each other. The relationships between classified objects will be established them as implicit relationships called *inheritance*. The relationships between encapsulated objects will be established as explicit relationships called *collaborations*.

6.3.2 How Is Encapsulation Used?

Similar to Process Decomposition

Object encapsulation is similar in concept to process decomposition in process-driven design. In process decomposition, you display the relationships between a known set of coupled processes and then examine the relationships to discover additional subordinate processes which may be needed to support your original processes. In object encapsulation, you list a known set of operations and attributes within an object, then examine their coupling to discover additional objects. Object encapsulation, like process decomposition, is a process of organizing and then downwardly expanding your list of requirements.

At first, you consider the relative cohesion among the operations and attributes within an object to divide it into objects. Later, you consider what is required to support the relationships between the original object and each of these new subordinate objects. For example, you might first divide a user-interface object (such as a keyboard) into a set of other objects representing its constituent parts (printable characters, control characters, graphical characters, and so on). You might then expand your list of operations by considering other things (generate character codes, acknowledge character printing, and so on) that apply specifically to the new objects. Similarly, you would expand the list of attributes attendant to these operations. The new operations and attributes are part of the new subordinate objects, but still represent requirements of the original keyboard object.

The Union of Requirements

In mathematical terms, encapsulation is a matter of representing the union between multiple sets of requirements. The sets are the objects and the requirements are the individual operations and attributes within the object. By definition, the union of two sets is the combined area, that

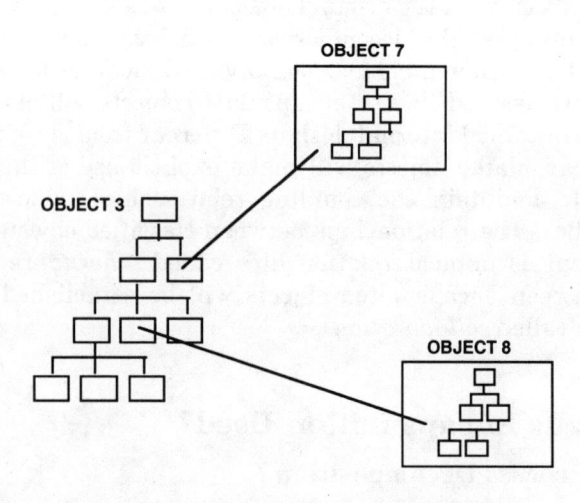

Figure 6-6. Encapsulated object structures.

CHAPTER 6: THE DEFINITION OF AN OBJECT **115**

is, all operations and attributes from both sets. We have introduced encapsulation as the division of a detailed breakdown of the operations and attributes of an object into separate objects. The full requirement of any object, therefore, is the union of its own internal requirements along with the requirements of all other objects encapsulated within it.

An encapsulated object is a wholly contained subset of another object. However, as an object, every encapsulated object still meets all of the

---

Equivalent Data Flow

The operations and attributes that remain within each object at the end of classification and encapsulation represent the processes performed and the data used specifically by that object. In the same way that you could derive a structure chart to show the hierarchical relationship among the members of an object, you can also represent the relationships between some members (the operations) at any level through the use of a data-flow diagram. As in process-driven design, a data-flow diagram may sometimes be the appropriate mechanism to describe the internal workings of a process oriented object.

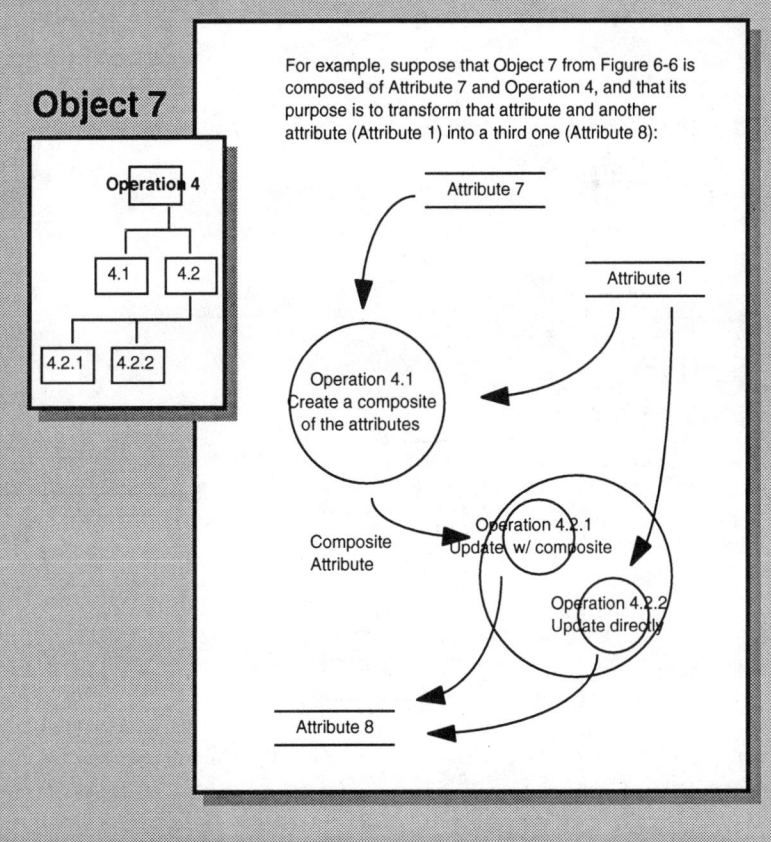

For example, suppose that Object 7 from Figure 6-6 is composed of Attribute 7 and Operation 4, and that its purpose is to transform that attribute and another attribute (Attribute 1) into a third one (Attribute 8):

Object 7

- Operation 4
  - 4.1
  - 4.2
    - 4.2.1
    - 4.2.2

Attribute 7 → Operation 4.1 Create a composite of the attributes
Attribute 1 →

Composite Attribute → Operation 4.2.1 Update w/ composite
Operation 4.2.2 Update directly

→ Attribute 8

116   OBJECT ENGINEERING

criteria of an object: It is composed of operations and attributes, it has its own internal design, and it has a well-defined interface. Encapsulated objects are server objects. The object in which an object is encapsulated is its client object. Furthermore, an object can be encapsulated within more than one other object if its server function is needed by more than one object.

Equivalent Entity Relationships

The operations and attributes that remain within each object at the end of classification and encapsulation represent the processes performed and the data used specifically by that object. In the same way that you could derive a structure chart to show the hierarchical relationships between the members of an object, you can also represent the relationships between some members (the attributes) at any one level through the use of an entity relationship diagram. As in data-driven design, an entity relationship diagram may sometimes be the appropriate mechanism to describe the internal workings of a data oriented object.

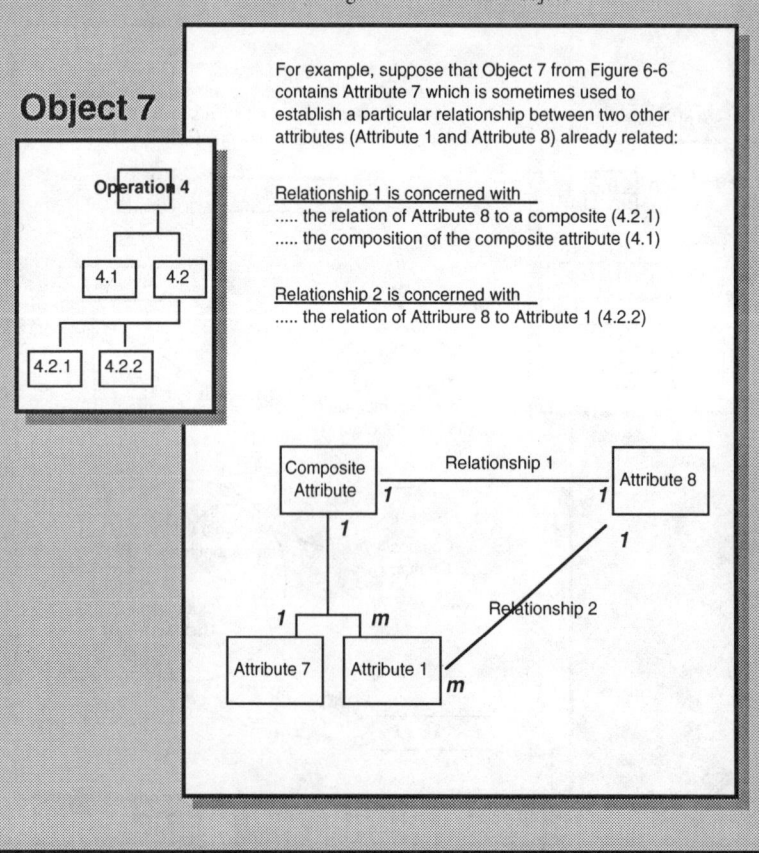

Object 7

Operation 4
- 4.1
- 4.2
  - 4.2.1
  - 4.2.2

For example, suppose that Object 7 from Figure 6-6 contains Attribute 7 which is sometimes used to establish a particular relationship between two other attributes (Attribute 1 and Attribute 8) already related:

Relationship 1 is concerned with
..... the relation of Attribute 8 to a composite (4.2.1)
..... the composition of the composite attribute (4.1)

Relationship 2 is concerned with
..... the relation of Attribure 8 to Attribute 1 (4.2.2)

Composite Attribute —— Relationship 1 —— Attribute 8
                1   1
                1
                                               1
                1   m   Relationship 2
Attribute 7 —— Attribute 1
                         m

Once encapsulated, an object can be treated just like any other object in your design. In the same way that the operations and attributes of any object can be represented in structure chart format, they can also be represented as data-flow diagrams. On a data-flow diagram of the internal design of an object, the operations become the process bubbles and the attributes become the data stores. Similarly, the operations and attributes of an object can alternatively be represented as entity relationship diagrams. On an entity relationship diagram of the internal design of an object, the attributes become the entities and the operations become abstracted as the relationships among the entities.

Collaboration Characteristics

The encapsulation of objects eventually results in the collaboration hierarchy of your domain. The operations and attributes of the objects are organized as subordinate sets of objects, and the relationships among these objects are known as the collaboration hierarchy. The object-oriented language compiler then uses the documented collaboration hierarchy to trigger operations and to access attributes in the subordinate objects much in the same way as subroutines are called in any conventional programming language.

For example, a keyboard module might be called in the source code from within an input/output module in an accounting system. The input/output object is said to collaborate with the keyboard object. Furthermore, the keyboard module may go on to call (to collaborate with) other subordinate modules (other server objects) to process keyboard characters, to process graphic input, or to process control characters. The calling modules are the client objects and the called modules are the server objects. Each call is a part of the collaboration between a client object and a server object.

The collaboration characteristics of an object, therefore, represent the client/server relationships, which must be established at design time in order for the system to properly satisfy its original requirements at runtime. The compiler will trigger operations and access attributes at runtime, based on the documented collaboration hierarchy. This represents the same type of operational structure as parent and child modules in conventional design.

CHAPTER REVIEW

The Definition of an Object

What is an object? A standardized component in the design of a system, it is a package of related operations and attributes with a well-defined interface and its own internal design.

What do operations represent? The process requirements of the objects in a domain, as in any process-driven design.

What do attributes represent? The data requirements of the objects in a domain, as in any data-driven design.

What is an instance of an object? A single run time copy of an object which can hold that object's state (a value for each of its attributes) like a row in a spreadsheet or a numerical array.

What is object classification? Upward grouping of objects which share distinct sets of common operations and attributes.

How is classification used? To organize the inheritance hierarchy among abstract classes of objects in a domain.

What is object encapsulation? The downward and outward division of objects which interact as clients and servers.

How is encapsulation used? To derive the collaboration interactions between concrete classes of objects in a domain.

7

The Definition of a Class

7.1 CLASSES AND INSTANCES

7.1.1 What Is a Class?

Objects Linked to Hierarchies

Classes in an object-oriented design are used to link a set of objects into organized groups called *inheritance hierarchies* and *collaboration hierarchies*. An object is a standardized way of representing a package of process operations and data attributes. The hierarchies enable you to represent these operations and attributes as organized requirements. Classes, therefore, play an important role in the organization of an object-oriented design.

The classes in an object-oriented design are organized to show two different hierarchical organizations of your requirements. The inheritance hierarchy represents the common process operations and the common data attributes required in your system. The collaboration hierarchy represents the operational interaction among the particular process operations and the particular data attributes which satisfy the requirements of your domain. Classes, therefore, are the design unit by which you manage the evolution of an object-oriented design.

A Group of Related Objects

The difference between a class and an object is probably the single most confusing concept in object-oriented design. These two terms are often used interchangeably, although they represent different things. The difference between a class and an object, however, need not be confusing if you stop to think of the definition of a class and contrast it with the definition of an object.

An *object* is a package of operations and attributes. A *class* is a group of related objects. By related, we mean that the objects which comprise a class have been derived based upon either the commonalty or the subordinate composition of a set of operations and attributes. Common objects derived by classification result in classes of objects. Subordinate objects derived by encapsulation also result in still more classes of objects.

As shown in Figure 7-1, the organization of a set of operations and attributes (those from the object shown in Figure 6-1) results in a set of or-

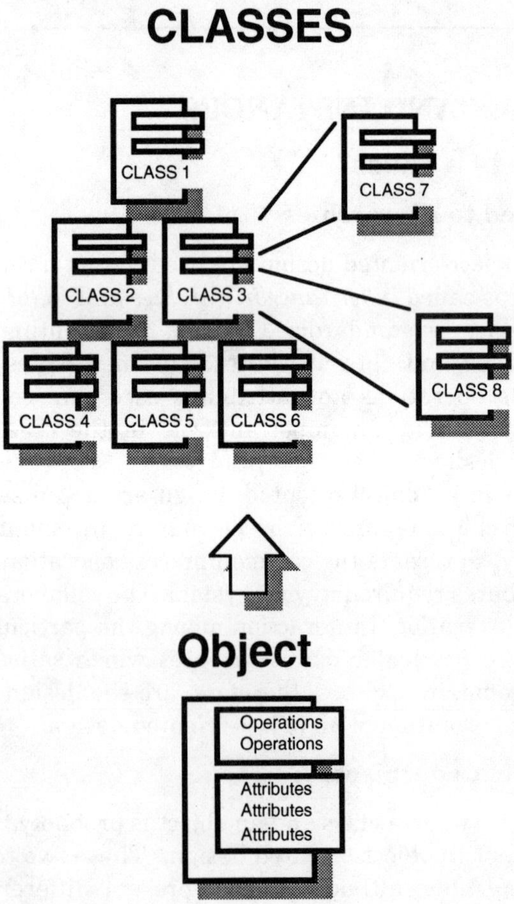

Figure 7-1. Class composition.

ganized objects which are called classes of objects. For example, the classes of objects labeled as Classes 1, 2, 3, 4, 5, and 6 were derived from the classification of the common operations and attributes in the original object. Similarly, the classes of objects labeled as Classes 7 and 8 were derived by the encapsulation of subordinate operations and attributes from within Class 3.

Objects and Classes

The concepts of objects and classes are interchanged all the time in discussions about object-oriented design. They are almost the same thing. In some ways, a class is a template for an object. An object is a package of operations and attributes. A class is a set of operations which can be inherited by the objects below it in the inheritance hierarchy (this is an *abstract* class), or which are part of every instance of a particular object (this is a *concrete* class). While the members of an object are its operations and attributes, the members of a class are either other classes or the instances of its object. The difference between an abstract class and a concrete class will help you to understand what the members of each type of class represent.

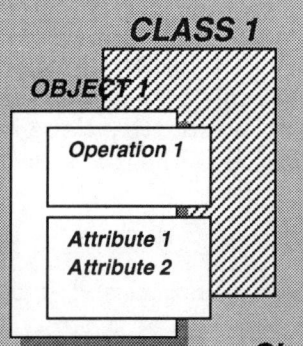

CLASS 1
OBJECT 1
- Operation 1
- Attribute 1
- Attribute 2

Consider an abstract class (Class 1) that contains a set of operations and attributes for the sole purpose of being shared by many objects. The set of operations and attributes it contains would constitute an object (Object 1) which cannot have any instances at run time. It just holds operations and attributes for use in other objects, for example, for Object 3. The class associated with that object, Class 3, therefore, is said to be a member of Class 1.

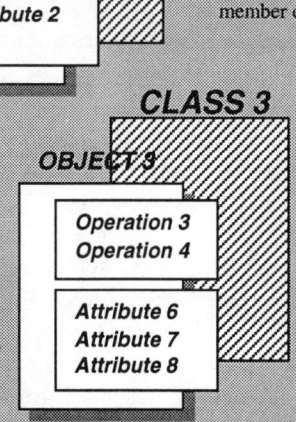

CLASS 3
OBJECT 3
- Operation 3
- Operation 4
- Attribute 6
- Attribute 7
- Attribute 8

Now consider a concrete class, in particular, the class (Class 3) whose object inherits operations and attributes from Class 1. Object 3 is the set of operations and attributes which are unique to Class 3. Each instance of Object 3 can use its own operations and attributes as well as any it needs from Object 1. Class 3 is a concrete class. Each instance of its object, Object 3, is said to be a member of Class 3.

In this example, the same number of operations and attributes as had comprised the original object now comprise the set of eight objects associated with these classes. This demonstrates the similarity between classes and objects. During the classification of objects, the set of operations and attributes which constitute one or more objects is distributed over a larger number of objects. Each new object contains a smaller set of the original operations and attributes. The operations and attributes of the objects are now better organized and represent classes of objects.

Each of the new objects derived during classification is said to represent a class of objects, in particular, those from which it was derived. This is the cause of the confusion about the difference between classes and objects. Each class is an abstract representation of a set of other objects but it also contains a package of operations and attributes of its own (which we call the object associated with the class). The object associated with a class contains the operations and attributes which tie the other objects together as a class.

A class is the organization around an object. In the Coad/Yourdon notation for a class, for example, the symbol for a class is drawn as a superstructure around an object. This is a good way to think of a class. There is a one-to-one relationship between a class of objects and the object associated with it. There is a one-to-many relationship, however, between the object associated with a class and the set of lower-level objects that belong to that class.

The differences between a class and the object associated with it are not as difficult to grasp as may first seem. All that is required is a simple understanding that a class is a grouping of objects, that there is also an object associated with the class at the class level, and that a class can be either abstract or concrete.

Abstract Classes of Objects

A class of objects derived by extracting common operations and attributes from within one or more other objects is said to be an *abstract class*. Therefore, the classification of objects results in abstract classes of objects. The objects which belong to the class are all those from which the common operations and attributes were originally extracted. The object associated with the class is the object which contains the common operations and attributes.

For example, if the operations and attributes which comprise the object associated with Class 1 in Figure 7-1 were derived by extracting the common operations and attributes from the objects associated with Classes 2 and 3, then the objects associated with Classes 2 and 3 are said to belong to Class 1. For simplicity, you would usually just say that Classes 2 and 3 are members of Class 1.

In this example, Class 1 is an abstract class since it serves no other purpose except to represent the common operations and attributes of other classes. Classes 2 and 3 are subclasses of Class 1. They may or may not be abstract classes themselves, depending on their relationship with their own subclasses. If either of the objects associated with Class 2 or Class 3 represents physical objects at runtime (that is, instances), then they are called *concrete* classes.

Concrete Classes of Objects

The classes of objects remaining after extracting common operations and attributes are said to be concrete classes. Therefore, the classification of objects results in concrete classes as well as abstract classes. The abstract classes represent the common objects extracted during classification. The concrete classes represent the physical objects which remain after classification.

For example, Classes 4, 5, and 6 in Figure 7-1 would represent concrete classes of objects. The objects in a concrete class are the instances of the object associated with it. As concrete classes, each of the objects associated with them represents a physical object which can be manipulated by the user (or by other program modules) at runtime. Concrete classes, therefore, represent the objects which become your runtime program modules.

Suppose that the object associated with Class 3 can have instances associated with it during runtime. It is, therefore, considered to be a concrete class even though it may also have a subclass of its own (in this example, its subclass is labeled Class 6). A concrete class always represents a class of object instances at runtime, and may or may not also represent common operations and attributes extracted from one or more other objects.

Additional sets of subordinate operations and attributes from within the object associated with a concrete class can be extracted after classification to form new encapsulated objects. Therefore, the encapsulation of objects identifies additional concrete classes of objects beyond those first derived by classification—an important feature of concrete classes. Some concrete classes are derived using object classification, but the vast majority of concrete classes in a large system are derived using object encapsulation.

For example, if some of the operations and attributes which comprise the object associated with Class 3 were extracted to form the subordinate sets of operations and attributes in the objects associated with Classes 7 and 8, then the objects associated with Classes 7 and 8 are said to be *encapsulated* within the object associated with Class 3. For simplicity, you would usually just say that Class 3 encapsulates Classes 7 and 8.

7.1.2 What Is an Instance of a Class?

A Composite Instance of an Object

A class, like an object, is often described in terms of its instances. An instance of an object is one of several parallel copies of all of its operations and attributes at runtime. An instance of a class is just an instance of the object associated with the class, adjusted to also include all of the common operations and attributes which can be inherited by the class of objects to which it belongs. An instance of a class is a composite instance of an object and all of the objects above it in an inheritance hierarchy.

For most purposes, you can think of the instances of a class as the instances of the object associated with it. These phrases are often used interchangeably in the literature. Fortunately, there is little substantial difference between the instance of a class and the instance of an object in terms of how it affects the design.

7.1.3 What Is a Member of a Class?

Subclasses of an Abstract Class

The members of an abstract class are the objects associated with its subclasses. Every abstract class has an object associated with it, but the objects associated with its subclasses are the members of that class. This is the essence of the original derivation of the term *class* in object-oriented design. It is a collection of objects, in particular, the collection of objects associated with a set of subclasses.

It is best to use the term *subclass* when referring to the members of an abstract class. Some authors and texts, however, will just refer to the subclasses of an abstract class as *the members of a class*. Unfortunately, this can be confused with the instances of a concrete class. To avoid this confusion, we will continue to refer to the members of an abstract class only as the *subclasses* of a class.

Instances of a Concrete Class

The members of a concrete class are the identical instances of the object associated with it. This is very different from the members of an abstract class. The members of an abstract class are the objects associated with its subclasses. The members of a concrete class are the instances of the object associated with the class itself. This is the more common use of the term *member of a class* that you will see in the literature—a collection of instances for a single object.

We feel that it is best to use the term *instances* when referring to the members of a concrete class. Some authors and texts, however, will just refer to instances of a concrete class as *the members of a class*. Unfortunately, this can be confused with the subclasses of an abstract class. To avoid this confusion, we will continue to refer to the members of a concrete class only as the *instances* of an object.

7.2 ABSTRACT CLASSES

7.2.1 What Is an Abstract Class?

The Result of Classification

An *abstract class* is one in which there is no physical representation of its associated object. In other words, the object associated with an abstract class can have no instances. Abstract classes are formed to represent the common operations and attributes extracted from objects during classification and are the upper-level classes on an inheritance hierarchy. The distinguishing feature of an abstract class is that it always has subclasses.

The role of an abstract class is to serve as a catalog of common parts. It is natural, therefore, to think of all classes as abstract classes. Consequentially, some authors and texts (for example, the Booch notation) refer to abstract classes simply as *classes*. Unfortunately, most object-oriented programming languages also use class constructs to implement concrete classes.

An abstract class is the organizational structure for a set of objects which share some common operations and attributes. The set of operations and attributes that they share, however, has no identity in and of itself at runtime. The operations and attributes exist only to support the purposes of the objects from which they were derived. They are said to be *inherited* by those objects.

A Catalog of Common Parts

An abstract class, most simply stated, is a catalog of common operations and common attributes. The operations and attributes in abstract classes are the common parts of your system. Each abstract class is an entry in the catalog of common parts. The catalog is used during runtime to resolve references to these operations and attributes. The inheritance hierarchy relates the abstract classes to one another. Inheritance, therefore, is the index to the catalog.

Figure 7-2 shows the internal design of the operations and attributes within the objects associated with two abstract classes (two of those from Figure 7-1). These operations and attributes are the cataloged common parts that are then available for use in their respective subclasses. Class 2, for example, represents the common operations and attributes that can be used in Classes 4 and 5 (its subclasses). Similarly, Class 1 represents those for Classes 2 and 3.

There is one operation (Operation 2) and three attributes (Attributes 3, 4, and 5) in Class 2. Any one of these can be referenced in the internal design of the objects of its subclasses. The internal design structure of these operations and attributes, however, is maintained in Class 2. This is the role of an abstract class. It contains the separately maintained internal designs of the operations and attributes which are common to its subclasses.

The operations and attributes contained in an abstract class tend to be separate and distinct from one another. They are merely cataloged together because they all serve the same set of lower-level objects. Each has its own internal design, which can be modified at any time without disrupting the integrity of the design of any other object. Just as the operations and attributes of an abstract class can be used in its subclass objects, an abstract class may also make use of the

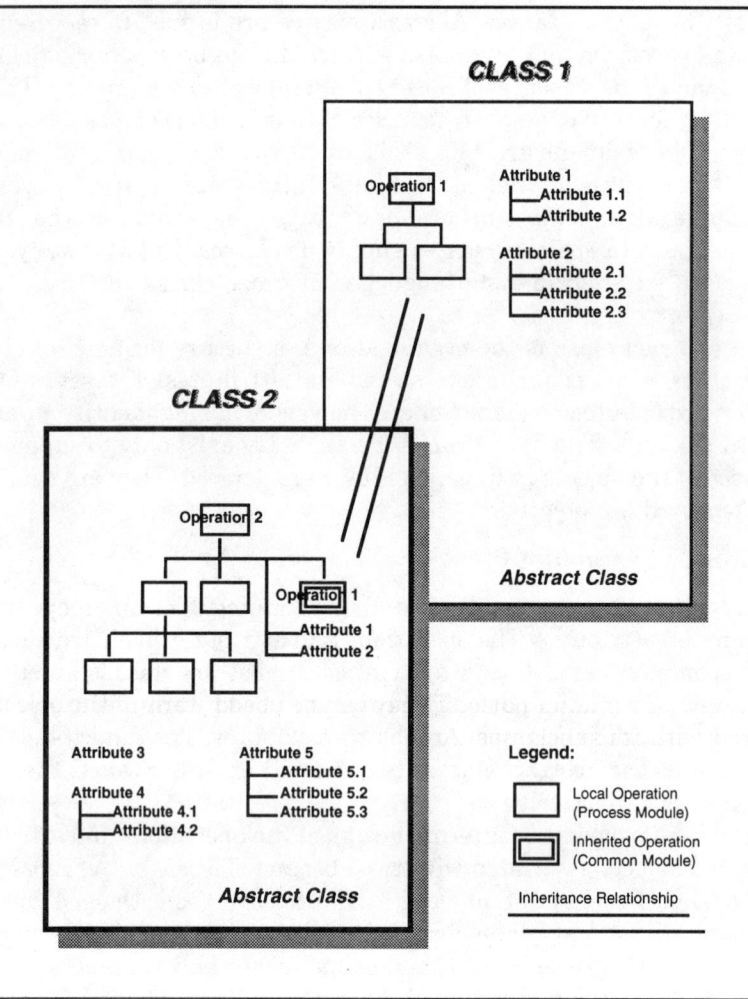

Figure 7-2. Abstract classes.

operations and attributes from within a higher-level abstract class to which it is a subclass.

For example, Operation 2 is structurally decomposed to contain various other operations and attributes. Among these are Operation 1 and Attributes 1 and 2, which are the common operations and attributes which Class 2 inherits from Class 1. The corresponding internal designs for those inherited operations and attributes are maintained in Class 1. This is how abstract classes are used to catalog common operations and attributes.

7.2.2 How are Abstract Classes Used?

Object-Oriented Representation

Abstract classes are a unique feature of object-oriented design used to represent the common characteristics of objects. You factor out the common traits of your objects which are then collected as new objects and represented as abstract classes. The representation of abstract classes in an object-oriented design results in better program maintainability than if you were to repeat the common traits as part of the design every time they were needed.

Abstract classes help to preserve the integrity of a large and complex design. Common operations and attributes are collected into abstract classes. The integrity of the system design is retained when you later modify the individual designs associated with these operations and attributes. The abstract class is a single point of maintenance for common processes and common data. You can modify code, fix bugs, expand functionality, and change environmental parameters for many different modules all in one place.

Abstract classes are often used to define default process operations and to set the initial conditions of data attributes. The operations and attributes of the object associated with an abstract class are the common characteristics of other objects. They can be used by any of the objects associated with its subclasses. An abstract class is the perfect place to define the default functions and initial conditions of other objects.

Abstract classes are also often used to define class-level operations and attributes. Class-level operations and attributes are administrative rather than functional in nature. They apply to how your design is implemented rather than to the original purpose it serves. Somewhere down an inheritance hierarchy, a set of abstract classes will have their operations and attributes inherited by the objects associated with a set of concrete classes. Each instance of any one of these objects will have its own identity, although there may be some need for administrative functions that span these multiple instances.

For example, a copy of a particular type of window on the computer screen might be an instance of an object associated with a concrete class. A function to track and list a menu of all open copies (instances) of a document window (the object associated with a concrete class) would most likely be a class-level function. It would be defined as an operation in a general-purpose window class (an abstract class), which can be inherited by the document window (a concrete class). The menu-listing function is a class-level function, which applies to the set of instances of a class rather than to any one instance.

The Inheritance Hierarchy

Abstract classes eventually become represented as an inheritance diagram in your object-oriented design. By definition, the abstract classes have a hierarchical relationship to one another. They were derived during object classification by extracting common operations and attributes among and within your initial set of objects. Inheritance is concerned with the hierarchical relationship between the groups of extracted operations and attributes and the groups of operations and attributes that use them.

The inheritance hierarchy is the diagrammed relationship between abstract classes and between concrete classes and abstract classes. Just as you transform objects into abstract and concrete classes, similarly, you then transform the classes into an inheritance hierarchy. The objects represent your system requirements. Your objective is to derive the inheritance hierarchy which best portrays the commonalty of those requirements. The inheritance hierarchy is your catalog of common operations and attributes. It is used to resolve operation and attribute references during runtime.

7.3 CONCRETE CLASSES

7.3.1 What Is a Concrete Class?

The Result of Classification

A *concrete class* is one in which there can be a physical representation of its associated object at runtime. In other words, the object associated with a concrete class can have instances. Concrete classes are the classes from which common operations and attributes are extracted during classification. They are the lower-level classes on an inheritance hierarchy and the only classes on a collaboration hierarchy. Concrete classes may or may not have subclasses, but the distinguishing feature of a concrete class is that the object associated with it can always have instances at runtime.

The role of a concrete class is to represent an operational module in the program. It is natural, therefore, to think of a concrete class as an object. Consequently, some authors and texts (for example, the Booch notation) just refer to concrete classes as *objects*. Unfortunately, object-oriented programming languages still refer to them as classes.

The Result of Encapsulation

Concrete classes are also the classes that are identified as containing subordinate sets of operations and attributes during encapsulation. They are divisions of the lower-level classes on an inheritance hierarchy that also have an operational relationship with one another as depicted on a collaboration hierarchy. Concrete classes compliment abstract classes by relating them to a physical representation of your system.

Concrete classes have relationships to abstract classes and other concrete classes. Some of the operations and attributes within the object associated with a concrete class are likely to also reference operations and attributes in the objects of other classes. They inherit some operations and attributes from the objects associated with abstract classes and collaborate with other objects associated with concrete classes.

Encapsulation is one way to derive an object associated with concrete class. It is similar to classification in that it is a means to divide an object into a more meaningful set of smaller objects. You can think of an encapsulated object as a subordinate part of another object. The encapsulated object can be a member of a different abstract class than the object in which it is encapsulated. Furthermore, an encapsulated object can be encapsulated by more than one other object.

An encapsulated object, like a classified object, can be common to several other objects. The distinguishing feature between an abstract class and a concrete class is whether the object associated with it needs to have instances at runtime. The object associated with an abstract class cannot have instances but the object associated with a concrete class can.

For example, the operations and attributes that support the creation of a routine to draw a chart in a computer program are likely to be designed as a concrete class. The chart is likely to be drawn in several different ways, using different parameter values, supplied by different users and/or different modules. Identifiable instances are required in order to separately track those different occurrences at runtime. The class associated with the chart drawing object is concrete.

In contrast, the operations and attributes that convert a date from one format to another are likely to be designed as an abstract class. A date-conversion routine will most likely be used by many modules with different parameter values, but identifiable instances are not required since the components of each occurrence of the calculation are not needed once the conversion is complete. Therefore, the class associated with the date-conversion object is abstract.

A concrete class is the operational structure for an object that makes use of its own operations and attributes as well as those of other objects. The operations and attributes of a concrete class can be shared through multiple collaborations. However, each instance (each use of the set of operations and attributes) will have its own identity at runtime. They support the purposes of the other objects with which they collaborate, but they also have their own identifiable purposes in the system.

Modules of the Operational Design

A concrete class, most simply stated, is an operational module of your computer program. The module is the object associated with a particular concrete class. It contains the operations and attributes which are needed to satisfy the purpose of that object in the system. The operations represent subordinate processes. The attributes represent subordinate data. The collaboration hierarchy relates concrete classes to one another. It represents the module-to-module interaction at run time.

130 OBJECT ENGINEERING

Figure 7-3 shows the operations and attributes within the objects associated with three concrete classes (three of those from Figure 7-1). Class 3 is one of the classes whose object will have instances during runtime, and is thus a concrete class. Furthermore, some of its subordinate operations and attributes have been extracted and encapsulated in Classes 7 and 8, which are two other concrete classes. The interaction between these three concrete classes demonstrates the operational design of part of a system.

The operations and attributes associated with a concrete class are usually interrelated to one another more than we've shown here. By *interrelated*, we mean that they can be subordinate to one another. To

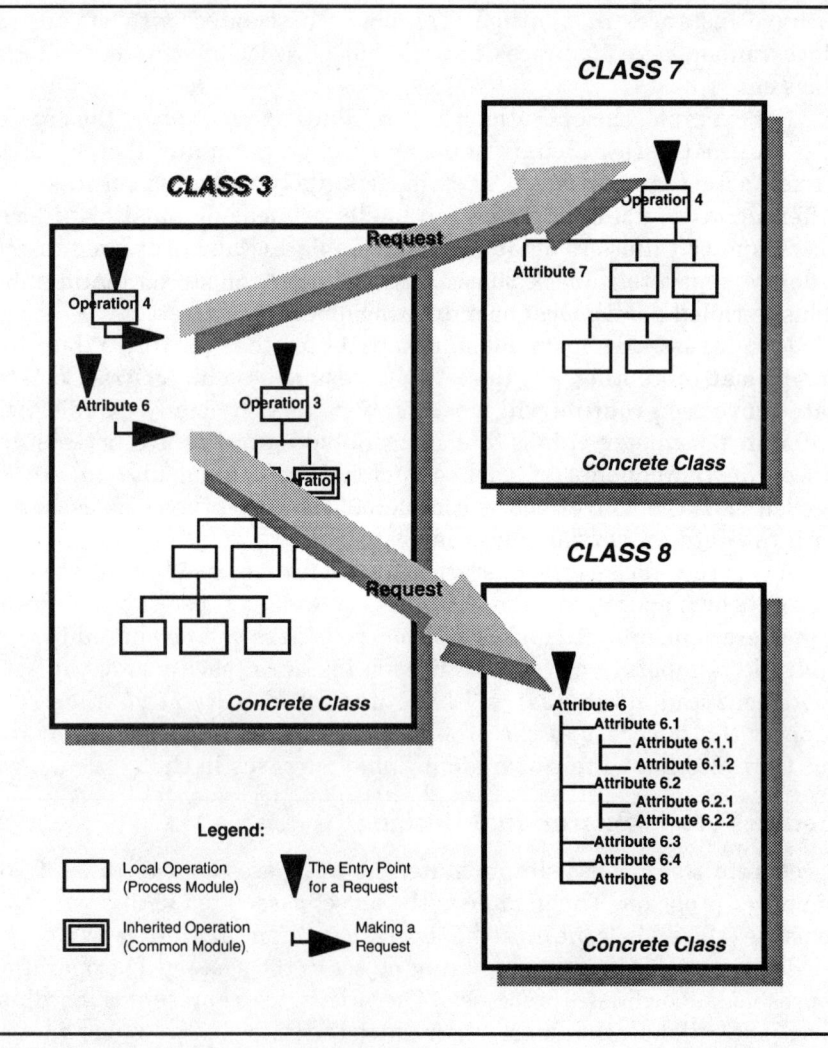

Figure 7-3.   Concrete classes.

simplify our discussion, however, we have shown these operations and attributes as independent design units rather than subordinate parts of a single larger structure.

Class 3 contains two operations (Operations 3 and 4) and one attribute (Attribute 6). These were the operations and attributes allocated to it during classification. Similar to the operations and attributes within an abstract class, these operations and attributes also have their own internal structural design. Operation 3, for example, is decomposed into various other operations (one of which, Operation 1, is inherited from elsewhere). Operation 4 and Attribute 6, however, are not decomposed here. Instead, they are encapsulated and their designs are contained in other classes.

For example, Operation 4 has been extracted from the object associated with Class 3 and encapsulated within Class 7. Its internal structure is now maintained in Class 7. It has been decomposed into the several lower-level operations and one lower-level attribute needed to support it. Class 7 will collaborate with (will be called from) Class 3 as well as from other classes not shown here. In particular, all collaborations with Class 7 will consist of triggering Operation 4.

Similarly, Attribute 6 has been extracted from Class 3 and encapsulated within Class 8. It also has been decomposed into several layers of lower levels of attributes. These attributes may be stored in a database (this is called *persistence*) or may just be stored in runtime memory. As an encapsulated concrete class, however, Attribute 6 will have its own identity distinct from any object which uses it, and its internal design will be maintained as part of Class 8.

Classes 3, 7, and 8 are all examples of concrete classes. The objects associated with each of these concrete classes represent the operational design of modules in a computer program. They collaborate with each other in triggering Operation 4 and in accessing Attribute 6. Class 3 represents the client object and Classes 7 and 8 represent the server objects. This is how concrete classes are used to represent modules in an operational design. The client/server collaboration of an object-oriented design is very much like any conventional design of module operation in a large system.

7.3.2 How Are Concrete Classes Used?

Conventional Representation

Concrete classes are used to represent the operational modules of a computer program in an object-oriented design. They serve the same purpose as program modules in a process-driven design or normalized data elements in a data-driven design. Concrete classes, program modules, and normalized data elements all represent the fundamental program unit in a system design. However, the use of concrete classes in an object-oriented design considers both the process requirements and the data requirements of your system and allows the program to operate in a more flexible manner.

The concrete classes in an object-oriented design, like the program modules in a conventional design, represent programmable units of the system. The common operations and attributes used by the objects associated with multiple concrete classes, however, are obtained at runtime by interrogating the inheritance hierarchy rather than by making explicit subroutine calls.

One advantage of representing a program module as a concrete class is the flexibility it gives you during design. It is much more modular. The set of operations and attributes of the class associated with a concrete object can be expanded as you learn more about how that object must operate to satisfy its purpose in the system. The object can inherit the operations and attributes of its class in order to achieve its basic function and can add its own specific operations and attributes to achieve its unique characteristics much later.

Another advantage of the concrete class representation is the flexible nature of its inheritance hierarchy. As the object instances refer to operations and attributes not contained within the object, the inheritance hierarchy is searched to locate a matching named operation or attribute. Multiple named operations and attributes may exist, but only the one nearest to the point of reference is used. This is called *polymorphism*. Polymorphism is used to resolve references at runtime which were unresolved at compile time.

A related advantage of polymorphism is the substitution of specific operations or attributes for more general ones. As the designer, you can include redundant operations or attributes within an object to be used at runtime instead of the corresponding inherited operation or attribute. This is called overloading. It allows you to refine local definitions of operations and attributes without disturbing their more global common definition.

The Collaboration Hierarchy

Concrete classes eventually become represented as a collaboration diagram in your object-oriented design. The objects associated with concrete classes have hierarchical relationships to one another. They were derived to represent those objects which are capable of having instances at runtime. The instances of the various objects have specific relationships to one another based on their encapsulation. Collaboration is concerned with the client/server relationships established between objects to enable their operation as program modules at runtime.

The *collaboration hierarchy* is the diagrammed relationship between concrete classes. Just as you transform objects into abstract and concrete classes, you then transform the concrete classes into a collaboration hierarchy. The objects represent your system requirements. Your objective is to derive the collaboration hierarchy that best portrays the interactions between those requirements. The collaboration hierarchy is your operation design for the operations and attributes of your system. It is used to turn your objects into program modules at runtime.

CHAPTER REVIEW

The Definition of a Class

What is a class? The superstructure around any object, which captures both its inheritance relationships and its collaboration relationships with the other objects in the domain.

What is an instance of a class? The composite instance of the operations and attributes of the object associated with that class and those of all of the objects associated with all of the abstract classes up its inheritance hierarchy.

What is a member of a class? The members of an abstract class are the other classes that inherit from it; the members of a concrete class are the instances of its associated object.

What is an abstract class? The representation of the operations and attributes inherited by objects in a domain.

How are abstract classes used? To catalog the common operations and the common attributes used by many objects.

What is a concrete class? The representation of an object as a module that collaborates with other modules.

How are concrete classes used? To portray the interaction between the client and server objects in a system.

8

The Definition of Inheritance

8.1 THE INHERITANCE HIERARCHY

8.1.1 What Is Class Inheritance?

An Object-Oriented Hierarchy

Every book, article, diagram, or person that you consult about object-oriented design will mention inheritance. *Inheritance* is a type of hierarchical relationship among objects in a class structure. This hierarchy (also called a *lattice structure*) is what makes a design object-oriented. An object-oriented programming language is one which accommodates inheritance in some manner, and which makes use of it to accomplish context-sensitive referencing. This is what makes an object-oriented program more flexible than a conventionally designed program.

The use of inheritance in the design of a computer program enables you to represent one aspect of the classes of objects in your system. In particular, inheritance portrays the commonalty shared among classes of objects. The objects represent packages of process operations and data attributes, which, in turn, are the fundamental requirements of your system. Inheritance, therefore, represents the organization of the common requirements of your system in an object-oriented manner.

Inheritance is the single most important feature that distinguishes object-oriented design from conventional design. Inheritance captures and catalogs the organized visibility of individual operations and attributes throughout your system. It is an integral part of your design.

The manner and the degree to which inheritance is implemented in your program, however, will vary from language to language and from compiler to compiler.

Diagrammed Classification

An inheritance hierarchy is a diagram of a set of classified objects. The inheritance relationship between a set of objects and their parent class is hierarchical. By hierarchical, we mean that there is a distinct parent/child relationship. The child objects are said to inherit the common operations and attributes contained in the object associated with the parent class. The primary purpose of representing an object as a class is to enable you to describe its inheritance relationships with other objects.

As shown in Figure 8-1, an inheritance diagram includes all of the classes in your domain. The concrete classes are those associated with objects which can have instances at runtime. They tend to be on the lower-level branches of an inheritance diagram. The abstract classes exist only to catalog sets of operations and attributes which are common to other classes. They tend to be in the middle and upper levels of an inheritance diagram.

INHERITANCE

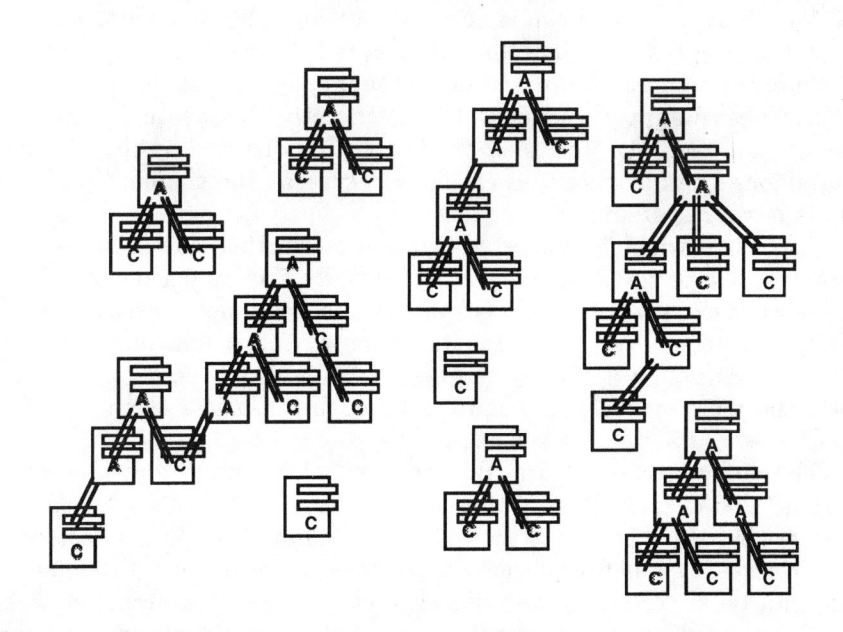

Figure 8-1. Inheritance relationships.

Concrete classes will inherit characteristics from other concrete classes or from abstract classes. The purpose of a concrete class is to represent an organized package of operations and attributes (an object) which can have one or more instances (similar copies) at runtime. You can think of the object associated with a class as a software module in your program. Inheritance, therefore, is the object-oriented representation of the common modules (abstract classes) overlaid on the operational modules (concrete classes) in your system.

Abstract classes provide a place to keep the common characteristics that will be inherited by the objects associated with other classes. The characteristics of a class are the operations and attributes of its associated object. The purpose of an abstract class is to catalog this type of organization. The purpose of the inheritance hierarchy, therefore, is to show the connection between any one concrete class and all of the abstract classes from which it can obtain common operations and attributes.

Abstract Class Interaction

Inheritance is concerned with the interaction of the abstract classes in your domain, however, an inheritance diagram shows the pattern of inheritance for all objects in your domain. Each class is associated with an object and each object represents an organized set of operations and attributes. The operations and attributes represent requirements. All of the connections down from a class on the inheritance diagram show which subclass will inherit the common operations and attributes associated with that class.

An inheritance diagram is one way in which the requirements of a system are represented in an object-oriented design. It shows the allocation of the common requirements throughout your entire domain. An inheritance diagram includes both concrete classes and abstract classes, however, the nature of the diagram is dictated by the interaction among the abstract classes. They represent the common requirements of your system.

Each class which is connected to one or more other classes below it is known as a *superior class* (this term is usually just contracted as *superclass*). Each class which is connected to one or more superclasses above it is known as a *subordinate class* (this term is usually just contracted as *subclass*). Although any class can be either a superclass, a subclass, or both, the most typical inheritance relationship consists of an abstract superclass and a concrete subclass.

The abstract classes form the structure of an inheritance diagram. Abstract classes are always superclasses, they are also often subclasses of other abstract classes, but they can never stand alone. In contrast, concrete classes are usually subclasses, but they can also stand alone and/or they can be superclasses of other concrete classes. A concrete class is usually a subclass of an abstract class, however, an abstract class can never be a subclass of a concrete class.

Factoring and Prototyping

Abstract classes represent the common characteristics shared by many objects. They are initially derived by extracting common groups of operations and attributes from among other objects during classification. New classes are first identified this way in an upward manner. This is a good way to think of the abstract classes on an inheritance diagram. However, this is not the way in which an inheritance diagram is used after it is first developed. New classes are later added to the inheritance hierarchy in a downward manner.

The identification of classes from objects is a discovery process. We have introduced the classification of objects as one of the first steps in organizing objects into classes. Classification is initially an upward identification of common classes of objects. Upward classification is called *inheritance factoring*. As an analyst, it is easier to start to organize your objects in this manner. Factoring common characteristics gives you the best understanding of the inheritance hierarchy and of its abstract classes.

Most discussions of inheritance in the literature present inheritance and classification as an outward and downward identification of new objects from existing classes. This is the most common use of an inheritance hierarchy once you have an initial diagram to modify. You derive new objects (usually new concrete classes) by identifying the unique operations and attributes which identify a specialized case of a more general preexisting object (usually an abstract class).

The identification of new classes from old classes is a modification process. Your inheritance hierarchy will expand outward as new classes are added to existing branches, and downward as new classes are increasingly augmented with new subclasses. This outward and downward classification of new objects from existing classes is called *inheritance prototyping*. The complete design of an object-oriented system involves both inheritance factoring (upward expansion of the diagram) and inheritance prototyping (outward and downward expansion).

Object-oriented analysts usually deal with both inheritance factoring and inheritance prototyping. Early in the design process, the analyst identifies the initial set of objects based on their operations and attributes. Common sets of operations and attributes define abstract classes, which in turn, define the initial inheritance hierarchy. Additional classes can be factored out later, but most often, new classes are prototyped under the existing ones.

Object-oriented programmers deal almost exclusively with inheritance prototyping. Once an object-oriented design exists, it is represented in part by an inheritance diagram. An object-oriented program has an inheritance hierarchy even if it is not documented in diagram form. An existing program design can be modified by adding new classes to the existing structure of the inheritance hierarchy. This is an important way in which an object-oriented design can be reused.

Single-Inheritance Hierarchies

The easiest way to understand how an inheritance hierarchy is used in an object-oriented design is to first consider the case of single inheritance. *Single inheritance* is a set of one-to-many parent/child relationships among the classes associated with objects. It is the most common type of inheritance hierarchy. Single-inheritance hierarchies can handle most types of object-oriented design problems that you are likely to encounter.

The upper-level classes on inheritance diagrams are called the *base classes*. Base classes are those abstract classes from which other classes inherit some of their characteristics. This is counterintuitive to the process of inheritance factoring, where the higher-level classes are derived from the lower classes. The concept of a base class is more consistent with the process of inheritance prototyping, where new lower-level classes are derived from existing classes. The existing classes are the base classes.

For example, a chart object in a particular program may inherit certain general functions from an input/output object in its inheritance hierarchy. The input/output object is associated with a base class. It contains certain common characteristics which can be augmented by its subclasses. The chart object adds its own specific process operations and data attributes needed to draw a chart while also making use of the general process operations and data attributes of the input/output object to read files and to interpret user input.

Inheritance prototyping occurs when you define new concrete classes as subclasses to an existing class. Just as the class associated with a chart object may be a subclass of an input/output class, you might use the input/output class as a base class to define still more subclasses. For example, you might define a document object as another subclass of the input/output class without worrying how to read files and interpret user input. The new object can inherit these functions from its base class.

8.1.2 What Is Multiple Inheritance?

Multiple-Inheritance Hierarchies

Inheritance hierarchies need not be limited to single inheritance. Some object-oriented programming languages allow and encourage the use of multiple inheritance. *Multiple inheritance* is a more complex situation to understand, but it follows the same principles as single inheritance. *Multiple inheritance* is a set of many-to-many parent/child relationships among the classes associated with objects. Often, however, multiple inheritance is just a finite number of composite single inheritance hierarchies, that is, several overlapping one-to-many relationships.

Figure 8-2 shows an example of a multiple-inheritance hierarchy. Some of the classes inherit from more than one other class. By definition, they display multiple inheritance. However, the way in which we have drawn the diagram allows you to identify three distinct single inheritance hierarchies which overlap one another—the six classes in the lower center, the three classes on the left (in addition to the three lower classes which inherit from them), and the three classes on the right (in addition to the two lower classes which inherit from them).

Multiple inheritance is useful in situations for which there are multiple groups of common characteristics which partially overlap one another.

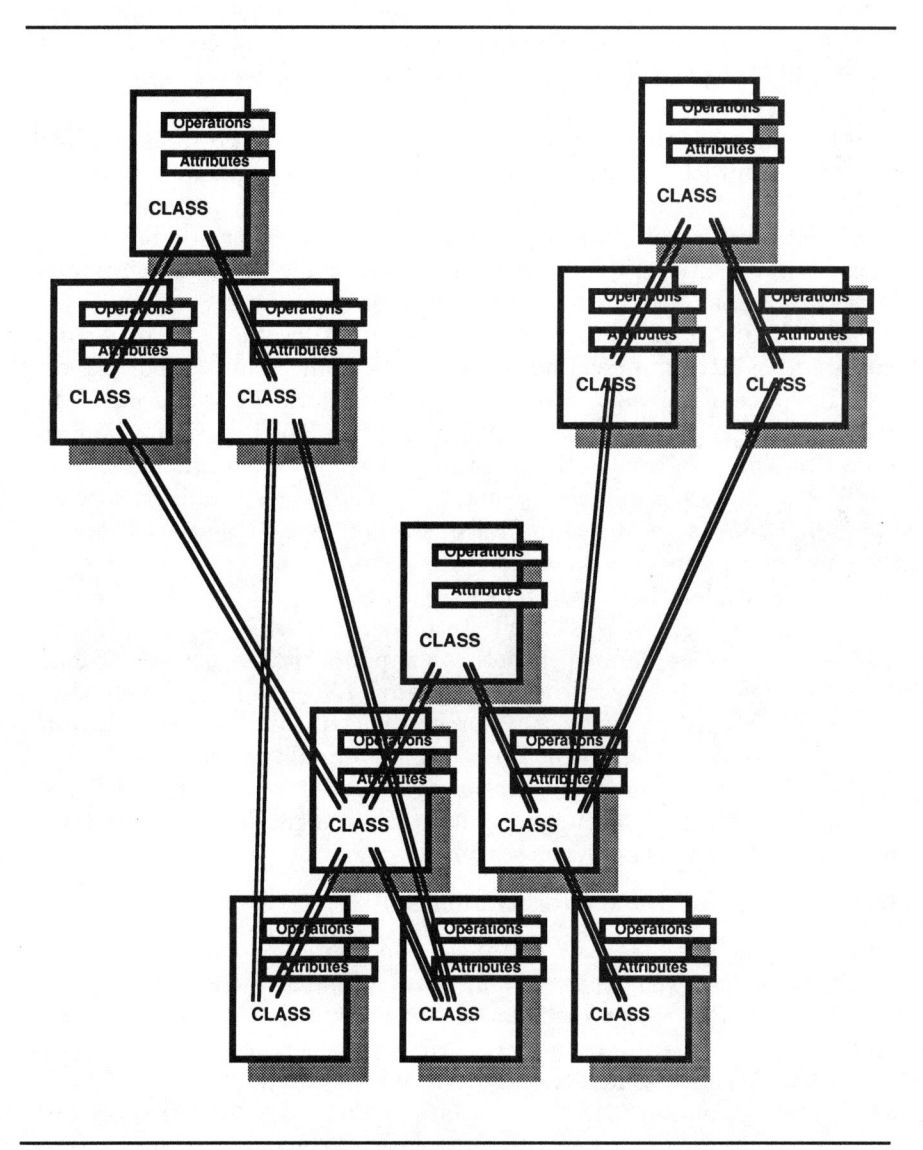

Figure 8-2. Multiple inheritance.

In addition to the sets of common characteristics which eventually become abstract classes on an inheritance hierarchy, you will find that there are some subsets of objects which are common to some of the same, but not all, other objects in a particular inheritance hierarchy. While you can always represent this as a partially redundant single hierarchy, it is cleaner to represent it using overlapping hierarchies.

For example, just as a chart object may need to inherit common input/output characteristics, it may also need to inherit font characteristics, color resolution characteristics, statistical calculation characteristics, and scale characteristics. A document object, however, may only need to inherit the input/output characteristics and the font characteristics. You could best portray this type of commonalty as overlapping inheritance hierarchies.

Multiple inheritance has its price, however, and that price is the need to provide conflict resolution. Any object-oriented language that allows multiple inheritance must include a conflict resolution algorithm in its compiler. Conflicts can arise when the same operation or attribute name is encountered in multiple base classes for a single object. Programmer intervention may be required to select the intended one.

In a single-inheritance hierarchy, the exact location of a particular operation or attribute need not be specified from within an object's design. It can be inherited at runtime (this is one form of polymorphism) by just referring to an operation or attribute name. The inheritance hierarchy will be used to resolve the reference based on the location of the object in which the reference is made. There are no conflicts between redundant names because the first one encountered (the closest one to the point of reference) is the one used, as was intended.

In a multiple-inheritance hierarchy, however, conflicts between redundant names cannot be so easily resolved. For example, an operation called *save* may be defined in both an input/output object and a font-definition object, to save the document onto a file, or to save the selection of the font type, respectively. A document object, which may inherit from both of these base objects, would need to fully qualify which operation is intended each time the save operation is triggered for a document. Thus, the use of multiple inheritance makes the design cleaner but dilutes some of the benefits of polymorphism.

Metaclass Inheritance Hierarchies

Inheritance hierarchies need not always be limited to objects. They may also be used to catalog the common characteristics of classes. Some object-oriented languages provide for an explicit hierarchy of common class characteristics separate from the hierarchy of common object characteristics. This is called a metaclass inheritance hierarchy.

By definition, a metaclass is a class of classes. All of the same concepts of abstract classes apply to metaclasses. They are abstract extractions of certain common characteristics of the objects that they represent, only in this case the objects that they represent are class structures. In theory, metaclasses are the next level of abstraction above classes. In practice, fortunately, metaclasses can be manipulated as a special case of multiple inheritance.

In theory, a metaclass is the treatment of a class as an object in order to define certain class-level characteristics common to many classes. Metaclasses are orthogonal to classes. They are another form of inheritance hierarchy. Metaclasses provide you with a separate place to define specific types of common characteristics, rather than to define them as part of the object associated with the class.

Metaclasses are used to define class-level characteristics. Class-level characteristics are the administrative functions needed to support your business functions in a particular design of a system. They may be such things as counting instances, ordering instances, or calculating memory. By using metaclasses, different class-level characteristics can be inherited by different groups of classes, and the class-level characteristics can be maintained separately from the common business characteristics of the class.

In practice, a metaclass is just a special form of multiple inheritance. A metaclass inheritance hierarchy provides a clearly defined separate hierarchy within which you are expected to define class-level operations and attributes. It is just a way to separate the common administrative characteristics of your system from the common business characteristics. Metaclasses are less confusing to use than multiple inheritance because the separate hierarchy is defined by language syntax rather than left up to the designer's interpretation.

8.1.3 What Does Inheritance Represent?

An *Is-a-Kind-of* Relationship

Inheritance is the object-oriented representation of an *is-a-kind-of* relationship. Each object associated with a subclass is-a-kind-of the object associated with the common parent class. All subclass objects share the same common operations and attributes of the parent object. The parent object represents a general case. Each subclass object, however, also adds its own particular set of operations and attributes to augment the common set. The child objects each represent different special cases.

The is-a-kind-of relationship indicates that two design components are similar enough to one another that one can be used as a template for the initial structural design of the other. In process-driven design, the structure of a particular design (its structure chart) may be used as a template to derive a modified structure which is-a-kind-of the original one. In data-driven design, special cases of a generalized entity may be labeled as an is-a-kind-of relationship on an entity relationship diagram. An inheritance diagram in an object-oriented design merely formalizes this template borrowing philosophy.

Inheritance is the representation of an is-a-kind-of relationship. Inheritance hierarchies are the cornerstone of any object-oriented design approach. The name of the type of diagram used to represent the inheritance hierarchy, however, may vary from author to author and from method to method. Some of the names that you will encounter for the diagrams which correspond to what we have been calling an inheritance diagram include:

Term for Inheritance Diagram	As referred to by these authors
Class Diagram	Booch
Gen-Spec Structures	Coad/Yourdon
Object Relationship Model	Embley/Kurtz/Woodfield
Inheritance Diagram	Shlaer/Mellor
Hierarchy Graphs	Wirfs-Brock/Wilkerson/Wiener

No matter what it is called, an inheritance diagram represents the inheritance hierarchy among the objects in your domain. During object classification, you extract common sets of operations and attributes to form new objects. As a result, you learn more about the needs of each object (that is, you identify more operations and attributes). The diagrammed pattern of inheritance relationships among your objects provides additional insight into the objects in your domain. It is a visual definition of the commonalty which exists among the requirements of your system.

A Pattern of Common Objects

You can use the pattern of an inheritance diagram to fine-tune the structure of your design. The separation of common operations and attributes into an organized inheritance hierarchy is conceptually similar to the creation of a suite of common modules in a conventional design and involves the same principles of cohesion maximization and coupling minimization to achieve a balanced structure appropriate to your system requirements.

The operations and attributes in the objects of an inheritance hierarchy have a greater measure of cohesion with one another than with those of other objects. You modify your inheritance diagram by further dividing your objects based on more detailed inspection of the cohesion among the operations and attributes they contain. The justification for removing a highly cohesive set of operations and attributes from one object to another is partially based on the relative amount of coupling that those operations and attributes exhibit with another object.

Cohesion and coupling is used in the same way to fine-tune the size and structure of an inheritance diagram as it is for a conventional structure chart. In fine-tuning your inheritance hierarchy, you address both the size of the objects in your design (how many operations and attributes they hold) and the composition of those objects (which operations and attributes they hold).

The size of an object associated with a class (and, therefore, the size of your inheritance hierarchy) is one measure of the level of detail represented by your design. The appropriate size of an object varies based on the size of the project, the importance of the mission of the system, the business function being addressed, and the personal style of the designers. An appropriate object is one that is small enough to be considered a unit and yet large enough to maintain a meaningful role in the system.

Classifying Members

Classification is a matter of finding the intersection of two sets of operations and attributes. The intersection contains the operations and attributes that would have been shown as common processes and data on an equivalent process or data structure chart. For example, in the object that was first introduced in Figure 6-1, Operation 1, Attribute 1, and Attribute 2 are subordinate to several other operations and attributes. They are common members (subsets) of the two objects shown below as circles. They can be extracted from the original object and cataloged as a set of common utility processes and common block data.

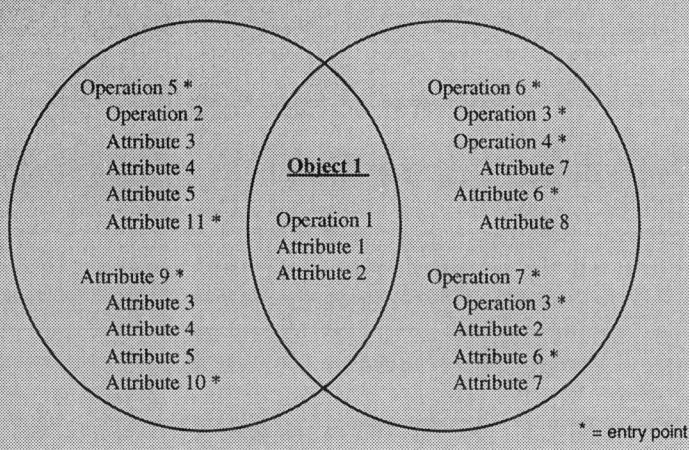

```
        Operation 5 *                          Operation 6 *
        Operation 2                            Operation 3 *
        Attribute 3                            Operation 4 *
        Attribute 4        Object 1            Attribute 7
        Attribute 5                            Attribute 6 *
        Attribute 11 *     Operation 1         Attribute 8
                           Attribute 1
        Attribute 9 *      Attribute 2         Operation 7 *
        Attribute 3                            Operation 3 *
        Attribute 4                            Attribute 2
        Attribute 5                            Attribute 6 *
        Attribute 10 *                         Attribute 7
```

* = entry point

Each group of extracted members becomes an object associated with a new higher-level abstract class on an inheritance diagram. Similar to the intersection area shown above (called Object 1), other common operations and attributes can also be extracted to form other objects. In particular, Attributes 3, 4, and 5 can be extracted from the left set to form another new object which we can call Object 2, and Operation 3 and Attributes 6 and 7 can be extracted from the right set to form another new object which we can call Object 3. These form new abstract classes. The remaining members constitute concrete classes which will inherit members from the abstract classes. Classification is the mechanism by which you derive abstract classes and determine their inheritance characteristics by the manner in which they were extracted from concrete classes.

The size of an object is usually anywhere from a handful to several dozen major operations and attributes per object.

The composition of an object is a more difficult measure of the level of detail appropriate in the design of an inheritance hierarchy. Different types of requirements will result in a very different distribution of operations and attributes among objects. The inheritance hierarchy may fan out, or may be subdivided to great depths to properly mirror the common portions of the business functions of your system.

For example, a very focused set of requirements (such as the I/O firmware on a particular network node device) may result in a thin but deep inheritance hierarchy to capture the several required characteristics in great detail. This might consist of only a few branches on the inheritance hierarchy, but each taken up a dozen levels to precisely define the common detail of the communication mechanism.

In contrast, a very broad set of requirements (such as the payroll system for a small company) may result in a wide but not so deep inheritance hierarchy to capture the many required characteristics in sufficient detail. This might consist of a dozen branches (for the many types of payroll functions) of only a few levels on each branch (the common arithmetic is all the same, consisting of only a few types of general calculations used in many places—totals, means, averages, balances, etc.).

The significant difference between object-oriented design and conventional design is embodied by the inheritance hierarchy. It represents an is-a-kind-of relationship between some requirements of a system. The is-a-kind-of relationship is sometimes described in certain diagrams of data-driven design and sometimes used manually during process-driven design. However, this type of relationship is not used in any meaningful way as a part of the design process of either case.

Inheritance is the feature of object-oriented design that is most often discussed in the literature. Object-oriented design adds value to software engineering by making explicit use of the is-a-kind-of relationship as an inheritance hierarchy. The inheritance hierarchy is used in designing and programming the common requirements of a system. All other distinguishing features of object-oriented systems are derived from inheritance. Polymorphism is made possible by inheritance, and modularity and reusability are derived from polymorphism.

Class Categories in a Domain

In concept, one inheritance hierarchy will cover an entire domain. However, not all parts of that hierarchy will necessarily be connected to one another, nor will it be feasible to represent them all in one physical diagram. It is advisable to divide the inheritance hierarchy for the objects in a large domain into mutually exclusive hierarchies which each represent specific aspects of the inheritance relationships.

In particular, the inheritance hierarchy for a domain may be broken up into several complementary hierarchies. Metaclasses are one example of this type of division of an inheritance hierarchy. They are used to separate common administrative characteristics from common business characteristics into different inheritance hierarchies. Other types of divisions of an inheritance hierarchy that you may find in the literature include class categories and utility classes.

There are many ways to divide an inheritance hierarchy into separate pieces. Class categories are functional divisions of a domain (divisions of business functions). You can think of class categories as vertical subdomains. Similarly, utility classes are divisions of a domain into separate inheritance diagrams based on support functions (data-structure maintenance, statistical calculations, etc). You can think of utility classes as horizontal subdomains.

One good example of the use of class categories is found in the Coad/Yourdon method of object-oriented design. They recommend that every domain be addressed by separately considering four complementary components. Each component of the domain simply represents one class category, in this case, class categories which are appropriate to the design of midrange graphical user-interface systems.

Class Categories recommended by Coad and Yourdon
Problem Domain Component—addressing business aspects
Human Interaction Component—addressing operational aspects
Task Management Component—addressing concurrency aspects
Data Management Component—addressing persistence aspects

Class categories, utility classes, and metaclasses are just artificial divisions of an inheritance hierarchy. They simplify the development process by dividing an inheritance hierarchy into complementary pieces. Divisions of an inheritance hierarchy are just a convenience to manage the complex inheritance relationships of a large domain. You use the same rules and the same diagram syntax to derive and represent different parts of the domain. Only the types of characteristics addressed in each division are different.

8.2 OBJECT VISIBILITY

8.2.1 What Is Object Visibility?

Access to Characteristics

Object visibility is an important principle in object-oriented design. It defines which objects have access to which other objects and to which characteristics of those objects. Visibility is the definition of an object's scope, in particular, the scope of its operations and its attributes. It can be explained best at a very gross scale, but it is at a more detailed scale that you will really work with an object's visibility.

At a very gross scale, inheritance and collaboration define the visibility of objects to one another. The objects associated with parent classes in an inheritance hierarchy are visible to the objects associated with their respective subclasses. Similarly, the server objects in a collaboration hierarchy are visible to client objects by means of the requests that they receive. However, objects are really packages of operations and attributes, and it is at that level that visibility is most meaningful.

At a more detailed scale, the internal design of an object defines the visibility of its individual operations and attributes. Some object-oriented languages, however, incorporate certain global definition rules for the declaration of an object's visibility. Therefore, you may encounter object-level visibility as well as operation- and attribute-level visibility. Object-level visibility, however, is only used to set and/or override the visibility of its operations and attributes. Visibility is really concerned with the availability of an object's operations and attributes to be used by other objects.

Each operation and attribute of an object can be visible or not. The visible operations and attributes of an object are available for public access from those of other objects that collaborate with it or that inherit from it. The nonvisible operations and attributes are private to the object in which they reside. Thus, an object's operations and attributes are usually divided into those which are public and those which are private.

Public Characteristics

The *public* operations and attributes of an object are those which are accessible from outside the object. In an inheritance hierarchy, a public operation can be triggered as if it were a part of the object associated with any subclass. In a collaboration hierarchy, a public operation can be triggered by any client object with which it collaborates. Similarly, public attributes can be accessed directly in subclasses and by clients.

The public operations and attributes of an object are those which can be entry points into the object from other objects. They are the major operations and attributes of an object. Public operations and attributes receive and respond to requests made from client objects. The operations and attributes that you identify early in the design process will be public members of your objects. They form the interface by which each object is known in the system.

For those operations and attributes of an object that are public, there is one more level of distinction which can be specified—whether they are protected or not. A public operation or attribute can be used within an object, it can be used by a client object which requests it, or it can be used by a subclass object that inherits its characteristics. However, a public operation and a public attribute can't necessarily be used by a client object of a subclass object.

Each public operation and each public attribute of an object can also be protected or not. The nonprotected public operations and attributes of an object are available for access in the clients of its subclasses. The protected public operations and attributes are available only within the scope of their inheritance hierarchy. Thus, an object's public operations and attributes are sometimes also divided into those that are not protected and those that are.

Some object-oriented languages make use of a special case of public visibility in which a nonlocal operation or attribute is granted public visibility status in an object of which it is not a member. This special case is called *friend visibility*. The use of friend visibility is an aspect of programming. It circumvents the otherwise good modularity of an

---

Class Categories

The inheritance hierarchy for the classes in your domain will consist of many different individual hierarchies. For most domains, the number of individual classes will number in the hundreds, so, even with the aid of a hierarchy diagram, it will be difficult to manage your classes and to make the best use of them in your design. To help solve this problem, the classes in an inheritance diagram are often grouped into categories of classes. The categories are merely a technique to help manage a large volume of classes, and do not necessarily imply any higher-level interrelationship.

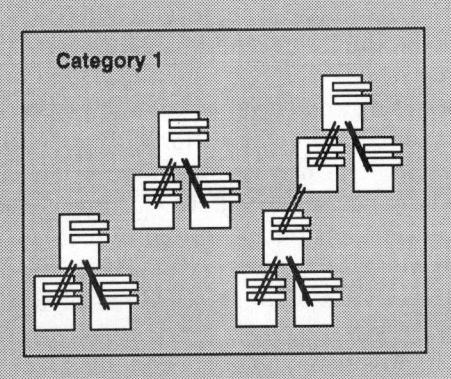

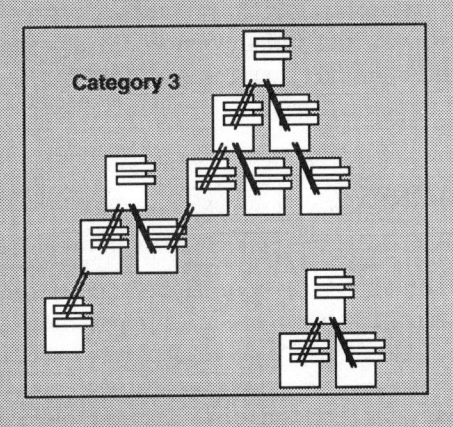

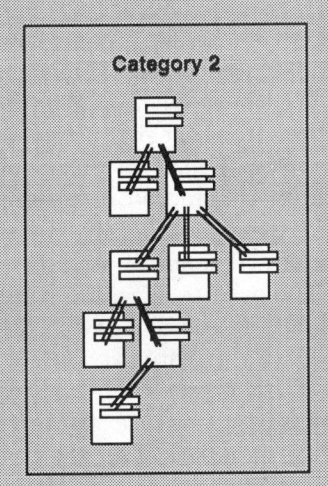

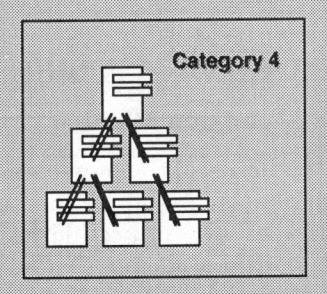

object-oriented design. You should avoid using it as part of your object-oriented design.

Private Characteristics

The *private* operations and attributes of an object are those which are accessible only by internal reference. By internal reference, we mean that private operations can only be triggered from within the design of a public operation in the same object (and a similar relationship holds true for accessing private attributes). This involves information hiding, which is a form of encapsulation.

The designation of private operations and attributes in an object is sometimes called *information hiding*. The information about the internal design of a public operation or about the internal composition of a public attribute is hidden as their private subordinate operations and attributes. By definition, therefore, the private characteristics of an object are the lower-level internal structures, which support its public operations and attributes.

Information hiding through the use of private characteristics is a limited form of encapsulation. Public members are the entry points to an object. Private members satisfy the requirements associated with those entry points. The private operations and the private attributes which support each entry point could be (and sometimes are) extracted and encapsulated as separate objects.

The concepts of information hiding and encapsulation are sometimes used interchangeably. It is best to think of information hiding, however, as a special form of encapsulation. The private members of an object could be considered to be implicitly encapsulated objects. For clarity of discussion, we generally reserve the term *encapsulation* to mean explicitly defined subordinate objects.

The private operations and attributes of an object are always subordinate to the public ones. The only way to trigger a private operation or to access a private attribute from outside an object is through the use of one of that object's public operations or attributes. Private operations and attributes constitute the lower-level internal design of an object. The private members of an object, therefore, are sometimes referred to as the *implementation* of an object.

8.2.2 How Is Visibility Used?

The Scope of a Member

The visibility of the members of an object (its operations and attributes) to other objects plays an important role in the use of polymorphism within an inheritance hierarchy. One form of polymorphism is context-sensitive referencing. *Context-sensitive referencing* is the ability to trigger a particular redundantly named operation, or to access a particular redundantly named attribute, most relevant to the object in which it is referenced. Context-sensitive referencing is the primary reason for the reusability of an object-oriented design.

The visibility of an operation or an attribute defines its scope which defines the context in which a reference to it is relevant. Therefore, the visibility of an object's members sets the scope for all context-sensitive referencing. The scope of the members of an object determine whether the object or the inheritance and collaboration hierarchies are used to define the context in which that member is relevant.

The scope of a private operation or attribute is limited to the object in which it resides. It can only be referenced by other members of the same object. The inheritance search algorithm of a particular language and compiler will search for a private operation or attribute name only within the object in which it is referenced. The context of a reference to a private member of an object, therefore, is limited to supporting the internal operation of the object.

The scope of a public operation or attribute is unconstrained (if not protected), or, at most, constrained to its own inheritance hierarchy (if protected). Therefore, the inheritance search algorithm of a particular language and compiler will find and select the nearest (that is, the most relevant) from among the redundantly named operations and/or attributes by searching the inheritance hierarchy up from an object that refers to the public operation or attribute. The context of a reference to a public member in an object, therefore, is limited only by the inheritance and collaboration hierarchies that contain the object.

8.3 OBJECT TYPES

8.3.1 What Is Object Typing?

Class Consistency

The use of object types in object-oriented design is often confused with the use of object classes. The two concepts are very similar, but represent different things. In fact, a *type* is a special case of a class, or more precisely, a type is a special case of a metaclass. In the same way that you can think of a metaclass as a predetermined form of multiple inheritance, you can think of an object type as a predetermined metaclass.

The class of an object is sometimes also referred to as its type, however, many languages provide for the definition of an object type separate from and in addition to its class. An object can have a type, but more important, an operation can have a type and an attribute can have a type. Fundamental operation types include the four functions (add, subtract, multiply, divide). Fundamental attribute types are commonly called data types (integer, real, character, etc.).

It is easier to understand the use of object types if you first consider the use of operation types and attribute types. As you use one operation as part of another (in process decomposition) or as you use one attribute as part of another (in data decomposition) their types may need to be consistent. Similarly, as you define instances of an object, their types may need to be consistent with the type of the object.

Typing is the enforcement of class consistency. An *object type* is a collection of objects that all share some fundamental characteristics, such that objects of the same type must be used in a similar way. Thus, an object type is the constrained use of an object class. A language, or more precisely, the compiler which implements a language, needs to check for the consistent use of object types in order to ensure proper operation at run time.

An object might be defined in terms of an attribute type, its class, or some programmer-defined type. A consistent use of object types might be required in an object-oriented design, which would prevent a programmer from attempting to trigger an operation or access an attribute in an instance of an object where it is not visible or prevent a user from attempting to create an instance of an object which is inconsistent with its definition.

Data-Attribute Types

Object typing is probably best explained in terms of the *data types* in a third generation language. Attributes are the data variables in an object. As such, attributes can have a type. The programming language in which a design is implemented defines the allowable types for an attribute. In third-generation languages such as FORTRAN and COBOL, data types usually include such things as short and long integers, single- and double-precision real numbers, exponential numbers, and character strings. In a similar way in an object-oriented language, an attribute can usually have a data type.

The data type of an attribute reflects the manner in which data storage is allocated in the memory of the base processor. Some of the more complex data types (double precision, long integers, strings, handles) are just higher-level composites of the fundamental data types (integer, real, character). In a third-generation language, the compiler or the operating system defines and maintains the composite definitions based on the fundamental data types. The fundamental data types are usually hardwired into the design of the central processing unit (that is, on the microprocessor chip).

In some object-oriented languages, programmers can define their own higher-level composite data types, and/or override the interpretation of the ones provided by the language. This is why it is important to know whether an object-oriented language compiler performs type checking. If you want to design your own data types, then you will want a strongly typed language, that is, one which checks for type consistency.

Process-Operation Types

Object typing can also be based on the *function types* of operations. Operations are the process functions in an object. As such, operations can also have a type. Like data types, the programming language in which a design is implemented may also define the allowable types for an operation. In third-generation languages such as FORTRAN and COBOL, function types usually include such things as signed and unsigned arithmetic, trigonometric functions, and the fundamental functions (add, subtract, multiply, divide), or can even be a data type (integer, real).

The function type of an operation reflects the manner in which data storage is manipulated in the memory of the base processor. Some of the more complex function types that you may have encountered (string concatenation, string comparisons, divide checks, multiply carries) are just higher level composites of the fundamental function types (add, subtract, multiply, divide). In a third-generation language, the compiler or the operating system defines and maintains the composite definitions based on the fundamental functions. The fundamental functions are usually hard-wired into the design of the central processing unit.

In some object-oriented languages, programmers can define their own higher-level composite function types, and/or override the interpretation of the ones provided by the language. You may choose, for example, to redefine how an array comparison operation takes place (assuming that you know something about the interface of the one supplied in the language). If you want to design your own function types you will want a strongly typed language.

8.3.2 How Is Typing Used?

Language Extensions

The issues of object typing may seem particularly extraneous to software engineers and programmers who are most familiar with third-generation languages. The compilers of third-generation languages all implicitly provide type consistency checking. It is a compiler service that they have come to expect. Unfortunately, this is not necessarily the case with object-oriented languages and their compilers. Many object-oriented language compilers include type checking as a language extension.

In object-oriented languages, object types are often more flexible than those of third-generation languages. Depending on your perspective, this flexibility may be a benefit or a burden. Programmers are sometimes allowed to define their own composite data types and/or function types. These programmers may work for the vendor of the compiler or they may be the same persons developing the end program (the business application) using a particular vendor-supplied language compiler.

Object types defined by programmers are stored for reuse in *type hierarchies*. Type hierarchies are manipulated and used in the same way as user-class hierarchies. The only difference is in the greater frequency in which types are reused in new programs. The types become extensions to the language for anyone who has access to the library in which they are stored. Eventually, a library of type definitions will be used by many application programmers as if it were a part of the language compiler.

The language extensions related to object typing are usually distributed as libraries of nested data type and function type definitions. These libraries may be source-code files that can be included in your program or they may be compiled executable modules that can be referenced from your programs. As the object-oriented language industry stabilizes, a standardized set of object types should evolve for each language and will be distributed as standard libraries with all object-oriented compilers that support that language.

Strong and Weak Typing

Since type definitions are most often distributed as language extensions in libraries rather than as embedded features of the compiler, the amount of type checking provided has become an issue in the selection of the compiler. Until a more standardized set of types evolves in this industry, you will continue to see object-oriented languages described as either *strong typed* or *weak typed*. A strong-typed language performs a lot of type checking using the libraries of type definitions provided with it or added to it. A weak-typed language does not.

The ability to define types is usually of greatest interest to systems programmers, and they may find that either a weak-typed or a strong-typed language may be suitable for their purposes. Flexible and expandable types are desirable if you are developing commercial end-user products or designing intricate communications software. However, if you are a business or scientific programmer developing an end-user application, you will most likely want a strong-typed language. There is not enough need for user-defined types in end-user programming to justify the conceptual burden of maintaining your own data types and function types.

Early and Late Binding

An issue often confused with object typing is that of *binding*. Object typing is the amount of consistency checking provided by a language using its libraries of type definitions. Binding is the place and time at which references are resolved. These may be object references, operation references, or attribute references. The time of binding affects the manner in which type checking occurs.

Early binding means that the compiler resolves references and checks for type consistency at compile time. In early binding, therefore, the programmer must resolve type conflicts. Compiler messages will identify unacceptable selections. This is no different from the compiler messages generated by third-generation languages. Because of its nature as a compile time feature, early binding is often called *static* binding.

Late binding means that references are resolved at runtime. In late-binding languages, therefore, the user must resolve type conflicts or otherwise accommodate them in some manner. As a result, your program must be designed to handle exception cases and recover gracefully from type inconsistencies. Thus, a late-binding language might provide a more flexible application but would require additional error checking and recovery as part of the application design. Because of its nature as a runtime feature, late binding is often called *dynamic* binding.

Binding is different from type checking. However, binding affects how type checking is implemented and it may affect the complexity required of your design. Most designers of large-scale object-oriented systems will want to use a strong-typed language. The implementation of some of these systems, however, may be best suited for early binding while others may be best suited for late binding.

For example, the design of a payroll system would benefit from a strong-typed language and early binding. A strong-typed language would screen out data type inconsistencies and an early binding would do that screening in advance of releasing the system to end users. You don't want to require that a payroll clerk make selection adjustments on the fly while printing checks.

In contrast, the design of a decision support system that reports sales figures from the best data available at the time would benefit from a strong-typed language and late binding. The program designer will not know what data will be available at any point in time. It is more desirable to allow the end user to make alternative selections based on some type of unavailability indication, such as a beep or a grayed-out area, to indicate a selection that is invalid at the time of usage (but might be valid at another time), rather than to require the programmer to accommodate all possible cases in advance.

CHAPTER REVIEW

The Definition of Inheritance

What is class inheritance?   The hierarchical relationship among the abstract classes in a domain, it is the single most distinguishing feature of object orientation.

What is multiple inheritance?   The capability to catalog more than one hierarchy of abstract classes in a domain.

What does inheritance represent?   An abstract between classes where the object of one class *is-a-kind-of* the object of another class in terms of its operations and attributes.

What is object visibility?   A form of limited encapsulation of the internal operations and attributes of an object, sometimes called information hiding.

How is visibility used?   To define the scope of the operations and attributes of an object when referenced from other objects.

What is object typing?   Automatic checking for consistency between the class of an encapsulated operation or attribute and the class of the object from which it was requested.

How is typing used?   As a supplemental form of context-sensitive referencing based on matching the types in addition to matching the names of operations and attributes.

9

The Definition of Collaboration

9.1 THE COLLABORATION HIERARCHY

9.1.1 What Is Class Collaboration?

A Conventional Hierarchy

Many discussions of object-oriented design overlook collaboration, but it is just as important as inheritance in the design of an object-oriented system. *Collaboration*, like inheritance, is a type of hierarchical relationship among objects in a class structure. In particular, collaboration is a hierarchy of object operation like the module hierarchy in a conventionally designed system. Collaborations are also sometimes referred to as *associations*, *implementations*, and *mechanisms*.

The use of collaboration in the design of a computer program enables you to represent one aspect of the classes of objects in your system. Collaboration portrays the operational interaction among the objects in your domain. The objects represent packages of process operations and data attributes, which, in turn, are the fundamental requirements of your system. A collaboration diagram, therefore, shows the operational requirements of your system in an object-oriented manner.

Collaboration is the feature of an object-oriented design which most resembles conventional design. Collaboration portrays the requests, which are made of the operations and attributes of different objects in your system. It is an integral part of your design. The manner and the degree to which collaboration is implemented in your program, however, will vary from language to language and from compiler to compiler.

Diagrammed Encapsulation

A collaboration hierarchy is a diagram of a set of encapsulated objects. The collaboration relationship between a server object and its client object is usually hierarchical but can sometimes be lateral. By *hierarchical*, we mean that the server object can be considered to be a subordinate part of the client object. By *lateral*, we mean that only some small part of the server object is used by the client object. For the most part, however, you can think of collaboration as a hierarchical relationship among objects.

Collaboration is the representation of the client/server model in diagram form. The client objects are said to *collaborate* with the server objects in order to achieve their prescribed functions or to obtain their prescribed properties. The server objects, like any objects, contain operations and attributes. Some of the client functions are achieved by collaboration with a server's operations. Some of the client properties are obtained by collaborating with a server's attributes.

The primary purpose of representing objects as clients and servers is to enable you to describe their collaboration relationships with one another. Collaboration provides an additional dimension to your design in conjunction with inheritance. Together, collaboration and inheritance contain the entire knowledge of an object-oriented design.

As shown in Figure 9-1, a collaboration diagram includes only the concrete classes in your domain. The concrete classes are those associated with objects which can have instances at runtime. They are the lower-level branches of your inheritance diagram. The collaboration diagram, therefore, supplements the inheritance diagram. It shows how the objects associated with the concrete classes will interact to meet the requirements of your system.

Concrete classes contain the characteristics of the physical objects in your system. The characteristics are the operations and the attributes of the object associated with each concrete class. The object will be represented by one or more instances at runtime. The object of a concrete class, therefore, has a physical representation in the operation of your program. You can think of it as an operational module in your program.

A collaboration diagram is the object-oriented equivalent of a structure chart in a conventional design. Each class on a collaboration diagram represents one module of your design. However, concrete classes only represent the noncommon portions of a module. The common operations and attributes have been extracted and cataloged as the abstract classes in your inheritance hierarchy.

The purpose of a collaboration diagram is to provide a representation of the operation of the modules in your design, concentrating only on the unique requirements of each module. The common requirements will be inherited according to the inheritance hierarchy. The collaboration diagram and the inheritance diagram, therefore, comple-

COLLABORATION

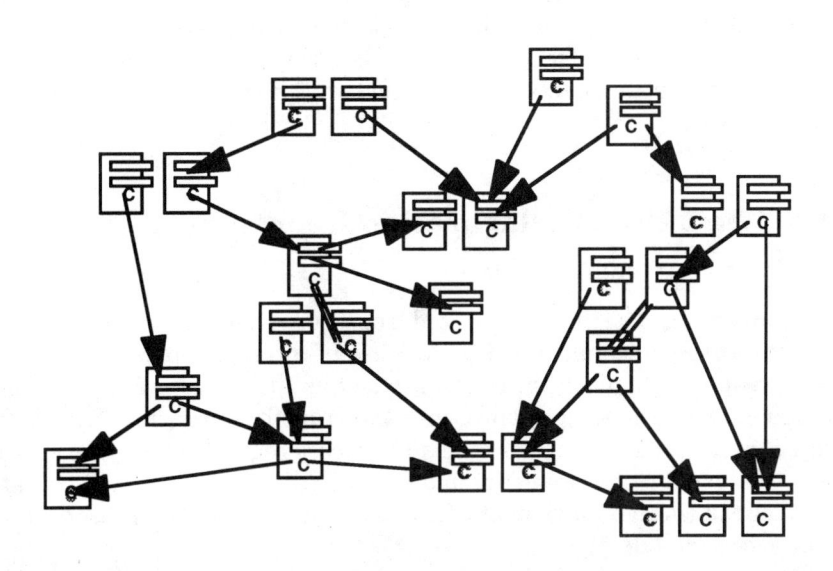

Figure 9-1. Collaboration relationships.

ment each other as two perspectives of the interactions between the classes of objects in your domain.

Concrete Class Interaction

Collaboration is concerned with the interaction of the concrete classes in your domain. The object associated with a concrete class can have instances at runtime. The instances are the physical representations of an object's operations and attributes. Therefore, collaboration addresses the physical interaction between the operations and attributes in different objects.

The objects of different concrete classes can be connected to one another in client/server relationships. Each connection between a client object and a server object on the collaboration diagram shows part of a potential thread of control during runtime. By *thread of control*, we mean the ordered triggering of operations or the ordered accessing of attributes. The operations and attributes are the requirements of your system.

A collaboration diagram is one way in which the requirements of a system are represented in an object-oriented design. It shows the allocation of the operational requirements throughout your entire domain.

The nature of a collaboration diagram is dictated by the interaction among the objects associated with the concrete classes, and represents the operational requirements of your system.

The collaborations between pairs of concrete classes represent the allowed interactions between the objects associated with those classes. This interaction is always directed so that there is one client object and one server object. An instance of a client object can make a request of an instance of a server object in each collaboration. A request from the client can trigger an operation in the server or it can access an attribute in the server.

9.1.2 What Does Collaboration Represent?

A *Makes-Use-of* Relationship

Collaboration is the object-oriented representation of a *makes-use-of* relationship. Each client object makes-use-of the server objects that satisfy its requests. You can think of a request as the transfer of a message. The transfer of a message represents the transfer of control. The client object represents a package of data and process requirements. The server object represents the particular means of accomplishing a subordinate part of one of those requirements. This the object-oriented representation of black-box modularity.

The makes-use-of relationship indicates that one design component is subordinate to another for a particular thread of control. In conventional design, this is represented as lower-level modules on a structure chart. At runtime, each module will pass control to a subordinate module as the situation warrants. A collaboration diagram is simply the equivalent representation of module operation in an object-oriented design.

Collaboration shows how some objects make-use-of other objects in your design. Collaboration hierarchies, therefore, represent the operational flow of control in an object-oriented design. The name of the type of diagram used to represent the collaboration hierarchy, however, may vary from author to author and from technique to technique. Some of the names that you will encounter for the diagrams which correspond to what we have been calling a collaboration diagram include:

Term for Collaboration Diagram	As referred to by these authors
Object Diagram	Booch
Message Connections	Coad/Yourdon
Object Interaction Model	Embley/Kurtz/Woodfield
Dependency Diagram	Shlaer/Mellor
Collaboration Graph	Wirfs-Brock/Wilkerson/Wiener

No matter what it is called, a collaboration diagram represents the operational hierarchy among the objects in your domain. During object encapsulation, you extract subordinate sets of operations and attributes to form new objects. As a result, you derive a description of the operation of the objects in your domain, that is, you identify the interactions between the operations and attributes in different objects. The diagrammed pattern of collaboration relationships between your objects is a visual definition of the operation of your system.

A Pattern of Object Operation

The pattern of object interaction portrayed on a collaboration diagram will mirror the pattern of operation required of your system. A particular client object may use many server objects, and a particular server object may be used by many client objects. Similarly, any one operation in a client object can make use of many operations in one or more server objects. The interactions among objects, and among their operations and attributes, take whatever form is dictated to satisfy the requirements of your system.

A collaboration diagram corresponds directly to some of the more conventional representations of software design that you may have used in the past. Client/server collaborations represent the same type of module to module hierarchy portrayed on a structure chart. The only difference is that the modules on a collaboration diagram are represented as objects, and that the objects are represented in terms of a specifically defined interface and internal design.

The client objects on a collaboration diagram are the *calling modules*, and the server objects are the *called modules*. Just like on a structure chart, a particular server object can also be a client object if it calls (collaborates with) other modules (other objects). The concrete classes associated with some client objects, because of their nature as high-level modules that contain many servers, are sometimes called *composite classes* and/or *container classes*.

Composite classes are one type of concrete class. In particular, a composite class is a concrete class which, by encapsulation, contains many other concrete classes. Like any other concrete class, a composite class has a separate physical representation in your system (that is, it can have instances) and represents a tangible object in the real world. It represents compound objects, made up of many components. Payroll systems, databases, computer hardware devices, automobiles, and automobile transmissions are examples of objects that could be represented as composite classes.

Container classes are also a type of concrete class. Similar to a composite class, a container class is a concrete class that contains information about other classes, can have instances, and represents a tangible object. Unlike a composite class, however, a container class is usually an artificial object whose purpose is only to track information about other objects in the system. Arrays, lists, files, and indices are examples of tangible objects in a computer program that could be represented as container classes.

The pattern of object operation portrayed by a collaboration hierarchy often confirms that the operations and attributes are appropriately distributed among the objects in your domain. Most objects (as represented by a concrete class) in a good design will collaborate heavily with one or two other objects. This indicates clean client/server relationships in which the operations and attributes are probably well distributed.

You can use the pattern of object operation to balance the assignment of operations and attributes among the objects in your domain. If a client object triggers many individual isolated operations in many different servers, and those servers also contain many other public operations and attributes that are never used in that client/server relationship, then you may consider reassigning the triggered operations into a single new concrete class or into the client object.

For example, consider a design in which a document object collaborates with three other objects. It collaborates with a utility object to recover chapters from storage, with a formatting object to display a page, and with a verification object to check spelling. This is not a good design. The document object collaborates with the other objects only to perform isolated operations in each (get chapter, display page, check word). These isolated operations are more closely related to the document than to the objects in which they are contained.

This type of collaboration pattern shows that these particular operations would be better placed within the client object (the document object). It is also likely that a similar reassignment of other operations in the server objects (the utility object, the formatting object, and the verification object) is likely to totally eliminate any need for those objects. They are not natural groupings of operations, although they may have seemed to be at one time.

Module Assemblies in a Domain

In theory, one collaboration hierarchy will cover an entire domain. However, the sheer size of that hierarchy may require that you present it as several related physical diagrams. It is advisable to divide the collaboration hierarchy for the objects in a large domain into several nested hierarchies, called *assemblies*, that each represent a specific physical layer of the collaboration relationships.

You can think of module assemblies in a domain as composite objects on a grand scale. Just as some client objects on a collaboration diagram may be composed of several subordinate server objects, a high-level collaboration diagram may be composed of one or more entire lower-level diagrams. The lower-level diagrams are represented as composite objects on the high-level diagram. The lower-level collaboration diagrams are nested within the high-level diagram.

In particular, nested-collaboration diagrams are usually used to represent different levels of physical hardware and/or software assemblies. Each level is used to isolate the collaboration issues relevant to a particular level of detail in your domain. Module assemblies are used in the same way as nested-process modules on a leveled set of data-flow diagrams. Each level represents a more highly decomposed definition of one component on a higher level.

One good example of the use of nested-module assemblies is found in the Booch technique of object-oriented design. Booch provides for different symbols to be used on similar diagrams for different assemblies. The different diagrams represent the collaboration relationship between objects at different levels in your domain:

Module Assemblies as represented by Booch
Processor Diagrams—interacting hardware units in a domain
Device Diagrams—interacting peripheral devices of hardware
Subsystem Diagrams—interacting software units of a device
Package Diagrams—interacting executable units of software
Program Diagrams—interacting programs in an executable unit
Task Diagrams—interacting separate modules within a program

Diagrams of these (or any other) nested-module assemblies are just artificial divisions of a collaboration hierarchy. They simplify the development process by dividing a collaboration hierarchy into separate pieces, each appropriate for a particular level of interest. Divisions of a collaboration hierarchy are just a convenient way to manage the many levels of collaboration relationships which are likely to exist in a large and complex domain. You use the same rules and the same diagram syntax to derive and represent different parts of the domain. Only the types of objects portrayed at each level are different.

Schema Assemblies in a Domain

In the same way that you might nest one part of a collaboration hierarchy within another to model levels of process module assemblies, you may also nest it based on *data-schema assemblies*. A process-module assembly represents objects which are more strongly characterized by their operations than by their attributes. A data-schema assembly is just the reverse. This kind of representation, however, has not yet been fully explored by the object-oriented industry.

A collaboration hierarchy nested to represent a data schema would be divided into nested assemblies similar to a set of nested-process modules, but this time nested along data lines. The objects in a schema assembly might represent *tuples* (records) in a normalized structure. In the same way that different types of process module objects represent different levels of operation (such as processor, device, subsystem, package, program, and task), different types of data schema objects might represent different levels of attributes (such as repository, dictionary, database, file, record, and element).

The subdivision of a collaboration hierarchy into nested-data-schema assemblies could be used to depict a normalized object-oriented database.

As the field of object-oriented databases develops, attribute assemblies might be used to divide an otherwise large collaboration diagram into nested sets of data-structure diagrams. Until then, nesting collaboration diagrams according to data-schema assemblies is not of as much practical use as nesting them into process-module assemblies.

9.2 OBJECT REQUESTS

9.2.1 What Is a Collaboration Contract?

A Package of Requests

A collaboration between two objects establishes a *contract* between them. The contract is represented as a package of requests. A *collaboration* may be composed of one or more contracts. Each contract may, in turn, be composed of one or more requests. The collaborations connect the objects. The contracts connect groups of related operations and/or attributes between those objects. The requests connect individual operations and/or attributes in one object with those of another object.

As shown in Figure 9-2, a collaboration between a client object and a server object can be composed of several contracts. A contract is just a more physical and somewhat artificial component of a collaboration. It helps you to organize the many requests which may be required in a particular collaboration. The important design aspects of collaborations and contracts, respectively, are the objects that they connect and the requests that they represent.

A collaboration is the general relationship between a client object and a server object. A contract is the agreement that the server perform

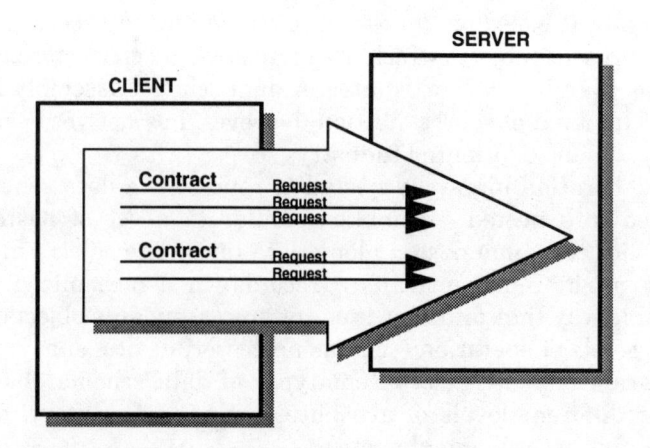

Figure 9-2. Contracts between objects.

a specific function or provide a specific property for the client. A contract is satisfied by the requests between the client and the server. Each request is associated with a particular operation or a particular attribute in the server object that fulfills a part of the contract.

If you choose to represent the collaborations in your design by one contract each, then there is little real distinction between a collabora-

Encapsulating Members

Encapsulation is a matter of finding wholly contained subsets of operations and attributes within an object. The organization of a package of operations and attributes into a hierarchy of common objects is called classification. The further subdivision of the lower-level objects on that hierarchy is called encapsulation.

Object 3

Operation 3 *
Operation 4 *
Attribute 7
Attribute 6 *
Attribute 8

Consider the internal dependencies of the members of Object 3, that we first introduced as part of Figure 6-5. When subordinate members are extracted from an object, they form a new object which is said to be encapsulated by the original object. In Object 3, Attribure 7 is subordinate to Operation 4 and Attribute 8 is subordinate to Operation 6. These members can be extracted to form two new encapsulated objects.

* = entry point

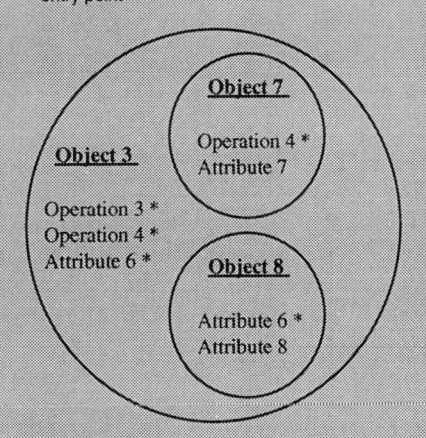

Object 3
Operation 3 *
Operation 4 *
Attribute 6 *

Object 7
Operation 4 *
Attribute 7

Object 8
Attribute 6 *
Attribute 8

Each set of extracted members becomes a new concrete class in a collaboration diagram. Object 3 is now a client object which makes use of two new server objects labeled Object 7 and Object 8. Encapsulation is the mechanism by which you derive new concrete classes of objects by dividing the old ones. The extracted members are grouped together because they are already known to be more highly related to one another than to the other members of the object.

Notice also that Operation 4 and Attribute 6 each appear in both the encapuslated objects and the original object. This indicates a full encapsulation, that is, one in which the public operations and attributes can still be triggered and accessed by making requests to "calling stubs" in Object 3, which subsequently trigger Operation 4 in Object 7 or access Attribute 6 in Object 8. This need not always be the case. You may decide to extract the encapsulated operations and/or attributes without leaving the "calling stubs" in the original object. As you make decisions like this, the nature of your collaboration diagram takes shape.

tion and a contract. For this reason, you will often see the terms collaboration and contract used interchangeably in the literature—they just represent different aspects of the same thing. A collaboration refers to the connection between the objects. A contract refers to the requests that connect them.

Requests, contracts, and collaborations are always directional, that is, they always represent a connection from a client object to a server object. Furthermore, the requests in a contract must always flow in the same direction as the contract, and the contracts in a collaboration must always flow in the same direction as the collaboration. You will need to use two separate collaborations if you require bidirectional flow between the same pair of objects.

Any particular object in your design may collaborate with several others. The other objects may be clients for which that object acts as a server. Similarly, there may several servers which an object uses as its clients. An object may also have multiple contracts with a single other object or with the several objects with which it collaborates. Within each contract, the client object can (and most often does) use many requests to request the services of a particular server object.

Interobject Relationship

A server object can be viewed as being encapsulated within each and every client object that makes use of it. All interaction with the server object, as far as the other objects in the system are concerned, is accomplished only through its client objects. The thread of control always runs through the client in a collaboration, satisfying some of the requirements of the client by a contract with the server, and using requests to trigger the particular operations or to access the particular attributes in the server which satisfy those requirements.

As shown in Figure 9-3, the collaborations between a client object (the object associated with Class 3) and two servers (Classes 7 and 8) are accomplished in terms of their contract requests. The collaboration between Class 3 and Class 7 is composed of two contracts. The collaboration between Class 3 and Class 8, however, is composed of only one contract. In turn, the contracts are composed of their constituent requests.

From the perspective of the thread of control, Classes 7 and 8 are both encapsulated within Class 3. The only way in which other objects can gain entry into either Class 7 or 8 is through the use of Class 3 (unless they too are designed to collaborate directly with either of these classes). Furthermore, Class 3 (or any other client) can only make use of these servers through their well-defined interface—the set of requests to which they can respond.

A client object makes use of a server that makes a request of it, by sending it a request. The request is part of a collaboration contract. It is used to satisfy part of some requirement in the client. An operation that is triggered in a server object to satisfy a contract is always a *public*

Contracts are a means of grouping sets of related requests between two objects. In the collaborations between these three objects, there are five separate requests and three separate contracts.

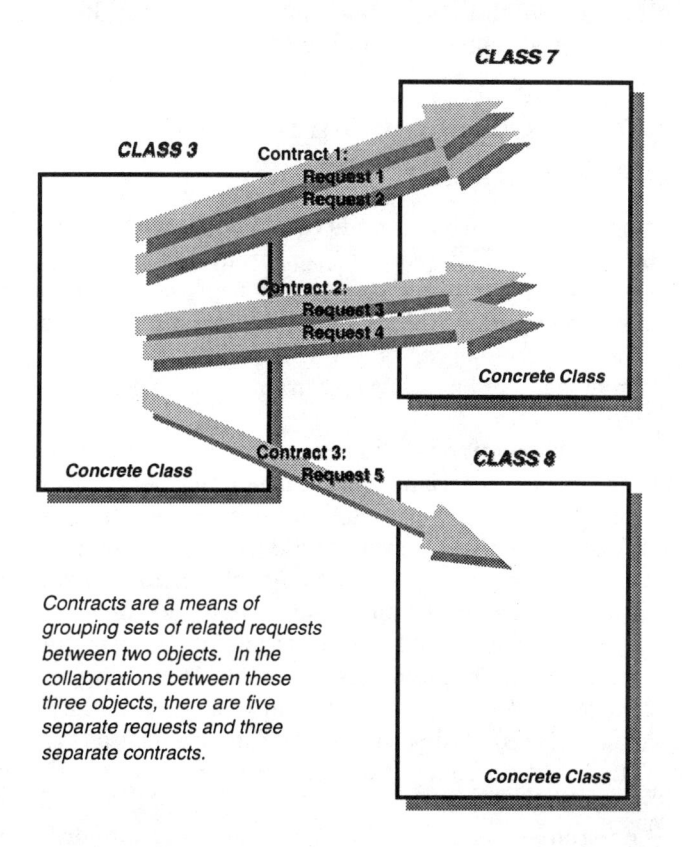

Figure 9-3.   Contract requests.

member of that object. A public member is an entry point into an object. A *public operation* in one object can be triggered from within any other object with which it collaborates.

In theory, you can also use a request in your design to access a public attribute in a server. However, currently available object-oriented programming languages generally do not support this type of request implementation. Rather, they require that you design operations to access attributes. The mechanism for accessing attributes using requests, however, would be the same as triggering an operation.

An object-oriented design achieves modularity using the well-defined interface of an object and its separately maintained internal design. The operations or attributes in a server object satisfy part or all of the requirement of an operation or an attribute in a client object. They may be entirely contained within the server object or may themselves encapsulate another server. The details of this arrangement, however, are of no concern to the original client object. The client only knows that the requirement will be satisfied by sending the request to its server.

9.2.2 What Is a Collaboration Request?

Interobject Communication

A collaboration between two objects is established by the requests which make up the contract. The requests represent the communication between the objects. In particular, a request represents the information passed between the member in the client object which requires a service and the member in the server object which provides that service. The members of an object can be either operations or attributes, but are most often operations.

Requests are abstractions of events in the same way that operations and attributes are abstractions of requirements. An operation is an abstract representation of a process requirement in an object. An attribute is an abstract representation of a data requirement. A request is just an abstract representation of an event which can trigger an operation or which can access an attribute from outside of the object.

A request is often described only in terms of its identifier, which is usually the same as the name of the operation it can trigger or the attribute it can access. A complete definition of a request, however, is its *signature*. A signature includes the name of the request as well as an ordered list of the input and output parameters needed to trigger the operation or access the attribute.

There is one request associated with each public member in an object. In some object-oriented programming languages, however, the signature of an individual request can have multiple protocols. A *protocol* is a format for a signature which is acceptable to the member. By acceptable, we mean that the member will recognize and respond to the request signature. The internal design of a member will have minor variations that accommodate each protocol of is request signature.

Figure 9-4 shows a closer examination of one of the requests between the client object presented in Figure 9-3 and one of its server objects. The signature of the request is composed of its name and its input/output parameters. The input parameters are called the *stimulus* of the request. The output parameters are called the *response* of the request. They represent the operational characteristics of a request. The stimulus determines the response—for any set of values for the input parameters, a particular set of values for the output parameters will be returned.

A request flows from a client object to a server object. The input parameters associated with that request flow in the same direction. The direction of a request, therefore, always follows the direction of its stimulus. The response of a request flows in the opposite direction. The response represents the result of the collaboration, that is, it represents the output from a server object.

The Request Stimulus

You can think of the stimulus of a request as the input parameters needed to trigger the operation associated with that request. In many ways, the mechanism is similar to calling a subroutine module. The called module (the server) performs specific functions based upon some input from the calling module (the client). In an object-oriented design, this input is called the *request stimulus*.

A public operation in an object is an entry point into that object. It can be triggered from outside the object. In particular, a public operation in a server object can be triggered by receiving a request from a client object. The signature of the request identifies the stimulus parameters as the input. *Stimulus parameters*, therefore, are similar to attributes. They are the data used to perform the functions of an object.

The *stimulus values* of a request can be derived from a variety of sources, depending on the scope of the attributes of the client and server objects. The stimulus may be composed of specific attributes contained in either the client or the server object, they may be inherited from within the inheritance hierarchy of either, they may be explicitly provided by another collaboration, or they may be derived from attributes and/or by operations elsewhere in the system.

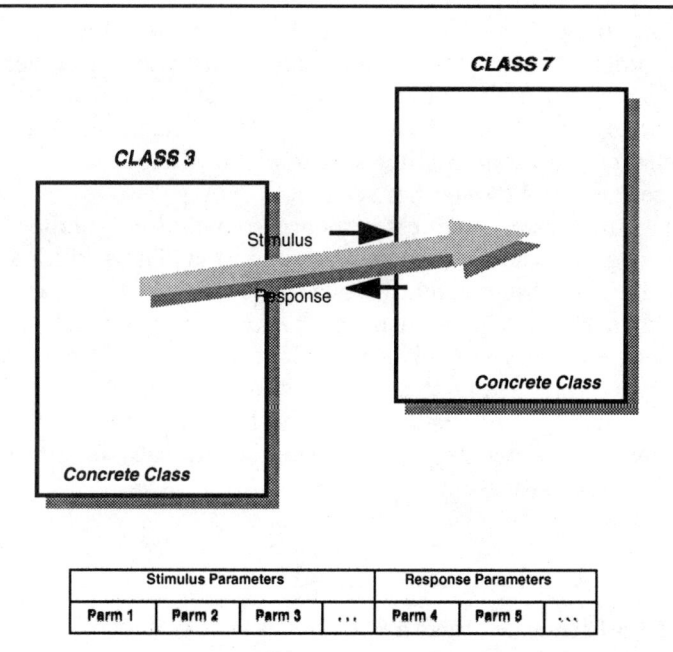

Figure 9-4. Request composition.

The protocol of a particular request stimulus might allow for many different combinations of stimulus parameters in a *request signature*. The signature of a request indicates which stimulus parameters are needed to trigger its operation. Often, however, a client object is allowed to trigger a server operation even if the full set of stimulus parameters is not available, as long as all of those required by a particular protocol are available.

The stimulus for a request identifies the external information needed by the operation or the attribute associated with that request. In some programming languages, this may be implemented in a literal sense by the creation and parsing of parameters in a request message. In other programming languages, the stimulus of a request is only implied by the data used in the internal design of the particular operation. It is always advisable, however, to explicitly list the stimulus of each request in your design, even if it only serves as a point of design clarification.

The Request Response

You can think of the *response* of a request as the output parameters produced after a client object triggers the operation associated with a request in a server. The response parameters correspond to the output of a called subroutine module. The called module (the server) produces certain data values which are returned to the calling module (the client) as output after it completes its function. In an object-oriented design, this output is called the *request response*.

You should be careful not to confuse the response of a request with a secondary encapsulation of a server from within another server. The response of a request is the set of values for the prescribed output parameters of the operation or attribute associated with that request. The further encapsulation of another server within the operation of a server object is represented by another request.

The parameters in a request response are usually a smaller and more constrained group than in the request stimulus. The stimulus parameters provide all of the information needed to perform the operation associated with a request. The response parameters need only return the information that has changed as a result of the operation performed by a request. As in the case of the request stimulus, the nature of the programming language will determine whether requests (and, therefore, their response parameters) are implemented literally or just used as a point of design clarification.

9.2.3 How Are Requests Used?

Hierarchical Encapsulation

Requests are used in an object-oriented design to represent the events which can occur between client and server objects. The client object can send requests to the server object. Requests can trigger a public operation in a server or they can access a public attribute. The requests, therefore, are used to model (and in some programming languages, to implement) the operation of your objects as the components of a system.

The operational relationship between client and server objects usually represents a hierarchical view of encapsulation. The server objects are considered to be encapsulated by the client objects. They are lower-level subordinate functions and properties of the clients. A collaboration diagram of this type of relationship would look like the hierarchy of a structure chart if it were not for the many collaborations among the many objects which create a more complex network of interaction.

Hierarchical encapsulation is the most typical case represented in a collaboration hierarchy. Collaboration represents what we have called a *makes-use-of* relationship among objects in a design. Some authors refer to hierarchical encapsulation as an *is-a-part-of* relationship (this is also sometimes called a *whole-part relationship*). It is one specific form of collaboration relationship.

The server objects in a collaboration diagram represent subordinate groups of operations and attributes in a design. These objects are most often first identified by extracting highly cohesive subsets of operations and/or attributes from other objects. The requests in a collaboration hierarchy are the events that can trigger the encapsulated operations, or in some cases, that can access the encapsulated attributes from within client objects in the system.

The server objects whose operations and attributes are encapsulated from the point of view of the client objects which use them are similar to decomposed processes in a process-driven design. Each process on a data-flow diagram can be decomposed into a lower-level set of subordinate processes and represented on another data-flow diagram. Similarly, each client object can be decomposed into the set of server objects that provide the subordinate services it needs to satisfy its requirements.

The server objects are probably even more similar to some of the components in a data-driven design. Server objects correspond to the subentities on a fully qualified entity relationship diagram. Client objects correspond to the major entities. Each entity is decomposed into its constituent parts. Similarly, each client object encapsulates many server objects in a fully diagrammed collaboration hierarchy.

Collaboration enables the reuse of objects in your design by defining their interface in a prescribed manner. The interface is composed of contracts, and, in turn, requests. Each request can be used by a client operation or attribute to trigger a needed operation or to access a needed attribute in a server. The requests are represented by known stimulus and response parameters. In this way, you can later substitute other servers as new modules to satisfy a collaboration. Only the signatures of the requests need be identical. The internal design of the server operations and attributes is independent of the interface.

Lateral Encapsulation

Limited collaboration between two otherwise unrelated objects is called *lateral encapsulation*. A lateral encapsulation is just another form of the makes-use-of relationship between objects in a design—a special case of collaboration. Lateral encapsulation is also called the *has-knowledge-of* relationship by some authors.

Class Assemblies

The collaboration hierarchy for the classes in your domain will consist of many different individual hierarchies. This is similar to the many different modules which may exist in a conventional design. Similar to class categories for an inheritance hierarchy, the classes in a collaboration diagram are often nested into assemblies. If your domain is very large, you may choose to represent it as assemblies such as processors, devices, subsystems, programs, packages, and tasks (as Booch recommends). The objects on a subsystem collaboration diagram, for example, would be the programs in each subsystem. These subsystems may represent divisions (as Coad and Yourdon recommend) such as a graphic interface, a database, a memory manager, and a business module.

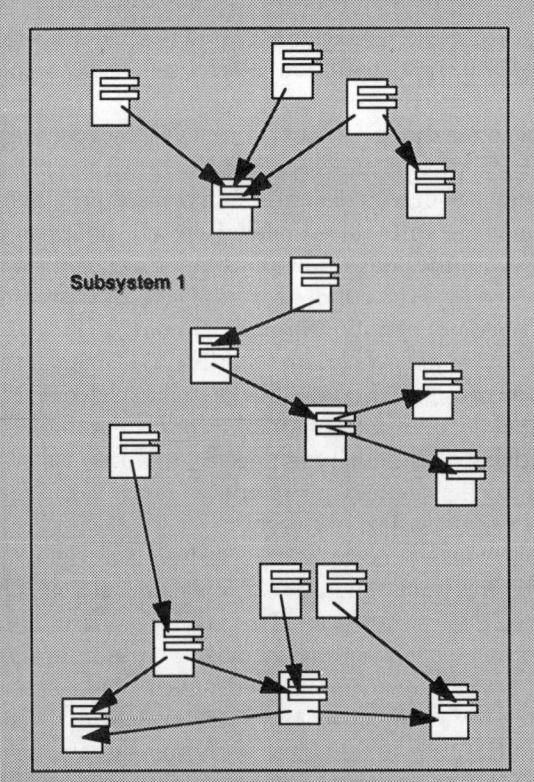

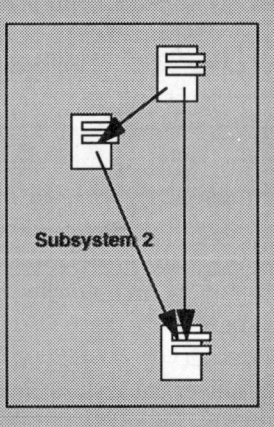

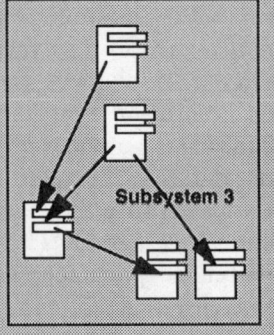

Lateral encapsulation, like hierarchical encapsulation, is the use of a server object by a client object, except that the server is not fully subordinate to the client. The client may access one attribute or it may trigger one operation in the server, however, most of the other operations and attributes in the server have no relationship to the needs of the client. They are not clearly subordinate to those of the client.

You can also think of a lateral encapsulation in terms of the relationships between modules in a conventional design. If hierarchical encapsulation corresponds to the module-to-module interaction portrayed on a structure chart, then lateral encapsulation corresponds to the process-to-process communication shown as off-page connectors on a data-flow diagram. Lateral encapsulation uses requests for direct communication between two objects which are otherwise server objects to another client.

Lateral encapsulation can be viewed as a shortcut in object communication facilitated by object-oriented design. An object is represented by a specific interface in terms of the requests that can be used to trigger its public operations and to access its public attributes. The requests that comprise the interface of an object, therefore, can be used by any object in the domain, not just the objects from which the server was originally intended to support.

CHAPTER REVIEW

The Definition of Collaboration

What is class collaboration? The hierarchical relationship between the concrete classes in a domain that corresponds to the module-to-module interactions of a conventional design.

What does collaboration represent? The *makes-use-of* relationships between the concrete classes of objects in a domain that request operations and attributes of one object be used within another.

What is a collaboration contract? A package of related collaboration requests between a particular client and server object in the collaboration hierarchy of a domain.

What is a collaboration request? The representation of an individual object-to-object interaction as a concatenated list of the input parameters supplied by the client object (called the *stimulus*) and the output parameters produced by the server object (called the *response*) when they collaborate.

How are requests used? To define the transient attributes (input/ouput parameters) needed to trigger a public operation or to access a public attribute in a server object by client objects in the domain.

10

The Definition of a Domain

10.1 OBJECT HIERARCHIES

10.1.1 What Is a Domain?

A Large-Scale Design

Object engineering is an organized approach for applying object-oriented design to large and complex systems. It makes use of the concept of a *domain* to characterize the requirements of a system, or more specifically, to characterize the *design* which satisfies those requirements. Your domain defines the problem that you are attempting to solve. Your design defines your solution to that problem. It is composed of your inheritance and collaboration hierarchies and their attendant classes, objects, operations, and attributes.

The true domain of a problem may be larger than the apparent domain represented by your design. Your design (its hierarchies, classes, objects, operations, and attributes) may only address some of the requirements of a complete domain, in particular those with which you were presented for your system. Therefore, you (or others) may modify and/or expand upon your initial design as time goes by until you meet all of the requirements of a particular domain.

A domain may also be larger than any one system, and therefore, your design may be partitioned into several systems that reflect either a natural division of functions within a domain or the historical sequence in which the functions were automated. In either case, the important point to remember is that you can develop an object-oriented design for a large system by treating it as a single domain even though it is likely to expand in the future.

Organized Requirements

A domain is a self-contained data-processing situation. It is usually expressed in terms of the requirements of a system, that is, as a system design. You can represent a domain, therefore, in terms of the components of a design as the inheritance and collaboration hierarchies for a set of objects. A domain contains the design for a system.

A domain is the set of requirements that characterize a problem. The requirements of a domain address a particular problem for which you will design a computer program. A domain, therefore, is an abstract representation of a complete set of requirements rather than any one particular system that addresses those requirements. Accounting, inventory, banking, order entry, purchasing, telemetry, and communications are all examples of things which could be considered to be domains.

A design is the solution to the problem represented by a domain. The domain is the abstract representation of the problem. The design is the specific and practical solution to that problem—for this reason, a design is one way to represent a domain. The design of a system solves the problem of a particular domain. The inheritance and collaboration hierarchies for an accounting system, for example, represent the requirements of an accounting domain.

As shown in Figure 10-1, you can think of a domain as the collection of components which constitute an object-oriented design. The domain is represented by two complementary class hierarchies—the inheritance diagram and the collaboration diagram. Supporting these hierarchies are descriptions of the individual classes on the diagrams, descriptions of the objects associated with each class, and descriptions of the requests, operations, and attributes that constitute each object.

Object engineering is an organized approach for the implementation of object-oriented design techniques and is a convenient way to address the design of a large distributed system. Much of the current literature on object-oriented design addresses only the techniques that you use to develop the design. Some authors, however, also place these techniques within the context of some particular approach. For example, Coad/Yourdon provide guidelines for applying object-oriented techniques by breaking down your domain into specific class categories, and Wirfs-Brock/Wilkerson/Wiener provide an even more specific set of recommended steps that constitute a well-organized approach.

The particular set of techniques that you would use to develop object-oriented diagrams is fairly consistent from author to author. Object engineering, like any other specific approach, just provides a framework for developing a similar set of object-oriented diagrams for the large and complex system that constitutes a domain.

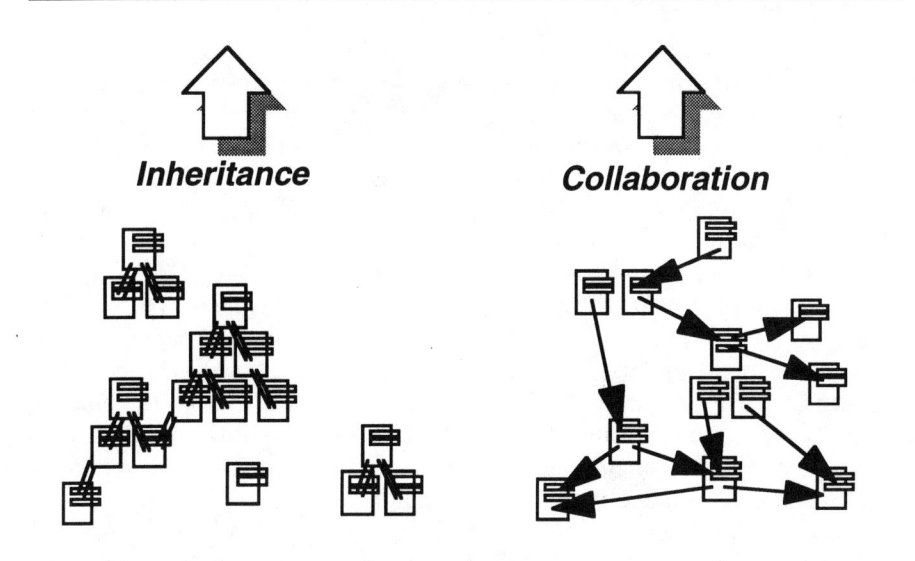

Figure 10-1. Domain compostion.

Inheritance and Collaboration

A complete object-oriented design for a domain is composed of two complementary class hierarchies. These are the *inheritance* hierarchy and the *collaboration* hierarchy. Inheritance represents the commonalty among the objects in the domain. Collaboration represents the operational interaction among the objects in the domain. Together, they provide a complete picture of an object-oriented design within a domain. However, there are many variations of diagramming conventions presented in the literature for representing a domain as an object-oriented design.

The Booch notation combines inheritance and collaboration on one physical type of diagram, the class diagram. A Booch class diagram is just a variation of the inheritance diagram and the collaboration diagram that comprise your domain. Object engineering, as presented in this book, therefore, can still serve as an approach to organize the development of the design for a large system even if you choose to use the Booch notation and techniques to develop your design.

The Coad/Yourdon notation provides another variation for developing the diagrams for a domain. The Coad/Yourdon notation, however, provides for separate inheritance and collaboration diagrams much like those recommended in this book. Although they also provide an approach to employ with their techniques, the Coad/Yourdon techniques can still be used within the object engineering approach presented in this book.

Classes and Objects

The classes on the inheritance and collaboration diagrams are the design units within a domain. You use classes to document the organizational information portrayed in the diagrams, as well as to document implementation considerations such as concurrency and persistence. Each class is also associated with an object. This association, however, may present itself in slightly different ways depending on the notation that you choose.

In a Booch notation, abstract classes (the classes primarily represented on an inheritance diagram) are simply called *classes*. The concept of the object associated with a class is dropped, and you instead assign the operations and attributes directly to the class. Similarly, concrete classes (the classes on a collaboration diagram) are just called *objects*. This variation in terminology aside, a Booch representation of classes and objects is still consistent with object engineering as an approach to organize a large-scale object-oriented design.

In a Coad/Yourdon notation, a composite symbol is used to represent a class and its associated object. This symbol is used on both inheritance and collaboration diagrams. The symbol is somewhat cumbersome to draw but it is a more accurate portrayal of the close relationship between the concepts of a class and its object. Like the Booch representation, a Coad/Yourdon representation of classes and objects is also consistent with object engineering.

In the diagram notation used in this book, there is little distinction between a class and its associated object. This representation is most similar to the Coad/Yourdon notation but it is still consistent with both the Booch and the Coad/Yourdon techniques. The important aspects of classes and objects are the same. You use them to represent the organization and the interaction of the requirements of a domain.

Objects (in any notation) represent the operations and the attributes allocated to the classes. The operations are the process requirements of the domain. The attributes are the data requirements of the domain. The purpose of defining objects, classes, inheritance, and collaboration is to organize these operations and attributes in some meaningful way as the design of a system for a particular domain.

Operations and Attributes

An operation in an object is the implementation of one specific process requirement in a domain. This is one of the ways in which object-oriented design is similar to process-driven design. At this level of your design, you are concerned with the implementation of processing requirements, except that the design is organized within the context of objects, classes, inheritance, and collaboration.

Most of the literature on object-oriented design addresses the implementation of operations in terms of *state transition diagrams*, primarily because of the types of domains in which object-oriented design was first applied. For example, both Booch and Shlaer/Mellor devote a significant part of their discussion to this topic. You should remember, however, that other forms of process-driven design may apply equally well, depending on the needs of your particular domain.

An attribute of an object is the implementation of one specific data requirement in a domain. This is one of the ways in which object-oriented design is similar to data-driven design. Like the design of op-

Multiple Relationships

Inheritance and collaboration each illustrate one aspect of the relationships between object classes. Although usually drawn separately, you could draw the inheritance relationships and the collaboration relationships between the classes in your domain on the same diagram. This type of combined diagram helps to illustrate that inheritance and collaboration are just different types of relationships which characterize the same set of classes.

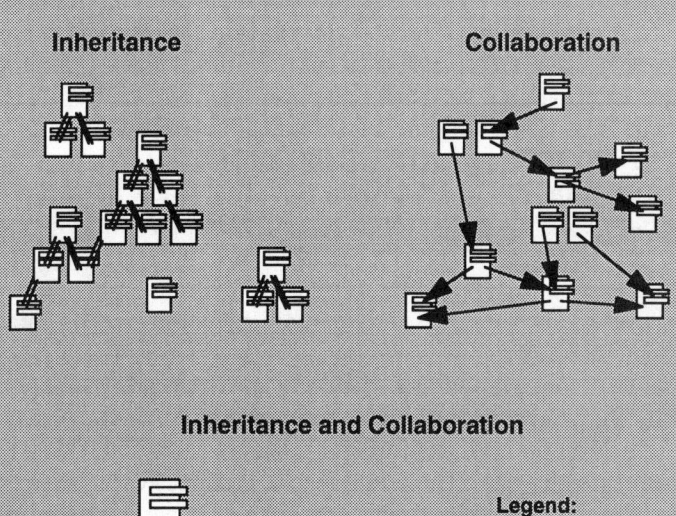

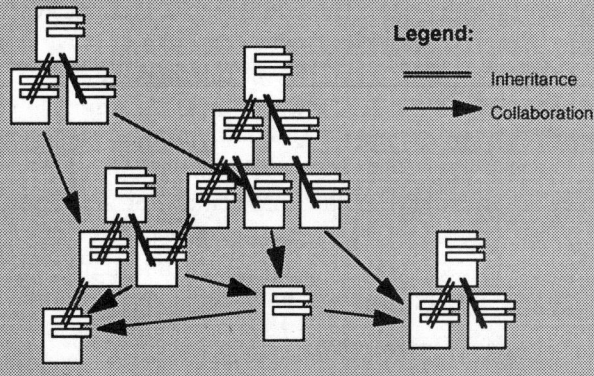

Inheritance

Collaboration

Inheritance and Collaboration

Legend:
═══ Inheritance
▶ Collaboration

erations, you are concerned with the implementation of requirements within the context of your object-oriented design, but in this case, they are data requirements.

As the field of object databases matures, more of the techniques of data-driven design will be applied to the design of the attributes within objects much in the same way as state-transition diagrams are already used in the design of the operations. For example, Andleigh/Gretzinger, Taylor, Rishe, Atre, and other authors have already started to address the design of object attributes as requirements for relational object databases within a domain. This is one aspect of an object-oriented representation which has not yet been fully exploited.

10.1.2 What Is Class Aggregation?

Organization of a Large Domain

A domain is just a frame of reference for developing a large-scale object-oriented design. In order to represent that design at a meaningful scale, you may wish to partition it into subordinate pieces similar to encapsulated objects, but at a higher level. Subordinate pieces of a domain usually show aggregate classes rather than individual classes. This is just a way to organize a particularly large domain.

A domain is composed of one inheritance hierarchy and one collaboration hierarchy. You portray these hierarchies as diagrams and will most likely partition the diagrams so that they each fit on a readable piece of paper or on a single screen image. Each partition of a domain represents an aggregation of classes that are loosely coupled to one another. You can partition a domain by separating portions of its inheritance hierarchy, by nesting portions of its collaboration hierarchy, or both.

One of the most apparent differences between the approaches presented by different authors is the manner in which they recommend partitioning a large domain using aggregate classes. The Coad/Yourdon approach stresses the use of mutually exclusive class categories of inheritance. The Booch approach stresses the use of specific nested physical groups of collaboration. The Wirfs-Brock/Wilkerson/Wiener approach describes a more general technique of nested frames of collaboration.

Regardless of the manner in which you may choose to partition your domain, you will use the same development approach and the same set of design techniques within each partition. The aggregate classes of each partition simply represent a particular perspective of your domain, each containing an inheritance and a collaboration hierarchy. Together, all of the partitions represent the complete domain.

An *Is-a-Part-of* Relationship

Nested partitions of a collaboration hierarchy for a large domain are often referred to as having an *is-a-part-of* relationship with one another.

This is very similar to the makes-use-of relationship of encapsulation shown on a collaboration diagram. They both represent a design unit contained within another design unit, however, the is-a-part-of relationship usually connotes no operational interaction. It is simply an artificial physical identification of an aggregate part of the design with the purpose of improving readability.

The is-a-part-of relationship signifies a cohesive set of aggregate classes, but there is no coupling between the different levels of classes. The cohesiveness is physical, but not operational. For example, an engine block is-a-part-of an automobile engine. The block is a physical part of the engine but there is no interaction between them. An engine is just an artificial name for the collection of components that includes a block.

Different authors handle class aggregation in different ways. The Coad/Yourdon notation provides an explicit diagram type (the whole-part structure) to show this type of relationship. The Booch notation doesn't particularly stress showing the relationship, however, it provides for different symbols (device, subsystem, etc.) on class diagrams to signify levels of aggregation.

You can represent aggregate classes in a large domain as either nested collaboration diagrams or as partitioned inheritance diagrams. The diagrams associated with the techniques discussed in this book, however, don't provide any explicit symbols or diagram types for this purpose. You simply divide and label your class hierarchies accordingly. If you wish to supplement our notation to explicitly show class aggregation, however, you can use either the Booch symbols for class levels and/or the Coad/Yourdon whole-part diagram.

10.1.3 How Are the Hierarchies Used?

Coding the Inheritance Hierarchy

The inheritance hierarchy plays an important role in any object-oriented design. You will encode the hierarchical relationship between object classes in some manner whether you are using a source language or some type of visual program definition environment. However, not all languages and environments that have some object-like features are object oriented. In order to be considered object oriented, a language or an environment must accommodate an inheritance hierarchy in some manner.

If you are using an object-oriented programming language, you will define the inheritance hierarchy as part of the source code statements for your program. This is usually done by naming each class and also declaring it as a member of some other class. By *programming languages*, we mean compiled languages such as C++, Smalltalk, ADA, and Object-Pascal (among many others), although not all object-like languages accommodate inheritance.

If you are using an object-oriented program definition environment, you will define the inheritance hierarchy as a property of an object

180 OBJECT ENGINEERING

definition on some type of screen form. By *object-oriented program definition environment*, we mean screen-oriented window tools such as Visual C++, Visual Basic, and Powerbuilder (among many others). These tools provide object-like features as supplemental characteristics to some type of programming language which, itself, may or may not be object oriented.

Booch Notation

There are many different notations for representing objects, classes, and their relationships to one another. One of the more popular ones is the Booch notation. Unlike the way in which we have used a single symbol to represent an object at any level of abstraction, the Booch notation makes use of different symbols for objects at different stages in the abstraction process:

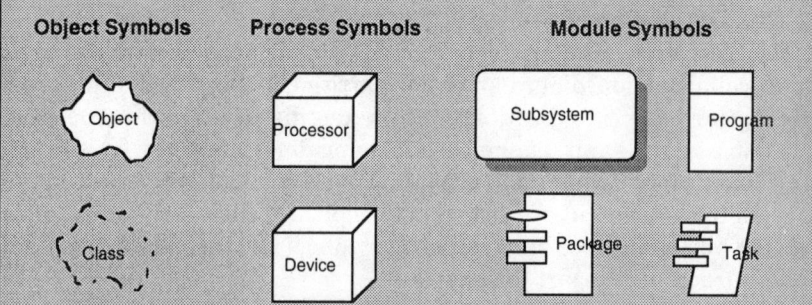

Object Symbols

- Object
- Class

Process Symbols

- Processor
- Device

Module Symbols

- Subsystem
- Program
- Package
- Task

In the Booch notation, objects still represent packages of operations and attributes (which Booch calls *method* and *properties*, respectively), and classes still represent the abstracted description of well-organized objects. The other types of symbols listed above just represent variations of objects. Modules represent software objects. Similarly, process symbols represent hardware objects. At some point in your design, you may wish to use these symbols in your collaboration diagrams to differentiate these kinds of objects from one another. However, for the purpose of explaining and deriving the diagrams, we will continue to use a single symbol for an object. Note that our symbol is very similar to the Booch package symbol.

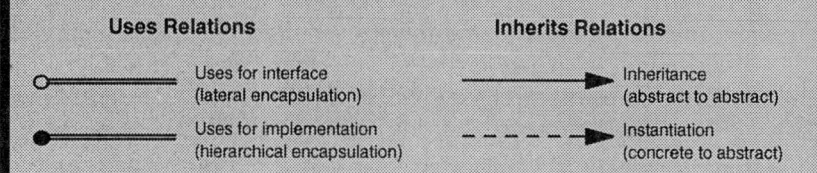

Uses Relations

- ○━━━━━ Uses for interface (lateral encapsulation)
- ●━━━━━ Uses for implementation (hierarchical encapsulation)

Inherits Relations

- ━━━━━▶ Inheritance (abstract to abstract)
- ─ ─ ─ ▶ Instantiation (concrete to abstract)

In the Booch notation, object classes still relate to one another in terms of collaboration and inheritance (which the Booch notation calls *uses relations* and *inherits relations*, respectively). The corresponding symbols are shown above.

Coding the Collaboration Hierarchy

The collaboration hierarchy also plays an important role in any object-oriented design. You will encode the relationship between the operations and attributes of an object in some manner within the source code of the language or the program definition environment. All program languages and environments, whether object-oriented or not, contain some accommodation for defining collaboration relationships between its modules.

In most cases, you will define the collaboration hierarchy as the interaction between operations and/or attributes within source code of the internal design of each object. In some cases, you will need to declare which other objects have contracts with a particular object at the beginning of its source code. In other cases, a mere reference to a public operation or a public attribute in another object will imply the collaboration.

The manner in which you implement collaboration will depend on the capabilities provided by the language or the environment you are using. For the most part, we have discussed object-oriented design independent of implementation issues. In this way we eliminate any bias towards the capabilities (or lack thereof) of current products. However, there are some language and environment peculiarities which bear mentioning.

For example, the popular object-oriented languages which are currently available usually require that you access attributes only through first triggering operations. Object-oriented program definition environments, however, tend to treat attributes on a more equal basis with operations. This book explains the accessing of attributes in the same way as the triggering of operations, even though you may not be able to implement it in the same way.

Coding the Object Internal Designs

After you have encoded the inheritance and the collaboration hierarchies in some manner, you will need to encode the internal design for the objects in your design. Regardless of the language or the environment that you may use to implement your design, you will eventually need to define the internal design of each object as source-code statements just as in any third-generation language you may have used in the past.

Each object is usually identified as a named class with a listed set of operations and attributes. You implement each operation, then, as a source-code procedure either in line or by reference as part of that class. Similarly, you identify the type and composition of attributes (which may contain other attributes as subordinate structures) within a class. In some languages and environments, you can also assign a type designation to the operations and/or objects.

The internal design for an object can be as simple or complex as you need to accomplish its function in the domain. Complex designs often encapsulate other operations and/or attributes, and may even be represented as entire object-oriented designs elsewhere. Simple ones often consist of only a few lines of code.

Operational Logic of the Program

The inheritance, collaboration, and internal designs for your objects will direct the operational logic of your program. The references to named operations and attributes from within the source code for each object will cause the compiler to trigger processes and/or access data as appropriate (that is, according to the accompanying inheritance and collaboration hierarchies). Although languages and environments may vary (and none are purely object oriented), the triggering of operations and the accessing of attributes demonstrates how the operational logic of your program is determined from your object-oriented design.

Triggering an operation in an object-oriented programming language is similar to calling a function or a subroutine in a procedural language. For the purposes of this discussion, no distinction is made between a function and a subroutine. You call a subroutine in a procedural language such as FORTRAN by using the name of the subroutine in a statement in your source code. Similarly, you perform an operation in an object-oriented language by using the operation name when you write the program statements for the object.

Accessing an attribute in an object-oriented programming language is similar to reading a common record in a database. For the purposes of this discussion, no distinction is made between a database and a file. You read (or write) a record in a database by using the record name in a statement in your source code. Similarly, you access an attribute in an object-oriented language by using the attribute name when you write the program statements for the object.

Examining how a program uses an object-oriented design to trigger operations and access attributes in other objects will help you to understand what the design represents. Operations in other objects can be common to a class of objects or local to the other object in which they reside. Similarly, attributes in other objects can also be common or local. Inheritance defines common referencing just as collaboration defines local referencing.

10.2 THE APPLICATION PROGRAM
10.2.1 How Are Operations Triggered?
Common Subroutine Inheritance

Inheritance defines the common subroutines of an object-oriented design. Your program will trigger common operations from within various objects by using the inheritance hierarchy that you develop as part of your design. Common operations in an inheritance hierarchy are similar to common subroutines in a process-driven design.

The common subroutines of an object are those operations that are internal to it but inherited from a higher class. The inheritance hierarchy is used to resolve references to internal operations that perform common functions. In conventional programming languages, common subroutines are sometimes called *utility functions*. You can think of operations in the upper levels of an inheritance hierarchy, therefore, as the utility functions for all objects below them along any subclass chain.

In process-driven design, every lower branch on a structure chart represents one call to a lower-level module. Common subroutines are just a special type of module. A common subroutine is a single lower-level module called by many main routines. You represent a common module as a process box replicated in many different places on a structure chart in your design.

In object-oriented design, an inheritance hierarchy serves the same purpose as common modules on a structure chart. However, instead of repeating the common module for every routine that needs it, you represent it as an operation in an inheritance hierarchy. An inheritance hierarchy is a tree structure that corresponds to a structure chart of common modules.

In object-oriented programming languages, you usually define the inheritance hierarchy at the declaration of your classes. This defines the object classes and their hierarchical relationship to one another, so that program modules (that is, objects) can call the common operations that they need. You can trigger specific operations in the inheritance hierarchy simply by using the name of the operation in a program statement within an object. The compiler will resolve the location of the appropriate operation by tracing up the inheritance hierarchy and matching names of operations.

Resolving subroutine calls is part of the overhead burden assumed by the compiler—just refer to the operation by name and let the compiler find it in the inheritance hierarchy. In a conventional design, the function names must be unique. In an object-oriented design, operation names need not be unique. Instead, the inheritance hierarchy will be used to find the right one.

Local Subroutine Collaboration

Collaboration defines the local subroutines of an object-oriented design. Your program will trigger local operations in other objects by using the collaboration hierarchy that you develop as part of your design. Local operations in a collaboration hierarchy are similar to local subroutines in a process-driven design.

In contrast to the inheritance hierarchy, collaboration hierarchies are used to trigger operations other than utility functions. These types of functions are usually called local subroutines. Server objects can be considered local subroutines. They are external to the calling client object. Local subroutines may be used more than once, but not with the same frequency that is characteristic of utility functions.

You can think of the operations of collaborating objects as the local subroutines called in an object-oriented design. Operations triggered in a collaboration hierarchy are similar to subroutine modules. In conventional design, local subroutine modules are shown as subordinate modules in a structure chart. In object-oriented design, the operations that correspond to local subroutine modules are represented as collaborations.

In object-oriented programming languages, you exercise the collaboration hierarchy by making explicit reference to a named operation. You can trigger a specific operation simply by making reference to its name and to the object where it is to be found. If the domain is also partitioned into levels of aggregate classes, you might also need to fully qualify (that is, class.class.class.object.operation) the position of the object in the aggregation scheme. This is similar in concept to a picture structure in COBOL, although it is applied in this case to processes rather than to data.

The Concept of Concurrency

The operations of the objects in a domain may be triggered in many different configurations. Often, the events that trigger operations (such as a mouse-button click) come from outside the domain in which the objects reside. Depending on the *object concurrency designation*, either the same operation (and its associated attributes) may be triggered more than once or a separate copy of that operation may be used for parallel processing.

You may trigger many operations within the same object over the course of running your program. In each case, you may use the same copy of that object or you may use multiple copies, each with their own identity. Multiple copies of the same object are called *concurrent instances* of that object. Each object in your domain may be either concurrent or nonconcurrent. Whether you trigger an operation by inheritance or through a collaboration, you must also consider whether or not it belongs to a concurrent object.

CONCEPT 22

A concurrent object is an object of a concrete class which can have more than one instance at run time.

Concurrency is usually described in terms of the operations of an object, however, it actually pertains to the whole object. By the *whole object*, we mean all of the attributes and operations which belong to the object. In conventional design, concurrency is called multithreaded processing. In object-oriented design, concurrency means that an object is duplicated and that those duplicate copies can each be used without interfering with one another.

The operations of a concurrent object can be triggered in parallel to one another, that is, by multiple threads of control. Since concurrency applies to the entire object, the attributes which may be used by a triggered operation are also duplicated. In effect, a separate copy of the data of an object (its attributes) will also exist for each concurrent instance of the object. Each concurrent instance is identified by a unique name called a *handle*.

Concurrent instances of an object correspond to multiple similar versions of an object. They all have the same set of operations and at-

---

Booch Class Diagrams

The Booch notation addresses both collaboration and inheritance relationships (called *uses relations* and *inherits relations*, respectively), but mixes their use on a single type of diagram. The advantage to a single diagram type, of course, is that the full nature of all of the relationships for an object is portrayed all in one place. The disadvantage is that collaboration and inheritance relationships are very different from one another, but when drawn on the same diagram, the distinction is lost in the noise. The derivation of concrete class collaborations and abstract class inheritance each drive the design in a different manner (i.e., encapsulation and classification). Therefore, we feel it is more important during design to use separate diagram types to represent the collaboration and inheritance hierarchies.

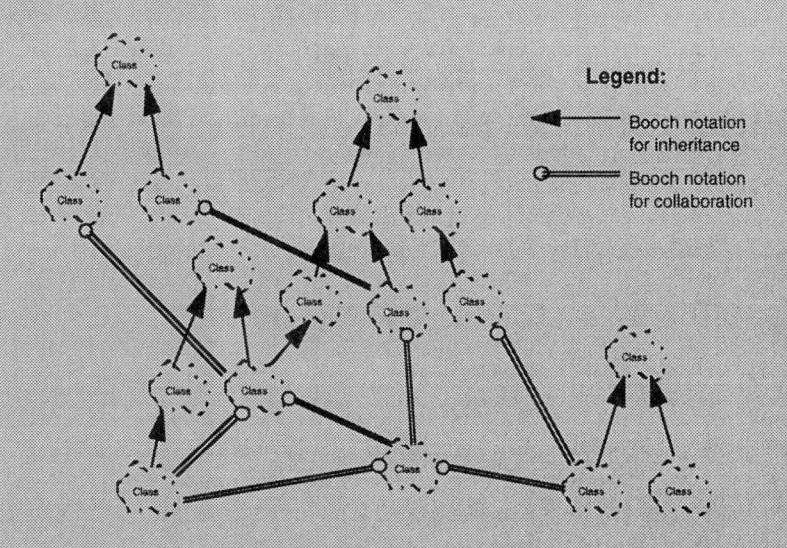

Legend:
⬅——— Booch notation for inheritance
○═══ Booch notation for collaboration

In the Booch notation, both collaboration and inheritance relationships are usually portrayed together in a combined class diagram. There are, however, three other variations of the class diagram which usually show only collaborations, each variation based on a specific physical type of object: object diagrams, process diagrams, and module diagrams. We recommend that you represent inheritance and collaboration on separate diagrams, although it is often helpful to divide the collaboration diagram in your domain to show nested assemblies of objects of a particular type (subsystem, program, module, etc.).

tributes but each version is a copy of the others with its own identity. You can trigger the operations in each copy of the object independent of the others and change the values of the attributes in one copy without affecting the values of those same attributes in another copy.

An object is said to be concurrent if another object or a user can create copies of it. A good example of concurrent objects is the multiple windows often found in a microcomputer GUI environment. Each new window on the screen is a concurrent copy (that is, an instance) of a window object in the program. The window object has certain operations (for example, it can be resized and moved) and certain attributes (such as height, width, location, and color). Other object modules and/or users are allowed to create new copies of the window object and to change the position and color of their copies.

An object is said to be nonconcurrent if the same copy of that object is used each time the object is used. The same set of server data attributes and the same set of executable server operation codes are used by any client object, that is, by any other program or module which calls it. A client that triggers a nonconcurrent server must wait until the server is ready (that is, done processing its prior requested operations) before any new requests can be made of it.

It is usually assumed that there is a unique instance of a concurrent object every time it is used as a server by another (client) object. In this way, there is no waiting if the operations of that same server are used by many clients. You use the handle of the instance of a concurrent object to identify it in your program statements. The handle allows the programmer to control which instance of a server is used by a particular client at a particular point in the program. You may also let the user choose which instance is to be used by some input mechanism, usually a screen pointer and a button click, that selects the instance and its handle.

10.2.2 How Are Attributes Accessed?

Common Data Inheritance

Inheritance defines the common data of an object-oriented design. Your program will access common attributes from within various objects by using the inheritance hierarchy that you develop as part of your design. Common attributes in an inheritance hierarchy are similar to common data in a data-driven design.

The common data of an object are those attributes which are internal to it but inherited from a higher class. The inheritance hierarchy is used to resolve references to internal attributes that hold common data. In conventional programming languages, common data is usually stored in records in a database. You can think of attributes in the upper levels of an inheritance hierarchy, therefore, as the common records for all objects below them along any subclass chain.

In data-driven design, every lower branch in a data-structure diagram represents one subordinate portion of a data entity. Database records are just a special type of data entity. Database records are stored in files rather than in program memory. You design database records by normalizing the data-structure diagrams in your design.

In object-oriented design, an inheritance hierarchy serves the same purpose as normalized data records in a data structure. However, instead of designing a database, you represent it as attributes in an inheritance hierarchy. An inheritance hierarchy is a tree structure that corresponds to a normalized database design. This is analogous to triggering process operations in the inheritance hierarchy, only now we are also using it to access data attributes.

The inheritance hierarchy lists the object classes and their hierarchical relationship to one another, so that program modules (that is, objects) can refer to the common data that they need. You can access specific data in the inheritance hierarchy simply by using the name of the attribute in a program statement within an object. The compiler will resolve the location of the appropriate data by tracing up the inheritance hierarchy and matching names of attributes.

Resolving data references is part of the overhead burden assumed by the compiler—just refer to an attribute by its name and let the compiler find it in the inheritance hierarchy. In a conventional design, variable names must be unique. In an object-oriented design, attribute names need not be unique. Instead, the inheritance hierarchy will find the right one.

Local Data Collaboration

Collaboration defines the local data of an object-oriented design. Your program will access local attributes in other objects by using the collaboration hierarchy that you develop as part of your design. Local attributes in a collaboration hierarchy are similar to local data in a data-driven design.

In contrast to the inheritance hierarchy, collaboration hierarchies are used to access attributes other than common records. These types of records are usually just called *local data*, meaning that they are local to the module in which they reside. The local data in a server object is considered to be external to the calling client object. Local data may be used more than once, but not with the same frequency characteristic of common records. You can think of the attributes in collaborating objects as local server data needed by client object modules.

Attributes that are accessed in collaboration hierarchies are similar to the local data within a subroutine module. An object's attributes represent the local variables shared by the local operations of that object. In conventional design, local data is accessed as part of the calling parameters of the subroutine in which it resides. In object-oriented design, a module's local variables are accessed from outside of the module (that is, from outside the object) in a collaboration.

In object-oriented programming languages, you exercise the collaboration hierarchy by making explicit reference to a named attribute. You can access a specific attribute simply by making reference to its name, the object where it is to be found, and the position of the object in the class aggregation scheme if the domain is partitioned in that way. Thus, you can access any attribute in any object. The collaboration hierarchy is just a diagram of the data-referencing logic between objects in different inheritance hierarchies.

The Concept of Persistence

The attributes of the objects in a domain may be accessed in many different configurations. Often, the events which access attributes occur many times over the course of one or more program sessions. Depending on the *object persistence designation*, an attribute may either retain the last value it was assigned during a program session or it may be reinitialized each time.

You may access attributes many times within the same object over the course of running your program. In each case, you may want to use the same values for those attributes or you may want to set new values. An object that retains the values for its attributes between uses is called a persistent object. Each object in your domain may be either *persistent* or *transitory*. Whether you access an attribute by inheritance or through collaboration, you must also consider whether or not it belongs to a persistent object.

CONCEPT 23

A persistent object is an object of a concrete class whose instances retain the values of their attributes between uses.

Persistence is usually described in terms of the attributes of an object, however, it actually pertains to the whole object. By the whole object, we mean all of the attributes and operations that belong to the object. In conventional design, persistence is the retention of variables in a subroutine between calls. In object-oriented design, persistence means that an object is saved between uses and that its attributes retain their values between subsequent usage.

The values of the attributes of a persistent object are retained between uses, that is, they are saved in memory. Since persistence applies to the entire object, however, the operations that are associated with the object are also saved in memory. In effect, a separate copy of the executable code for an object (its operations) is saved along with its attributes. The next time that your program or a user triggers operations in that object, control passes to the prior memory locations without reloading program code or reinitializing data.

Persistent values for an object's attributes correspond to saving data in that object. The prior state of that object is reactivated when you use it later. If the object is also concurrent, each concurrent instance of that object is saved in its own memory area. In that case, the object instance's

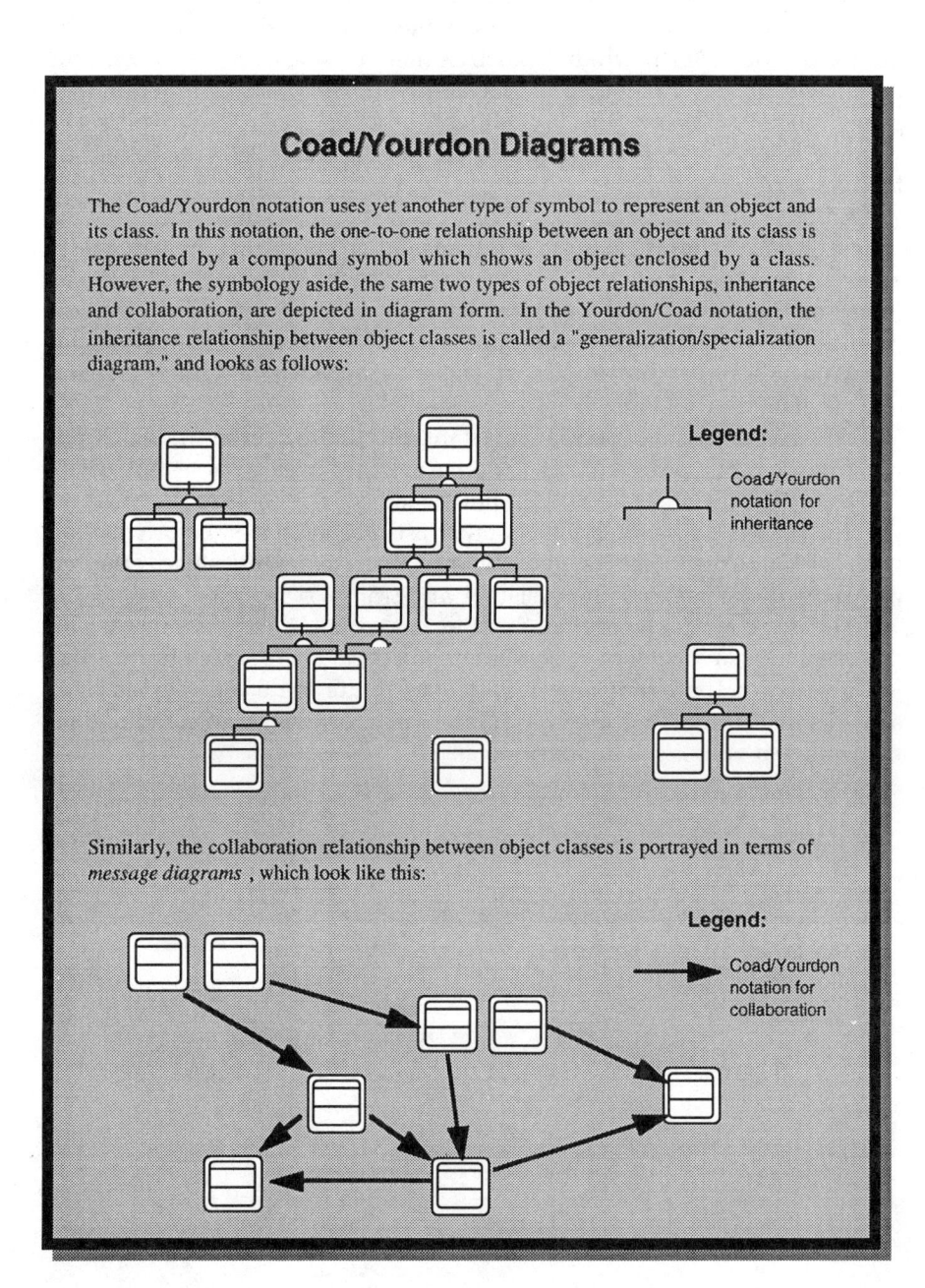

Coad/Yourdon Diagrams

The Coad/Yourdon notation uses yet another type of symbol to represent an object and its class. In this notation, the one-to-one relationship between an object and its class is represented by a compound symbol which shows an object enclosed by a class. However, the symbology aside, the same two types of object relationships, inheritance and collaboration, are depicted in diagram form. In the Yourdon/Coad notation, the inheritance relationship between object classes is called a "generalization/specialization diagram," and looks as follows:

Legend:
Coad/Yourdon notation for inheritance

Similarly, the collaboration relationship between object classes is portrayed in terms of *message diagrams*, which look like this:

Legend:
Coad/Yourdon notation for collaboration

handle must also be used to identify the desired copy of the object. However, whether it is concurrent or not, the operations of a persistent object can be retriggered at any time to operate on the last set of values for its attributes.

An object is said to be persistent if its state is saved between uses. A good example of persistent objects is the hiding and minimization of windows in a microcomputer GUI environment. A window that is put away but not closed is a good example of a persistent object. The attribute values of the window (such as height, width, and color) and the executable operation modules associated with them are retained in program memory. Other object modules and/or users can redisplay the window later without reinitializing its position and color or reloading the executable code.

An object is transient (nonpersistent) if it must be reinitialized each time it is used. A good example of a transient object is a window in a GUI environment that is closed by a user action or by some condition in the program. The values of the window's attributes are reset to their default conditions each time a new client accesses it. The executable modules for the window's operations are also reloaded each time a new client triggers one of them.

Whether or not an object is persistent affects the manner in which you must design your program code. A program that uses a persistent object must manage the allocation of computer memory during execution. A program that uses a transitory object must provide some means for tracking whether the server object is active when it is needed. Most object-oriented programs make use of both persistent and transitory objects.

The state of an object is defined as a particular set of values for all the attributes of an object. A persistent object saves its state after control is returned to the client object that uses it. Its state may be changed again later by any other client at a later time. It always reflects the last-known set of values for its attributes.

CONCEPT SUMMARY - Using Objects

CONCEPT 22. A concurrent object is an object of a concrete class which can have more than one instance at run time.

CONCEPT 23. A persistent object is an object of a concrete class whose instances retain the values of their attributes between uses.

CHAPTER REVIEW

The Definition of a Domain

What is a domain? A self-contained problem area, or more precisely, the system design solution that solves that problem, as represented by the inheritance and collaboration hierarchies in an object-oriented design.

What is class aggregation? A nested grouping of classes or class hierarchies in a domain, used to achieve an intermediate level of organization between the classes and the domain, and often expressed either as categories of abstract-class inheritance hierarchies or assemblies of concrete-class collaboration hierarchies.

How are hierarchies used? Inheritance and collaboration hierarchies are encoded as class relationships in an object-oriented programming language, within which the internal designs of the operations and attributes of the object associated with the class are encoded in a conventional manner.

How are operations triggered? Either as a common routine called within the inheritance structure or as a subordinate routine called within the collaboration structure.

How are attributes accessed? Either as a common data element within the inheritance structure or as a subordinate data element within the collaboration structure.

Part III
OBJECT-ORIENTED METHODOLOGY

The next six chapters of this book present the object-engineering approach and a corresponding set of detailed techniques for developing an object-oriented design. Object engineering is a three-layered approach in which you concentrate on the domain, the classes in the domain, and the objects associated with those classes.

Chapter 11 shows you how to use the object-engineering model to design large scale object-oriented systems. This is a definition of the layered approach for developing the object-oriented programs of a client/server system.

Chapter 12 discusses domain design as the top layer of the model. The result of domain design is called the domain model. A domain model describes the requirements of your system by identifying a preliminary set of object classes organized according to their inheritance and collaboration relationship to one another.

Chapter 13 discusses class design as the middle layer of the model. The result of class design is an interface model within a domain. An interface model allocates the requirements of your system to the objects from your inheritance and collaboration hierarchies.

Chapter 14 discusses object design as the bottom layer of the model. The result of object design is an implementation model for the objects associated with each class in the domain. The implementation model provides the source code for each operation and the data schema for each attribute.

Chapter 15 discusses the design of individual object operations as the process-oriented part of object design. This is the implementation of each public operation of an object as a small and well-contained process-driven design using structured design techniques.

Chapter 16 discusses the design of individual object attributes as the data-oriented part of object design. This is the implementation of each public attribute of an object as a small and well-contained data-driven design using information engineering techniques.

11

The Object-Engineering Model

11.1 THE MODEL COMPOSITION

An Object-Oriented Approach

Object engineering is an organized approach for developing large-scale software systems using object-oriented design techniques. It has many similarities to the conventional approaches associated with process-driven and data-driven design techniques. It has the same framework for transforming requirements into a working computer program. Object engineering, however, is a model-based approach rather than a procedure-based approach.

The object-engineering model organizes the design of a system in the same way as conventional software development approaches. The same type of transformation of requirements must take place in any approach—from a functional design to a physical design, to a program design. In object engineering, the functional design is called the *domain model*, the physical design is called the *interface model*, and the program design is called the *implementation model*.

As you can see in Figure 11-1, object engineering is a layered approach for designing large-scale object-oriented systems. You construct and/or modify each layer using of a set of techniques to design a particular aspect of your system.

The layered model accommodates a *recursive design*, that is, you can approach the model at any layer to derive design components at that layer and at the more detailed layers below it. You can also move up layers to provide and/or modify the higher-layer components as your design

CHAPTER 11: THE OBJECT-ENGINEERING MODEL **195**

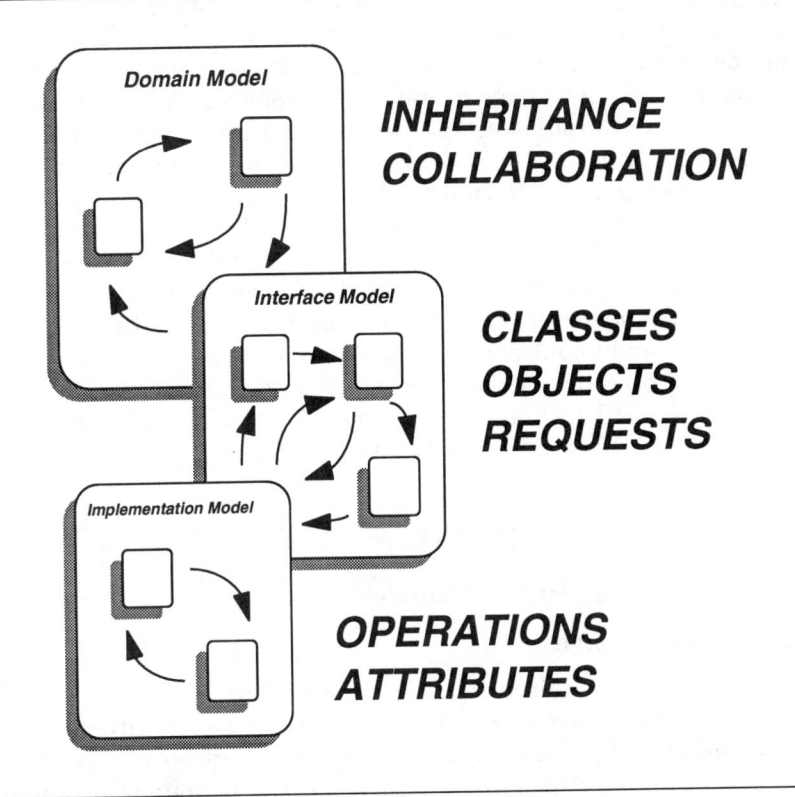

Figure 11-1. The object-engineering model.

evolves. This is an important point to remember, since it is likely that you will first encounter an object-oriented design at some point other than at the beginning of the design of a new domain.

Object engineering is a model-based approach which employs object-oriented techniques. This is different from conventional software engineering approaches. By model based, we mean that much more emphasis is placed on the model as the objective of the approach rather than on the steps to get there. Furthermore, the object-oriented techniques employed within the approach lead you to develop portions of the model in layers of increasing detail rather than in sequential phases.

An object-oriented design for a large-scale system can be represented by a sequence of layers that roughly correspond to the phases in a conventional approach. Each lower layer in the approach provides you with a more detailed view of the components from the layer above it. You apply different techniques to design different aspects of your system at each layer. You can use the techniques described in this book, or you can incorporate techniques described elsewhere.

You will find considerable agreement in the literature about the nature of an object-oriented approach to software design, even if everyone does not describe it exactly the same way. Coad and Yourdon, for example, discuss a model of five layers and four components. Their five layers address the same purposes as the three layers presented here as the object-engineering model. Their four components are just four specific categories of classes in a typical domain.

Classes are often divided into specific groups for better manageability. The divisions can be called a number of things depending on which author you read. Coad and Yourdon call the divisions of classes in a domain either *components* (for the specific class divisions that they list) or *subjects* (for the additional class divisions that users may list). Similarly, Booch calls the divisions of classes in a large domain either *class categories* (when applied to inheritance hierarchies) or *module assemblies* (when applied to collaboration hierarchies).

11.2 THE DOMAIN MODEL

11.2.1 What Is a Domain Model?

A Domain Perspective

The top layer of the object-engineering model is called the *domain model*. The domain model portrays the high-level interaction among classes of objects. Third-party vendors often sell libraries of classes tailored for specific uses in object-oriented design. If your organization makes use of such libraries, then you will never enter the object-oriented life cycle at this layer, since you will be using, rather than designing, these high-level classes.

The objective of object engineering at the top layer is to build a model of your domain, that is, to identify objects. If you have a large domain you will spend a significant amount of time constructing this model. If you have a small domain, or if you are working within an existing domain, then you may just sketch this model in your head. Either way, the domain model defines the nature of the object-oriented design that you will develop.

The domain model is the functional design of an object-oriented system. This is the highest layer of an object-oriented design for a large system. It is mostly associated with starting a new design and/or modifying an existing one. The domain model corresponds to the essential model in a process-driven design and to the information strategy plan in a data-driven design. The domain model consists of the inheritance diagram (a hierarchy of abstract classes) the collaboration diagram (a hierarchy of concrete classes) and the interface model (the detailed description of those classes).

The domain model defines the structure of your program. Each part of the domain model documents one aspect of your domain. The inheritance diagram documents the sharing of common operations and attributes. The collaboration diagram documents the operational interaction between the operations and attributes of different objects. The interface model then defines the interfaces for the operations and attributes of the objects in a collaboration diagram.

The Components of the Model

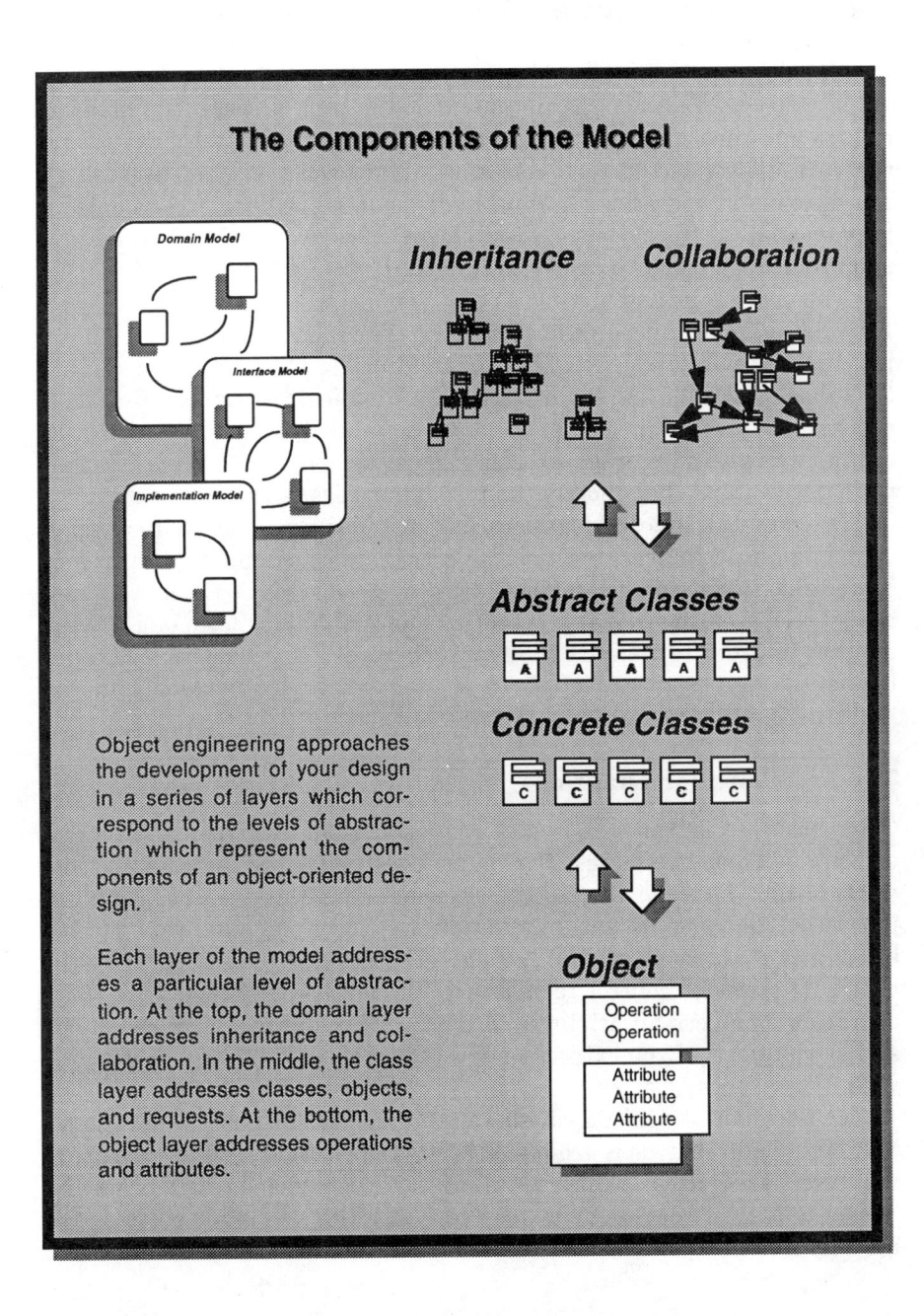

Object engineering approaches the development of your design in a series of layers which correspond to the levels of abstraction which represent the components of an object-oriented design.

Each layer of the model addresses a particular level of abstraction. At the top, the domain layer addresses inheritance and collaboration. In the middle, the class layer addresses classes, objects, and requests. At the bottom, the object layer addresses operations and attributes.

The Inheritance Diagram

Inheritance diagrams show the relationship among abstract classes of objects in terms of their common operations and attributes. Each abstract class in the domain model represents a set of operations and attributes which are shared by objects of more than one class. The shared operations and attributes of each abstract class can be used (or *inherited*) by any of the objects that belong to that class (that is, that share its characteristics).

You develop the initial inheritance diagram to show the relationships among the abstract classes in your domain, and between the abstract classes and the concrete classes. You gather objects together into groups that are all connected to a common set of operations and attributes. These common operations and attributes can be represented as objects, in particular, as the objects associated with new abstract classes. This results in a tree structure called an inheritance diagram.

The operations and attributes that you use to identify objects are not very definitive at this point in the design. The initial abstract classes are just the first-cut tree structure of the inheritance hierarchy. You will use the inheritance diagram to further refine your abstract classes, that is, to redistribute some of the common operations and attributes. You draw the common classes in a tree structure above the objects from which they were derived and then modify the tree for a more efficient structure.

Drawing the inheritance hierarchy provides you with further opportunity to refine your abstract class descriptions. You modify the tree by combining some classes, further dividing (classifying) them into new abstract classes, and moving operations and attributes from one class to another in order to simplify the tree structure. You restructure the tree by identifying new abstract classes similar to the way in which you originally derived them.

The Collaboration Diagram

Collaboration diagrams show the requests passed between the objects of different concrete classes. The requests establish the client and server relationships between the objects associate with those classes. The collaboration diagram is the foundation for specifying the well-defined interfaces of an object-oriented design. The requests will be used by the clients to transfer control to the servers. Each request will trigger an operation or access an attribute in a server at runtime. The operations and attributes that you extract as new server objects, are each associated with a new concrete class.

You develop the initial collaboration diagram to show the hierarchical relationship between groups of related operations and attributes at the lower levels in your inheritance hierarchy. Some objects will use requests to trigger operations or to access attributes in other objects. The need for a request between two classes is identified based on the manner in which the subordinate sets of operations and attributes were extracted to form concrete classes.

You use the collaboration diagram to define additional concrete classes, that is, to further redistribute some of the subordinate operations and attributes. The initial concrete classes become a tree structure in the diagram. The subordinate objects (servers) are drawn connected to and usually below the original objects (clients) from which they were derived. You then modify this tree for a more efficient structure.

Drawing the collaboration hierarchy provides you with further opportunity to refine your concrete class descriptions. You modify the tree by combining some classes, by further dividing (encapsulating) them into new concrete classes, and by moving operations and attributes from one class to another. The tree is reconstructed by encapsulating new concrete classes from existing ones, usually because they either act to either transform the same attribute or represent transactions associated with the same operation.

You may group several operations because they transform the same attribute. The new group can become a new encapsulated object (a new concrete class). In order to do this, you need to consider the relationships between the operations and the attributes within a class of objects. Often, this type of analysis occurs using the interface model, although it affects the domain model.

You may also group several attributes because they serve as alternative transactions to the same operation. This group can also become a new encapsulated object (a new concrete class). This type of analysis is also based on the interaction between operations and attributes within the classes of objects in the interface model.

11.2.2 How Do You Design a Domain?

Identify Objects in a Domain

The goal of the top layer of object-oriented design is to identify the object requirements of your domain. You might do this to develop the design for an entirely new domain, or you may simply use an existing domain to select and arrange objects in a new manner. Domain design is the definition of the functions required in your design. As shown in Figure 11-2, domain design results in the development of a domain model.

You identify object requirements by representing the structure of your classes in diagram form. As you diagram your class structure, you develop further insight into the nature of the operations and attributes that make up your objects, and you tend to derive more classes by dividing your original set of classes. The domain model represents the interaction among the modules in your system in terms of their inheritance relationships and their collaboration relationships.

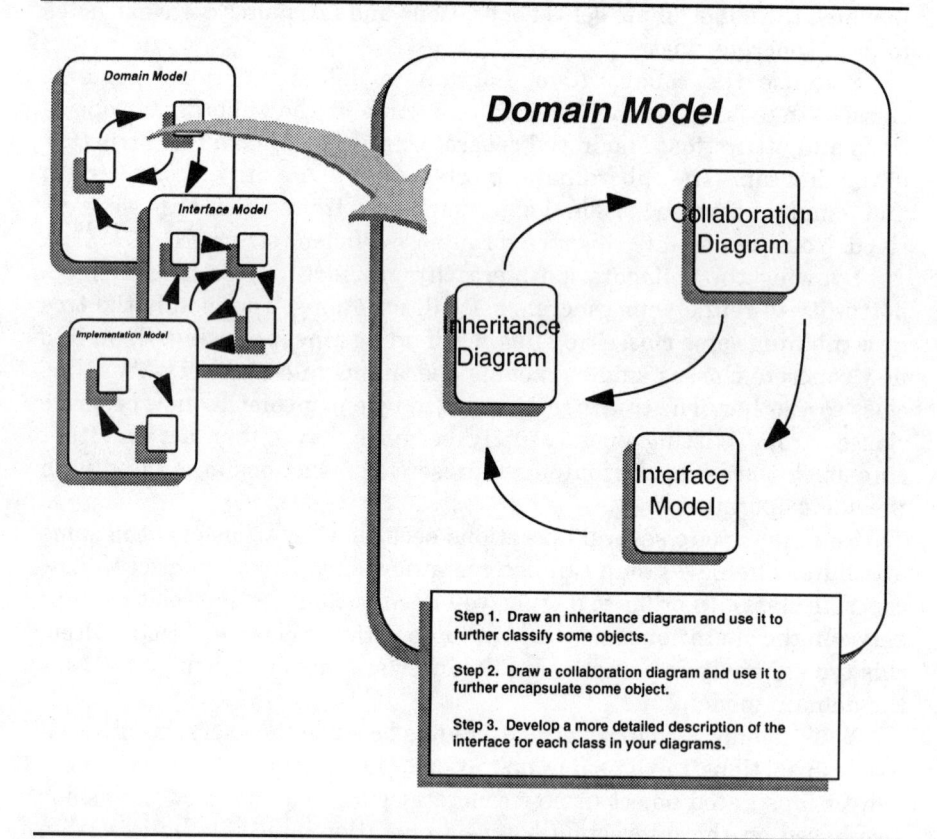

Figure 11-2. The steps in domain design.

The domain model represents the functional design of an object-oriented system. A typical technique to derive a domain model involves the steps listed on the bottom of Figure 11-2. Although you may use them many times durng the design process, these steps show one pass at the process of diagramming the inheritance and collaboration hierarchies. You can then use the diagrams to identify the need for additional abstract and concrete classes.

You may find other techniques in the literature that also address the development of a domain model and which are equally suitable to use within the object-engineering approach. The purpose of domain design is the same whether you use our specific design techniques or some other techniques. Domain design provides you with the perspective of your design which enables you to take advantage of context-sensitive referencing. This is called polymorphism, and it is the single most important feature of an object-oriented design. It is the domain model that makes polymorphism possible.

The Domain Provides Polymorphism

The domain model makes your design truly object oriented. You will use the inheritance characteristics in the description of each class in your design to construct an appropriate header statement for each class at the beginning of blocks of source code, much like a conventional subroutine. You will also use the collaboration characteristics to identify and then design the specific operations and attributes within each object.

References to the operations and attributes in the context of an inheritance hierarchy make use of a feature of object-oriented design called *polymorphism*. Polymorphism is the characteristic of an object-oriented design that enables a program to refer to a commonly named operation or attribute, knowing that the compiler will find and use the one most appropriate to the context in which it is needed.

The context for a polymorphic reference is the object in which the reference is made, or more specifically, it is the inheritance hierarchy in which that object is classified. The operation or attribute appropriate to that context is the one nearest to the object in the hierarchy. In this way, you can design many operations and/or attributes with the same name, but designed individually for slightly different purposes. Therefore, different operation or attribute designs will be selected based on the context in which they are used at runtime.

11.2.3 How Do You Use the Domain?

Inheritance Polymorphism

Polymorphism is a concept of an object-oriented program that can appear in many forms, depending on the capabilities of the programming language and its compiler. For the most part, you can think of polymorphism as the substitution of a particular member in a particular context. Members can be either the operations or the attributes of an object. The context is the position of the object in the inheritance hierarchy.

Polymorphism is most often described in terms of the selective use of an inheritance hierarchy to establish context-sensitive referencing in your program. This provides the flexibility that is characteristic of an object-oriented program. Inheritance polymorphism can come in two forms, *inclusion polymorphism* or *ad hoc polymorphism*, depending on the nature of your compiler and programming language.

The most typical form of inheritance polymorphism is inclusion polymorphism. Inclusion polymorphism is also called *overloading*, and is the substitution of an appropriate operation or attribute at its reference using the inheritance hierarchy of your design. This is the single most useful purpose of an inheritance hierarchy. It is the fundamental reason to develop an inheritance hierarchy as part of your design.

Another form of inheritance polymorphism in an object-oriented program is ad hoc polymorphism. Ad hoc polymorphism is the substitution of a particular operation or attribute based on the some other criteria in addition to its position in the inheritance hierarchy. The additional criteria are usually the state of the object or the type of the operation or attribute.

Both inclusion polymorphism and ad hoc polymorphism make use of the inheritance hierarchy to determine the context of a reference to a foreign operation or attribute. Inclusion polymorphism (i.e., overloading) makes use of the normal class hierarchy. Ad hoc polymorphism, however, often requires a special metaclass hierarchy (for example, for the class type).

Collaboration Polymorphism

Collaboration polymorphism is similar to inheritance polymorphism, except that it makes use of the collaboration hierarchy rather than the inheritance hierarchy to establish the context for a reference to an operation or to an attribute. However, it is still the substitution of one member for another one with the same name.

Collaboration polymorphism is less common than inheritance polymorphism, but provides the same type of flexibility. When it is supported in a language or programming environment, collaboration polymorphism is also called *parametric polymorphism*. It usually makes use of a request protocol to resolve name conflicts.

Parametric polymorphism is the substitution of one member from among many identically named members in the same object. Each alternative member of the same name is a variation to be used as in a case structure in conventional languages. Usually, the protocol of the request determines which member is used. Your programming language and compiler must support multiple protocols for the same request if you are to use parametric polymorphism.

11.3 THE INTERFACE MODEL

11.3.1 What Is an Interface Model?

A Class Perspective

The middle layer of the object-engineering model is called the *interface model*. This is the layer at which you will most often work with object-oriented designs, both in using them and in tailoring them to your particular purposes. It represents a view of your design from the perspective of the classes that you are using as your building blocks. The interface model portrays the full set of externally accessible parameters by which one object sees another. This provides the well-defined interface for all the objects in your domain which makes them reusable.

The objective of object engineering at the middle layer is to build a model of your classes called the interface model, that is, to allocate the requirements of your system to the objects in your domain. This is a model of your design at the class layer. Most discussions about object-oriented programming focus on this aspect of the model.

The interface model is the physical design of an object-oriented system. This is the middle layer of an object-oriented design for a large system. It contains the activities and models most associated with the standardized documentation of an object-oriented design. The interface model corresponds to the environmental model in a process-driven design and to the business area analysis in a data-driven design. It consists of the class descriptions (defining object relationships) the object descriptions (defining each object's purpose) the request descriptions (the input/output parameters for using objects) and the implementation model (the detailed description of the objects).

The interface model defines the characteristics of the objects in your domain. Each part of the interface model documents one portion of a general description of your design. The class descriptions document the relationships among objects. Abstract classes document inheritance relationships. Concrete classes document collaboration relationships. The object descriptions then document the lists of operations and attributes which constitute each object. Finally, the request descriptions document the use of these objects in a black-box manner, and the implementation model provides the corresponding internal designs for each one.

The Class Descriptions

A class catalogs the relationship among the objects in your domain, that is, the inheritance and collaboration hierarchies. Eventually, the source-code statements for an object are programmed as part of a class in your program. The statements describe the operation of each operation and the structure of each attribute in an object. Classes are most often associated with the inheritance hierarchy, however, classes also document the collaborations between objects.

Class descriptions are a means of documenting the hierarchical relationships among objects (both the inheritance hierarchy and the collaboration hierarchy). A class description is usually a single page of text which describes its object's purpose and capabilities. Classes can be either abstract (representing inheritance classes) or concrete (representing collaboration classes).

Class descriptions document the inheritance diagrams and the collaboration diagrams of your domain. They are a textual record of the visual information in the diagrams. The diagrams and the descriptions each serve a different purpose. The diagrams facilitate the manner in which you develop the design and class descriptions facilitate the manner in which you program the design.

The Object Descriptions

You define one object for each class in your domain by assigning it a descriptive name and by listing the specific operations and attributes it contains. The names of your objects should characterize their overall purpose. The operations and attributes that they contain should substantiate that purpose. The objects should have names which reflect the people, places, things, and documents that they represent.

You will eventually represent each of your objects as a class. Classes are just abstract representations of objects. There are two types of class descriptions: one for concrete classes and one for abstract classes. Each object description will eventually become a concrete class. Analysis of the operations and attributes within an object will eventually lead to the identification of abstract classes of objects.

Some objects are associated with concrete classes. Concrete classes represent the operations and attributes of the physical objects in your domain. Concrete classes always represent one or more object instances and can also be composed of further subclasses themselves. Concrete classes are used to derive other concrete classes (by encapsulation) and to derive abstract classes (by classification). Most concrete classes will belong to one or more abstract classes.

Other objects are associated with the abstract classes in your domain. Abstract classes represent the additional higher-level operations and attributes which can be inherited by the objects of its subclasses. Abstract classes never represent object instances and are always composed of subclasses. Subclasses of abstract classes may, themselves, be either abstract classes or concrete classes.

The Request Descriptions

Requests are used to represent the collaborations between the physical objects in your domain. They are used by a client object to trigger operations and to access attributes in other (server) objects. Requests are the detailed definitions of the connections shown in a collaboration diagram. They correspond to data couples on a structure chart (hierarchical collaborations) and to off-page data flows on data-flow diagrams (lateral collaborations).

Hierarchical collaborations are used primarily to trigger subordinate operations in encapsulated servers. They are characterized by stimulus-based requests, where there is often no response expected. In a process-driven design, a hierarchical collaboration is a data couple connection, with the stimulus being the down-flowing data couple. It represents the calling parameters of a child module.

Lateral collaborations are used primarily to access sibling attributes in encapsulated servers. They are characterized by response-based requests, where there are often no stimulus parameters. In a process-driven design, a lateral collaboration is an off-page data flow. The response represents incoming data from a module in another group.

Request descriptions define the calling parameters of requests and associate them with a particular operation or attribute. Each request is an event which passes control to an encapsulated object. Triggering a particular operation in a server is one type of event; accessing a particular attribute is another. A collaboration between objects will have a separate request for each operation or attribute in a server that is used by other client objects.

Each request is associated with either an operation or an attribute. However, all operations and attributes are not associated with requests. Only public operations and attributes require explicit requests. Private operations and attributes are treated as local processes and data for the exclusive use of the other operations and attributes within the same object. In contrast, the public ones can be accessed by requests from other objects in collaboration relationships.

11.3.2 How Do You Design Classes?

Allocate Object Requirements

The goal of the middle layer of object-oriented design is to allocate the specific requirements of your system to the objects in your domain. This is known as *class design*. Class design is the physical design of systems and programs to satisfy the functional requirements of your domain. It results in the development of an interface model, as shown in Figure 11-3. In software engineering terms, this is known as a *general design*.

The class layer of an object-oriented design is usually the point at which most people enter the object-oriented life cycle. Requirements are allocated by listing the operations and attributes of the objects in your domain as part of your interface model. The interface model represents the general requirements of your system in terms of the operations and attributes of its objects and how those objects are grouped as classes.

The development of the interface model involves repetition of a two-step process: expanding objects by listing more operations and attributes, and then contracting the size of each object by grouping the operations and attributes into subsets which become new objects. The subsets can either represent the common characteristics of several objects, or the subordinate characteristics within a single object. Common subsets are derived by classification. Subordinate subsets are derived by encapsulation.

A typical technique for designing classes involves the steps listed on the bottom of Figure 11-3. You may find other techniques in the literature that also address the development of a interface model. The purpose of this book is to provide you with a comprehensive approach for object-oriented design, that also includes a workable set of techniques to employ. Other techniques, however, may apply equally well. Class design provides you with a perspective of your design that enables you to use portions of it more than once. The interface model makes your design extensible.

206 OBJECT ENGINEERING

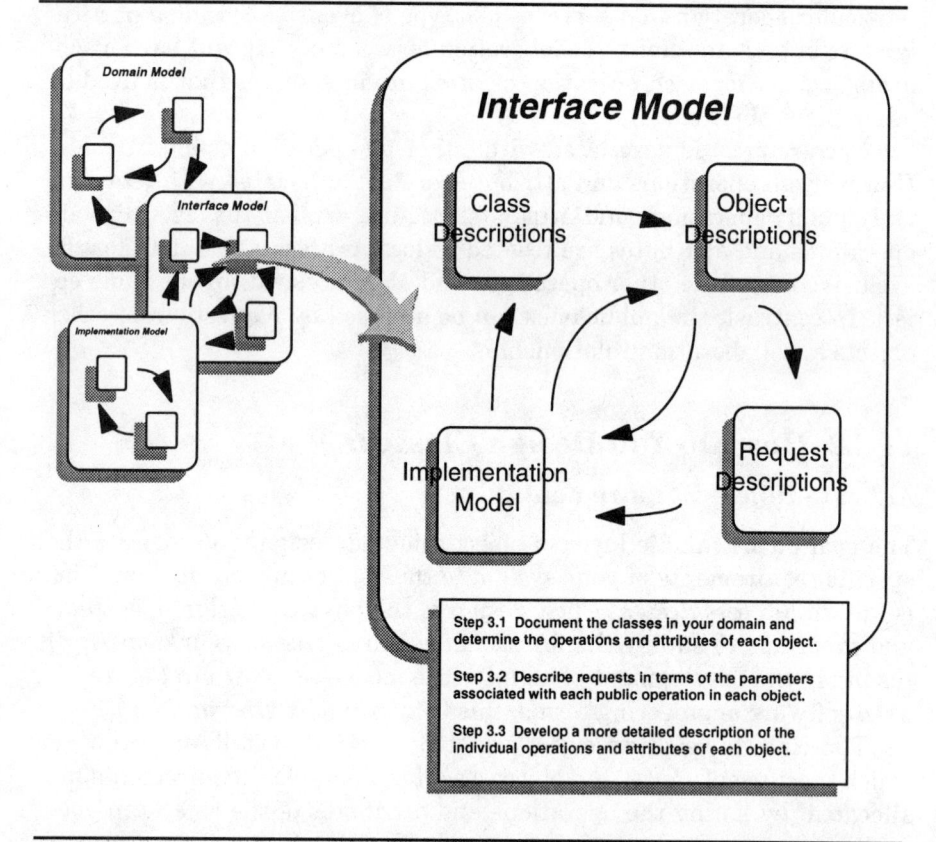

Figure 11-3. The steps in class design.

The Classes Provide Extensibility

The interface model enables you to reuse the classes in your domain more easily. This is the layer of the object-engineering model that best characterizes the benefits of object-oriented design. In the design of small-scale object-oriented systems, this is trivial. In the design of large systems, however, you will need to properly document the interfaces and the class relationships of your objects so that you can reuse them in many applications.

The classes that are cataloged as part of your overall domain can be reused in new applications within your domain. Each new application is just a new collaboration diagram, which may consist of either new or existing concrete classes of objects. These concrete classes may also inherit existing operations and attributes from the abstract classes cataloged in your inheritance diagram. The existing abstract classes become, in effect, extensions to the programming language for programmers who use them in this way.

An existing cataloged inheritance hierarchy is often called a *class library*. The use of class libraries in conjunction with a language compiler provides a feature of object-oriented design called *extensibility*. Extensibility is the characteristic of an object-oriented design that enables the common aspects of many classes to be reused in many application system designs as if they were a part of the original programming language.

An object-oriented programming language is extended through the use of inheritance libraries. The libraries use the abstract class structure of an object-oriented design to organize common utility modules and common data types. The classes in the library extend the language. These libraries may be the result of your own prior designs or may be aquired from third parties for general use by everyone in your organization.

11.3.3 How Do You Use the Classes?

Static Source Libraries

The most typical form of extensibility in an object-oriented programming environment is through the use of *source libraries*. Source libraries are files of related abstract classes that are distributed to extend the nominal capabilities of a programming language. As abstract classes, they provide operations and attributes that can be inherited by concrete classes of your design, which is how they extend the capabilities of the language.

Source libraries contain definitions of abstract classes for you to use from within and as a part of your object-oriented programs. Because they contain abstract classes, source libraries provide you with a predesigned inheritance hierarchy. The abstract classes in the source library extend the programming language by providing you with a set of standardized classes that you will use as classification names in many programs.

Source libraries contain source-code statements that define abstract classes, that is, that contain common operations and common attributes that you can reference in your own source statements. You generally purchase the source libraries from the vendors of the compilers or from third parties in those markets. You use the operations and attributes in these libraries as if they were a part of the programming language, and thus, they extend the language.

Source libraries may be associated with a particular vendor's compiler, a particular programming language, or a particular type of application function. Which libraries you select determines the nature of the extensions to the language that you are using. Each source library usually addresses one aspect of a programming language by providing abstract classes for such things as graphical-user interfaces, standard data types, database access, mathematical functions, and peripheral hardware access.

Dynamic Link Libraries

Another form of extensibility in an object-oriented programming environment is the use of *dynamic link libraries* (DLLs). Like source libraries, link libraries are files of operations and attributes packaged as classes which extend the nominal capabilities of a programming language. Link libraries are different from source libraries in that they contain concrete classes and they are pre-compiled and distributed as executable modules which can be called from within your application source code.

Link libraries are used to extend the capabilities of many languages, both conventional and object oriented. A DLL for an object oriented language contains functions and data organized as classes, in particular, organized as concrete classes. As concrete classes, they provide operations and attributes that can be used as servers in collaborations with other concrete classes of your design, which is how they extend the capabilities of language.

Link libraries contain definitions of concrete classes for you to use from within and as a part of your object-oriented programs. Because they contain concrete classes, link libraries provide you with a predesigned collaboration hierarchy. The concrete classes in the link library extend the programming language by providing you with a set of standardized classes which you will use as encapsulated objects in many programs.

Link libraries are used for a variety of purposes. Often, the original language vendor distributes their compiler with DLLs that contain the fundamental functions of the language. New DLLs can then be distributed to provide a new version of the language, or to make it capable of understanding additional kinds of statements. Third-party vendors often market dynamic link libraries to customize a language compiler for a particular platform or to provide specific application program interfaces (APIs) between otherwise nonintegrated products.

11.4 THE IMPLEMENTATION MODEL

11.4.1 What Is an Implementation Model?

An Object Perspective

The bottom layer of the object-engineering model is called the *implementation model*. It represents a view of your design from the perspective of the objects that form the basis for every class in your domain. This is the layer at which you will work when you tailor an existing domain for the needs of a particular program by adding more objects (as subclasses) to the existing classes in your domain. This provides the separately maintained internal designs for the operations and attributes used by your system(s).

The objective of object engineering at the bottom layer is to build a model of the internal design of your objects called the implementation model, that is, to implement your requirements within the structure that you've established at the prior layers. This is a model of your design at the object layer and the layer at which you transform your conceptual design to a design for a computer program that can be coded.

The implementation model is the program design in an object-oriented model. This is the lowest layer in an object-oriented design, and as such, the part of your design that will be implemented as your computer programs. The implementation model of an object-oriented design corresponds to the implementation model in a process-driven design and to the business system design in a data-driven design. The implementation model consists of the operation descriptions, the internal process designs for each object; and the attribute descriptions, the internal data designs for each object.

The implementation model defines the individual structure of every component in your program. Each part of the implementation model documents one portion of a detailed design to be programmed. The operation descriptions document the individual process requirements of each object. The attribute descriptions document the individual data requirements of each object. Together, they form the basis for the complete internal design of an object as a self-sufficient and reusable software module.

The Operation Descriptions

Eventually, you must define the operational procedure of each object in your inheritance and collaboration hierarchies. You implement the collaborations in a collaboration hierarchy by making function calls to external operations, and/or by making data references to external attributes, from within the program statements associated with an object. These operations, however, must be designed by someone.

Operation descriptions are the designs for the operations of an object. They may consist of source code and/or some type of diagram or diagrams. The diagrams show the operational interactions and/or timing relationships between the operations and attributes within each object. In this sense, they are no different from the detailed structure charts of a conventional process-driven design.

Operation diagrams address the structure of an object in terms of its operations and their relationships to its attributes. The types of diagrams that you use depend on the nature of your domain. You may choose to use conventional process-driven diagrams to design the operational processes within your objects, or treat certain public operations as encapsulated objects, themselves.

A well-designed object will result in only a handful of operations and attributes. Many operations and attributes will be classified into separate abstract classes. Other operations and attributes will be encapsulated into separate concrete classes. The remaining operations and attributes within an object, however, still require a conventional type of source-code design for implementation.

The source-code design for the operations in each object is no different from any other conventional program design, except that it has a well-defined interface (the request protocol) and is maintained separately from the other objects. The operation design itself, however, often makes use of conventional diagrams such as state transition diagrams or data-flow diagrams.

The Attribute Descriptions

Often, you will need to define the data structure of some objects in your inheritance and collaboration hierarchies. You implement the relationships of an inheritance hierarchy by making implied function calls to either internal or inherited operations, and/or by making implied data references to either internal or inherited attributes when those attributes are persistent (that is, when they are stored in a database), their schema must be designed at some point.

Attribute descriptions are the database design of an object. They may consist of simple descriptive statements about each attribute and/or some type of diagram or diagrams. The diagrams show the structural interactions and/or state relationships between the operations and attributes within each object. In this sense, they are no different from the normalized data structures of a conventional data-driven design.

Attribute diagrams address the structure of an object in terms of its attributes and their relationships to its operations. The types of diagrams you choose depend on the nature of your domain. You may choose to use conventional data-driven diagrams to design the data structure within your objects or treat certain public attributes as encapsulated objects, themselves.

As in the case of the operation descriptions, a well-designed object will result in only a handful of operations and attributes. These attributes, however, still may require a conventional type of data structure design for implementation. For example, you may find that the best way to represent the attributes within an object is through the use of entity relationship diagrams and normalized data structure diagrams.

11.4.2 How Do You Design Objects?

Implement Individual Objects

The goal of the bottom layer of object-oriented design is to implement the requirements of your interface model as the design of a computer program. The building blocks for that program are the objects from your design. The design of your objects is a physical statement of the program modules needed to satisfy the requirements in your domain. Object design results in the implementation model, as shown in Figure 11-4. In general software engineering terms, this is known as a *detailed design*.

You implement the design of each object class by completing the detailed design for each operation and each attribute in your interface model. You design the internal mechanisms of your program modules at this layer of object engineering. The program modules are the objects in your design. The internal mechanisms are the operations and attributes that each object contains. The object layer of an object-oriented design is the most tangible part of the object-engineering model.

The implementation model is the literal expression of the program statements for the operations and attributes of each object in your domain. This will most often include designing the detailed operational transitions of attributes from one state to another, the detailed design of the individual operations, and the detailed designs of the individual attributes. You eventually write the source code for each object in your domain from the implementation model.

A typical technique to derive the implementation model involves the steps listed at the bottom of Figure 11-4. In many ways, object design is no different from program design in a conventional methodol-

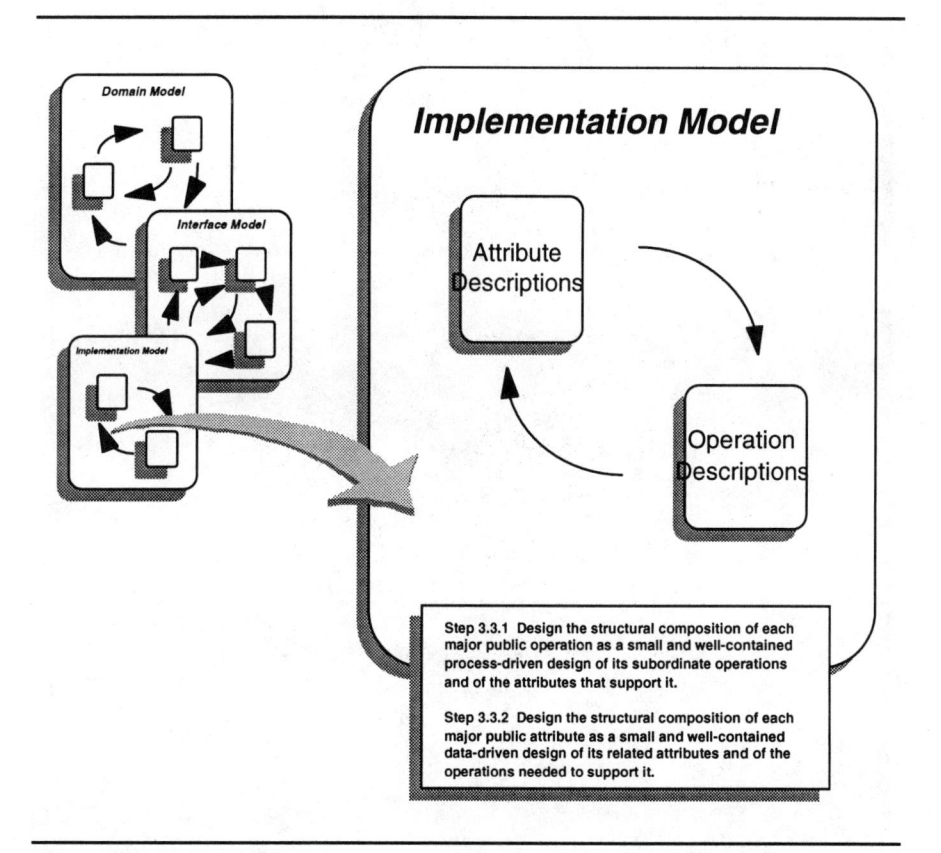

Figure 11-4. The steps in object design.

212 OBJECT ENGINEERING

ogy. Each object is a self-contained module. In the design of each object, apply the techniques most appropriate to its nature. This may involve using conventional design techniques as well as reapplying object-oriented design techniques.

As with the techniques for domain design and class design, you may find other techniques in the literature that also address the development of the implementation model. In fact, this is the most written-about area

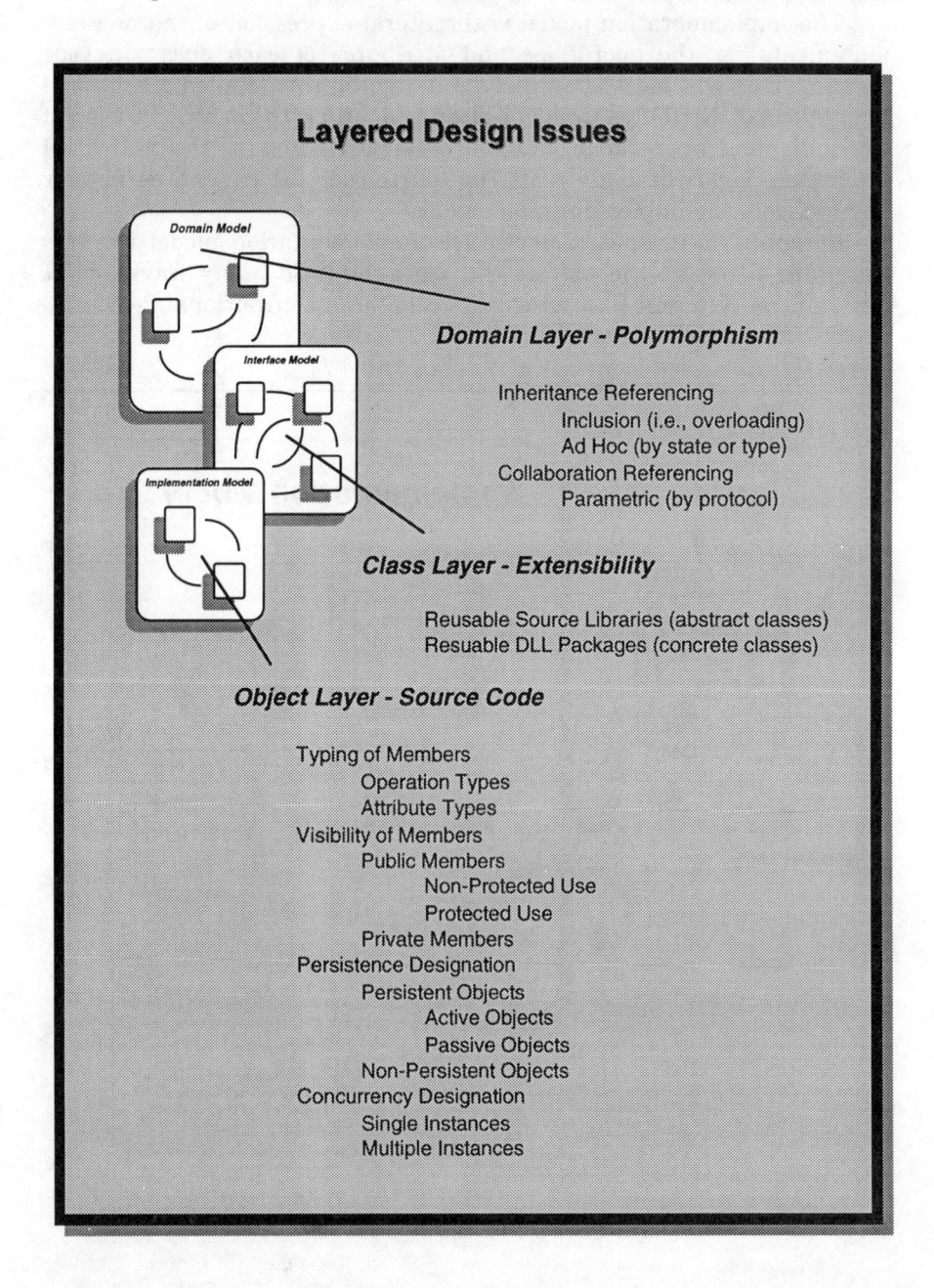

Layered Design Issues

Domain Model
Interface Model
Implementation Model

Domain Layer - Polymorphism

    Inheritance Referencing
        Inclusion (i.e., overloading)
        Ad Hoc (by state or type)
    Collaboration Referencing
        Parametric (by protocol)

Class Layer - Extensibility

    Reusable Source Libraries (abstract classes)
    Resuable DLL Packages (concrete classes)

Object Layer - Source Code

    Typing of Members
        Operation Types
        Attribute Types
    Visibility of Members
        Public Members
            Non-Protected Use
            Protected Use
        Private Members
    Persistence Designation
        Persistent Objects
            Active Objects
            Passive Objects
        Non-Persistent Objects
    Concurrency Designation
        Single Instances
        Multiple Instances

of publication in the field of object-oriented design. The purpose of object design is the same regardless of which particular detailed techniques you use for individual operation and attribute design.

Object design provides you with the design of program modules in much the same manner as does any conventional program design. The implementation model defines the source-code statements for your object-oriented program. However, it is the class layer and domain layer that are overlayed on the object layer that make your program object oriented.

The Objects Provide Source Code

The next layer below the implementation model is programming. While this topic is beyond the scope of this book, it still warrants some mention. After all, the purpose of object engineering is to develop an object-oriented design, and the purpose of developing an object-oriented design is to implement it as an object-oriented program. You can interpret the elements of your object-oriented design as the corresponding elements of an object-oriented program.

The bulk of the source code for your object-oriented program comes from the implementation model developed as the result of the object-design layer. This is the lowest layer of an object-engineering approach, and the one which is most similar to conventional design. The operation and attribute descriptions become source code preceded by header declarations which identify the various classes to which they belong.

In object-oriented programming, you transcribe each operation description and each attribute description into a block of source code preceded by an appropriate operation or attribute header declaration. These blocks of source code are usually grouped together and preceded by an appropriate class declaration. The operation and attribute descriptions, therefore, are the detailed designs for each object, which then become your program source code.

The characteristics of each object in your design determine how to transcribe the operation and attribute descriptions into source code. The syntax for a particular programming language (that is, the statements available in the programming language that you will use) determines exactly how you write the source code for your program. Your implementation model describes your program units (your objects) in object-oriented terms (their operations and attributes). An object's type, visibility, persistence, and concurrency determine how their operations and attributes are also transformed into source code.

11.4.3 How Do You Use the Objects?
An Object's Range is Determined by Its Type

The *range* of permissible values that a data element can take and the set of language statements in which it can be used is determined in conventional programming languages by its type. A type in a conventional programming language is a language-specific modifier for a data element. A type in an object-oriented language is used in the same way. It determines the range of usage for an object, an operation, or an attribute.

The range of an object is the permissible set of values its attributes can take, and is determined by its type. Object typing is most often applied only to attributes, although operations and even the objects themselves can have a type designation. The type of an object, the type of an attribute, and the type of an operation, are all similar to the type of a variable in conventional languages.

Object-oriented languages, like conventional languages, usually have some mechanism to declare the type of an attribute (and sometimes the type of an operation as well). Typing in object-oriented languages, however, is usually more flexible than in conventional languages. Often, you can use a class structure to define an inheritance hierarchy of type characteristics for use in your application program.

An Object's Scope Is Called Its Visibility

The *scope* of a data element describes where (in which different program units) it can be used in relation to its definition (its declaration) in that program using a conventional programming language. The scope of an object, of an operation, and of an attribute means the same thing in an object-oriented programming language. It defines which other program units (this object, its subclass objects, etc.) can make use of an object, an operation, or an attribute.

The scope of an object is determined by the visibility of its operations and attributes. Visibility is just the object-oriented way to declare an object's scope, that is, the places in which its operations and attributes can be referenced. This is determined by visibility in conjunction with inheritance.Visibility can be either public or private, which in turn dictates which operations and attributes of one object can be used as part of another by way of either an inheritance or a collaboration relationship.

Object scope is very similar to variable scope in conventional programming environments. In conventional languages, the scope of a variable is determined by the rules of language syntax regarding when and how they are declared. In object-oriented languages, these rules involve both visibility and inheritance, and the particular rules will vary from language to language and from vendor to vendor.

An Object's Extent Is Called Its Persistence

The *extent* of a data element in a conventional language is the time period (or more likely, the conditions within which) it will retain a value while other processes are performed. Extent is usually defined by terms such as *static* (retained between calls) or *dynamic* (reinitialized between calls) while declaring the data element as a variable name. The extent of an object, an operation, and an attribute in an object-oriented language is handled in much the same way.

The extent of an object is determined by the *persistence*, or *life span*, of its operations and attributes. Persistence is just the object-oriented way to define an object's memory status. The life span of an attribute is the same as that of a data parameter in a conventional language. As with visibility rules, the manner in which you declare objects persistent or not will vary from language to language and from vendor to vendor.

Persistence is very similar to the extent of variables in conventional programming languages. An object's attributes can retain their values (their state) between collaborations in a single program session. In conventional languages, this is known as the extent of a variable. In object-oriented languages, this is known as persistence. An object's attributes may retain their values between program sessions as stored data just like any other computer program.

Object Instances Depend on Concurrency

The *concurrency* of an object is a concept that has no regularly used analogy in conventional programming languages. In most conventionally designed and programmed systems, the processes and data are assigned once for any one particular run of the program. In object-oriented programming languages, however, you can designate muliple copies (instances) of a program unit (an object) to be used together and in conjuction with one another. This concept is called *concurrency*.

In most object-oriented languages, an array of parallel object states can be maintained and used as the concurrent instances of a single object. Instances are distinguished from one another by unique names (handles) in addition to their object name. Concurrency is the characteristic of an object-oriented design which enables you to replicate objects as arrays of identical operations and attributes but with their own identity. They can be manipulated like one another, but they will each have a different state.

CHAPTER REVIEW

The Object Engineering Model

What is object engineering? A layered approach for the organized design of a large-scale object-oriented system.

How do you design a domain? By identifying the inheritance and collaboration relationships between physical objects as the top layer of your design, called the *domain model* .

How do you use the domain? Inheritance and collaboration define the contexts (called *polymorphism*) used to resolve references to named operations and attributes at runtime.

How do you design classes? By allocating specific operations and attributes to the objects in your domain as part of the middle layer of your design, called the *interface model* .

How do you use the classes? Classes of objects from prior designs can often be used in new designs, and thus, those class names become extensions to the programming language.

How do you design objects? By implementing the design of each object operation and each object attribute as part of the bottom layer of your design called the *implementation model* .

How do you use the objects? To write source code for your object operations and data schemas of your object attributes.

12

Design at the Domain Layer

12.1 IDENTIFYING OBJECTS IN A DOMAIN

12.1.1 What Does a Design Represent?

The Domain Model

The top layer of object engineering is concerned with the design of the domain model. This is the part of object engineering that makes it object-oriented. The steps which we suggest for designing a domain model outline the activities that you are likely to perform, although the detail will certainly vary from project to project. The model that you develop to represent the domain layer will also vary in its form from project to project, but the basic components will be the same.

The products of the top layer of object engineering are shown in Figure 12-1. The model developed is called the *domain model*. The domain model consists of the inheritance hierarchy, the collaboration hierarchy, and the interface model. We will address the detailed development of the interface model in the next layer of design. However, it is important to consider it part of the overall domain model. You will eventually develop your interface model as a direct result of the inheritance and collaboration hierarchies of your domain model.

The classes in a domain are organized sets of objects which define how common operations and attributes are inherited among objects and how objects communicate with one another. You develop a domain model by drawing two diagrams that show two respective kinds of hierarchical relationships among classes. You draw an inheritance diagram to show

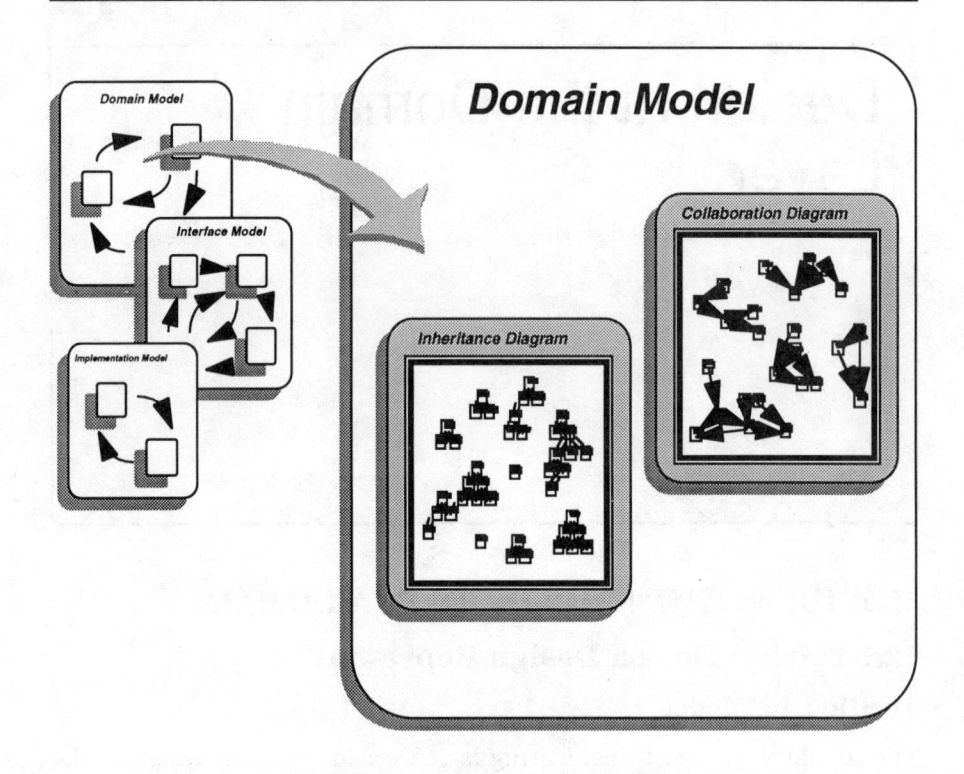

Figure 12-1. Working at the domain layer.

the hierarchical relationships among the abstract classes in your domain. Similarly, you draw a collaboration diagram to show the same thing among the concrete classes.

The inheritance diagram shows the priority of inheritance for the common operations and the common attributes in your design. It will be used by the compiler to resolve references when there is more than one operation (or attribute) with the same name in your domain. It is common for many objects to use the same names to identify similar but slightly different processes (or data). The inheritance diagram is an object-oriented catalog of the common operations and the common attributes in your domain.

The collaboration diagram shows the operational interaction between the objects in your design. It will be used by the compiler to set up the runtime pointers between memory locations which correspond to subordinate module calls. This is no different than the corresponding process structures and/or data structures of a conventional design. The collaboration diagram is just the object-oriented equivalent of a structure chart.

12.1.2 How Do You Start Your Design?

Designing a New Domain

Object engineering in its pure form is an organized analysis of a self-contained business area that will be automated by the system that you are designing. Object engineering leads you to the design of a new object-oriented system by analyzing the requirements of its domain. You analyze a domain by identifying and comparing the attributes, operations, and objects in the domain. You identify lists of attributes, operations, and objects and then reorganize them, look for more, and reorganize them again.

Objects are most easily characterized by the attributes they possess. Therefore, an easy way to start to identify the objects in your domain is to identify groups of attributes. You should look for adjectives to identify the attributes of objects in your domain. You find these by examining the real-world objects that you are modeling, by examining existing systems, and by examining written descriptions of the requirements of your domain.

Objects are also characterized by the operations they possess. Therefore, you can also identify the objects in your domain by identifying operations. You should look for verbs to identify the operations of the objects in your domain. You will find the operations in the same sources of information in which you find the attributes. Furthermore, the related groups of verbs and adjectives will point you toward related groups of operations and attributes. Related groups of operations and attributes are objects.

You can also identify the initial set of objects in your domain by looking for nouns in the same sources of information used to identify operations and attributes. This initial set of objects will only contain public operations and attributes. As you later expand and reorganize the objects in your design, you will start to identify their private operations and attributes. Private operations and attributes are those which support the public ones.

The objects that you identify from the descriptions of the requirements of your domain will be the persons, places, and things that you model in your design. In particular, you should be concerned with physical things, with the roles played by those things, with the events that happen to those things, and with the places in which those things reside.

As you start to identify objects, it is important to name them. Wirfs-Brock, Wilkerson, and Wiener provide a good discussion of the mechanism for identifying initial objects. Naming objects helps you to eliminate unnecessary and redundant objects. Not all nouns in a description of a domain will become objects in your design. Look for the nouns that are the subjects of the sentences. Change sentences from the passive voice (the cost is stored) to the active voice (the invoice stores the cost) to identify hidden objects (an invoice).

You will not need all the objects that you first identify in your system design. Some objects mentioned in a description of your domain may reside outside that domain. They are only mentioned to help to explain the requirements of the objects in your domain. Ross provides a good list of the criteria that you should apply to determine the valid objects from among all those which you may first identify. Put most simply, a valid object must have a reason to exist in the domain. It should:

1. Have operations and/or attributes that characterize it.
2. Be capable of retaining values for its attributes.
3. Accomplish some identifiable requirement in the domain.
4. Have a discernable structure and form.
5. Be identifiable in the real-world by a name.

Modifying an Existing Domain

One of the major benefits of an object-oriented design is that it can be reused in whole or in part as a component of a new system designed at a later time. You can reuse portions of one design in another because of the well-defined interface of the objects. Therefore, parts of the inheritance hierarchy derived for one system can often be reused by many systems in a domain. The process of reusing parts of the inheritance hierarchy of an existing domain model is called *commonalty analysis*.

Commonalty analysis of a domain can take many forms. It can be an informal process of streamlining an initial set of objects, or it can be a very formal and organized process above and beyond the object-oriented design of your system. For the purpose of this book, we will keep our discussion of commonalty analysis limited to streamlining the diagrams that comprise the domain model rather than introducing any particular analysis techniques.

An in-depth analysis of preexisting objects would take place solely at the domain layer. For example, the application of commonalty analysis to large-scale system design is usually described in terms of multiple refinements of the domain model—first by considering similar systems in the same domain, then by considering different systems in the same domain, and finally by considering systems in different domains.

Regardless of whether or not you perform commonalty analysis and regardless of the specific techniques that you use to identify objects and their classes, the objective of domain design is always the same. The objective is to derive a model that satisfies the requirements of your domain. This then drives the design of the systems in that domain at the lower layers of object engineering.

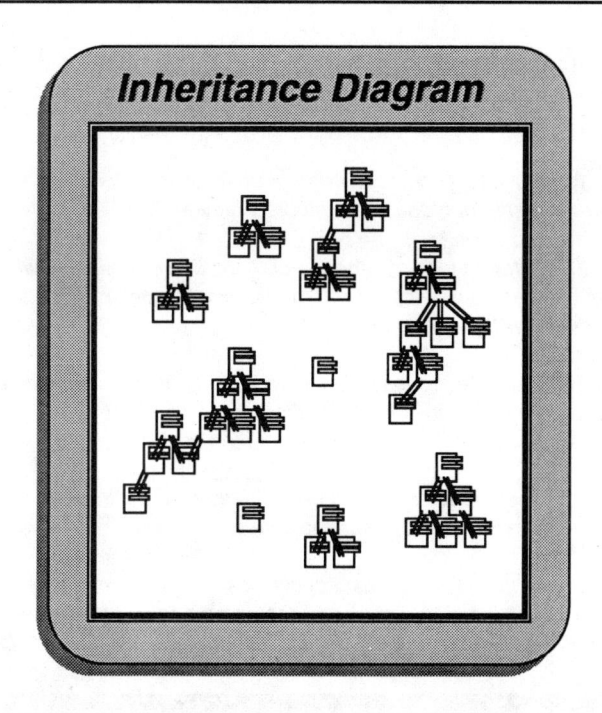

12.2 THE INHERITANCE DIAGRAM

12.2.1 How Do You Determine Inheritance?

A Hierarchy of Common Requirements

Inheritance diagrams are pictorial representations of the sharing of common operations and attributes among abstract classes of objects. These are the operations and attributes that are extracted from your initial objects during classification. An inheritance diagram is a hierarchical drawing of all or part of the abstract classes of your domain. As shown in Figure 12-2, the fundamental components of inheritance diagrams are:

Component	*Component Definition*
Class Shapes	named symbols representing each abstract class
Inheritors	lines connecting classes to their subclasses

Each abstract class is a set of common operations and attributes and therefore is already related to one or more lower-level classes. Each inheritor line drawn on the diagram corresponds directly to the definition of a class to superior class relationship in an abstract class description. This type of relationship (inheritance) is also known as an is-a-kind-of relationship. Each class is a kind of its superior class.

Figure 12-2. The inheritance diagram.

A suitable technique for developing the inheritance diagram is defined in Table 12-1. Most techniques of inheritance modeling will be composed of similar steps for diagramming the relationships among abstract classes and then using the diagram to find more classes. As you diagram the inheritance relationships between abstract classes, look for additional clusters of similar operations and attributes. These become new abstract classes in your domain.

Many of the branches of your inheritance hierarchy may reflect the organization of operations and attributes that are similar to those which you have designed before or which belong to standardized libraries. You can eliminate the detail of these from further consideration in your design and just refer to the existing class as the superior class at that point in your hierarchy. This is one of the benefits of object engineering. Domain models can often be reused in new systems.

In designing the rest of your domain model, you may find that you can combine some of the initial abstract classes that you have identified into less pure but more efficient representations of an inheritance hierarchy. You should balance the number of abstract classes against the

Table 12-1. Steps to identify inheritance.

Step 1.1 List a preliminary set of objects that you know are likely to be a part of your design.

Step 1.2 LIst a few operations and/or attributes that best characterize the purpose of each object on your list.

Step 1.3 Extract those common operations and/or attributes which appear in several objects, or that are known to exist in objects already defined in your domain.

Step 1.4 Draw the groups of common operations and attributes as abstract classes of objects above those from which they were extracted and in which they will be inherited.

Step 1.5 Repeat the entire process to further extract additional abstract classes from your abstract classes.

Step 1.6 Combine some abstract classes to simplify an overly complex diagram of too many classes with too few operations and attributes, and repeat the entire process again.

number of operations and attributes within each class in the same way in which you would balance the number of modules against the number of program statements in a module for a conventional design.

You may also find that you can divide some abstract classes into more precise groups of common operations and attributes by examining them for added similarity beyond simply being shared by the same set of physical objects (their concrete classes). Often, if you can name subordinate sets of operations and attributes within an abstract class, you can also extract them as another separate abstract class which you may expand upon in the future.

Just as in conventional design, you will need to apply some common sense and some knowledge of the characteristics of the programming language that you are using in order to streamline your inheritance hierarchy. One operation or attribute per class is not an efficient design. At the other extreme, dozens of public operations and attributes in the same abstract class will limit the value of your inheritance hierarchy.

The Classification of Requirements

Domain design is a repetitive activity. You examine your classes to determine if you need more or different classes of objects to fully satisfy the requirements of your domain. You use the inheritance diagram as a guide to expand and contract your initial abstract classes into a more effective organization than existed in your initial design. This analytical process is called *classification*.

The clusters of operations and attributes that you extract during classification become new objects, each of which represents an abstract set of operations and attributes. The new object is abstract because it is not intended to represent a real-world object. It is just a holding area for the cluster of related operations and attributes that are used by the object from which they were extracted. These operations and attributes represent common requirements that are also likely to be used by other objects either in your current design or in subsequent designs.

At a very high level, abstract classes may be so abstract that they just represent categories of related abstract classes. A category is an abstract class that has no member operations or attributes, but exists solely to better organize a large group of abstract classes. You should use categories to organize a particularly large domain by separately considering different categories of classes, such as utility classes and subject areas.

There are many ways to organize a large set of abstract classes into categories. Coad and Yourdon, for example, suggest that you consider four components for any design that you develop. Booch suggests that you develop separate categories for each situation. No matter what particular techniques you use, the approach is always the same. Categories of abstract classes are just the next higher level of abstraction for representing the inheritance hierarchies of a large domain in an understandable manner.

Abstract classes differ from the physical objects that remain after classification and are used differently in the design. The remaining physical objects represent real-world objects, which will eventually become interacting program modules. They are eventually drawn as concrete classes in collaboration diagrams. The extracted operations and attributes of abstract classes represent the requirements which are (or can become) common to several other objects. They are eventually drawn in inheritance diagrams.

Diagram the Inheritance Relationships

The class shapes depicted on an inheritance diagram are symbols representing abstract classes of objects. Each one of these class shapes represents one object, in particular, one object derived from one or more other objects that contain the common operations and attributes shared by those other objects. Abstract classes are sometimes just referred to as *classes*, and inheritance diagrams are sometimes referred to as *class diagrams*.

There is one class shape on an inheritance diagram for every abstract class in your domain. However, sometimes a particular class is repeated on several diagrams to show multiple inheritance or to divide a large domain into readable pieces. This type of division may be informal and left to the discretion of the person who draws the diagram, or it can follow a predefined set of diagram-naming conventions for specific groups of abstract classes in the domain.

Many developers divide the inheritance hierarchy of a large domain into separately drawn pieces to depict different organizational perspectives. Each piece could represent one very high-level abstract class that is part of the inheritance hierarchy, or it could represent some other arbitrary collection of similar abstract classes. These pieces of an inheritance hierarchy can either be called *subjects* or *categories*.

Categories of classes are often useful for maintaining good project-management control of a large inheritance hierarchy. However, they really just represent artificial divisions of your domain. By artificial, we mean that there is no express sharing of operations or attributes among the classes in a category in the way there is among the subclasses of a class. Class utilities and metaclasses are other examples of specific types of organizational divisions of inheritance.

Concrete classes are usually added to an inheritance diagram at its lower levels to tie them to their appropriate higher-level abstract classes. The relationships among concrete classes, however, should not be depicted on the inheritance hierarchy. The purpose of the inheritance diagram is to show the class-to-class inheritance relationships for the objects they represent. The relationships among concrete classes are better left to the collaboration diagram.

The inheritor lines depicted on an inheritance diagram show the class to superior class relationships for both the abstract and the concrete class. These are the lines connecting each class with the classes from which it will inherit some operations and attributes. These are usually drawn as lines connecting the classes, with the superior classes drawn above the classes from which they are referenced (implying that inheritance flows down). The direction in which the inheritance flows (down), however, is the reverse direction of that in which a request would flow (up) if these were client and server objects.

If you have chosen to include implementation information in your class descriptions, you may also want to represent it on your inheritance diagrams. There are standardized symbols to indicate object visibility (called *class adornments* by Booch) for this purpose. These special symbols are optional, however, based on how much detail you want to include in your design. The important relationships between abstract classes are the inheritance relationships themselves.

12.2.2 How Do You Diagram Inheritance?

Draw the Abstract Classes

You develop your initial inheritance diagram to show the interaction among the objects in your domain, in particular, to show the other common objects that they share. There should be one class on an inheritance diagram for every abstract class description in your domain. There are a number of different symbols that you can use to represent an abstract class. It doesn't really matter what symbol you use, so long as you understand it to represent an abstract class and use it consistently.

There is only one inheritance hierarchy for a domain, although it may have many branches drawn as individual diagrams. You can diagram your inheritance hierarchy in pieces to separately represent different branches or different levels within the same branch. As a result, a particular class is sometimes repeated on several diagrams. When breaking up a large inheritance hierarchy into separate diagrams, keep the number of repeated classes to a minimum. This makes for the cleanest set of complementary diagrams.

Multiple inheritance is difficult to represent on a single diagram. The easiest way to diagram multiple inheritance is to draw separate single-inheritance diagrams, each one representing one layer of the multiple hierarchies. Unfortunately, this masks the multiple inheritance characteristics and results in many repeated classes. It is usually better to divide the hierarchy into small branches and pieces of branches and try to show the multiple relationships on a single diagram for each piece.

If you divide the inheritance of your domain into separate *class categories*, you should keep the classes from each category separate from one another. Each category should represent a logical and meaningful high-level grouping of classes based on similar inheritance features. In fact, you can consider a category to be a subdomain. The inheritance diagrams for each class category should have little, if any, overlap. They should be composed of completely disjointed branches of your inheritance hierarchy, such as: a user interface category of abstract classes, a memory management category of abstract classes, an instance scheduling category of abstract classes, and a business functions category of abstract classes.

Draw the Concrete Classes

Concrete classes are always the lowest level on the inheritance diagram. Sometimes, one concrete class can inherit from another concrete class, but eventually they will inherit from some abstract class in the inheritance hierarchy. You should add the concrete classes to your inheritance diagram only after it has stabilized. You may make minor revisions to the inheritance hierarchy as you connect the concrete classes to it, but it is usually only the abstract classes that lead you to dramatically restructure it.

Like the abstract classes, there are a number of symbols shown in the literature from which you may choose to represent concrete classes. The Booch notation, for example, uses a solid depiction of the dotted symbol that they recommend for abstract classes. The Coad/Yourdon notation uses the same compound symbol to represent either abstract classes or concrete classes. We favor using the same symbol for both abstract classes and concrete classes, with a minor notation to distinguish between them when necessary (such as A for abstract classes and C for concrete classes).

It is neither necessary nor advisable to show the interaction among concrete classes on an inheritance diagram. Since you will usually divide your inheritance hierarchy into different diagrams for different categories or branches, the client/server relationships between concrete classes are not guaranteed to be on the same diagram. Even if it is possible to connect them, the interaction among concrete classes will distract from the real purpose of the inheritance diagram.

The purpose of an inheritance diagram is to show the paths used to resolve polymorphic references to common operations and attributes. In contrast, the interaction among concrete classes is achieved by passing requests. The inheritance paths are clearer if no requests are shown on the inheritance diagram. Although it is sometimes acceptable to show them when you are examining limited portions of a domain, it is usually not a good idea to show collaborations on an inheritance diagram as a rule.

Draw the Inheritance Lines

You draw the inheritance lines on an inheritance diagram to show the class-to-class relationships between each pair of abstract classes and between each concrete class and abstract class in an inheritance hierarchy. Each class on your inheritance diagrams should be located near the other classes to which it has an inheritance relationship. More specifically, each superior class should be drawn directly over (or at least higher on the page than) the classes which inherit its members.

Like the class symbols, you can draw the inheritance lines in any way you think suitable. Some designers choose to draw a different type of line to indicate inheritance from that which they use to indicate collaboration. Since we recommend that you separate inheritance from collaboration on different diagrams, this issue becomes trivial. However, if you find that it adds clarity, you can indicate inheritance as we do—by using a double line from a class to its superior class. If the identity of the superior class is not apparent from its position on the page, you should also anchor the superior class by an arrow or some other marker.

12.2.3 How Do You Organize the Diagrams?

Define Class Categories

Class categories are a good way to divide a large domain into more manageable groups of classes. Class categories, in particular, are applied to abstract classes. Often, you can see a relationship among groups of abstract classes that is more conceptual than physical. They may comprise entirely separate branches of an inheritance diagram, but you might wish to group several branches together as a category for better management and control of your domain. Class categories are also called *subjects* or *components* of a domain.

Each class category is a separately maintained set of inheritance diagrams for a domain. Therefore, if you make use of class categories, you can compare the categories of your design to those already available within your domain (or in other domains) as a first-level check for reusable classes. Class categories are a good way to support the extensibility of a domain. They help you to find the classes that you need to reuse.

Define Utility Classes

Utility classes are just a special case of class categories. Most class categories that you define in your domain will be standard components of a design (such as a user-interface category or a data-access category), or subjects typical of the function of your domain (a billing category or inventory category). Utility classes are low-level categories which are more universally applicable across many designs.

Utility classes may include such things as input modules, output modules, statistical functions, numeric conversions, instance handles, memory managers, and imaging modules or character code translators. Utility classes tend to be technology related. They are the most popular variety of static-source libraries that you can purchase to extend the capabilities of an object-oriented language. They are standardized abstract classes that make your own inheritance hierarchy more robust.

Define Metaclasses

Finally, you may find that you need to define metaclasses of classes in order to apply the same type of inheritance features to your inheritance hierarchy. Usually, metaclasses are realized as object types, or more precisely, as operation types and attribute types. *Operation types* are such things as the add, subtract, multiply, and divide functions represented by particular character symbols in your source code. *Attribute types* are such things as the integer and real number declarations in attribute header statements.

The concept of an inheritance hierarchy in object-oriented languages is modeled after the type hierarchy in conventional languages. It stands to reason, therefore, that object-oriented languages enable you to extend the types available to designers within a domain in the same way that you can extend the inheritance features of its classes. A type is just one specific form of a metaclass.

If the programming language that you use supports extendable type definitions, you can extend your inheritance hierarchy with new types. In the same way that you can design or purchase utility classes, you would also be able to design or purchase custom-built type hierarchies. Thus, you could redefine the syntax of an addition statement for programs in your domain, or more likely, define your own higher-level operations (for example, an arithmetic mean) or types of attributes (for example, a window handle).

12.3 THE COLLABORATION DIAGRAM

12.3.1 How Do You Determine Collaboration?

A Hierarchy of Operational Requirements

Collaboration diagrams are pictorial relationships of the client/server relationships between the objects associated with concrete classes. These are your real objects, that is, those that become subroutines in your computer program. A collaboration diagram is a hierarchical drawing of all or part of the real objects in your domain. As shown in Figure 12-3, the fundamental components of collaboration diagrams are:

Component	Component Definition
Class Shapes	named symbols representing each concrete class
Collaborations	lines connecting client and server classes

Each concrete class is a subordinate set of operations and attributes. Each collaboration line drawn on the diagram corresponds directly to a set of contracts between two classes in a concrete class

CHAPTER 12: DESIGN AT THE DOMAIN LAYER **229**

[Collaboration Diagram illustration]

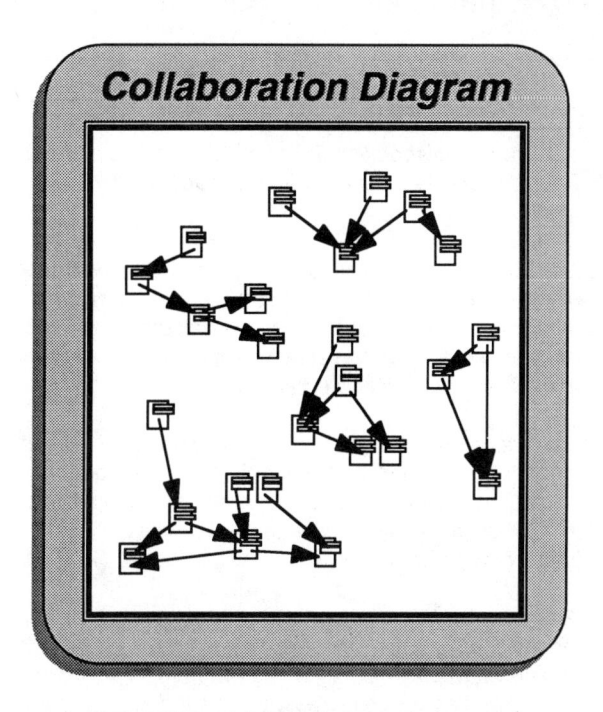

Figure 12-3. The collaboration diagram.

description. This type of relationship (a collaboration) is also known as a *uses* relationship. A collaboration can be either of two general types—hierarchical or lateral. A *hierarchical collaboration* represents *uses-for-implementation* relationship. A *lateral collaboration* represents a *uses-for-interface* relationship.

A suitable technique for developing a collaboration diagram is defined in Table 12-2. You may choose to use some other technique for diagramming collaboration relationships between concrete classes but it will most likely be composed of similar steps. As you diagram the collaboration relationships between concrete classes, you may discover that different arrangements of operations and attributes within a class would make your design easier to understand, easier to construct, and more efficient to operate. You should modify your collaboration diagram accordingly.

You modify your collaboration diagram by combining some concrete classes after you expand others. This process is outlined in Table 12-3. Your initial set of concrete classes are defined as a result of classification. *Classification* is the process of extracting the common operations and attributes to identify abstract classes in your inheritance hierarchy. The remaining groups of operations and attributes (the remaining objects)

Table 12-2. Steps to identify collaborations.

Step 2.1 Draw a collaboration diagram showing the interaction between the preliminary list of objects that you used to develop your inheritance diagram.

Step 2.2 Examine the lists of operations and attributes that remain in each concrete class after you extracted some to derive your inheritance diagram, and look for natural groups of highly related ones to extract as server objects represented as new concrete classes on your collaboration diagram.

Step 2.3 Examine the collaborations between your objects and look for additional groups of related objects that perform transformations on specific attributes, and draw them as server objects represented by new concrete classes on your collaboration diagram.

Step 2.4 Examine the collaborations between your objects and look for additional groups of related objects which process specific transactions between attributes, and draw them as server objects represented by new concrete classes on your collaboration diagram.

---

become your initial concrete classes. These are what you represent in your collaboration hierarchy.

Your initial set of concrete classes may be suitable for design directly without any further modification. Often, however, an examination of the operational interaction (the collaborations) between the objects associated with these classes will suggest better ways to group these remaining operations and attributes. Pairs of highly coupled objects (those with many requests between them) may need to be combined, or their members may need to be regrouped into other objects. Your collaboration diagram allows you to picture how your program will operate, and thus, will help you to streamline it.

The Encapsulation of Requirements

One way to identify more concrete classes using a collaboration diagram is to look for additional subordinate sets of operations and attributes for encapsulation within an object. As with conventional design, you can find candidates for encapsulation by performing transform analysis and transaction analysis within your objects. You can then extract these transform objects and transaction objects as new encapsulated objects in your design. This analytical process is called *encapsulation*.

You can perform transform analysis on an object's attributes by looking for process transform centers as you would in process-driven design. An outline for this process is provided in Table 12-4. Groups of attributes that interact with a single operation are *transform centers*. The concept is the same as examining transform centers on a data-flow diagram. An operation which transforms many attributes is just an object transform center.

You can perform transaction analysis on an object's operations by looking for process transaction centers as you would in process-driven design. An outline for this process is provided in Table 12-5. Groups of operations that interact with a single pair of attributes are similar to a transaction center. The concept is the same as examining transaction centers on a data-flow diagram. A set of parallel operations all tied to the same pair of attributes is just an object transaction center.

Encapsulation is not unique to object-oriented design. It is the same analytical concept as process decomposition that is used in process-driven design, except that you now apply it to both the processes and the data. Hierarchical encapsulation corresponds to the decomposition of process modules on a structure chart. Lateral encapsulation corresponds to the direct interaction between modules on different branches of a leveled set of data-flow diagrams (i.e., off-page connectors).

At a very high level, even concrete classes tend to get somewhat abstract, yet they still represent real-world objects. In the same way that

Table 12-3. Look for encapsulated objects.

> Step 2.2.1 Look for additional groups of closely related operations and attributes within each class, and separate them into new encapsulated concrete classes.
>
> Step 2.2.2 Combine some concrete classes which share many similar operations and/or attributes, and consider creating new abstract classes on your inheritance diagram based on those similarities.
>
> Step 2.2.3 Adjust your collaboration diagram accordingly and repeat the entire process of looking for and extracting additional sets of subordinate operations and attributes.

Table 12-4. Look for transform objects.

> *Step 2.3.1 Identify groups of operations within an object which read/write the same pair of attributes.*
>
> *Step 2.3.2 Create a new operation (a transform center) to represent this group of operations.*
>
> *Step 2.3.3 Create a new concrete class whose object contains this new operation, its subordinate operations, and the pair of attributes transformed.*
>
> *Step 2.3.4 Adjust your collaboration diagram accordingly and repeat the entire process of looking for and extracting additional sets of subordinate operations and attributes.*

you encapsulate one object within another, you may encapsulate an entire collaboration hierarchy as an object within another collaboration hierarchy. In a particularly large domain, you can nest complete collaboration hierarchies within others so that you can concentrate on the interactions at a particular level of detail.

There are many ways to nest collaborations in a large domain. Booch, for example, suggests that you consider several specific levels of collaboration which correspond to identifiable levels of abstraction in the physical world (processor, device, subsystem, package, task, module). Wirfs-Brock, Wilkerson, and Wiener suggest that you address different levels of physical interaction by framing one layer within another to whatever degree your situation warrants. No matter what particular techniques you use, the approach is always the same. Nested levels of concrete classes are just the next higher level of abstraction for representing collaboration hierarchies for a large domain in an understandable manner.

Diagram the Collaboration Relationships

The class shapes depicted on a collaboration diagram are symbols representing concrete classes of objects. Each one of these class shapes represents one object, in particular, one of the remaining real objects after common operations and attributes have been extracted. Concrete classes are sometimes just referred to as *objects*, and collaboration diagrams are sometimes referred to as *object diagrams*.

There is one class shape on the collaboration diagram for each concrete class in your domain. However, sometimes a particular concrete class is repeated on several collaboration diagrams that comprise a large domain. This type of division of the collaboration hierarchy may be informal and left to the discretion of the person who draws the diagram, or it can follow a predefined division of the collaborations in your domain.

Some developers divide the collaboration hierarchy into assembly diagrams to depict different operational perspectives of a domain. The different perspectives correspond to nested levels of a design. Usually, each level represents a particular physical aspect of the implementation environment. You should break up a collaboration hierarchy into nested assembly diagrams to maintain better control of the concrete classes in a large domain. It complements the use of class categories to manage a large inheritance hierarchy.

Assemblies of a collaboration hierarchy are just specific nested groupings of concrete classes. For example, device diagrams (for hardware platforms) and subsystem diagrams (for software platforms) are typical of nested groupings of concrete classes. You may develop several device collaboration diagrams, one for each type of hardware platform in your domain. You may then develop individual subsystem collaboration diagrams within each device diagram to define the interaction among the major objects on each platform.

12.3.2 How Do You Diagram Collaboration?

Draw the Concrete Classes

You develop your initial collaboration diagram to show the interaction among the physical objects in your domain. Each concrete class repre-

Table 12-5. Look for transaction objects.

> Step 2.4.1 Identify groups of operations within an object that read/write the same pair of attributes.
>
> Step 2.4.2 Create a new operation (a transaction center) to represent this group of operations.
>
> Step 2.4.3 Create a new concrete class whose object contains this new operation, its subordinate operations, and the pair of attributes transformed.
>
> Step 2.4.4 Adjust your collaboration diagram accordingly and repeat the entire process of looking for and extracting additional sets of subordinate operations and attributes.

sents a real object in your domain, that is, an object which can have instances at runtime. There should be one class on a collaboration diagram for every concrete class in your domain. As with abstract classes, it really doesn't matter what symbol you use as long as you use it consistently.

There is only one collaboration hierarchy for a domain, although you can draw it as separate assemblies representing nested levels of your domain. Assembly diagrams of collaboration are similar to nested objects within a collaboration diagram. A standard list of typical types of *assembly diagrams* may include such things as: processor diagrams of the hardware platforms, device diagrams of the peripheral equipment, subsystem diagrams of the business software systems, package diagrams of the programs in schedule groups, task diagrams of the individual programs, and module diagrams of the internal program designs.

Draw the Collaboration Lines

Collaboration diagrams show the contract relationships between concrete classes in your domain. Contracts represent the operational interaction between the objects associated with concrete classes. Each interaction is a client/server relationship established by a group of requests between the members of those objects. The objects will be represented by instances at runtime. They represent the real-world objects that correspond to subroutines in the source code of your computer program.

You draw the collaboration lines on a collaboration diagram to show the contract relationships between the concrete classes in your domain. Each collaboration on your collaboration diagrams represents a call from one program module to another in the same way as modules are connected on a structure chart in conventional design. The object-oriented collaboration hierarchy, however, is more like network structures than pure hierarchical structures.

The collaboration lines depicted on a collaboration diagram show the contract relationships between the concrete classes of objects listed in your domain. Each collaboration line represents a set of contracts. Contracts are groups of requests between a single pair of objects. You can draw these in any way that you find suitable but you should somehow indicate the direction of the requests. We recommend a line with an arrow at the server end of each collaboration, as shown in Figure 12-3.

If you have chosen to include implementation information in your class descriptions (such as cardinality) you may also want to represent it on your collaboration diagrams. *Cardinality* represents the number of allowed object instances for a particular concrete class. This applies to the server object in each collaboration. Like adornments for inheritance diagrams, these special symbols are also optional on your collaboration diagram. The important relationships between concrete classes are the collaboration relationships themselves.

12.3.3 How Do You Nest the Diagrams?
Draw Separate Hardware Diagrams

You can break the collaboration hierarchy for a domain into several smaller related hierarchies. Usually, you divide collaboration by nesting different levels of collaboration diagrams within one another representing different parts of a domain within each level. You can usually develop a nested collaboration hierarchy by first considering the different levels of hardware processors and devices on which your software will be implemented.

Processors are the different central processing units, or computers, that form the primary environment for any computer program. Processor diagrams are just collaboration diagrams that are drawn for the concrete classes at the processor level. Mainframe computers, minicomputers, desktop microcomputers, spooling printers, graphical scanners, programmable firmware, and programmable chips can all be considered processors of some sort. You may wish to draw a separate collaboration diagram for each processor in your domain.

Devices are the different kinds of peripheral support hardware that are connected to processors. Devices would first appear as server objects on a processor diagram. Device diagrams are just the separate detailed collaboration diagrams of the internal designs of these servers. Printers, keyboards, display terminals, and mouses can all be considered devices of some sort. You may wish to draw a separate collaboration diagram for each device on each processor in your domain.

Draw Separate Software Diagrams

Similar to the hardware platforms in your domain, you may wish to divide your collaboration hierarchy into separate levels of software within each device on the hardware platform. Descriptions of the different levels of software in object-oriented design are the same as in conventional design. They include such things as subsystems, packages, tasks, and modules.

Subsystems are the independent collections of programs in your domain. They act together to accomplish one major function. Subsystem diagrams are the separate collaboration diagrams that you would use to represent the client/server interactions within a subsystem in a particular hardware device in your domain. Subsystems are usually such things as inventory, purchasing, billing, accounting, and personnel systems.

Packages are the scheduled groups of programs within any one subsystem in your domain. Package diagrams are just the separate collaboration diagrams that you would use to represent the client/server interactions within a subsystem. The online programs, nightly batch programs, and periodic reconciliation programs of a billing system are examples of packages within a subsystem.

Tasks are the individual computer programs usually found within a package (a *program* is an implementation term, while a *task* is the equivalent design term). Task diagrams are just collaboration diagrams at the task level. If you choose to nest your collaboration hierarchy in this manner, the task diagrams will show the program designs within each package in the subsystems in your domain.

Finally, *modules* are component parts of a well-organized program. They correspond to subroutines and sections within a computer program. Module diagrams are the best example of the similarities between object-oriented design and conventional design. A module-level collaboration diagram is just an object-oriented name for a conventional structure chart. Usually, you will draw separate subsystem, package, task, and module diagrams that contain concrete classes at those levels.

CHAPTER REVIEW

Design at the Domain Layer

What does a design represent?   The objects that comprise your domain, including their interaction with one another, their component operations and attributes, and their internal design.

How do you start your design?   By identifying the objects necessary to meet the requirements of your system, and either developing them in their entirety or analyzing them against existing objects which may meet some of those requirements.

How do you design inheritance?   As the hierarchy of abstract classes of objects which contain the common operations and attributes which are inherited by other objects.

How do you organize the diagrams?   The abstract classes in a large domain are often organized at an intermediate level into categories of classes and drawn as separate diagrams.

How do you design collaborations?   As the relationships between concrete classes of objects that contain the operations and attributes that interact at run time.

How do you nest the diagrams?   The concrete classes in a large domain are often nested within one another and portrayed as different levels of hardware and/or software assemblies and drawn as separate nested diagrams.

13

Design at the Class Layer

13.1 ALLOCATING OBJECT REQUIREMENTS

The Interface Model

The middle layer of object engineering is concerned with the design of the interface model. It focuses your attention on the classes that comprise the hierarchy diagrams in your domain. As with the prior design of the domain layer, the steps suggested here for designing classes outline the activities that you are likely to perform during class design, although the details will certainly vary from project to project. The model that you develop to represent the class layer will also vary in its form from project to project, but the basic components will be the same.

The products of the middle layer of object engineering are shown in Figure 13-1. The model developed is called the *interface model*. The interface model consists of class descriptions, object descriptions, and request descriptions, which define the interfaces of all objects, and the implementation model, which provides their internal designs.

We will address the internal design of objects in the next layer of design. However, it is important to consider the implementation model as part of the overall interface model. You will eventually develop it as a direct result of the class, object, and request descriptions of your interface model.

You develop an interface model by examining the objects in your domain and then reorganizing them. The objects that you use can come from an existing domain that you will expand to meet your needs or can be developed as a part of a new domain. You reorganize your objects by

238 OBJECT ENGINEERING

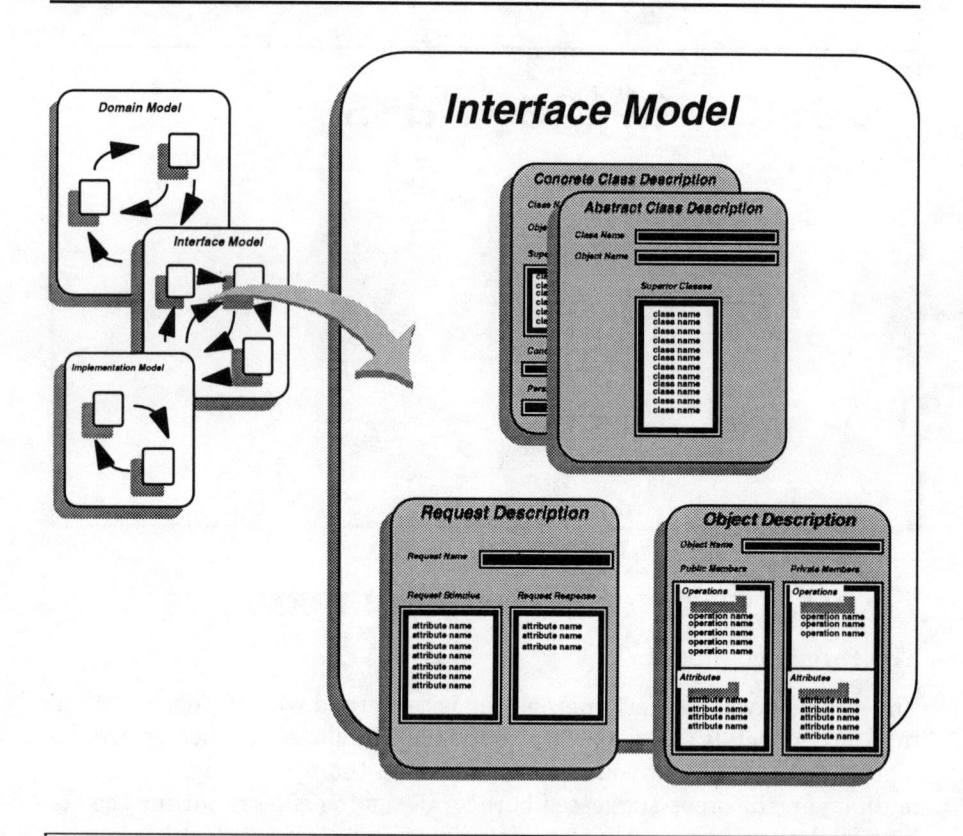

Figure 13-1. Working at the class layer.

classifying them into more detailed inheritance relationships and by further encapsulating some of those classified objects within one another.

You further classify objects by identifying and then grouping new sets of common operations and attributes in the objects of your domain. Each new common set of operations and attributes becomes another abstract class in your domain. This process is somewhat similar to clustering in the early steps of a data-driven design. Sets of common operations and attributes are usually closely related to one another. It is therefore helpful to look for clusters of operations and attributes as candidates for classification.

You can also further encapsulate some operations and attributes within an object by grouping them into new subordinate sets. Each new set of operations and attributes becomes another concrete class in your domain. The new subordinate set represents a new server object encapsulated within the original (client) object. It is therefore helpful to look at the interaction between operations and/or attributes within an object to identify candidates for encapsulation.

The majority of encapsulated objects have collaborations that are of a hierarchical nature. This is the more typical form of a client/server collaboration. Hierarchical collaborations correspond to data couples on a structure chart. They represent the relationship of a child subroutine function to its parent module. Hierarchical collaborations are found by a technique very similar to process decomposition.

In contrast, lateral collaborations represent the interactions among objects with no clear parent-child relationship. In this type of collaboration, the server is not fully encapsulated within the client. Lateral collaborations are really just the exception to the rule to simplify your design. They correspond to off-page data flows between two processes on different diagrams in a leveled set of data-flow diagrams.

13.2 THE CLASS DESCRIPTIONS

13.2.1 How Do You Determine Classes?

The Interaction between Objects

Objects are groups of operations and attributes. They are already organized into preliminary groups in your inheritance and collaboration diagrams. You now analyze the interrelationships within and among these groups to organize them into a more robust set of classes. As part of that analysis, you divide your original groups into new and better organized groups (abstract classes) as suggested in Table 13-1. This is a straightforward process of reorganizing your objects using techniques known as *classification* and *encapsulation*.

Abstract classes represent the operations and attributes that you extracted from your original (physical) objects because they are common to several objects in your domain. These objects can often be divided further to derive more abstract classes (classification). Abstract classes will not be represented as real object instances. They will only be parts of other object instances, that is, their operations and attributes will be inherited by the objects associated with concrete classes.

The concept of extracting abstract characteristics from objects is unique to object-oriented design and programming. A class description for an abstract class is a single page of text that describes the inheritance characteristics between the abstract class(es) derived from and then used by other classes in your domain. As shown in Figure 13-2, the fundamental components of an abstract class description are:

Component	Component Definition
Class Name	the name used to identify this class
Object Name	the object associated with this class
Superior Class	names of the higher classes to which it belongs

Concrete classes correspond to those objects remaining after you extract the sets of common operations and attributes by classification.

Table 13-1. Steps to define classes.

Step 3.1.1 Document the name of each abstract class and each concrete class from your inheritance diagram, and identify the abstract classes (if any) from which they inherit additional operations and attributes.

Step 3.1.2 Identify (by name) the object associated with each abstract class and each concrete class.

Step 3.1.3 Document the purpose of each object by listing all of its operations and all of its attributes, and by identifying which ones are public and which ones are private.

Step 3.1.4 Document the contracts that each concrete class has with another concrete class from your collaboration diagram, and identify any additional pertinent information such as its concurrency or persistence.

Step 3.1.5 Examine the relationships among classes, both in terms of their inheritance and their collaboration relationships with one another, to consider additional changes to their relationships and modify those diagrams accordingly.

These objects can often be divided further by encapsulation to derive more concrete classes, which are smaller and more specific than your original objects. A class description for a concrete class is a single page of text that describes the collaboration characteristics of the object to which it corresponds. As shown in Figure 13-3, the fundamental components of a concrete class description are:

Component	*Component Definition*
Class Name	the name used to identify this class
Object Name	the object associated with this class
Superior Class	the abstract class(es) to which this class belongs
Contracts	a list of groups of requests sent to other classes
Concurrency	indicator for single or multi-threaded processing
Persistence	indicator for reinitialized or saved data values

Notice that the first three components of a concrete-class description are the same as those of an abstract-class description. Concrete classes are just a different kind of class from abstract classes. Abstract classes hold the common operations and attributes that were extracted from objects.

Concrete classes represent those remaining objects. The core of the definition of either kind of class, therefore, contains the same components.

Notice also that the second component of a class description (the associated-object name) is a pointer to an object description. This should be no surprise since there is a one-to-one relationship between a class and the object associated with it. You use concrete classes to represent real objects—those that will have instances. An instance of an object will be a program module or subroutine at runtime, which may also inherit some of its operations and attributes from other objects associated with abstract classes.

Inheritance Defines Abstract Classes

You represent the organization of the objects in your domain as inheritance relationships between abstract classes. Abstract classes represent common objects which, by themselves, can never have instances at runtime. These common objects are represented as sets of operations and attributes that can be inherited into the objects below them in the inheritance tree. The inheritance tree is simply an object-oriented way of cataloging these common operations and attributes for later use in your program.

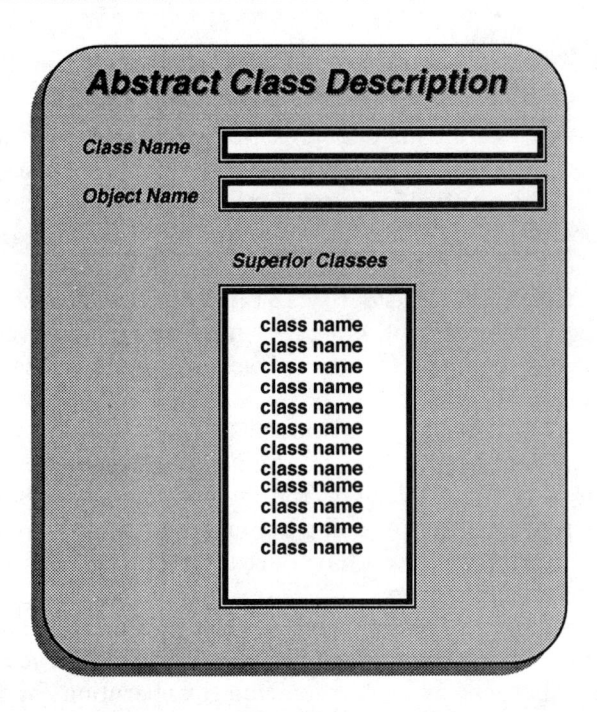

Figure 13-2. The abstract class description.

Concrete Class Description

- Class Name
- Object Name
- Superior Classes
  - class name
  - class name
  - class name
  - class name
  - class name
  - class name
- Contracts (other classes)
  - class name
    - request name
    - request name
    - request name
  - class name
    - request name
    - request name
    - request name
  - class name
    - request name
    - request name
    - request name
- Concurrency
- Persistence

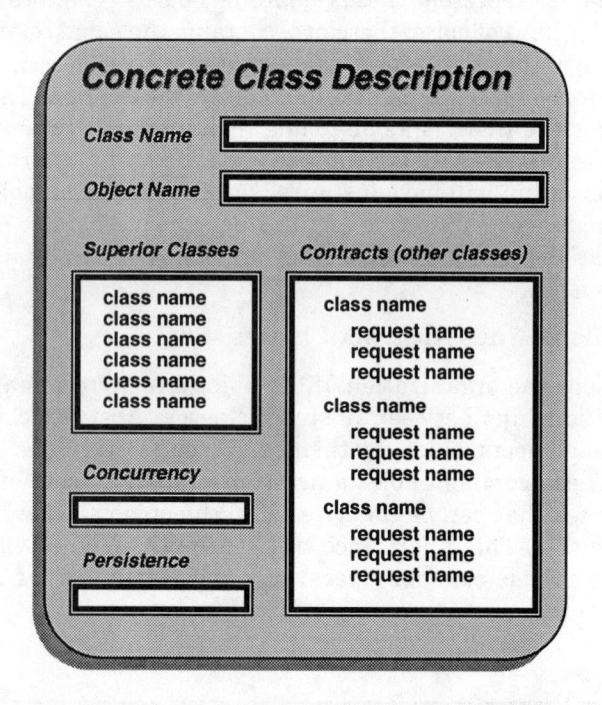

Figure 13-3. The concrete class description.

Classification is a means of representation that is unique to object-oriented design, however, it is the same analytical process as clustering, which is used in the entity-analysis portion of a data-driven design approach. In a conventional data-driven design, you allocate groups of related data and process elements into clusters on a cluster matrix and then represent the clusters as entities on an entity-relationship diagram. Classification of objects in an object-oriented design involves the same analytical process. You look for and extract clusters of related attributes and operations.

You expand the lists of operations and attributes that apply to the objects of your system by drawing on the same concepts that you might have used in conventional design. You identify more attributes by considering their relationships to each other and identify more operations by decomposing the ones that you have already identified. As a result, the objects themselves grow larger.

You then expand the list of objects by considering the expanded lists of operations and attributes within each object. You divide your expanded objects into smaller objects by reorganizing the operations and attributes within each object. Sometimes you may divide one object into several objects, at other times you may shift operations and/or attributes from one object to another. As you further classify the abstract classes in your domain, you should also modify your inheritance diagram accordingly.

Encapsulation Defines Collaboration

You represent the operation of the objects in your domain as collaboration relationships between concrete classes. Concrete classes represent real objects, that is, those which can have instances during run time. Some objects (servers) are represented as encapsulated within other objects (clients). The entire sets of operations and attributes in the servers are hidden from view and characterized in the clients only by the requests associated with them. They are said to be encapsulated.

Encapsulation is the design process of further organizing the concrete classes of objects in your initial collaboration diagram into a more robust set. Like the steps for classification, the steps for encapsulating objects within one another are intended to guide your thought processes to transform your initial objects into an organized set based on their operational interaction with one another. Depending on the type of interaction they display, encapsulation can be either hierarchical or lateral.

Hierarchical encapsulation is the process that you use to discover and represent additional hierarchical collaborations between the objects in your domain. This is the most typical form of encapsulation. It represents the division of a large physical object into a set of smaller subordinate physical objects. Hierarchical encapsulation is similar to the process decomposition that you may have used in process-driven design.

Lateral encapsulation is the process that you use to discover and represent additional collaborations of a lateral nature between the objects in your domain. This is more of an exception than a normal way of thinking about the interaction between objects. *Lateral collaboration* is used when you need to use a part of another object but not enough of its operations or attributes to consider it as a fully encapsulated subset. Lateral collaborations allow you to reuse operations and attributes without extracting them as separate objects just because of a few external references.

Collaborations are the operational interaction between the physical objects in your design. The physical objects are those that remain after you extract abstract sets of operations and attributes in classification. In many ways, encapsulation is just the object-oriented equivalent of conventional process decomposition. Similarly, collaboration diagrams are the object-oriented equivalent of process-structure charts in conventional design. As you further encapsulate the concrete classes in your domain, you should modify your collaboration diagram accordingly.

13.2.2 How Do You Define Classes?

Name the Classes

The *class names* in a class description are the unique identifiers for each class. There is a one-to-one correspondence between a class and an object.

The object associated with an abstract class is simply the specific set of operations and attributes inherited by its subclasses (in the case of an abstract class) or included within its instances (in the case of a concrete class).

The name of a class, either abstract or concrete, will usually be the same as the name of the object it represents. Classes always represent the organizational characteristics of one and only one object in your design (although they may have multiple instances at runtime). The description of a class is just a more general representation of the object it represents.

Once you have established a set of abstract classes, you have also established a mechanism for reusing the common operations and attributes that they represent. You can now add new classes into the existing inheritance hierarchy underneath the existing abstract classes. The new classes can inherit operations and attributes from the abstract classes above it in the hierarchy. This is the means by which you can reuse an existing design to develop new designs.

Identify the Superior Classes

The listing of a superior class in a class description is just a reference pointer from one class to another class which contains the common operations and attributes that it needs. This is the relationship that distinguishes object-oriented design from conventional design. These are the relationships depicted between the abstract classes on your inheritance diagram.

You will often find that some abstract classes can be grouped together as similar classes under the same superior class even if you can't identify any specific operations or attributes that belong to that superior class. This is called a *class category*. Class categories are just artificial abstract classes for organizing a large domain. You might eventually represent some of the higher-level abstract classes that you first identify as class categories.

In addition to the class-to-superior-class relationships between abstract classes, you may wish to also note additional implementation information about your classes as part of the abstract-class description. In particular, some object-oriented programming languages allow you to designate an object's visibility in the same way that you would describe an operation's visibility or an attribute's visibility: *public objects* are those whose members are available to clients, *protected objects* are those whose private members can be inherited, and *private objects* are those whose members cannot be used by clients.

The meaning of an object's visibility will depend on the particular language in which it is used. Visibility ultimately applies to the operations and the attributes of an object. However, a visibility designation at the object level can be used to supercede individual operation and attribute visibility or to set the otherwise unspecified visibility of some operations or attributes. Object visibility, however, is really a programming concern and not a design concern.

Identify the Contracts

Concrete classes are different from abstract classes in that they represent real-world objects. This means that the objects associated with concrete classes will have instances at runtime. Therefore, in addition to identifying the superior classes from which they will inherit operations and attributes, you also need to identify the collaboration contracts that they possess with the objects of other concrete classes. You should list each other concrete class with which a concrete class collaborates, each contract within a collaboration, and all of the request names within a contract.

Each contract is a package of requests among the objects of concrete classes. In many ways, a contract is just a way to organize a set of events (the requests) in much the same way that an object is a way to organize a set of operations and attributes. The concrete classes that you encapsulated within other classes will become the server objects in collaborations. The original concrete classes in which they are encapsulated become their clients.

Many of the operations and attributes within a concrete class may be related to one another. They may use the same set of private operations and/or attributes within the object to accomplish their purposes or communicate with each other. Some groups demonstrate a moderate degree of cohesion, yet not so much that they have been extracted as separate objects. You can use contracts to bundle the requests sent to these groups of somewhat cohesive operations and attributes in the same object.

Each encapsulation relationship between one concrete class and another signifies a collaboration. Each collaboration should be documented as one or more contracts. Even if you always bundle all the requests between two objects into a single contract, you should still identify it with a name. This helps you to identify each collaboration in your design, especially when you reuse portions of an existing design.

The list of contracts in a concrete-class description are the reference pointers between concrete classes. This relationship is similar to the class pointers between abstract classes. The superior class lists are abstract class pointers for inheritance purposes. These are the relationships depicted on your inheritance diagrams. Similarly, the contract lists are concrete-class pointers for collaboration purposes. These are the relationships depicted on your collaboration diagram.

In addition to the contracts, you may also wish to note implementation considerations as part of your concrete-class descriptions. In particular, many designers like to note the cardinality of the object collaboration and sometimes the manner in which the object will be linked into the program. The cardinality and the link characteristics of objects are just specific environmental considerations related to the collaborations between the objects of concrete classes.

Cardinality is just an identification of the number of object instances which is allowed for (or expected of) a particular collaboration between two objects. This concept is borrowed directly from data-driven design, and in particular, from entity-relationship diagrams. It means the same thing as the cardinality between two entities on an entity-relationship diagram and is noted in the same way.

Each object associated with a concrete class can have one or more instances at runtime (this is the definition of a concrete class). The cardinality of a concrete class, therefore, is just the declaration of the specific number of instances anticipated. Cardinality is usually noted once for the class and applies to its role as a server to the other classes in terms of: one (1), the object cannot have any concurrent instances; number (n), the object can have up to n separate concurrent instances; or many (M), the object can have an undertermined number of concurrent instances.

The manner in which objects of concrete classes will eventually be linked together in the program has little bearing on the design process. For this reason, we do not recommend that you consider it at this point. However, if you choose to document the type of linking that you will use when compiling your program, you should note it as part of your concrete-class descriptions. Linking is usually described in terms of three designations for classes: imported, server classes which reside in external program units; local, those which reside in the same program unit as their client; and exported, imported classes from within the external program units.

Signify the Concurrency

The designation of a class's concurrency in a class description is primarily *binary* (it either is or is not concurrent). *Concurrency* identifies whether there can be multiple threads of control. A concurrent designation signifies that the object of that concrete class can have multiple threads of control (multiple instances at runtime). This is called *synchronous operation*. A nonconcurrent designation signifies that the object can only have one instance, and therefore, the system can only have a single thread of control through that object. This is called *sequential operation*.

The concept of managing multiple threads of control is, of course, not new to object-oriented design. Conventional third-generation programming languages and, in particular, database management systems, have long been managing multiple threads of control in a shared environment. Unlike conventional approaches, however, object-oriented design enables you to address threads of control on a module-to-module basis. Objects are the modules in your program.

Although the concurrency of a class is described here as binary, there can be gradations between these two extremes in practice. For example, a particular compiler may apply concurrency either at the object level or at the instance level. At the object level, concurrent but different objects can perform their respective functions parallel to one another. At the instance level, concurrent instances of the same object can also operate parallel to one another as an array of objects.

The concept of concurrency at the objectlevel describes the parallel operation of the many different objects in your domain. This is also called event-driven operation. Each object can be activated by an event, and many events can occur before any one activated object completes its operation. This type of concurrency is presumed for all programs that are described as object oriented. Object concurrency is addressed as part of the request and operation design.

The concept of concurrency at the instance level describes the parallel operation of different instances of the same object. The identity of each instance of an object at runtime is usually referred to as its *handle*. You must consider whether an object can have multiple instances as part of the design of the other objects in your system that use it (they need to manipulate its instance handles). For this reason, object concurrency should be designated as part of your concrete-class descriptions.

Signify the Persistence

The designation of a class's persistence, like its concurrency, is also best described as binary (either persistent or not). *Persistence* signifies that an object instance will be retained after control passes out of the object (back to its calling client object). Nonpersistence signifies that an object instance will not be retained. A nonpersistent object is also called a *transient object*.

Unlike third-generation languages, most object-oriented programming languages require that you expressly allocate and release the memory area to store an object's attribute values. The point at which you release the memory area determines the extent of an object's persistence. The persistence of an object determines whether or not it must include constructor and destructor operations.

Although the persistence of an object is described here as binary, in practice there are usually gradations between these two extremes. For example, if an object is persistent, it may be retained either until the next call, or until the program to which it belongs terminates, until it is expressly deleted by a program command. If your programming environment distinguishes among these levels of persistence, you should also note this distinction as part of the persistence designation on your concrete-class descriptions.

A persistent object is usually one in which the state of its attributes (and possibly the executable instructions for its operations) will be retained between program sessions. This will usually best be handled by some type of automated management system. A management system that addresses both the operations and the attributes in persistent objects is called *active*. One that only manages the attributes in persistent objects is called *passive*.

13.3 THE OBJECT DESCRIPTIONS

13.3.1 How Do You Determine Objects?

The Requirements of Objects

The requirements of the objects in your domain are the operations and the attributes that they contain. You may have already used your knowledge of the types of operations and the types of attributes that each object is most likely to contain as you derived your objects and portrayed them in inheritance and collaboration diagrams. Now, however, you must transform that general sense of requirements (your preliminary list of operations and attributes for each object) into a definitive list of operations and attributes.

An *object description* is a means of documenting the detailed characteristics of each object associated with the classes in your domain. An object description is a single page of text that describes the object's purpose in the domain. As shown in Figure 13-4, the components of an object description are:

Component	Component Definition
Object Name	the name used to identify the object
Public Members	accessible from any object
Operations	a list of processes belonging to the object
Attributes	a list of data belonging to the object
Private Members	accessible only within this object
Operations	a list of processes used within this object
Attributes	a list of data used within this object

The lists of operations and attributes within an object associated with a concrete class are sometimes called *instance operations* and *instance attributes*, respectively. This distinguishes them from those which can be inherited to several objects (those of abstract classes). At this stage in class design, you are not concerned with class designation anymore (abstract or concrete). You can just think of all operations and attributes in an object as the characteristics of its instances, regardless of whether they will be inherited or whether they are local.

You now need to determine the specific requirements for the objects in your domain as suggested in Table 13-2. The system that you are designing will represent some real-world set of requirements. Therefore, one source of information to determine the specific requirements of each of your individual objects is that real-world process that will be served by your system. Observe, consider, and examine that process. Talk to experts who operate and manage that process today. The objects in your design should parallel the real-world objects from which they were derived.

Other sources of information about the requirements for your design are the existing systems that address the same or similar requirements. Often, a complex process in the real world is already supported by some type of system. The existing system may be a computer program that

CHAPTER 13: DESIGN AT THE CLASS LAYER   249

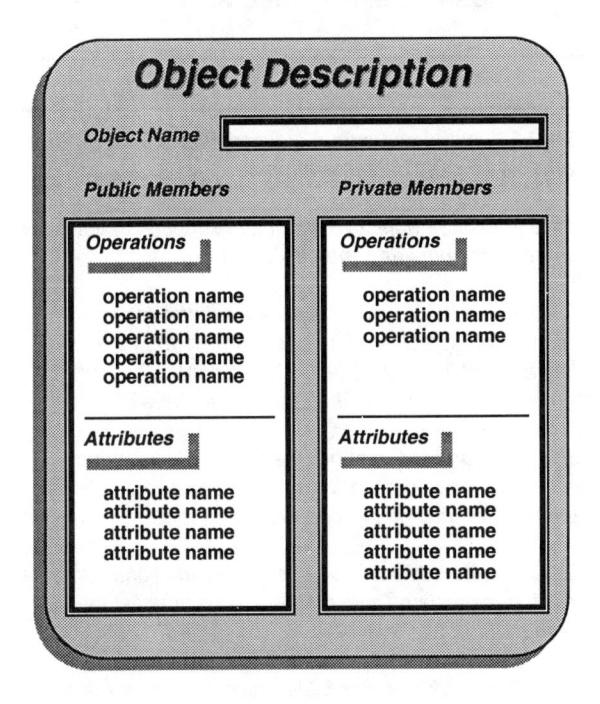

Figure 13-4. The object description.

needs improvement or needs to be upgraded to take advantage of new technology. The existing system may just as well be a manual process that needs to be automated. Either way, you can examine the existing system to identify an initial set of objects for your design.

Finally, the most obvious source of information about the requirements for your design is the written material generated to request and/or justify the design of a new system. The written material may be in the form of lists of requirements, descriptions of functions, designs of data structures, memoranda, informal diagrams, or formal specifications. All are sources of information to identify the operations and attributes that will comprise the objects for your domain.

13.3.2 How Do You Define Objects?

Name the Objects

The *object name* in an object description is the unique identifier for the group of operations and attributes that constitute each object. The object name is a convenience during design and programming. You will tend to use this name to refer to the entire set of operations and attributes of an object. This name should be both unique and descriptive. Many designers use the name of a major operation in an object as its object name.

Table 13-2. Steps to define objects.

> Step 3.1.3.1 List the verbs from a description of your program requirements as candidate operations.
>
> Step 3.1.3.2 List the adjectives from a description of your program requirements as candidate attributes.
>
> Step 3.1.3.3 List the nouns associated with the verbs (operations) and adjectives (attributes) which you have just identified to identify which objects should contain which operations and attributes as their public members.
>
> Step 3.1.3.4 Examine the public members of your objects to determine what additional private operations and additional private attributes may be needed to support them.
>
> Step 3.1.3.5 List additional operations and additional attributes that are often associated with the objects on your list to determine more public members.
>
> Step 3.1.3.6 List additional objects which may be needed to support the operations and the attributes on your lists, then modify your class descriptions and diagrams accordingly and repeat this entire process.

The lists of operations and attributes in an object description provide the sense of definition for each object—the operations and attributes are called the *members* of the object. Notice that the lists of operations and attributes in an object description are separated into two lists, which define the visibility of the members as either public or private. At this stage of your design, most (if not all) of your operations and attributes will be public members, since you have not yet developed sufficient detail to be concerned with the more private internal workings of your objects.

If you have trouble naming an object, this may be a sign that the object is more conceptual than tangible. Some objects are needed in a design to fully model the conceptual aspects of the more tangible objects. The tangible objects are easy to identify and name. Their names come from the physical objects that they represent or from the major operation that characterizes the object. The supporting conceptual objects are more difficult to name. Conceptual objects usually contain many attributes that support the definition of other more tangible objects. Therefore, you should examine the attributes within conceptual objects to help you arrive at an appropriate object name.

If the attributes of a conceptual object are grouped in a logical manner their collective name will be easy to determine. If you still cannot determine a suitable name for an object, then you should consider whether you should further rearrange the contents of your objects by dividing the unnameable object into several objects or by reassigning its members to other objects.

Identify the Operations

List the operations of each object in your domain to characterize the process requirements of your design. Each operation corresponds to one process requirement for your system. These lists help you to define your objects or to rearrange them into more meaningful groups of operations and attributes. A meaningful set of objects is one that can be easily assembled into collaboration and inheritance hierarchies and can therefore be reused in many new systems.

Expanding your lists of operations to develop a robust interface model is similar to process decomposition in process-driven design. The primary means by which you identify new operations from known ones is to consider the details of the processes required. You decompose general operations into more specific operations. The general operations tend to be the public operations in your objects and the detailed operations to be the private ones.

Another way to expand your list of operations is to consider their relationships with the attributes and objects in your design. You can identify additional operations by looking for their responsibilities to maintain the attributes in your domain and by listing the services that it must provide to other objects. The responsibilities and services of an object may include such things as performing calculations on attributes, monitoring or changing the states of attributes, and managing other objects.

In conventional design (using third-generation languages), memory management is transparent to the programmer. In most object-oriented programming languages, however, you must design your own memory-management processes. The operations needed to perform this function must be specified just like any other functional operation. You will usually find that standard names are reserved for the operations to allocate and release memory areas in these languages.

Object-oriented programming languages usually require that you manage memory at the instance level. Operations to allocate memory are usually called *constructors* and those to release memory are usually called *destructors*. The identification of a reserved memory area for a particular instance of an object is usually called its *handle*. Constructors, destructors, and handles are just examples of some standard operations (constructor and destructor operations) and standard attributes (handles) that you may need to consider for all of the objects in your domain.

Identify the Attributes

You list the attributes of each object in your domain to characterize the data requirements of your design—each attribute corresponds to one data requirement for your system. Like the operation lists, these attribute lists help you to define your objects or to rearrange them into more meaningful groups of operations and attributes. Your objective is to derive a meaningful set of objects by considering both their process requirements and their data requirements.

Attributes address the data requirements of the objects in your domain. You expand your lists of attributes in a similar manner to entity analysis in data-driven design. The primary means by which you identify new attributes from known ones is to consider the relationships between them. Your initial attributes tend to be the public attributes in your objects. Attributes that support your original ones tend to be the private attributes.

You find new attributes in your objects by considering what is needed to support the known attributes in your initial design. You should consider the information that an object needs to retain, what finite states that information can take, and what is needed to describe those states. Then distribute these added attributes among your objects by dividing large objects but keeping related attributes together.

13.4 THE REQUEST DESCRIPTIONS

13.4.1 How Do You Determine Requests?

The Interface of an Object

Request descriptions define the parameters used to trigger operations in a server object. Therefore, each public operation will have a corresponding request. An operation's request is the only means by which another operation in another object can interact with it. Requests are associated with a server (where the triggered operation resides), but are used by clients (from whence the request is made). Together, all the requests for a server object represent the entire interface for that object.

The way in which you document the interface of your objects is through their request descriptions. A request description is a single line of text describing the content of a request between a pair of objects. This is sometimes also called a *request signature*. It provides a complete identification of everything that signifies the difference between one request and another. As shown in Figure 13-5, the fundamental components of each request in a request description are:

Component	Component Definition
Request Name	name of the associated operation or attribute
Stimulus	list of calling parameters (input attributes)
Response	list of result parameters (output attributes)

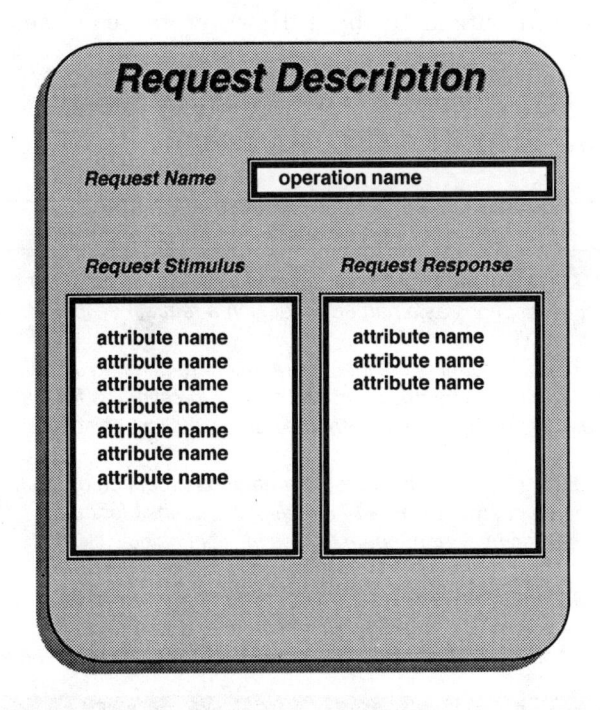

The request descriptions provide a convenient way to document the interfaces for all of the objects in your system. You should have one request description for each public operation in each object. A technique to derive request descriptions is outlined in Table 13-3. The steps are rather simple: look for and list the input and output required of each request.

Only the public operations in your design will require request descriptions. Public operations are the ones that act as entry points into server objects from clients. They receive requests. The purpose of a request description is to help you to later design the client operations that trigger an external operation. You design the contents of a request based on consideration of the needs of the server operation that will receive and act upon a request.

The *stimulus parameters* are the set of input calling parameters sent with the request into the server object from the client object in a collaboration between two those objects. The operation in the client that sends the request must assemble these parameters in order for the server operation to perform its function. Therefore, determine the stimulus parameters for a request by looking at an operation in a server object. This is why request descriptions are associated with (and usually have the same name as) the operation that they trigger in a server object.

Request Description

Request Name: operation name

Request Stimulus:
- attribute name
- attribute name
- attribute name
- attribute name
- attribute name
- attribute name
- attribute name

Request Response:
- attribute name
- attribute name
- attribute name

Figure 13-5. The request description.

The *response parameters* are the set of output parameters returned to the client from the server when it completes the process associated with the triggered operation. The server must calculate or otherwise assemble these parameters in order to fully satisfy its requirement. Determine the response parameters for a request by looking at the reasons that a client object needs to collaborate with a particular server.

Request parameters are sometimes called *transient attributes* because they are data elements, just like the attributes in an object. Many times, in fact, the request parameters are just alias names for attributes in the client object. The stimulus parameters (input) of a request are often used as parts of calculations in the server operation design. The response parameters (output) are often the result of those calculations. Thus, if you can identify your request descriptions early, they will guide you in designing your public operations.

Request Documentation

You can think of a request that triggers an operation as the call to a subroutine or a function. Similarly, you can think of a request that accesses an attribute as a call with no parameters. A request for an operation, however, is composed of input and output parameters. The input parameters are called the *request stimulus*. The output parameters are called the *request response*.

Each request represents either the triggering of an operation or the accessing of an attribute in an object. However, there are no parameters

Table 13-3. Steps to define requests.

Step 3.2.1 List each public operation in each object from your object descriptions as a named request in a request description.

Step 3.2.2 Determine the input parameters required to trigger each associated operation and list them as the stimulus for that request, preferably by their attribute names in client objects.

Step 3.2.3 Determine the output parameters produced by each associated operation and list them as the response for that request, also by their attribute names in client objects.

Step 3.2.4 Organize the requests between each pair of objects into the groups of contracts as listed on your concrete class descriptions, and document the name and contract for each one.

involved in accessing attributes directly (if this is even allowed in the language that you are using). Therefore, you only need request descriptions for those requests that will trigger operations. For this reason, many authors interchange the concepts of requests and operations in their discussions. While this is usually not a problem, it is still important to remember that there is a difference.

An operation is similar to a subroutine or a function in a conventional programming environment. Its request, therefore, is analogous to a subroutine or a function call. This analogy correlates very well with conventional design representations. A request would be the data couple, which links a parent module with a child module that it calls in a process-driven design. The parent module would be a client object. The child module would be a server.

A subroutine is a program module with a well-defined interface and an internal design that is maintained separately from the calling agent. Subroutines can be characterized by the calling parameters, which define the required input and the expected output. Functions are just subroutines that also return a separately identified value as part of the output. Requests are just an object-oriented way of representing a call to a subroutine or a function.

Subroutines, functions, and objects all have well-defined interfaces and separately maintained internal designs. If you understand how to call subroutines and functions in a conventional language, it will be easier to understand how to trigger operations and access attributes in objects. The requests of an object constitute its interface. The operation and attribute descriptions of an object constitute its internal design.

13.4.2 How Do You Define a Request?

Name the Requests

It is typical to give a request the same name as the operation it triggers. In this way, you never lose track of which request belongs to which operation. Furthermore, if you define a particular operation with the same name in several different objects (as is the case if you plan on using inclusion polymorphism), then the single request description will act as a template of the common interface for all of the redundantly named operations in your domain.

You should have one request for each uniquely named public operation of an object. Requests trigger only public operations. Private operations do not use requests; they are triggered directly from within the source-code statements of the other operations of an object. You need only develop request descriptions, therefore, for the public operations in the objects in your design.

The programming language that you use to implement your design will determine how you use requests in your program. It is always a good idea, however, to document the request descriptions for each public operation even if your language doesn't make explicit use of them. They serve as a good point of reference of the data needed to trigger operations in server objects from the clients in which they are encapsulated.

Some object-oriented programming languages allow multiple protocols to be defined for a single named request (*parametric polymorphism*). A *protocol* is the formatted string of stimulus and response parameters that are required within each request. If multiple protocols are allowed in the language you are using and you wish to make use of them, list all protocols for each request as part of the request description.

List the Stimulus Parameters

You should list the data elements needed by a particular operation as the stimulus parameters for its corresponding request. The parameters in a request stimulus represent the same thing as the downward data couple on the module connection between a parent module and a child module in a conventional structure chart. The parent module corresponds to the client object and the child module to the server object.

The stimulus in a request description is the set of calling parameters, which will be needed by the operation which is triggered. However, because you can make use of context-sensitive referencing within an operation's design, you do not need to provide all of those parameters as part of the request stimulus. Any parameters needed by a triggered operation, but not supplied in the stimulus, will be found in your design based on the object's context at runtime (either in the server object or by searching up its inheritance hierarchy).

A *request stimulus* is a list of the client attributes needed by a public operation in a server object. This would be called the input parameters of a subroutine module in conventional design. Request input is packaged in this way for the same reason that operations and attributes are packaged as objects—to provide a standardized way to describe the internal design of a module. Request input is packaged as stimulus parameters to provide a standardized way to describe the input interface of objects.

The parameters of a request stimulus are data elements. These data elements may be attributes contained in the client object or they may be obtained from its inheritance hierarchy. In conventional programming languages, the stimulus parameters are part of the call statement. In object-oriented programming languages, the values for the stimulus parameters are explicitly loaded into a corresponding formatted message. The message is sent from the client object to the server object. Messages, therefore, are one way to implement requests.

If your programming environment can distinguish between different protocols for the same request, you can also make use of parametric polymorphism. *Parametric polymorphism* is the ability to use alternative protocols for the same request to trigger alternative processes for the same operation. To define alternative protocols, you should list the input parameters for each protocol separately in the stimulus column on a request description.

List the Response Parameters

You should list the data elements returned by a particular operation as the response parameters for the request that triggers it. The parameters in a request response represent the same thing as the upward data couple on the module connection between a parent module and a child module in a conventional structure chart. The parent module corresponds to the client object and the child module to the server object.

Request responses are the opposite of request stimuli. The response in a request description is the set of return parameters sent back when a triggered operation completes its processing or is used to unload an attribute value in a server object. These would be called the output parameters of a subroutine module in conventional design. Request responses are just a standardized way to describe the output interface of objects.

Like the stimulus parameters, response parameters are often attributes derived in the server objects but needed by and used in the client objects. Similarly, if your programming environment can distinguish different protocols for the same request and you wish to make use of parametric polymorphism, you should list the output parameters for each protocol separately in the response column on a request description.

Define Request Handling

In addition to the name, the stimulus, and the response, some developers also like to document the operational characteristics of a request when received by its operation. Such characteristics usually describe how the request will be handled under concurrent operation. The handling characteristics for each request can usually be documented as either synchronous, asynchronous, balking, or timed. Synchronous requests indicate that the system waits until the operation is ready. Asynchronous requests indicate that other objects process while waiting. Balking requests indicate no triggering if the operation is busy. Timed requests indicate that the system is to wait for a prescribed period.

Concurrency affects your design at the class level and at the object level. Request handling is the class level aspect of concurrency. Memory management is the object level aspect of concurrency. The level at which you are considering the concurrency of your objects will determine the point in your design at which you need to address the related issues.

Concurrency at the class level means level of control is required in the operations environment for your program. That is where request handling fits into your design. It defines the nature of the control that must be applied to your objects to manage an event-driven program. You will need to address these control issues as part of your request descriptions.

Concurrency at the instance level means that you will need to design constructor operations to allocate memory, destructor operations to release it, and handle attributes to track which instances are being used. You will need to address these design issues as part of your operation and attribute descriptions.

CHAPTER REVIEW

Design at the Class Layer

How do you determine classes? As the common parent objects on your inheritance diagram (the abstract classes) for the other objects (the concrete classes) in your domain.

How do you define classes? In terms of the inheritance and collaboration relationships to one another, and in terms of the objects which contain their operations and attributes.

How do you determine objects? By listing the specific person, place, thing, or event associated with each class.

How do you define objects? By identifying the operations and attributes that meet the business needs for the part of your system represented by each particular object.

How do you determine requests? By examining the interface requirements of an object, that is, the parameters needed to trigger its public operations.

How do you define requests? As a named request associated with a particular operation, and by listing its required input and output parameters.

14

Design at the Object Layer

14.1 IMPLEMENTING INDIVIDUAL OBJECTS

The Implementation Model

The bottom layer of object engineering is concerned with the design of the implementation model. This is the part of an object-oriented design that is most directly related to programming—the design of your individual objects. It provides the outline for your program's source code. However, the power of an object-oriented program is derived from the higher layers of design which precede it. The domain provides the framework which facilitates polymorphism in your program. The classes provide the framework by which you can reuse portions of a domain in many programs.

You may design an object as an embedded system, or you may design it as detailed and specific object operation descriptions and attribute descriptions. An embedded system would be designed in the same way as any system in your domain—using the object-engineering approach. As shown in Figure 14-1, the design of an object as an entire embedded system results in the recursive use of object engineering. This is one of the benefits of object engineering as a model-based approach. Its life cycle can be applied recursively more easily than those of conventional life cycles.

At some point however, you will need to design lower-level objects in your domain. The steps that we suggest for designing objects outline the activities that you are likely to perform, although the details will certainly vary from project to project. The steps involved are called *object design* and the model developed is called the *implementation model*.

260 OBJECT ENGINEERING

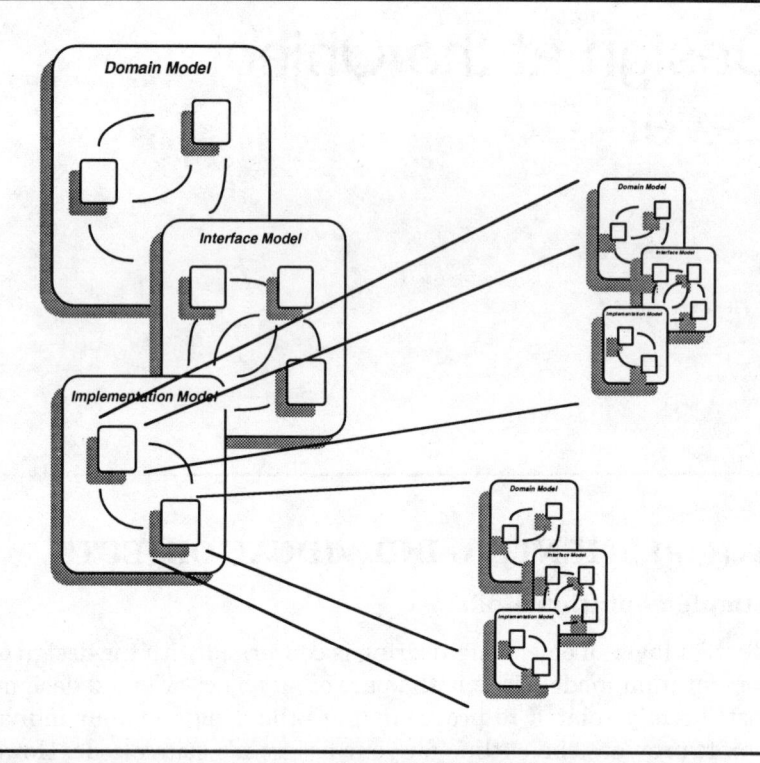

Figure 14-1. Embedded object-oriented design.

As shown in Figure 14-2, the implementation models consist of a set of operation descriptions and attribute descriptions for each object in your design.

Objects include both operations and attributes, so the implementation model must address both operation design and attribute design. Just like a process description in a conventional design, the implementation model contains descriptions of the processing logic for the individual operations in your objects. Like a data description in a conventional design, the implementation model may contain descriptions of the data structures of their attributes.

The operations represent the process requirements of your system, but organized in an object-oriented way. An operation description can take many forms, depending on the complexity of the process that you need to represent. It can be expressed as an entirely separate object-oriented design, as a conventional state-transition diagram, as a conventional data-flow diagram, or just as a text description of the process it represents.

The attributes represent the data requirements of your system. Like the description of an operation, the description of an attribute can also take many forms depending on the complexity of the data that you need to represent. An attribute description can be expressed as an entirely separate object-oriented design, as a conventional entity-relationship diagram, as a conventional data-structure diagram, or just as a text description of the data element it represents.

Although operations and attributes individually resemble processes and data, there is still a significant benefit to packaging them as objects. The structure of a domain model provides you with significant flexibility. It enables you to more easily develop prototypes and pilot programs from the classes in an existing domain. Similarly, the interface model enables you to reuse objects to develop entirely new systems using whole pieces of existing objects. The implementation model then provides the internal design for each object, which makes this possible.

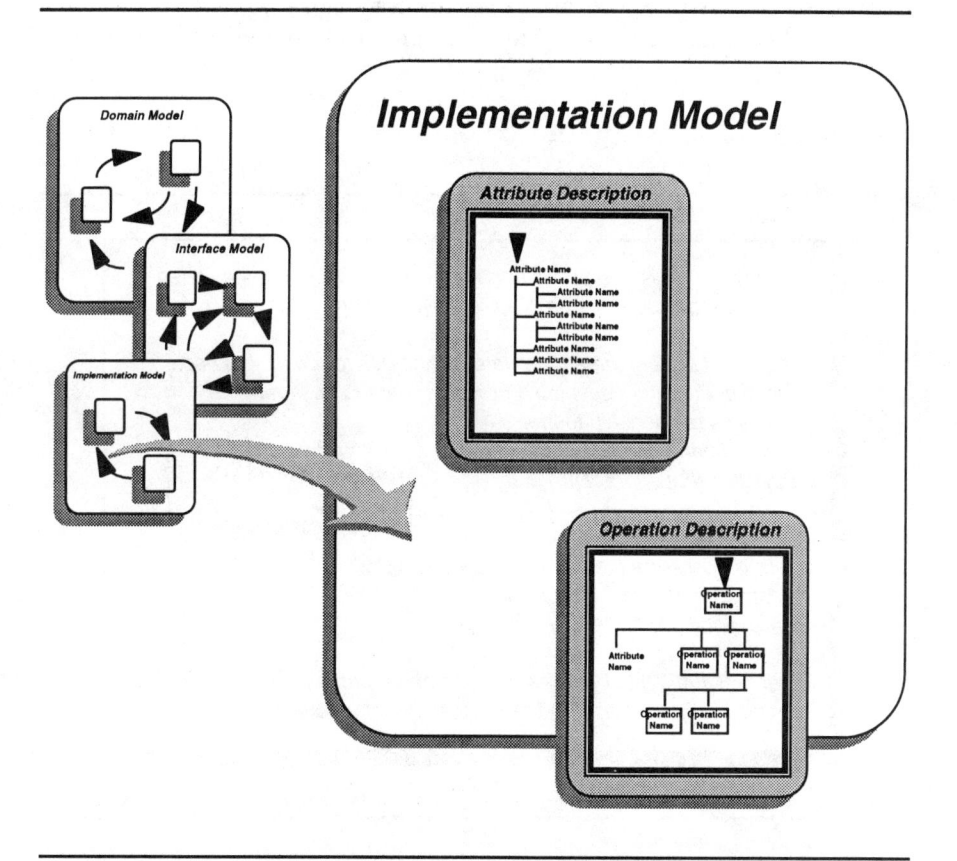

Figure 14-2. Working at the object layer.

14.2 THE OPERATION DESCRIPTIONS

14.2.1 How Do You Design Operations?

Examine Process Requirements

Designing the internal workings of each operation in an object is a relatively easy process because of all of the organization you have already designed around it. Each operation is a single processing requirement. At this point, simply use the same techniques that you would have used in a process-driven design. Your operations are just individual process-intensive applications. Just like in conventional process-driven design, you need to consider the complexity of each operation in order to select the appropriate process-driven technique to design it.

The design of an operation is called an *operation description*. We suggest steps to develop an operation description in Table 14-1 as an outline for developing a small process-driven design. Just like any other process-driven design, you will use different techniques depending on the complexity of each operation. Some operations may be sufficiently complex to be further encapsulated within other objects. These would warrant their own complete embedded life-cycle development. Other operations may be

Table 14-1. Steps to design operations.

Step 3.3.1.1 List the public operations which will not be designed later as separate systems in a recursive design.

Step 3.3.1.2 Use the appropriate techniques for designing each public operation to develop a process-oriented design which shows its relationship to the private operations and the attributes that support it.

Step 3.3.1.3 Transcribe each such process-oriented design for an operation into a structural representation.

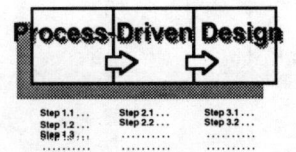

Step 3.3.1.4 Write brief descriptions of the processing logic for each private operation on the process structure chart.

designed as part of the object in which they reside using either state-transition diagrams or data-flow diagrams.

Operation descriptions are the designs of the individual processes in an object-oriented design. In some cases, an operation in an object may be an entirely separate but encapsulated object. There is no need to develop a design for such an operation, since the encapsulated object will satisfy that process requirement in its own internal design. Sometimes, an encapsulated object may even represent an entire nested design of another system.

Most operations within an object, however, will not be embedded systems and will require specific operation designs as part of your domain. You need to select and use an appropriate process-driven technique to design each public operation that belongs to your domain. The private operations, however, only need brief text descriptions. They will all be subordinate to some public operation in the same object.

Design Public Operations

The majority of the operations in your design will not be sufficiently complex to be treated as embedded systems within your design. Therefore they must have their own operation designs as part of your system. Although you may use a variety of diagram types to derive the design of any one particular public operation, you should eventually represent it using a process-structure chart as shown in Figure 14-3.

You will usually need to develop a small conventional process-driven design to describe each public operation in each object in your domain. The complexity of the design that you develop for an operation depends on the complexity of the operation—public operations are more complex than private operations.

Public operations are those that serve as entry points into an object for requests from other objects. *Private operations* are those that can only be used within an object. They support public operations or other private operations. Therefore, you should focus your attention on the designs for the public operations and the designs of the private ones will fall into place.

The design of a public operation involves the design of its processing logic, just like in a structured-design approach. This can take on a simple form such as a data-flow diagram, or it can be as complex as needed to accomplish its required function. Since object-oriented designs can be used to model multiple threads of control (concurrent objects), an operation design often takes the form of a state-transition diagram.

The management of multiple threads of control usually requires a dynamic model of processing logic. Static models show the interaction between modules without differentiating between the various states they may assume during operation. Data-flow diagrams and structure charts are static models of operation. Dynamic models, on the other hand, consider the transition of a module through various states. State-transition diagrams are dynamic models of operation.

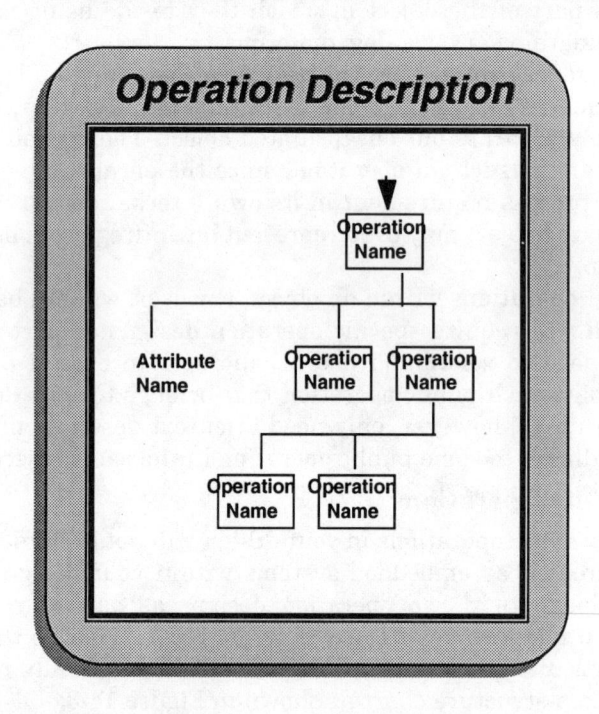

Figure 14-3. An operation description.

The type of model that you should use will depend on the complexity of your requirements. You can design the operations of your objects using state-transition diagrams, data-flow diagrams, or some other mechanism. Which model you use depends on the same criteria that you would have applied in a conventional design. The design of each operation at this point is the same as if you were using process-driven techniques to develop any scientific or process-intensive application.

Describe Private Operations

Some operations are so small that a simple text definition of its process operation is all that is required. This is usually the case for private operations. If an operation is self-contained (such as a lowest-level private operation in the design of a public one), then a text definition of its design will be sufficient. If a simple definition of an operation meets your needs, that is what you should develop as your operation descriptions.

In conventional design, this type of textual description of an elemental operation is called a *minispec*. It is just a single page English language or process-design language (PDL) statement of the required processing logic. In object-oriented design, it is typical to use minispec operation descriptions to design small self-contained object-oriented programs developed to run on desktop computers.

14.2. When Do You Use State-Transition Diagrams?
Complex Public Operations

State-transition diagrams are discussed by almost every author of object-oriented related material. This can be misleading since not every operation in every object will require state-transition diagrams. Historically, object-oriented design has usually been applied to the development of real-time distributed systems, so it was the nature of the requirement in those domains which called for state-transition diagrams. You should evaluate whether each public operation in your design requires a state-transition diagram as its design or whether some other diagram is more appropriate.

State-transition diagrams are appropriate for the design of some of the more complex public operations in your objects. Although these operations may be relatively complex, this does not mean that their designs are difficult to develop. It just means that you should use a design technique that is robust enough to adequately model its complexity. The transitions between the various states modeled on the state transition diagram for a public operation often become its subordinate private operations.

The state of an object is defined as a unique set of values for its attributes. In theory, there can be an astronomical number of unique states for any one object (computed as a *combinatorial value*) based on the number of attributes and the range of values they may take. In practice, however, program developers are usually only concerned with only a few very specific states. A state-transition diagram allows you to model the transition between those specific states.

Object state-transition diagrams are very similar to state-transition diagrams for real-time systems in conventional design. You characterize your objects according to the several states that they can take in your particular situation, diagram the changes (transitions) from one state to another in state-transition diagrams, and then use these diagrams to derive the detailed process-operation design in terms of a structure chart.

The objective in using state-transition diagrams in object-oriented design is the same as in conventional process-driven design. State-transition diagrams allow you to identify the appropriate lower-level processes needed to support a major function that is state dependent. The lower-level processes become private operations. The major function is a public operation. The end result is a process-structure chart of each major function in your design and their lower-level processes.

14.2.3 When Do You Use Data-Flow Diagrams?

Simple Public Operations

You may choose to use data-flow diagrams to derive the inner workings of some of the public operations in your domain. At this level (the operation level), you are working with the process requirements for a relatively simple and small system. Process-driven techniques are usually appropriate in the design of these operations. They are really just small and well-contained process-intensive applications that lead you to the structural design of each operation.

If your operations are small and well-contained but more physical than functional, you may decide to develop process-structure charts (or maybe flow charts) directly without any data-flow diagrams. The complexity of the diagrams for your operation descriptions depends on what suits your needs at this level. This is just one way in which object-oriented design doesn't replace conventional design but enhances it.

14.3 THE ATTRIBUTE DESCRIPTIONS

14.3.1 How Do You Design Attributes?

Examine Data Requirements

Designing the internal structure of each attribute in an object is a relatively easy process because of all of the organization you have already designed around it. Each attribute is a single data requirement. At this point, you simply use the same techniques that you would have used in a data-driven design. Your attributes are individual data-intensive applications. Just like in conventional data-driven design, you need to consider the complexity of each attribute in order to select the appropriate data-driven technique to design it.

The design of an attribute is called an *attribute description*. Steps to develop an attribute description are suggested in Table 14-2 as an outline for developing a small data-driven design. Just like any other data-driven design, you will use different techniques depending on the complexity of each attribute. Some attributes may be sufficiently complex to be further encapsulated in another object. These would warrant their own complete embedded life-cycle development. Other attributes may be designed as part of the object in which they reside using either entity-relationship diagrams or data-structure charts.

In the same way that some operations will represent entire systems that need to be developed as embedded systems, some attributes may also represent large embedded data structures. You develop a large embedded attribute structure just like any other object-oriented design. You should use the layered approach to develop a domain model, an interface model, and an implementation model. Its development would mirror the

Table 14-2. Steps to design attributes.

> Step 3.3.2.1 List the public attributes that will not be designed as separate systems in a recursive design.
>
> Step 3.3.2.2 Use the appropriate techniques for designing each public attribute to develop a small data-oriented design for it that shows the other attributes to which it is related and the operations that support those relationships.
>
> Step 3.3.2.3 Transcribe each such data-oriented design for an attribute into a structural representation.
>
> Step 3.3.2.4 Write a brief description of the data definition for each attribute on the data structure chart.

development activities for your entire design, except that it is smaller and it has its own objects, operations, and attributes.

Most attributes in your design, however, will not be sufficiently complex to be treated as entirely embedded structures. Instead, they will require individual attribute designs. Compound public attributes may require individual data-driven designs in the same way that some operations require process-driven designs. Simple attributes that support other attributes and operations will only require brief text descriptions.

Design Public Attributes

The public attributes of your objects are the most likely candidates for those that will require designs of their own. In these cases, you will find that an attribute design is just a small and well-contained conventional data-driven design. The design technique that you use may involve several diagram types, such as the hierarchical data structure shown in Figure 14-4.

You will make use of the same techniques and the same diagrams used in information engineering. These may include entity-relationship diagrams and data-structure charts. As with operation design, you can usually concentrate on the design of your complex public attributes, and the private ones will most likely appear as supporting elements in those designs.

The design of a public attribute involves the design of the relationships among data elements. This can take on a simple form such as a data-structure chart, or it may require a more complex form such as entity-relationship diagrams. Data-structure charts are sufficient to document the attribute relationships inside a nonpersistent object, while entity-relationship diagrams are more appropriate to model the attributes inside a persistent object.

A *persistent object* is one in which the existence of its instances can extend beyond the life of the program in which it is created. An object-oriented database is the structure in which a persistent object would be stored. Object-oriented databases, like conventional databases, are best when accompanied by a set of access tools, called its *management system*. They provide the automated interface into the stored object structures, but you still have to design that structure.

As with programming languages, the nature of a particular management system will determine the precise use of the data diagrams that you develop, but the fundamental concepts are always the same. You develop the design of the public attributes in the persistent objects of your design in the same way as you would develop any conventional data-driven design for a business application in a database environment.

Attribute Description

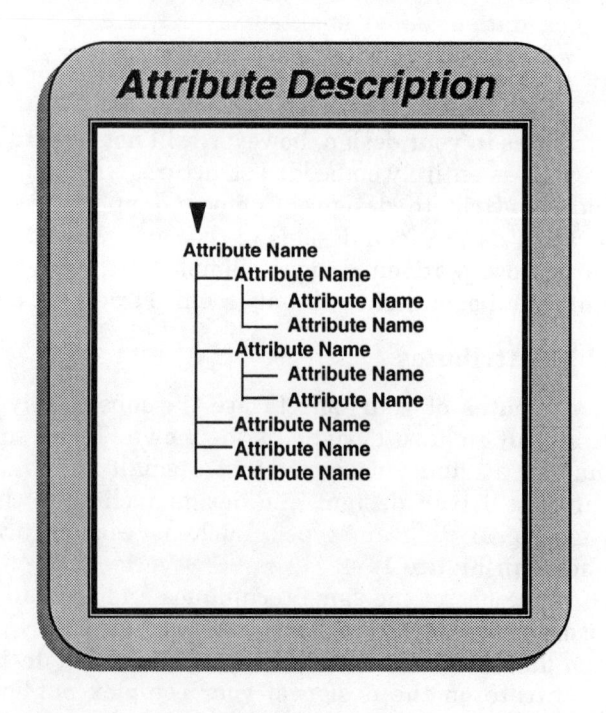

```
▼
Attribute Name
   ├── Attribute Name
   │      ├── Attribute Name
   │      └── Attribute Name
   ├── Attribute Name
   │      ├── Attribute Name
   │      └── Attribute Name
   ├── Attribute Name
   ├── Attribute Name
   └── Attribute Name
```

Figure 14-4. An attribute description.

Describe Private Attributes

The attributes in the objects of many systems are often functionally subordinate to the operations. These supporting attributes help to define the objects but are usually not meaningful alone. For such cases, a text definition of each attribute will be sufficient. This is certainly the case for the private attributes, and can often be the case for any public attributes that are not composed of other attributes. If a simple definition of an attribute meets your needs, that is what you should develop as your attribute descriptions.

In conventional design, this type of text description of an elemental attribute is called a *data definition*. It is just a single-line structured statement of the meaning of a data element. In object-oriented design, it is typical to simply provide attribute descriptions in the form of data definitions for small, self-contained programs developed to run on desktop computers.

14.3.2 When Do You Use Entity-Relationship Diagrams?

Complex Public Attributes

Entity-relationship diagrams are appropriate for the design of each public attribute that is composed of other lower-level attributes. In other words, complex data-oriented objects may require entity-relationship diagrams to help you to model a network of attributes connections in the same way that you would in any conventional data-intensive application.

You should develop entity-relationship diagrams for the public attributes in persistent objects. This is particularly warranted when you plan on implementing your design in conjunction with a database. Just like in conventional design, the entity-relationship diagram will help you to establish an appropriate storage structure. The storage structure for an object-oriented design is called an *object base*. If you plan on using a commercial management system to maintain a base of objects, you should develop entity-relationship diagrams for all the public attributes in your design.

A management system to maintain a base of objects is said to be *passive* if it stores only the attributes of objects and *active* when it stores both the attributes and the operations. A passive object manager is a good platform as you transform your existing database applications into object-oriented representations. However, you may then later make another conversion to an active one. An active object manager provides you with a complete object-oriented storage and retrieval mechanism.

Entity-relationship diagrams allow you to identify the appropriate attribute relationships needed to support each major data element in a conventional database. The same is true of object bases. The major elements are the central entities on the diagram and are your public attributes. The lower-level elements are the supporting entities and become your private attributes. The end result is a data-structure chart of the data elements in your design. It shows the structural relationships among all attributes in your objects.

14.3.3 When Do You Use Normalized Data Diagrams?

Simple Public Attributes

You will most often choose to use some type of simplified data-structure representation to model the inner workings of the public attributes in your domain. At this level (the attribute level), you are working with the data requirements for a relatively simple and small system. Data-driven techniques are usually appropriate in the design of these attributes (if they require any design at all). They are really just small and well-contained data-intensive applications that lead you to the structural design of each attribute.

There are a variety of simple data structure representations that may be appropriate for your design. One of the more common representations is a normalized data-structure chart. It is just a more direct way to display the simple structural composition of small but compound attributes. This is just one way in which object-oriented design doesn't replace conventional design but enhances it.

CHAPTER REVIEW

Design at the Object Layer

How do you design operations? As a process-driven design for each major public operation, which is composed of its private operations and of the attributes needed to support it.

When do you use state-transition diagrams? To design the operations of an object that represents a complex process, usually implemented in a concurrent manner.

When do you use data-flow diagrams? To design public operations in an object that represent rather simple processes of transforming attributes or making calculations based on the values of some attributes.

How do you design attributes? As a data-driven design for each major public attribute, which is composed of its private attributes and of the operations needed to support it.

When do you use entity-relationship diagrams? To design the attributes of an object that represent a complex structure, usually implemented in a persistent object base.

When do you use normalized data diagrams? To design public attributes in an object which represent rather simple storage requirements in a conventional database.

15

Designing Object Operations

15.1 THE OPERATIONS IN AN OBJECT

Structured Design of Operations

You design an operation as a small process-intensive and self-contained application. An object-oriented design has a framework that organizes all of the operations in your design. The steps that you may have gone through up to this point will have identified and allocated the process requirements of your system in an object-oriented manner. Now you need to concentrate on the individual design of those process requirements. They are the operations that an object is able to accomplish.

Each part of the object-engineering model provides one aspect of a well-controlled process-driven design. The domain model provides an object-oriented structure within which you can represent the process requirements of your system, the interface model then defines how those process requirements are specifically distributed within that structure, and finally, the implementation model defines the packages of operations that satisfy those process requirements. The design of each individual operation within the implementation model is now a rather straightforward and simple exercise in conventional design.

You can often design each public operation in your objects by applying the techniques of structured design. As shown in Figure 15-1, each operation is a part of a larger design (addressed by your domain), which is organized in an object-oriented manner. Objects have well-defined interfaces and separately maintained internal designs. The

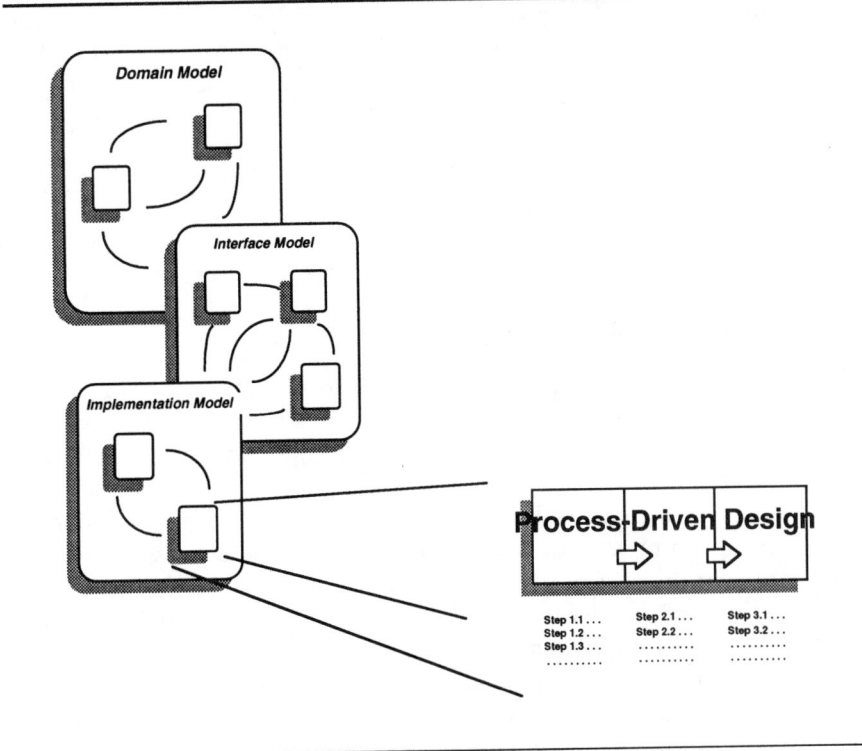

Figure 15-1. Embedded operation design.

internal design for each object consists of the design of its public operations and public attributes. The operations are just individual processing requirements.

Although the design of operations is addressed separately from the design of attributes, they are related to one another. As you apply process-driven design techniques to the design of an operation, you will also use, refer to, and otherwise modify your lists of attributes in the same objects. Attributes support operations, so the design of each operation must also consider its interaction with the attributes of the same object. This is consistent with process-driven design, which leads you to a design that eventually considers both processes and data, even though it approaches that result from the perspective of the process requirements.

Structured design is a process-driven approach for the design of a system. It can be applied to the design of either hardware or software systems, but usually addresses software systems. As a process-driven approach, structured design drives the transformation of the requirements for a system from the perspective of its process requirements. This usually takes the form of a transformation through a functional design phase called the *essential model*, to a physical design phase called the *environmental model*, and finally to a program design phase called the *implementation model*. The design of each major operation in an object follows a similar progression.

15.2 PROCESS-DRIVEN DESIGN

15.2.1 When Do You Use Process-Driven Design?

Object Operations Are Processes

A process is called an *operation* in the object-oriented world. This is significant if you already understand how to use process decomposition to design software. Object-oriented design techniques seem very different from conventional techniques but they rely on many of the same concepts. An object is composed of operations and attributes, so its design partially relies on process decomposition to transform operation requirements into a working computer program.

If you think of an operation in an object as a process that that object can perform, then you will start to see how process decomposition applies to object-oriented design. You used the concept of process decomposition to fully identify all object operations as functions in a domain and to group them within the domain's physical architecture. It's now time to implement them as specific process designs.

The techniques used to design objects reflect the combined use of operations and attributes, not merely the sum of operation design and attribute design. However, you will find that the concept of process decomposition helps you to visualize an object operation and what it represents. You implement object operations using all the same concepts and procedures of process-driven design. An operation is a process requirement.

Implementing object operations is quite similar in concept to the design of a process-driven design and sometimes quite similar in practice. In object-oriented design, you define some object operations as subroutines capable of responding to specific request protocols. In some cases, subroutines become additional independent objects and are portrayed in collaboration diagrams. In other cases, however, they remain as the public operations of an object and structure charts might be used to represent their design.

Operations represent half of the nature of an object (the other half being attributes). You can think of an *operation* as the object-oriented world's name for a process. Therefore, if you are accustomed to manipulating processes and representing them in data-flow diagrams and structure charts, then you are already halfway to understanding the concepts of operation design.

Designing the Major Operations

Designing the operations in an object is a relatively easy process in object engineering. You have already organized the many requirements in your domain into logically related packages of operations and attributes called *objects*. Each public operation in an object is a single major processing requirement. You now can use the same techniques that you would have used in a process-driven design to complete its design as a small individual process-intensive application.

As shown in Figure 15-2, the design of the operations in your domain follows a process-driven approach. Therefore, you should expect to use the same principles, techniques, and diagrams that you would have used under a structured-design life cycle. The only difference is that you can eliminate the first phase of identifying your requirements (the lists of operations in your object descriptions are your known process requirements) and you can move more quickly through the remaining phases since each public operation is so much smaller than an entire conventional processing system.

Each public operation serves as an entry point into an object for requests from other objects. They are, therefore, the focus of your attention as you design the internal logic of your objects. The design of a public operation involves the design of its processing logic, just like in a structured-design approach. This may involve transforming the operations of an object into data-flow diagrams, state-transition diagrams, or process-structure charts.

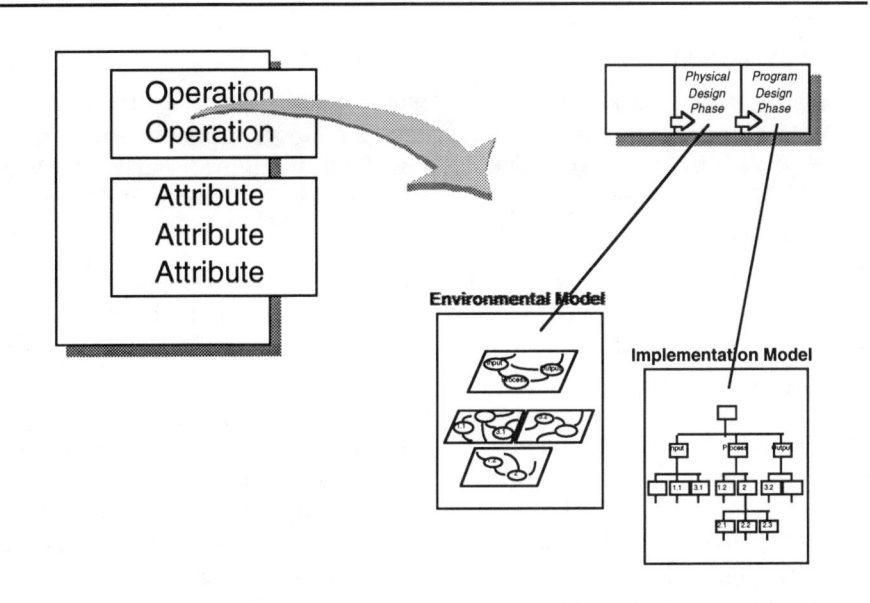

Figure 15-2. A process-driven design cycle.

The criteria for developing a good design for an object operation is the same as for any process-intensive application. It requires the use of process-driven design techniques. In designing the operations in your objects, you should:

- Minimize the coupling between operations in different objects. If you have too many parameters in your request protocols (more than 5) or if you have parameters that are just passed along in subsequent requests (these would be called *tramp data*), then you should consider further encapsulating some of the operations in that object into new server objects, which can be triggered from within the original client.

- Maximize the cohesion between the operations in a single object. Examine the public operations in your objects to ensure that they perform related functions and that they will likely make use of many of the same lower-level private operations—otherwise, consider separating the operations into other objects.

- Maximize the cohesion between the objects in an inheritance hierarchy. Examine the pattern of operations inherited from each abstract class to ensure that most of the operations are inherited by most of the same subclasses—otherwise, consider separating the operations into objects of separate abstract classes.

- Streamline the definition of each operation. It should carry out one and only one function as its role in satisfying the requirements of the object in which it resides—otherwise, you should create new operations, one for each purpose that the object serves.

- Apply size constraints to the design units. Keep the size of each object understandable (7 operations per object, plus or minus 2, is a good size) so that the design will be straightforward, thereby increasing the probability that it can be easily identified for reuse at a later time.

- Apply size constraints to the components of your design. Keep the size of your diagrams readable (use class categories to divide a large inheritance hierarchy and use nested class assemblies to divide a large collaboration hierarchy).

The criteria in the list above should seem familiar to you. These are the same principles you would have applied in the use of structured design. So even though the manner in which you develop a design may have changed, the principles of a good design remain the same. If you have learned to develop good process-driven designs in the past, then you can learn to apply that knowledge to the design of the operations in an object-oriented design now.

15.2.2 How Do You Program the Design?

Object-Oriented Programming Languages

The objective of object-oriented design, of course, is to develop an object-oriented program. It is important, therefore, to remember that you will eventually need to convert your design into a computer program. There are source languages designed particularly for this purpose. You program your design using one of these languages just as you would using any other programming language, except that there are additional language constructs to implement the object-oriented concepts.

Individual languages will vary in how they implement the concepts of an object-oriented design but they should all include some type of mechanism to implement each concept or they are not fully object-oriented languages. These concepts are classes, inheritance, collaboration, visibility, persistence, and concurrency. Primarily, each object class is implemented like a program in a conventional design, and each operation in that object is implemented like a subroutine of that program. However, some classes are abstract and used only for inheritance, while others are concrete and can have instances used in collaborations at runtime.

The object classes in a programming language are usually declared in the same manner as a program in a third-generation language—that is, the name of the class is usually specified in a header statement followed by the source-code statements which define the class. The header usually includes the information that you have documented in your class descriptions. The source code statements usually include the information from your operation descriptions.

The inheritance relationships among classes are usually declared as part of the header declaration of a class along with its name. This is usually accomplished by referring to the names of its *superclasses*, which are pointers up the inheritance hierarchy. Sometimes the type of the object associated with a class is also declared as part of the class header, just like a data type in conventional language.

The collaboration relationships among concrete classes may or may not be explicitly declared at the beginning of the body of the source-code statements for a class. Often, collaboration is just a call to an operation like a conventional subroutine call, or a reference to an attribute in another object, and may only be discernable by inspecting the source code for each operation. Similarly, a particular language may or may not use explicit requests to trigger operations in a collaboration. It all depends on how the language that you are using implements these features.

In an object-oriented programming language, the majority of the statements that will be new to conventionally trained programmers will be those which involve the structure of your object-oriented design (the upper layers of your design). Eventually, however, you will program the internal designs of the operations in your objects in language form.

You will still write the source-code statements for each operation in some type of programming language.

Application Development Environments

In addition to object-oriented programming languages, object-oriented application development environments on desktop computer platforms are becoming more widely available. An application-development environment is a set of interrelated tools, usually using a graphical-user interface (GUI) mechanism, which allows a programmer to implement the components of an object-oriented design without entirely resorting to the written statements of a programming language.

Individual-development environments will vary in how they implement the specific concepts of an object-oriented design, however, like an object-oriented programming language, they should all include a mechanism for each concept of an object-oriented design. You define the classes, inheritance, collaboration, visibility, persistence, and concurrency from your design in some manner by menu and pointer selections on your video screen.

In an object-oriented application development environment, the majority of the GUI input of your design will involve encoding its structure (the upper layers of your design). Eventually, however, you usually program the internal designs of your objects (the implementation model) in language form. Thus, the structure of your design can be more readily implemented than with a programming language, but you often still have to write the source-code statements for each operation in some type of embedded programming language.

Using the Implementation Model

Programming your design in either an object-oriented programming language or using an application-development environment will be no different from programming a design using a conventional language. You will need to represent the design for your process operations and/or the schema for your data attributes directly from your implementation model into the program statements of a programming language.

You usually declare the individual operations and attributes of the object associated with each class within the body of the class to which it belongs (after its declaration). Each operation and each attribute is declared similar to the class itself by a header statement (using its name) followed by the source-code statements, which implement its internal design. The complete definition of an operation or an attribute usually also includes an indication of its visibility, its type, and its persistence.

You usually indicate the visibility of each operation or attribute by listing the public members followed by the private members or by declaring each as either public or private as part of its declaration. Similarly, you usually declare the type of an operation and/or an attribute as part of its header statement. You define the persistence of each object in a manner similar to declaring the extent of a variable as static or dynamic in conventional programming languages. It may also be necessary to design specific operations and attributes to manage runtime memory.

You manage the concurrency of each object through the use of its instance handles. This may also involve resolving request contention for the same object instance. The burden may fall on the designer to provide for this logic as part of each object. Similarly, most object-oriented programming languages require that you define explicit operations in each object to allocate and release runtime space for the attributes of each instance of an object (called *constructors* and *destructors*, respectively).

Often, however, you will not be designing an object-oriented program from the ground up. One of the chief benefits of object-oriented design is the manner in which you can reuse existing objects as building blocks for new systems. Therefore, many components of the object-oriented model will already exist in some form when you start your design. You will examine them and select those which seem to meet some of your needs. Your design activities, therefore, will often revolve around examining parts of interface models and domain models, rather than deriving them from scratch.

Using the Interface Model

One way in which you can reuse the objects in an existing domain is through the use of the interface model. Classes of objects are cataloged in the interface model as part of your domain. If you find a set of existing classes that meets your needs, you might either reuse the objects of those classes in their entirety or add your own new objects by creating additional concrete classes that can inherit from some of the existing abstract classes in that domain. This type of reuse dramatically reduces your design effort. This effect is usually called *extensibility*.

The interface model is the key to making use of the extensibility of an object-oriented design. The interface model consists of the descriptions of existing objects in terms of their class relationships and the requests to which they can respond. These classes, and the objects that they represent, can be used as the basis for constructing additional lower-level tiers of the inheritance hierarchy in a domain. Once declared as part of your new inheritance hierarchy, the operations and attributes already designed as part of the abstract classes in the existing inheritance hierarchy can be triggered or accessed by a simple request.

Often, highly reusable branches of the classes in a domain are distributed as source libraries and reusable-link libraries by third parties. It is common in an object-oriented environment to obtain such libraries as the basis for developing new designs that reuse existing high-level abstract classes or low-level concrete classes. Source libraries contain abstract classes of common source code which can be included in (inherited by) your program. Link libraries contain concrete classes of precompiled executable modules that can be called (as collaborations) from within your program. The libraries represent highly reusable portions of an existing domain.

Using the Domain Model

Another way in which you can reuse the objects in an existing domain is through the use of the domain model. The inheritance hierarchy of the domain model provides the framework by which you can use any one particular operation or attribute in many objects. Furthermore, you can define different operations (or different attributes) with the same name in several different objects, and let them be resolved at runtime based on their context, that is, based on the location of the objects in the domain model. This is called *polymorphism*.

Polymorphism enables you to refer to an identically named operation or attribute from within any object without specifying which one should be used. The compiler (if you are using a programming language) or the interpreter (if you are using an online programming environment) will find and use the operation or attribute that is most appropriate to the context in which it is needed. It does that by searching up the inheritance hierarchy from the object in which the reference is made.

In this manner, the operations and attributes within abstract classes can be reused by different concrete classes at runtime. Each collection of collaborating concrete classes represents one system in your domain. These concrete classes can inherit operations and attributes from the abstract classes to which they are connected in the inheritance hierarchy. The objects associated with the abstract classes of your domain can be reused by any or all of your systems.

15.3 PROCESS-DRIVEN TECHNIQUES

15.3.1 How Do You Identify Process Requirements?

The Essential Model

The first goal of conventional process-driven design is to identify the process requirements. You do this by listing the major process functions of your program and then decomposing those process functions hierarchically. This represents the functional design of your program. The concepts are the same whether you are building an essential model using structured design or if you are applying those same techniques to the design of a major operation in an object using object engineering.

Although you will never need to develop an essential model as part of your operation description, it is still useful to examine the concepts involved in developing one in order to understand how to develop the internal designs for each operation. You will develop the design of each operation in the same way that you would in a conventional process-driven approach from the point of a completed essential model.

In object engineering, operation design is the same as developing a conventional design. An operation is a process. Therefore, in designing an operation, you should consider how you would design a small process-oriented program using conventional techniques. Designing processes conventionally, you would usually start with an essential model. It is a functional representation of system requirements using data-flow diagrams.

You identify additional lower-level object operations in the same way that you identify process requirements in an essential model (also called *new logical model*). You decompose object operations to further define their function. In doing so, you identify more of the private operations of an object (and more of the data attributes that they support). However, rather than starting with data-flow diagrams, your initial object-oriented model of process functions is just the lists of operations in your object descriptions. It serves as the essential model of a process-driven design.

In the earlier versions of structured design, you would determine the major process functions based on the functions of preexisting programs, systems, and manual procedures. You would prepare a series of leveled sets of data-flow diagrams using process decomposition. The final form of these diagrams is called the *new logical model*. It represents the major process functions for your system.

In the later versions of structured design, you would determine the major functions by looking at each input and/or output requirement and then listing the respective process required to support it. Once you determine these requirements, you decompose them to fully define these major functions in the essential model.

In an object-oriented design, the object descriptions from your domain model replace the need to develop an essential model of functions. The functions of an object are already defined in terms of the list of operations of which they are comprised, so there is no need to perform the first phase of a process-driven design. However, your operation design progresses in the same manner from this point further. It's just a smaller and more well-contained design.

15.3.2 How Do You Allocate Process Requirements?

The Environmental Model

The second goal of conventional process-driven design is to allocate the process requirements to process groups. In conventional design, you do this by revising the functional design represented in the data-flow diagrams, which represents the physical design of your functions. In the design of an object operation, you follow the same procedure of allocating your known lower-level process operations into physical groups.

In the design of your operations, you pick up the conventional design approach at this point in the process-driven model. Your process requirements are the known operations listed in your object descriptions. This replaces the need for an essential model. You now proceed, however, with the development of a small environmental model in the same way that you would under any structured design approach. It will represent the initial physical allocation of the private operations which are needed to support each public one.

The concept of allocating operations in object-oriented design is similar to allocating process requirements in process-driven design. You allocate process requirements in a process-driven design by the steps listed in Table 15-1. These steps convey the concept of allocating a program's operation into process groups. In structured design, this is called the *environmental model*. In object engineering, the processes are the operations listed in the object descriptions of your interface model.

The environmental model of structured design is the definition of the requirements of your system in a physical form. In object engineering, you design the physical structure of the operations in an object in the same way. You identify the process requirements of your objects in terms of their operations, and then allocate those operations into a physical structure in preparation for implementation.

The design of the structure of your object operations corresponds to the second phase of a process-driven design. This involves the develop-

Table 15-1. An environmental model.

Step 3.3.1.2.1 Examine the physical environment to determine the nature of the programming language, the operating system, the peripheral devices, any networking, and any other hardware or software constraints.

Step 3.3.1.2.2 Develop data-flow diagrams or state-transition diagrams to reflect groups of operations and the attributes which support them, based on the physical environment, on known organizational preferences, on known performance criteria, and on known security requirements.

Step 3.3.1.2.3 Identify additional operations and attributes needed to perform the custodial functions to support these groups.

Step 3.3.1.2.4 Further decompose these restructured operations into additional private operations and attributes to fully define the restructured requirements.

ment of physical data-flow diagrams or state-transition diagrams as a physical model of each public operation and the attributes that support them. You allocate the private operations below the public operations. The public operations will be triggered from outside the object. The private operations will be used by (called by) the public ones.

Data-Flow Diagrams

The allocation of processes is an exercise in reorganization. In a conventional design, you would use the leveled set of data-flow diagrams of your essential model to prepare another leveled set of data-flow diagrams. In object-oriented design, you use your list of operations. In both cases, you use process decomposition principles to better organize the process requirements that you just identified.

You move operations into new groups, add new operations, and combine others. New groups might be needed for operations that pass information back and forth. New operations might be needed to define new functions that are related to how data is stored in, or processed for, the new groups. Other operations may be combined if they perform very similar functions. These things would be discovered during operation decomposition.

You determine the new groups of processes based on common characteristics or connectivity. If you can identify several process bubbles that all have data flows connected to a single other process, then you often create a new group for these processes. This is especially true when the other process to which they are all connected represents some particular physical module (such as a database, a user screen, or another program).

You can regroup processes both within a single level as well as from several different levels. When you find several processes connected to a particular process, they are often not on the same diagram or even close to one another. Their commonalty is not readily apparent. As a result, a seemingly minor regrouping will often result in a significant change to the structure of your data-flow diagrams.

The lower-level processes that are subordinate to the processes you group together will remain subordinate and be carried along into the new group. Many of the lower-level data-flow diagrams in the leveled set will not change in content, just in location within the leveled set. However, you will usually have to reconnect the data flows connected to process bubbles on these lower-level diagrams.

In conventional process-driven design, this reorganization process simply results in another version of your data-flow diagrams. You have expanded, rearranged, and further decomposed your processes into a more robust and better organized set of requirements. Your original essential model has been transformed into an environmental model. The same holds true in the design of the public operations for a particular object in object-oriented design.

In object-oriented design, the same kind of reorganization of the process requirements takes place within the public operations of an object. The public operations are those that can be triggered by requests from other objects. The private operations are those which implement the required behavior of the public ones. The public operations can be expanded, rearranged, and further decomposed into a more robust set of private operations without affecting the interface characteristics of the object to which they belong.

State-Transition Diagrams

Sometimes, the processing requirements of a particular public operation are sufficiently complex to require the use of state-transition diagrams. State-transition diagrams are dynamic versions of data-flow diagrams. By *dynamic*, we mean that they focus on the several changes of the state of one or more attributes rather than the simple movement of a value from one attribute to another. Although they really provide more of a combined data-driven and process-driven perspective to design, state-transition diagrams are usually associated with the process-driven design of real-time systems.

Real-time systems require closer attention to the changes in the state of their data because of the communication constraints associated with the distributed environments that characterize them. Distributed environments are well suited to the client/server model of object-oriented design, so it stands to reason that state-transition diagrams have been widely used as one of the first mechanisms to design the operations in objects.

In conventional design, a state-transition diagram is a representation of the process logic required to maintain a specific set of changes to a specific set of data entities. In object-oriented design, a state-transition diagram is used in the same way. It represents the operation logic required to maintain a set of changes to a specific set of attributes—those that belong to a particular object. The changes are the transitions from one state to another.

State-transition diagrams are also called *state networks* (state nets) or *finite state machines*. They are usually modeled as a set of states connected by the transitions that are experienced to go from one state to another. They may also be drawn to show exceptions and/or conditions that differentiate the probability of a transition to change from or to one of the several states to which it may be connected as input or output, respectively.

States are recognized sets of attribute values or, sometimes, the finite operations of an object. A state, however, is most often an abstract condition (set of particular values) for a compound set of attributes. The set of attributes is either all those of a particular object or some subset thereof. Each state characterizes one particular condition of the object. Each transition represents a particular public operation required of that object.

Transitions are changes from one state to another. In conventional design, transitions are represented as condition/action pairs. Each transition is defined by a particular condition that causes the transition, and a particular action that takes place to accomplish the transition. The condition is also called a *trigger*. It represents the request required to cause a state change. The action represents the public operation required to change the state.

In conventional process-driven design, the action part of a transition on a state-transition diagram becomes a lower-level process module called by one of the major process modules in your design. The major process modules are those in the data-flow diagram of your essential model (your public operations). You start with a functional set of leveled data-flow diagrams and then develop state-transition diagrams for those processes on the diagrams that have complex state changes. This allocates those requirements into a more physical form called the *environmental model*.

In object-oriented design, the actions in the transitions become the private operations, which support the public ones (from your original object descriptions). Therefore, state-transition diagrams are just another way of discovering private operations. They are a specific form of process decomposition used to allocate process requirements into a physical design, the same as you would in a conventional process-driven design. A state-transition diagram is another way to represent the environmental model of your operations.

15.3.3 How Do You Implement Process Requirements?

The Implementation Model

The third goal of conventional process-driven design is to restructure the design again so as to best implement your process requirements on a particular platform. You do this by restructuring the process requirements, which are represented in the physical data-flow diagrams of the environmental model. This represents your program design. In the design of an object operation, you follow the same procedure of developing structure charts from your environmental model.

In the design of your operations, you continue to use a conventional design approach to allocate your private operations within (below) the public ones. You now proceed to develop a small conventional implementation model for each public operation from its corresponding environmental model. The design process, however, is much more informal than it would have been under a conventional process-driven approach due to the much smaller size of each individual operation.

The concept of implementing operations in object-oriented design is similar to implementing process requirements in process-driven design.

You implement process requirements in a process-driven design by following the steps listed in Table 15-2. In structured design, this is also called the *implementation model*.

The implementation model of structured design is the restructuring of the requirements of your system in its final physical form as a program module. In object engineering, you design the program structure of the operations in an object in the same way. You allocate the process requirements of your objects into a physical structure in your environmental model and then implement those operations by restructuring them for processing efficiency.

The design of your object operations as a program module corresponds to the third phase of a process-driven design. This involves the development of process-structure charts for each public operation in an object. The private operations are all nested below one or more of the public operations. You reorganize some of them in order to improve efficiencies based on similarities in program function. For example, you may group all input modules together on one branch of the structure chart.

Table 15-2. An implementation model.

Step 3.3.1.3.1 Partition the data-flow diagrams or state-transition diagrams into a set of separate software units (such as jobs, programs, etc.).

Step 3.3.1.3.2 Further partition the data-flow diagrams (or develop them from the state-transition diagrams) within each separate unit by separating transaction groups and transform groups from the other remaining processes.

Step 3.3.1.3.3 Create a structure chart from the data-flow diagrams for each separate unit showing its major business operations, transaction groups, and transform groups.

Step 3.3.1.3.4 Identify more private operations to perform the specific functions needed to support these new groups according to the nature of the language in which the design will be programmed.

Step 3.3.1.3.5 Further decompose any new or restructured private operations to fully define the restructured process requirements.

The purpose of developing the implementation model is to create new groups of processes more suitable for programming. Two specific techniques to determine these new groups are transaction analysis and transform analysis. *Transaction analysis* is a technique to design new groups for handling multiple parallel data flows. *Transform analysis* is a technique to design new groups for handling a transformation of several input flows into several output flows at one location.

In transaction analysis, you look for transaction centers. A *transaction center* is a set of parallel processes that are each connected to the same two input and output processes. Those parallel processes can be grouped as a new higher-level process (the transaction center). The transaction center is a new substructure that can process many alternative data flows (transactions).

In transform analysis, you look for transform centers. A *transform center* is a single process that is connected to multiple strings of input and output processes. These processes can be grouped as another new higher-level process (the transform center). The transform center is a new substructure that can process a related set of input data flows into a related set of output data flows.

The goal of creating a program design is to convert the physical design into a form ready to be programmed. Transaction centers and transform centers are specific implementation considerations usually addressed in process-driven design. They may, however, also be used as criteria to group certain operations and attributes as new objects.

Process-Structure Charts

The restructuring of processes for implementation involves the transformation of your requirements from one form to another. The physical design is represented in one form (data-flow diagrams or state-transition diagrams), while the new program design will be represented in another (structure chart). This transformation is not just a regrouping but also a change in perspective. Your diagramming perspective changes from the top view shown in the data-flow diagrams or state-transition diagrams to the side view shown in the structure chart.

The implementation model starts out as just a side view of the environmental model, but can then evolve into a completely different structure. In a similar manner to the change from functional design to physical design, this transformation focuses on regrouping processes based on a particular set of physical criteria. The physical criteria this time, however, are specifically governed by the programming language.

Structure charts are the primary mechanism used to represent the implementation model. A structure chart consists of one high-level process, represented as a named box, shown connected to a set of lower-level named process boxes. Each lower-level process is, likewise, connected to its subordinate processes. The information flowing up and down between process boxes is called a *data couple*. You can think of a structure chart as the full side view of a leveled set of data-flow diagrams.

If your design has only a few levels, you can show the entire structure on one structure chart. However, a single design is usually subdivided into several structure charts. Each structure chart in the set is related to the other structure charts much in the same way as a leveled set of data-flow diagrams or a nested set of collaboration diagrams. Usually, an object operation is well contained enough to be represented by a single structure chart of no more than five levels.

CHAPTER REVIEW

Designing Object Operations

When do you use process-driven design? To develop the internal design of the process-intensive objects in your domain.

How do you use process-driven design? Design the public operations in an object as small stand-alone process modules, within the confines defined by the object and to meet the requirements allocated to that class of objects.

How do you identify process requirements? Use the list of operations in an object in place of an essential model of the structured design life-cycle approach.

How do you allocate process requirements? Transform the list of operations into an environmental model for the public operations in an object using either data-flow diagrams or state-transition diagrams as you would in the structured design life-cycle approach.

How do you implement process requirements? Transform the data-flow diagrams and/or state-transition diagrams for the operations of each object into an implementation model using process structure charts as you would in the structured design life-cycle approach.

16

Designing Object Attributes

16.1 THE ATTRIBUTES IN AN OBJECT

Information Engineering of Attributes

You design an object attribute as a small data-intensive and self-contained application. An object-oriented design has a framework that organizes all of the attributes in your design. The steps that you may have gone through up to this point will have identified and allocated the data requirements of your system in an object-oriented manner. Now you need to concentrate on the individual design of those data requirements. They are the attributes that characterize an object.

Each part of the object-engineering model provides one aspect of a well-controlled data-driven design. The domain model provides the object-oriented structure within which you can identify the data requirements of your system, the interface model then defines how those data requirements will be specifically distributed within that structure, and the implementation model defines the specific packages of attributes that satisfy those data requirements. The design of each individual attribute within the implementation model is now a rather straightforward and simple exercise in conventional design.

You can often design each major public attribute in your objects by applying the techniques of information engineering. As shown in Figure 16-1, each attribute is a part of a larger design (addressed by your domain), which is organized in an object-oriented manner. Objects have well-defined interfaces and separately maintained internal designs. The internal design for each object consists of the design of its public operations and public attributes. The attributes are individual data requirements.

Although the design of attributes is specifically addressed separately from the design of operations, they are related to one another. As you apply data-driven design techniques to the design of an attribute, you will also make use of, refer to, and otherwise modify your lists of operations in the same objects. The operations are supported by attributes, so the design of each attribute must also consider its interaction with the operations in the same object. This is consistent with data-driven design, which leads to a design which eventually considers both processes and data, even though it approaches that result from the perspective of data requirements.

Information engineering is a data-driven approach for the design of a system. It can be applied to the design of either hardware or software systems, but it usually addresses software systems. As a data-driven approach, information engineering drives the transformation of the requirements for a system from the perspective of its data requirements. This usually takes the form of a transformation through a functional design phase called the *information strategy plan* to a physical design phase called the *business area analysis*, and finally to a program design phase called the *business system design*. The design of each major attribute of an object follows a similar progression.

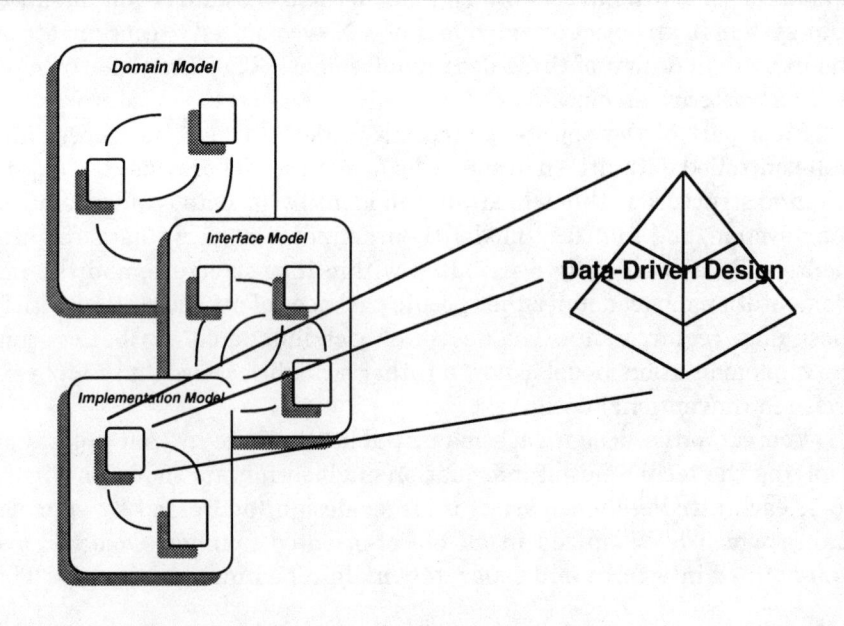

Figure 16-1. Embedded attribute design.

16.2 DATA-DRIVEN DESIGN
16.2.1 When Do You Use Data-Driven Design?
Object Attributes Are Entities

An entity is called an *attribute* in the object-oriented world. The is significant if you already understand how to use entity analysis to design software. Object-oriented design techniques seem very different from conventional techniques but they rely on many of the same concepts. An object is composed of attributes and operations, so its design may partially rely on entity analysis to transform attribute requirements into a working computer program.

An entity is usually defined as a *data item*, and is also sometimes called a *field*. An attribute is usually defined as a nondivisible characteristic of an entity. In a very practical sense, however, an attribute is the same as an entity. The difference is only a matter of size. You use entity analysis to derive a robust set of entities, which are the attributes of your program.

If you think of an attribute in an object as an entity that that object contains, then you will start to see how entity analysis applies to object-oriented design. You used the concept of entity analysis to fully identify all object attributes that characterize the functions of a domain and to group them within the domain's physical architecture. It's now time to implement them as specific data designs.

The techniques used to design objects reflect the combined use of attributes and operations, not merely the sum of attribute design and operation design. However, the concept of entity analysis helps you to visualize an object attribute and what it represents. You identify, allocate, and implement object attributes using all of the same concepts of data-driven design, and some of the same practices. An attribute is a data requirement.

Implementing object attributes is quite similar in concept to a data-driven design, and sometimes also quite similar in practice. Attributes represent half of the nature of an object (the other half being operations). You can think of an attribute as the object-oriented world's name for an entity. Therefore, if you are accustomed to manipulating entities and representing them in entity relationship diagrams, you are already halfway to understanding the concepts of attribute design.

Designing the Major Attributes

Designing the attributes in an object is a relatively easy process in object engineering. You have already organized the many requirements in your domain into logically related packages of operations and attributes called *objects*. Each public attribute in an object is a single major data requirement. You now can use the same techniques that you would have used in a data-driven design to complete its design as a small individual data-intensive application.

292 OBJECT ENGINEERING

As shown in Figure 16-2, the design of the attributes in your domain follows a data-driven approach. Therefore, you should expect to use the same principles, techniques, and diagrams that you would have used under an information engineering life cycle. The only difference is that you can eliminate the first phase of identifying your requirements (the lists of attributes in your object descriptions are your known data requirements) and move more quickly through the remaining phases since each public attribute is so much smaller than an entire conventional data system.

Each major public attribute can define the state of an object in terms of its relationship with other objects in your domain. The design of a public attribute involves the design of its data structure, just as in an information engineering approach. This may involve transforming the attributes of an object into entity relationship diagrams, process sequence diagrams, or normalized data structure charts.

The criteria for developing a good design for an object attribute are the same as for any data-intensive application. It requires the use of data-driven design techniques. In designing the attributes in your objects, you should consider their relationships to the other attributes within the same object, and if necessary, in other objects. These relationships are implemented by the operations in your objects. If you haven't identified any operations that you can map to those relationships, you should add new operations to your objects. Thus, just like in conventional

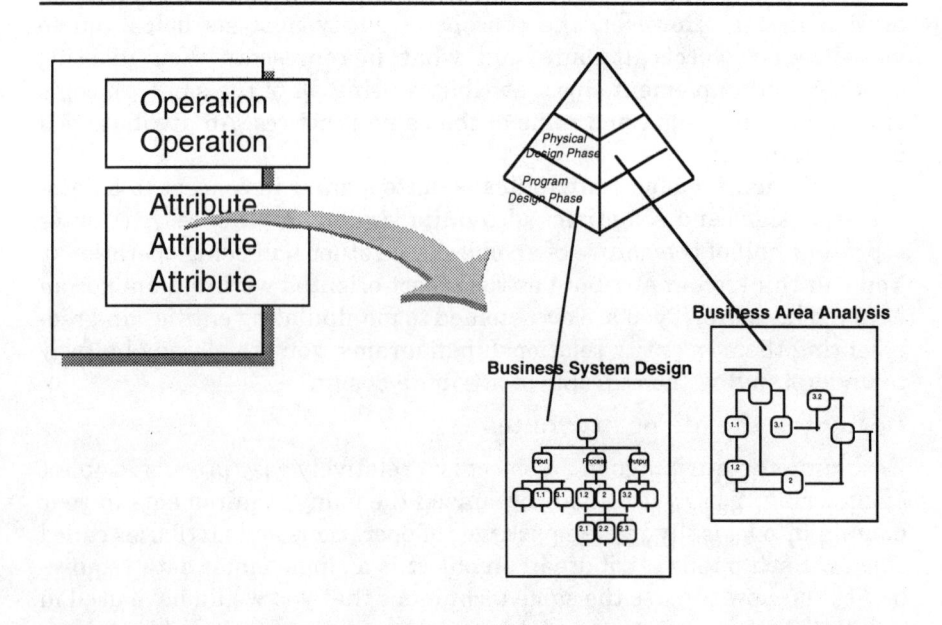

Figure 16-2. A data-driven design cycle.

data-driven design, attribute design can also be a means of discovery for identifying additional operations.

16.2.2 How Do You Design Object Bases?
The Persistence of Objects

The persistence of some of the objects in your design will involve (at a minimum) the storing of the states of the attributes of those objects. Therefore, the design of your attributes may take on a different form than the design of your operations. It may, in fact, resemble the design of a conventional database in many respects. The attributes in an object correspond to the data elements in a program, which may be stored in a database for certain applications.

An object-oriented design is different from a conventional design in that it models the inheritance as well as the collaboration between objects. This means that the storage of attributes should consider both types of relationships. Furthermore, objects also contain both attributes and operations. This, too, may impact how you design your object base.

The state of the art of object-oriented storage and retrieval tools is still evolving. To date, there is no standard set of capabilities that can be expected of all tools. Some tools may address only attribute storage, while others may address both attributes and operations. Some tools may address only conventional collaboration types of relationships, while others may address both collaboration and inheritance.

Database managements systems (DBMS) are automated mechanisms to store and retrieve organized data in a conventional program. They are data-oriented tools that correspond to programming language compilers, which are process-oriented tools. Therefore, just as the design of your operations requires that you consider the use of specific object-oriented programming languages, the design of your attributes may require that you consider the use of specific types of object-oriented databases.

We will refer to an object-oriented storage and retrieval tool as an *object-base management system* (OBMS). They are the next generation of database management systems in the same way that hierarchical databases gave way to network databases, and then to relational databases. However, commercial development of object-base management systems has been trailing developments in languages and compilers. This is still a developing field.

The evolution of conventional database management systems has provided added functionality at each stage in their development. Hierarchical databases provided for a single relationship between data elements, network databases provided for multiple relationships, and relational databases then provided a dynamic mechanism for representing network relationships. The next logical step is to build upon relational database theory and technology to develop object-oriented databases, called object bases:

- **DATABASES:** store the values (states) of data (attributes) as their elements, including knowledge of the structural relationships (collaborations) between those elements.

- **OBJECT BASES:** store the values (states) of objects (operations and attributes) as their elements, including knowledge of the structural hierarchies (inheritance and collaboration) of the domain to which they belong.

Object-Base Management Systems

In designing the structure of the attributes within the objects of your domain, you may need to consider how and where you will store their state at various points during and between runs of your program. You can, of course, store the values of attributes in a conventional database using a conventional database management system. It would be preferable, however, to use an object-oriented storage mechanism specifically designed to accommodate the nature of an object-oriented design.

There are two primary types of object-base management systems (OBMS), those which maintain passive object bases and those which maintain active object bases. The majority of commercially available products in this field address passive object bases. They are a good platform to use while you transform your existing database applications into object-oriented representations. The full benefits of object-oriented design, however, can only be realized with active object bases. They provide you with a complete object-oriented storage and retrieval mechanism.

Similar to the evolution of conventional databases, an OBMS adds more functionality to the current version of automated storage and retrieval mechanisms in accordance with the added capabilities of object-oriented programming languages. An OBMS maintains knowledge about two types of relationships between the objects in your design. One type of relationship is inheritance, the other is collaboration. An OBMS also maintains two types of information about the objects in your design. One type of information describes the logic of the operations, the other describes the values of the attributes.

Passive Object-Base Design

A passive object base is usually just an extension of existing relational database management system technology. This is most often referred to as an object database management system (ODBMS). It is capable of storing the schema-type collaboration relationships between the attributes of the objects in your domain, as well as storing their inheritance relationships, but it doesn't address the operations of those objects at all.

A passive object manager stores persistent objects in a relational structure, maintains both inheritance and collaboration information, and stores the state of variables but not their accompanying processing logic. Most object-oriented database products that you will come across are of this type (passive). They are extensions of existing relational database management systems to accommodate the storage and use of the inheritance relationships between objects in order to access the state of persistent attributes.

The design for a passive object base, therefore, is similar to the design of a relational database. You must determine how your data elements (attributes) are related to one another in order to model their interaction and then relax some of the rigid constraints of that model in order to implement it within the physical constraints of the tool that you are using. You focus your attention on the collaboration relationships between attributes in the design of a passive object base.

Normalize the collaboration relationships between the attributes in your design in the same way that you would normalize the schema relationships between the data elements in a conventional design. The collaboration between objects (when applied to the attributes) is just the object-oriented description of conventional data-element relationships. This may involve the revision of your collaboration hierarchy in the same way that a data schema might be revised in order to be implemented on a particular database management system.

The added advantage of a passive object base over a conventional database is that it is capable of storing and utilizing your inheritance hierarchy. The inheritance hierarchy would then be used by the programming language to resolve references to the appropriate attribute at runtime. Thus, just like in conventional programming, the use of object-base management systems requires some compatibility with the programming language that you are using.

Active Object-Base Design

An active object base addresses the entire object, that is, the operations as well as the attributes. It is capable of storing the collaboration schema relationships between the objects in your design (like a conventional database) and the inheritance relationships between those objects (like a passive object base), but will also store both the attributes and the operations of those objects.

An active object manager is also called an *object broker*. It stores persistent objects in a relational structure, maintains both inheritance and collaboration information, and stores process logic as well as the state of the variables. This is the eventual goal for object-oriented storage and retrieval tools, and will possibly be part of the second wave of improvement after the industry establishes itself with passive object managers. The manner in which they address the storage of persistent operations will differentiate object brokers from one another.

The design for an active object base, fortunately, should be no different from the design of a passive object base. It is only the capabilities of the resulting object base that differ. You should be primarily concerned with the collaboration schema of the attributes of your objects. The inheritance relationships will be stored and utilized as with a passive object base. However, in an active object base, the operations will now also be stored.

In the same way that a passive object base stores and utilizes an inheritance hierarchy to give it additional capabilities over a conventional database, an active object base stores and utilizes the designs of the operations of objects to give it additional capabilities over a passive object base. In practical terms, this means that the benefits of centralized storage will be extended to the libraries of source and executable code that comprise a computer program.

The substitution of alternative source libraries plays an important role in the reusability of parts of an existing inheritance hierarchy, similarly, the substitution of alternative executable libraries plays an important role in the reusability of parts of an existing collaboration hierarchy. This is one of the primary benefits of object-oriented design. Active object bases and the object brokers that manage them will help to realize that benefit.

Although you can manage objects by simply loading and linking libraries by their text name (as is done in conventional programming), it will be much more efficient and effective if it is done by an object broker as an integrated part of the object base. This will require additional intelligence on the part of the programming environment in which your design will be implemented. That is the role of the object broker.

The programming runtime environment will need to act as the object broker to make use of the inheritance hierarchy to select operations and attributes when needed. This is partially true in order to institute the use of passive object bases and absolutely required in order to make use of active object bases. These are some of the areas currently under development in the industry.

16.3 DATA-DRIVEN TECHNIQUES

16.3.1 How Do You Identify Data Requirements?

The Information Strategy Plan

The first goal of conventional data-driven design is to identify the data requirements of your program. You do this by constructing a comprehensive model of major entities and then elaborating on them. This represents the functional design of your program. It is based on examining the business functions of your enterprise and on describing the data subjects needed to support it.

Although you will never need to develop an information strategy plan as part of an attribute description, it is still useful to examine the concepts involved in developing one in order to understand how to develop the internal designs for each attribute. You will develop the design of each major attribute in the same way as you would in conventional data-driven approach from the point of a completed information strategy plan.

In object engineering, you identify object attributes in the same way that you identify data requirements in the information strategy plan. You analyze object attributes to further expand your list of functions. In doing so, you identify more individual attributes (and the operations needed to support them). However, rather than developing such a plan, you just use the lists of attributes in object descriptions as your model of data requirements.

The concepts are the same whether you are developing an information strategy plan using information engineering or if you are applying those same techniques to the design of a major attribute in an object using object engineering. Therefore, it is helpful to recall how you would have developed the information strategy plan for a conventional data-driven design.

In developing an information strategy plan, you prepare lists of organizations, departments, divisions, locations, business goals, functions, and data subjects in order to assemble an enterprisewide picture of your business. Usually, these various lists are displayed as matrices, which cross-reference one list against another. However, you concentrate on the business-function list and the data subject list to develop your design.

Decompose business functions by further listing the processes needed to support them. As the list of business functions grows, it can be segmented into separate sublists based on organizations, locations, and/or business goals. However, the important concept is the decomposition of these business functions into specific business processes. These business processes eventually are displayed as rows in a process/data matrix.

Decompose data subjects by further listing the data entities that they contain. The data-subject list can also be segmented by organizations, locations, and/or business goals, and eventually the data entities become the columns in a process/data matrix. You identify your data requirements in this organized manner. The process/data matrix identifies specific business areas for which you need to design programs.

In an object-oriented design, the object descriptions from your interface model replace the need for developing an information strategy plan. The data requirements of an object are already defined in terms of the list of attributes of which they are comprised, so there is no need to perform the first phase of a data-driven design. However, your attribute design progresses in the same manner from this point further. It's just a smaller and more well-contained design.

16.3.2 How Do You Allocate Data Requirements?

The Business-Area Analysis

The second goal of conventional data-driven design is to allocate the data requirements into groups. In conventional design, do this by regrouping the entities on the entity-relationship diagrams into a leveled set of process-sequence diagrams, which represents the physical design of your functions. In the design of an object attribute, particularly when designing an object base, you follow the same procedure of allocating your known lower-level data attributes into physical groups.

In the design of your attributes as part of an object base, you would pick up the conventional design approach at this point in the data-driven model. Your data requirements are the known attributes listed in your object descriptions. This replaces the need for an information strategy plan. You now proceed, however, with the development of a small business-area analysis model in the same way as you would under any information engineering approach. It will represent the initial physical allocation of the private attributes that are needed to support each public one in an object base.

The concept of allocating attributes in object-oriented design is similar to allocating data requirements in data-driven design. You allocate data requirements in a data-driven design by the following steps listed in Table 16-1. These steps convey the concept of allocating a program's attributes. In information engineering, this is called the business-area analysis. In object engineering, the data requirements are the attributes in your object descriptions.

Table 16-1. A business-area analysis.

Step 3.3.2.2.1 Develop entity-relationship diagrams for the major public attributes in each object.

Step 3.3.2.2.2 Expand the entity-relationship diagrams by adding physical entities to support the relationships among the major public attributes.

Step 3.3.2.2.3 Create a leveled set of process-sequence diagrams from the entity-relationship diagrams.

Step 3.3.2.2.4 Restructure the diagrams based on the physical environment, on known organizational preferences, on known performance criteria, and on known security requirements.

Step 3.3.2.2.5 Identify public operations needed to support the relationships between the attributes and that perform custodial functions for them.

The business-area analysis of information engineering is the definition of the requirements of your system in a physical form. In object engineering, you design the physical structure of the attributes in an object in the same way. You have identified the data requirements of your objects in terms of their attributes. You then allocate those attributes into a physical structure in preparation for implementation in a conventional DBMS, a passive OBMS, or an active OBMS.

The design of the structure of your object attributes corresponds to the second phase of a data-driven design. This involves the development of entity-relationship diagrams or process-sequence diagrams as a physical model of each public attribute and the operations that support them. You allocate the private attributes below the public attributes. The public attributes will be accessed from outside of the object. The private attributes will be used by (as part of) the public ones.

Entity-Relationship Diagrams

Entity-relationship diagrams are the primary mechanism used to represent the physical design in a data-driven approach. They represent the relationships among major groups of data elements in a system. These data elements are called *entities*. They are similar to objects except that they do not contain any operations. They are groups of closely related attributes, or in more general terms, they are large undecomposed attributes.

A business area is the complete set of entities for a single system. In theory, one comprehensive entity-relationship diagram should be drawn for each business area. In practice, a number of overlapping diagrams are usually drawn for a single business area, one diagram showing all the relationships for a particular entity. As a result, each diagram shows the complete neighborhood around each entity.

The neighborhood diagrams are somewhat redundant in relation to one another. An individual entity may appear on several neighborhood diagrams if it has relationships with many other entities. However, there will be only one entity-relationship diagram that shows the neighborhood for any one entity. It is just a way of subdividing an otherwise large diagram into its constituent perspectives. You then look for the processes needed to support these entities.

You identify processes in order to accomplish the physical movement of data between data entities. The steps to develop process-sequence diagrams are very similar to the allocation of processes in process-driven design. The groups of processes here, however, tend to be more data oriented since the processes have been defined specifically to support the data manipulation. Although you are using processes, you are really reorganizing data requirements.

In object-oriented design, you would primarily use entity-relationship diagrams as a means of documenting the relationships between the attributes within an object or as a step in the development of fully normalized data structure diagrams. You would only need fully normalized data structure diagrams if you are making use of some type of storage and retrieval mechanism (a DBMS or an OBMS) to maintain your persistent objects.

Process-Sequence Diagrams

Process-sequence diagrams are another mechanism used to represent the physical design. They represent the set of processes needed to support the manipulation of the data reflected in the entity-relationship diagrams. They are usually derived from the processes in a process/data matrix from an information strategy plan and the entities in an entity-relationship diagram. They show the sequential actions taken on the entities.

Process-sequence diagrams are, for all practical purposes, data-flow diagrams. They contain processes, data stores, and data flows. Like data-flow diagrams, process-sequence diagrams are generally organized as a leveled set of related diagrams. Each lower level shows the internal workings of one process on a higher diagram.

The process-sequence diagrams can be derived from entity-relationship diagrams. Each entity from the entity-relationship diagrams becomes a data store on the process-sequence diagrams and each relationship between a pair of entities on the entity-relationship diagrams becomes the set of processes between the corresponding pair of data stores. The sequence connections between these processes are the data flows.

You derive the processes in the process-sequence diagrams in order to support the data stores (entities). In this way, your functional design (entity-relationship diagrams) becomes more physical. You are allocating your data requirements (entities) into physical groups in the leveled set of process-sequence diagrams.

In object-oriented design, you would not typically make use of process-sequence diagrams. Our only purpose in discussing them at this point was to demonstrate that a data-driven design arrives at the same point as a process-driven design (that point being a structure chart representation of process and data). This is important to understand if you are to accept the design of objects as the integrated replacement of data-driven and process-driven design.

16.3.3 How Do You Implement Data Requirements?

The Business-System Design

The third goal of conventional data-driven design is to restructure the design again so as to best implement the data requirements on a particular platform. You do this by restructuring the process-sequence diagrams into process-structure diagrams and data-structure diagrams. This represents your program design. In the design of an object attribute, you follow the same procedure of developing data structure charts from your business-area analysis.

In the design of the attributes that may be particularly complex or part of an overall object-base design, you would continue to use a conventional design approach to allocate your private attributes to support the public ones. You would proceed to develop a small conventional business-system design for each major public attribute from its corresponding business-area analysis model. The design process, however, is much more informal than it would have been under a conventional data-driven approach due to the smaller size of each individual attribute.

The concept of implementing attributes in object-oriented design is similar to implementing data requirements in data-driven design. You implement data requirements in a data-driven design by the following steps listed in Table 16-2. These steps convey the concept of implementing a program's attributes. In information engineering, this is called the *business-system design*.

The business-system design of information engineering is the restructuring of the requirements of your system in its final physical form as a program module. In object engineering, you design the data structure of the attributes in an object in the same way. You have allocated the data requirements of your objects into a physical structure in your

Table 16-2. A business-system design.

> *Step 3.3.2.3.1 Partition the leveled set of process-sequence diagrams into a separate operation structure and data structure.*
>
> *Step 3.3.2.3.2 Partition the operation structure into separate units (jobs, programs, etc.) based on known hardware and software platform requirements.*
>
> *Step 3.3.2.3.3 Create process-structure diagrams that reflect the hierarchical structure of the partitioned operations.*
>
> *Step 3.3.2.3.4 Identify additional lower-level private operations to perform the specific functions needed to support these new groups according to the nature of the language in which the design will be programmed.*
>
> *Step 3.3.2.3.5 Normalize the attribute structure into a form suitable for implementation in the environment you will be using.*

business area analysis and you then implement those attributes by restructuring them for accessing efficiency.

In developing the structure diagrams, you perform the same fundamental transformations as you would using process-driven design. You move processes into new groups based on platform considerations such as the capabilities of the computer language in which you will be programming. You move data into new groups (called *normalizing*) based on platform considerations such as the type of database management system (such as hierarchical, networked, or relational) you will be using.

The design of your object attributes as a data structure corresponds to the third phase of a data-driven design. This involves the development of data-structure charts for each public attribute in an object. The private attributes are all nested below one or more of the public attributes. You reorganize some of them in order to improve efficiencies based on similarities in program function. For example, you may group substructures together on one branch of the structure chart in order to eliminate redundancies in data storage (normalization).

Data-Structure Diagrams

In conventional data-driven design, you derive the process structure for your program at this phase of development. In addition to a process structure, you can also derive a data structure. Data-structure diagrams are a popular mechanism used to represent the database design for your system. They contain the same information as structure charts in a process-driven design: named boxes representing each data element subdivided into lower-level named boxes. They are derived from the process-sequence diagrams in the same way that structure charts are derived from data-flow diagrams.

Data-structure diagrams are similar to process-structure diagrams. They convey the hierarchical relationships between the data stores at various levels on the process-sequence diagrams in the same way that process-structure diagrams convey the hierarchical relationships between processes. This complements a conventional program design, in effect, with a conventional database design. Similarly, your object-oriented attribute designs should complement your object-oriented operation designs.

CHAPTER REVIEW

Designing Object Attributes

When do you use data-driven design? To develop the internal design of the data-intensive objects in your domain.

How do you use data-driven design? Design the public attributes in an object as small stand-alone data entities, within the confines defined by the object and to meet the requirements allocated to that class of objects.

How do you identify data requirements? Use the list of attributes in an object in place of an information strategy plan of the information engeering life-cycle approach.

How do you allocate data requirements? Transform the list of attributes into a business-system analysis for the public attributes in an object using entity-relationship diagrams and process-sequence diagrams as you would in the information engineering life-cycle approach.

How do you implement data requirements? Transform the process-sequence diagrams for the attributes of each object into a business-system design using data-structure charts as you would in the information engineering life-cycle approach.

17

Conclusion

17.1 SUMMARY

17.1.1 How Do You Perform Object Engineering?

Identify Objects in Your Domain

At the top layer of object engineering, you are concerned with two types of interactions between objects—inheritance and collaboration. The set of objects identified in this manner constitutes the domain for your system. In object engineering, this is called the *domain model*. It is the initial design of your system. A domain model provides you with the information by which you can manage the components of your design, and more important, by which you can find and reuse those components in new designs.

The domain model is the functional design of an object-oriented system. It represents the functional requirements of your system. In the design of small programs, you may not need to develop a domain model. You know your requirements and you have a design (an initial list of objects) in mind. In the design of large-scale systems, however, you will get lost without a domain model. It provides the map of your requirements and holds the rest of your design together.

In identifying the objects in your domain, you apply many of the same principles of process-driven and data-driven design that you may have used in the past. In particular, you classify objects according to their inheritance characteristics by examining their relationships to one another much like entity analysis from data-driven design. Similarly, you encapsulate objects according to their collaboration characteristics by decomposing them much like process decomposition from process-driven design.

Allocate Requirements to Objects

At the middle layer of object engineering you are concerned with the descriptions of the classes, objects, and requests, which constitute the structure of your design. This is where you allocate specific requirements to the objects in your domain. In object engineering, this is called the *interface model*. The objects of the classes in your domain interact with one another in very specific ways. The objects interacting with one another in your inheritance hierarchy will become abstract classes; the objects interacting with one another in your collaboration hierarchy will become concrete classes.

The interface model is the initial physical design of an object-oriented system. It represents the high-level physical implementation of the objects in your domain. By *high level*, we mean that only the external characteristics of your objects are defined here. This includes documenting the class relationships of the objects in your domain, the lists of public operations and public attributes that comprise each object, and the list of requests that can be used to trigger those operations and access those attributes.

Each object is a package of operations, and the attributes are organized within either abstract or concrete classes. In the abstract classes, objects are comprised of the common operations and attributes used by the objects of concrete classes. In the concrete classes, objects are comprised of the operations and attributes which interact with one another at runtime. The interactions among the operations and attributes in different objects are accomplished by making requests. The requests, therefore, are the sole means of representing the nature of one object to another in your domain.

Implement Individual Object Designs

At the bottom layer of object engineering you are concerned with the implementation of the specific operation requirements and attribute requirements of the objects in your domain. You develop the design of each as a small well-contained conventional design. Public operations can be designed using process-driven techniques. Public attributes can be designed using data-driven techniques.

The operations and attributes for the objects in your domain establish the full set of requirements for your system. The internal designs for the public operations and the public attributes of the objects in your domain establish the design for an object-oriented program and/or the schema for an object-oriented database, respectively. In object engineering, this is called the *implementation model*.

The implementation model is the completed physical design of an object-oriented system. It represents the low-level physical implementation of the objects in your domain. By *low level*, we mean that the internal characteristics of your objects are defined here. This includes documenting the integrated design of the public operations and attributes in terms of their subordinate operations and attributes that support each. These designs can be accomplished either as separate subordinate object-oriented or conventional designs, depending on their size and nature.

The design of the operations in each individual object is quite similar to the design of a small and well-contained process-driven application. Public operations in an object act as subroutines, receiving requests from other objects. In some cases, you might extract these subroutines to become additional independent objects. In other cases, however, they remain within the object and you use process-structure charts to represent their design. The implementation design of the public operations establishes the process-oriented part of the internal design of the objects in which they are contained.

The design of the attributes in each individual object is quite similar to the design of a small and well-contained data-driven application. Public attributes in an object are used as state variables of the objects in which they reside. In some cases, you might extract these variables to become additional independent objects. In other cases, however, they remain within the object and you use data-structure diagrams to represent their design. The implementation design of the public attributes establishes the data-oriented part of the internal design of the objects in which they are contained.

17.1.2 How Is It Different from Conventional Design?

A Model-Based Development Approach

Object engineering is different from the conventional approaches of structured design and information engineering. It is a model-based approach that employs object-oriented techniques. This leads you to develop your design in layers. Although the layers correspond to the phases in a conventional approach, they help to focus your attention on the model that you are constructing rather than the steps that you may use. Each lower layer provides you with a more detailed view of a part of another layer.

A model-based approach is more conducive to being used in a recursive manner. Each layer of your design is composed of specific design models. As you complete the design at any one layer, you may find that some parts of that layer are sufficiently important or complex to warrant a completely separate pass through the entire development life cycle. Other parts of the design, however, can be addressed sufficiently by continuing with the next layer of design.

A model-based approach also results in a better-defined system than would be developed by conventional approaches. Your design is composed of an inheritance hierarchy, a collaboration hierarchy, the classes within the hierarchies, and the objects associated with the classes. The objects are individual packages of operations and attributes. Each object has a well-defined interface and its own internal design, which makes for better control over your design, more opportunities to reuse portions of your design, and more flexibility in making subsequent design changes.

Considering Both Processes and Data

An object-oriented design, unlike a conventional design, makes use of both the process requirements and the data requirements of your system to drive its design. An object is a package of operations and attributes, which represent process requirements and data requirements, respectively. Because of this dual nature of objects, it is much easier to develop a balanced design from the start. The process requirements of the operations and the data requirements of the attributes guide you as you transform your design from a functional level to a physical level and, finally, to a program level.

In conventional approaches, you use either a process-based perspective or a data-based perspective to drive your design. In object-oriented design, you use both perspectives. In a manner similar to process-driven techniques, you decompose objects using a concept called *encapsulation*; as with data-driven techniques, you expand and regroup objects using a concept called *classification*. Object-oriented design combines the best aspects of both process-driven design and data-driven design.

17.1.3 How Is It Similar to Conventional Design?

A Life-Cycle Development Framework

Despite some differences, object engineering is similar in many respects to conventional approaches to software development. The goals of object engineering are the same as conventional approaches — to transform a set of requirements into a working computer program. Like conventional approaches, it makes use of a life-cycle framework to organize your design activities. The life cycle guides you in identifying your requirements, allocating them into a physical structure, and implementing the details of that structure as a design for a computer program.

Object engineering is the framework used to develop an object-oriented design for a large-scale system. Objects, at first, seem very different from program modules and data structures but they are really not very different at all. Objects are composed of operations and attributes. Operations are just the object-oriented term for process modules, and attributes are just the object-oriented term for data structures.

Process-Driven Design Techniques

The general approach of object engineering is similar in concept to many aspects of structured design. *Structured design* is a process-driven software development approach that employs the use of process decomposition. You use process decomposition to decompose large objects into smaller objects much like you would in structured design. The decomposition of objects is called *encapsulation*. If you have used structured design in the past, you will be able to apply the same principles to object engineering.

Many of the detailed design techniques that you use in object engineering are also the same as those you may have used in structured design. You use conventional process module design techniques in the design of the process operations within your objects. The design for each operation is just a small, well-contained, process-intensive conventional design. It stands to reason, therefore, that process-driven techniques of structured design are still applicable to the operation portion of the design of your objects.

Data-Driven Design Techniques

The general approach of object engineering is also similar in concept to many aspects of *information engineering*. Information engineering is a data-driven software development approach that employs entity analysis. You use entity analysis to examine the relationships between specific objects in order to determine a more general set of objects. The analysis of objects as entities is called *classification*. If you have used information engineering, you will be able to apply the same principles to object engineering.

Many of the detailed design techniques that you use in object engineering are also the same as those you may have used in information engineering. You use conventional data schema design techniques in the design of the data attributes within your objects. The design for each attribute is just a small, well-contained, data-intensive conventional design. It stands to reason, therefore, that data-driven techniques of information engineering are still applicable to the attribute portion of the design of your objects.

17.2 FUTURE TRENDS

17.2.1 How Will Programming Change?

More Flexible Computer Programs

Object-oriented design will have a measurable (and presumably beneficial) effect on computer programming in the 1990s and beyond. Computer programming is likely to continue changing in the manner in which it has already started to change—by further embracing the principles and concepts of object-oriented design. In particular, the flexibility and reusability of object-oriented designs that has proven itself on desktop platforms will be extended to the design of large-scale industrial systems.

Specifically, programming will increasingly employ the object-oriented programming languages and application development environments that are already available, and new releases of those languages and environments will incorporate the object-oriented model more fully by addressing the following areas:

- **INHERITANCE:** More compilers will contain object-oriented extensions into the syntax of their languages. By *extensions*, we mean that they will accommodate the definition of an inheritance hierarchy in some manner and make use of it for polymorphism.
- **COLLABORATION:** Those languages will also expand their syntax to access attributes in the same manner that they already trigger operations—through the use of explict requests. The wider use of a standard object request syntax will better enable cross-product communications.
- **VISUAL PROGRAMMING:** There will be more visual-application development environments for object-oriented programming, integrated with established object-oriented programming languages. These environments will provide graphical means for specifying the inheritance and collaboration hierarchies of a domain model.
- **OBJECT BASES:** There will be more complete object-base management system environments for persistent operation and attribute storage, integrated with established object-oriented programming languages and their visual programming environments.

More Reusable Design Components

The use of programs and program modules designed in an object-oriented manner will also continue to impact computer programming. In particular, the more definitive way in which an object is defined (that is, in terms of its interface) will finally allow the realization of some of the objectives of modular programming.

The design process can be more fully automated because of the manner in which the individual designs of objects can evolve in a layered model. Similarly, their well-defined interfaces will facilitate the cross use of modules and programs on different platforms. Components of an object-oriented design will be more reusable both during the design process and in production with the continuing advancement of:

- **CASE TOOLS:** There will be computer aided software engineering (CASE) tools for the design of object-oriented systems. These tools should incorporate both the syntax (diagramming notation) and the spirit (a dual process and data perspective) of the object-oriented model. These tools will provide graphical means for specifying both the inheritance and the collaboration hierarchies of a domain model.
- **OBJECT MANAGERS:** There will be runtime object management environments to select and schedule the use of persistent object modules from an object base. For example, the Common Object Request Broker Architecture (CORBA) is one set of standards for the implementation of an integrated set of object management components. In

a similar manner, the de facto message standards set by the Microsoft Object Linking and Embedding (OLE) and Open Data Base Connectivity (ODBC) protocols are other examples of an emerging object management environment, sometimes also referred to as the Windows Open Services Architecture (WOSA). These types of environments enable objects of different programs to share certain information and operating characteristics based on the interface model of an object-oriented design.

- **OBJECT LIBRARIES:** There will continue to be libraries of pre-designed abstract classes (static-source libraries), which you can include into your own program design, and libraries of predesigned concrete classes (dynamic-link libraries), which you can call from your own programs. These libraries will become even more integral to the use of object-oriented programming languages and environments.

17.2.2 How Will the Design Environment Improve?

A Repository for Object-Oriented Designs

Computer aided software engineering (CASE) tools are automated mechanisms for the development of computer programs. A CASE tool represents the automation of a software-development approach. The diagrams employed within a particular CASE tool represent the design techniques associated with its approach. The diagrams represent the design; however, an effective CASE tool should be repository based, rather than diagram based, in its storage of the design.

Repositories store the basic constructs of your design rather than the diagrams of those constructs. This was a hard-learned lesson in the early failures of CASE tools for conventional design. Unfortunately, these failures are being repeated with early object-oriented CASE tools in the rush to capitalize on the support of object technology. A good repository still needs to be centralized and to address the design rather than its representation.

Furthermore, the concept of a repository should be taken to its logical conclusion. It should be based on a formal model, which will ensure the tighter fit implied by an object-oriented description of a system. By *formal model*, we mean a minimum collection of base components that have rigid isomorphic transformation relationships with their various alternative diagrammatic representations.

In mathematical terms, this type of repository design is called a *closed-form model*. By closed form, we mean that the transformation from one form to another is deterministic. The same set of components appears on all diagrams. These components will always be portrayed in the same way in relation to one another on any type of diagram. There is no magic, no subjective interpretation, and most of all, no gap between analysis and design. Likewise, there is no gap between design and programming. Only in this way can the entire life cycle be automated.

A Formal-Based Model Representation

A formal model only requires the storage of the base constructs of a design. The failure to incorporate this concept has been one of the chief failings of conventional CASE tools. The base constructs for an object-oriented CASE repository are operations, attributes, and the events that connect them. These base constructs can be grouped as objects, which in turn can be diagrammed as classes and drawn to show inheritance hierarchies and collaboration hierarchies, but only the base constructs need to be stored in the CASE repository.

The base constructs in a formal-based repository can be portrayed in any diagram form that you find appropriate. The base constructs in an object-oriented design include the operations and attributes of your design. The diagrams in which they can be portrayed can include data-flow diagrams, entity-relationship diagrams, state-transition diagrams, or structure charts as well as the objects in inheritance and collaboration diagrams. These different diagram forms are just isomorphic representations of the same underlying basic constructs (operations and attributes).

Isomorphism in this context means that you can transform the representation of those base constructs from one diagrammatic form to another, and likewise, that you can enter information about your design using any diagrammatic form. The diagrams are all integrated because they use the same underlying constructs. They simply represent different perspectives of the process operations and the data attributes of your design. The knowledge of your design is represented by the base design constructs in your repository, not by their portrayal in any one type of diagram.

The various object-oriented diagrams (inheritance and collaboration) and the accompanying descriptions (object and class) used in the various layers of object engineering can all be derived from a layered formal model of the interrelationships between operations and attributes. Similarly, all of the various conventional diagrams (data flow, entity relationship, state transition), which may be useful in the design of the operations and the attributes at the lowest layer, can be derived from a single formal model of their intrarelationships.

The principle of isomorphism could be applied equally as well to conventional design, although it has not been implemented within any of the popular conventional CASE tools. Data-flow diagrams are just a process-oriented view of both the processes and the data required in a system. Entity-relationship diagrams are just a data-oriented view of the same thing.

In object-oriented design, collaboration diagrams portray a combined view of both process (operation) and data (attribute) requirements. The use of a formal-based model seems to be particularly appropriate for automating object technology. Formal-based object-oriented CASE tools would represent the dual nature of data and processes in a more isomorphic (internally integrated) manner, and thus, would avoid the failings of their conventional predecessors.

Support for the Object-Engineering Model

Object-oriented CASE tools serve the same purpose in software engineering as conventional CASE tools—the automation of a particular development approach through the integrated use of a set of design techniques. That approach and its techniques, of course, should be object oriented. In particular, an object-oriented CASE tool should support all three layers of the object-engineering model (domain, class, and object) and do so in an isomorphic manner (showing alternate perspectives) using a formal-based repository containing only the basic constructs (operations, attributes, and requests).

In object engineering, the domain layer is the entry point for the design of any system in an object-oriented manner, the class layer provides the general design for those systems, and the object layer provides the detailed design for their programs. Furthermore, the design of the internal object operations should be supported in a process-driven manner and the design of the internal object attributes should be supported in a data-driven manner.

In an object-oriented CASE tool, you should be able to visually manipulate the inheritance and collaboration hierarchies of your domain model, browse through the class libraries of your interface model to identify candidate structures for reuse, and develop the internal designs of each object in your implementation model in an integrated manner.

At the Domain Layer (the Domain Model):
Domain Identification—the ability to manage multiple domains
Class Categories—segmented inheritance diagrams
Inheritance Diagrams—pictorial representations of shared objects
Module Assemblies—segmented process collaboration diagrams
Schema Assemblies—segmented data collaboration diagrams
Collaboration Diagrams—pictorial representation runtime of object

At the Class Layer (the Interface Model):
Abstract Class Descriptions—for identifying inheritance relations
Concrete Class Descriptions—for identifying collaboration relations
Object Descriptions—templates for packaging operations and attributes
Request Descriptions—parameters for public operations and attributes

At the Object Layer (the Implementation Model):
Data-Flow Diagrams—static operation interactions
State-Transition Diagrams—dynamic operation interactions
Entity-Relationship Diagrams—attribute interactions
Process-Structure Charts—nested operation hierarchies
Data-Structure Charts—nested (normalized) attribute hierarchies

Bibliography

Andleigh, Prabhat K. and Gretsinger, Michael R. *Distributed Object-Oriented Data Systems Design*. Englewood Cliffs, N.J.: Prentice Hall Press, 1992.

Berry, John T. *The Waite Group's C++ Programming*. Carmel, Ind.: Macmillan Computer Publishing, 1988.

Booch, Grady. *Object-Oriented Design with Applications*. Redwood City, Cal.: The Benjamin/Cummings Publishing Company, Inc., 1991.

Coad, Peter and Yourdon, Edward. *Object-Oriented Analysis*. Englewood Cliffs, N.J.: Yourdon Press, Inc., 1990.

Coad, Peter and Yourdon, Edward. *Object-Oriented Design*. Englewood Cliffs, N.J.: Yourdon Press, Inc., 1991.

Coad, Peter and Nicola, Jill. *Object-Oriented Programming*. Englewood Cliffs, N.J.: Yourdon Press, Inc., 1993.

Date, C. *An Introduction to Database Systems*. Reading, Mass.: Addison-Wesley Publishing Co., Inc., 1981.

DeMarco, Tom. *Structured Analysis and System Specification*. New York: Yourdon Press, Inc., 1978.

Embley, David W.; Kurtz, Barry D.; and Woodfield, Scott N. *Object-Oriented Systems Analysis: A Model Driven Approach*. Englewood Cliffs, N.J.: Yourdon Press, Inc., 1992.

Gane, Chris and Sarson, Trish. *Structured Systems Analysis*. Englewood Cliffs, N.J.: Prentice Hall Press, 1979.

Inmon, William H. *Data Architecture: The Information Paradigm*. Welleseley, Mass.: QED Technical Publishing Group, 1992.

LaLonde, Wilf R. and Pugh, John, R. *Inside Smalltalk*. Englewood Cliffs, N.J.: Prentice Hall Press, 1990.

Martin, James. *Information Engineering, Book II: Planning and Analysis*. Englewood Clifs, N.J.: Prentice Hall Press, 1990.

Martin, James. *Principles of Object-Oriented Analysis and Design*. Englewood Clifs, N.J.: Prentice Hall Press, 1993.

McMenamin, Stephan and Palmer, J. *Essential Systems Analysis*. New York: Yourdon Press, Inc., 1984.

Microsoft. *Microsoft Windows Software Development Kit: Guide to Programming*. Redmond, Wash.: Microsoft Corp., 1990.

OMG. *The Common Object Request Broker: Architecture and Specification*. Framingham, Mass.: Object Management Group and X/Open Consortium, 1992.

Rao, Bindu R. *C++ and the OOP Paradigm*. New York: McGraw-Hill Inc., 1992.

Rishe, Naphtai. *Database Design: The Semantic Modeling Approach*. New York": McGraw-Hill, Inc., 1992.

Ross, Ronald G. *Entity Model: Concepts and Applications*. Boston: Database Research Group, 1987.

Scharbach, P.N., ed. *Formal Methods: Theory and Practice*. Boca Raton, Fla.: CRC Press, Inc., 1989.

Shlaer, Sally and Mellor, Stephen J. *Object Lifecycles: Modeling the World in States*. Englewood Cliffs. N.J.: Yourdon Press, Inc., 1992.

Shumate, Kenneth C. and Keller, Marilyn M. *Software Specification and Design: A Disciplined Approach for Real-Time Systems*. New York: John Wiley and Sons, Inc., 1992.

Taylor, David A. *Object-Oriented Information Syustems: Planning and Implementation*. New York: John Wiley and Sons, Inc., 1993

Tse, T.H. *A Unifying Framework for Structured Analysis and Design Models*. Cambridge, England: Cambridge University Press, 1991.

Wirfs-Brock, Rebecca; Wilkerson, Brian; and Wiener, Lauren. *Designing Object-Oriented Software*. Englewood Cliffs, N.J.: Prentice Hall Press, 1990.

Yourdon, Edward and Constantine, Larry. *Structured Design*. New York: Yourdon Press, Inc., 1979.

Young, Douglas A. *Object-Oriented Programming with C++ and OSF Motif*. Englewood Cliffs, N.J.: Prentice Hall Press, 1992.

Index

A

abstract classes, 62, 78, 89, 174, 198, 207, 239, 305
  in an inheritance hierarchy, 136, 222, 224, 227
  role in design, 122, 124
abstraction, 62
actions, 99
ADA, 3, 74, 179
aggregate classes, 179
allocating classes, 305
allocating requirements, 16, 90, 205
  by classification, 91
  by encapsulation, 91
  data requirements, 297
  process requirements, 281
assembly diagram, 312
  examples of, 233
associations, 155
asynchronous requests, 257

attribute analysis, 17
attribute description, 210, 261
attribute design, 266, 267, 289
  design criteria, 297
  functional design, 296
  physical design, 297
  program design, 300
attributes, 17, 21, 22, 25, 28, 260, 307, 311
  accessing an attribute, 74, 182, 255
  also known as, 99
  attribute design, 291, 295, 299
  data-driven requirements, 31, 43, 52, 55, 62, 63, 84, 86, 87
  external attributes, 93
  internal attributes, 66
  private attributes, 71, 148, 149, 269

317

318 INDEX

attributes *(continued)*
  protected attributes, 146
  public attributes, 71, 146, 149, 205, 267, 291, 305, 306
  role in design, 97, 100, 101, 103, 145, 174, 177, 211, 252
  scope of an attribute, 149
  transform analysis, 287
  use in abstract classes, 122, 127
  use in concrete classes, 123

B

balking requests, 257
base classes, 139
binding, 151–153
  early binding, 152
  late binding, 152
business applications, 30, 32, 76
business area analysis, 46, 298
business functions, 297
business system design, 48, 301

C

C, 32
C++, 3, 75, 179
cardinality, 245, 246
CASE tools, 310, 311
  object-oriented criteria, 312
class categories, 144, 196, 223–225, 227, 312
  examples of, 145
class description, 203, 312
  composition of, 239
class design, 26, 205, 237
class diagram, 142
class libraries, 152, 196, 207
class relationships, 305
class shapes, 224, 232
classes, 62, 119, 134, 174, 217, 224, 237, 279, 311
classification, 28, 50, 65, 78, 84, 90, 304, 307, 308
  intersection of requirements, 110
  role in design, 108, 109, 111, 120, 137, 223, 243
client objects, 98, 116, 146, 158, 159, 162, 166
clients, 55, 57, 68, 73, 85, 88, 156
client/server model, 4, 131, 156, 284
client/server relationship, 169, 234
  member visibility, 244
cluster matrices, 44, 88
COBOL, 3, 33, 150, 151, 184
cohesion, 108, 142, 276
collaboration, 40, 62, 64, 72, 82, 145, 304, 309, 311
  also known as, 155
  collaboration relationships, 68, 199, 243, 295
  encoding collaboration, 180, 279
  role in design, 162, 175, 182, 183, 187
  standard object modules, 111
  use of concrete classes, 129
collaboration diagram, 2, 41, 89, 132, 156, 169, 174, 198, 218, 234, 288, 312
  also known as, 158
  composition of, 228
collaboration graph, 158
collaboration hierarchy, 85,

117, 119, 156, 178, 208, 306
collaboration lines, 234
common characteristics, 127
common data, 187
common modules, 183
commonality analysis, 220
component classes, 196
composite classes, 159
concrete classes, 62, 78, 89, 176, 198, 208, 239, 305
   in a collaboration hierarchy, 156, 229, 232, 234
   in an inheritance hierarchy, 136
   role in design, 123, 128
concurrency, 184, 213, 215, 279
   impact on operations, 246
   impact on requests, 256
conflict resolution, 140
constructors, 251
container classes, 159
context-sensitive referencing, 70, 75, 81, 134, 148, 200
   using polymorphism, 226
contract, 162, 164, 234, 245
conventional design, 26, 29, 30, 98, 264, 269
CORBA, 309
coupling, 112, 142, 276

D

data-driven design, 17, 22, 26, 30, 76, 267, 291, 296, 297, 300
database, 33, 93, 187, 283, 293
   database design, 302
   database management system, 293, 299, 302
   definition of a database, 294
   hierarchical database, 294
   network database, 294
   normalization, 302
   object-oriented usage, 161, 178, 268, 293
   relational data base, 294
   relational objects, 178
data couple, 287
data definition, 269
data-flow diagram, 19, 38, 88, 102, 171, 263, 266, 281–283, 312
data management component, 145
data referencing, 26
data relationships, 21
data requirements, 27, 30, 55, 84, 103, 177, 252, 261, 289, 307
data structure, 270, 302
data structure chart, 267, 297, 312
data structure diagram, 22, 302, 306
data structures, 260
dependency diagram, 158
design documentation, 14
destructors, 251
development approach, 9
   data-driven, 41
   formal models, 310
   model based, 14, 306
   object-oriented, 82
   procedural based, 13
   process-driven, 33
development environment, 309
device diagram, 161, 233, 235
distributed applications, 69, 72, 75, 81, 284
domain, 57, 60, 61, 175, 178

domain *(continued)*
  the apparent domain, 173
  the true domain, 173
domain design, 26, 199, 219, 220
domain model, 82, 85, 87, 196, 200, 217, 281, 304
  composition of, 196, 312
domain partitions, 178
dynamic link libraries, 86, 208, 310

E

encapsulation, 28, 40, 68, 78, 84, 90, 304, 307
  role in design, 113, 117, 120, 129, 148, 164, 169, 230, 243
  union of requirements, 114
entities, 17, 21, 22, 31, 87, 291
entity analysis, 43, 50, 56, 84, 109, 252, 291, 304, 308
entity relationship diagram, 21, 33, 44, 88, 103, 267, 269, 292, 299, 312
environmental model, 38, 282
essential model, 37, 280
event-driven programs, 72
events, 72, 247
extensibility, 76, 207, 227, 279

F

fields, 99
finite state machines, 284
flexibility, 93, 201, 306, 308
flow chart, 36, 266
FORTRAN, 36, 150, 151, 182
friend visibility, 147
functional design, 16, 18–21, 37, 44, 200, 281, 296, 304

G

gen-spec diagram, 142

H

handle, 186, 215, 247, 251
has-knowledge-of, 170
hierarchical collaboration, 73, 88, 204, 229, 239
hierarchical encapsulation, 73, 169, 231, 243
hierarchy graphs, 142
horizontal domain, 60, 145
human interaction component, 145

I

identifying objects, 304
identifying requirements, 16, 86, 199
  by a collaboration hierarchy, 88
  by an inheritance hierarchy, 88
  data requirements, 296
  process requirements, 280
implementation model, 39, 82, 92, 208, 211, 259, 285
  composition of, 209, 305
implementations, 155
implementing attributes, 291, 305
implementing operations, 274, 305
implementing requirements, 16, 210
  data requirements, 300
  process requirements, 285
information engineering, 9, 17, 31, 42, 60, 267, 290, 297, 308

information hiding, 148
information strategy plan, 44, 296
inheritance, 62, 64, 70, 82, 304, 309, 311
  common object modules, 111
  encoding inheritance, 179, 279
  inheritance factoring, 137, 139
  inheritance prototyping, 137, 139
  inheritance relationships, 65, 199, 294
  multiple inheritance, 139, 225
  referencing common attributes, 72
  referencing common operations, 71
  role in design, 134, 145, 175, 182, 186, 198, 241
  single inheritance, 139
  use of abstract classes, 125
  use of concrete classes, 129, 132
inheritance diagram, 2, 50, 51, 88, 127, 135, 174, 198, 218, 225, 213
  also known as, 142
  composition of, 221
inheritance hierarchy, 85, 111, 119, 135, 178, 179, 183, 187, 207, 306
inheritance lines, 225, 227
instances, 62, 106, 124
  class instances, 123
  concurrent instances, 185
  instance attributes, 248
  instance handle, 186
  instance operations, 248

object instances, 123
integrated design, 83
interface, 252, 309
interface model, 82, 89, 202, 205, 237, 282, 305
  composition of, 203, 312
  in a CASE tool, 312
is-a-kind-of, 141, 144, 222
is-a-part-of, 178

L

language extensions, 152
lateral collaboration, 74, 89, 204, 229, 239
lateral encapsulation, 74, 171, 231, 243
lattice structure, 134
layered approach, 82, 194, 310
life-cycle approach, 10, 16
  bar form, 11, 29
  embedded objects, 263
  object-oriented model, 55, 196
  prototyping model, 13
  pyramid form, 11, 31
  recursive use, 84, 194
  waterfall model, 13
life-cycle check points, 14
life-cycle framework, 10, 23, 307
life-cycle model, 12
life-cycle phases, 14
link libraries, 279, 310

M

makes-use-of, 158, 169
  for implementation, 229
  for interface, 229
mechanisms, 155

members of a class, 124
members of an object, 110, 250
memory allocation, 247, 251
memory management, 251
message connections, 158
messages, 158, 256
meta-classes, 140, 144, 224, 228
methodology, 2
methods, 99
module assemblies, 160, 312
  examples of, 161
module diagram, 236

N

naming classes, 243
naming objects, 219

O

object-oriented analysis, 137
object-oriented design, 2, 9, 16, 18, 22, 27, 84, 99, 308
  designing attributes, 291
  designing operations, 274
  its general usage, 54, 69, 76, 307
  within object engineering, 173, 213
object-oriented languages, 69, 179, 183, 184, 187, 207, 214, 251, 277, 293, 310
object-oriented model, 81
object-oriented programming, 137, 208, 213, 277
Object-Pascal, 179
object base, 296
  active objects, 269, 294, 295
  definition of, 294
  object-base management system, 293, 294, 299, 309
  object management environment, 310
  passive objects, 269, 294
  repository, 310, 311
object description, 204, 312
  composition of, 248
object design, 26, 210, 259
  design criteria, 220
  separate internal design, 76, 81, 86, 96, 98, 100, 113, 169, 181, 209, 306
  well-defined interface, 76, 81, 86, 93, 96, 98, 101, 113, 169, 198, 202, 306
object diagram, 158
object engineering, 8, 10, 16, 81, 173, 304
  in a CASE tool, 311
  layered development, 194, 217, 237, 259
  model-based development, 194, 306
  recursive nature, 84
  using object-oriented design, 54, 55
object interaction model, 158
object name, 249
object relationship model, 142
object structure chart, 312
objects, 2, 22, 55, 61, 63, 83, 87, 311
  associated with a class, 176
  classification, 120
  composition of, 144
  conceptual objects, 250
  concurrent objects, 186
  definition of, 97
  extent of an object, 215
  object design, 239, 260, 269

object interface, 55
persistent objects, 190, 247, 268, 269
role in design, 96, 100, 174, 176
scope of an object, 214
tangible objects, 250
the size of an object, 143, 276
transient objects, 190, 247
ODBC, 310
OLE, 310
operation decomposition, 17
operation description, 209, 260, 263
operation design, 262, 272
   design criteria, 276
   functional design, 281
   physical design, 281
   program design, 285
operations, 17, 18, 22, 25, 28, 307, 311
   also known as, 99
   external operations, 93
   internal operations, 66
   operation design, 260, 274, 283
   private operations, 71, 148, 149, 263, 264, 301
   process-driven requirements, 29, 30, 35, 41, 55, 62, 63, 84, 86, 87
   protected operations, 146
   public operations, 71, 146, 149, 167, 205, 253, 263, 275, 282, 305, 306
   role in design, 97, 100–102, 146, 174, 176, 211, 251
   scope of an operation, 149
   transaction analysis, 287
   triggering an operation, 73, 182, 255, 309
   use in abstract classes, 122, 127
   use in concrete classes, 123
over-loading, 132, 201

P

package diagram, 161, 235
parameters, 99
PASCAL, 32
persistence, 188, 213, 215, 247
   impact on attributes, 293, 294
physical design, 16, 18–20, 22, 38, 46, 281, 297, 305, 306
polymorphism, 70, 132, 140, 148, 200, 201, 226, 280, 309
   ad hoc polymorphism, 201
   for data referencing, 71
   for function calling, 71
   inclusion polymorphism, 201
   parametric polymorphism, 201
private members, 71, 148
private objects, 244
problem domain component, 145
process-driven design, 17, 18, 26, 29, 76, 263, 275, 280, 281, 285
process decomposition, 18, 35, 40, 56, 84, 113, 231, 251, 274, 304, 307
process design language, 20, 32, 39, 264
process referencing, 26
process requirements, 18, 27, 29, 55, 84, 102, 176, 251, 260, 272, 284, 307

process sequence diagram, 22, 46, 297, 299, 300
process structure chart, 266, 306, 312
process structure diagram, 48
processes, 17, 18, 22, 30, 87, 274
processing logic, 260, 264
processor diagram, 161, 235
program design, 16, 18, 20, 22, 39, 48, 285, 300
program diagram, 161
programming environment, 179
programming language, 207
protected objects, 244
protocol, 166, 168, 202, 256
   parmeteric polymorphism, 256
public members, 71, 148, 166, 250
public objects, 244

R

range, 214
re-usability, 61, 64, 76, 81, 93, 98, 148, 220, 308, 310
   pilot systems, 86
   prototypes, 86
   re-usable classes, 206, 227, 279
   re-usable hierarchies, 85, 296
   re-usable libraries, 279
   re-usable modules, 5, 55
   re-usable objects, 65, 68, 86, 148, 202, 279
real-time systems, 265, 284
request description, 204, 252, 312
   composition of, 252
request name, 255
requests, 93, 174, 202, 234, 245, 254, 305, 309
   examples of, 257
   in a collaboration hierarchy, 158, 162, 166, 168, 198, 204
   receiving requests, 57, 306
   sending requests, 59, 164
requirements, 96, 99, 110, 114, 164, 173
response, 57, 166, 168, 169, 257
response parameters, 254, 257
responsibilities, 99

S

schema assemblies, 161, 312
scientific applications, 29, 32, 76
scope, 149
sequential operation, 246
server objects, 98, 116, 146, 158, 159, 162, 166
servers, 55, 59, 68, 73, 85, 88, 156
services, 99
signature, 166, 168
Smalltalk, 179
software development, 29, 30
software engineering, 5, 8
source code, 213
source libraries, 207, 227, 279, 298, 310
state dependency, 265
state nets, 284

state of an object, 103, 190, 215, 247, 252, 265
   changes in state, 284, 285
   storing the state, 293, 294
state transition diagram, 20, 22, 39, 176, 263, 265, 282, 284, 312
state variables, 306
stimulus, 57, 166, 167, 169, 256
   stimulus parameters, 253, 256
   stimulus values, 167
structure chart, 20, 26, 39, 48, 171, 287, 312
   data structure, 267
   process structure, 266
structured design, 9, 17, 20, 30, 33, 34, 60, 263, 273, 275, 280, 307
sub-classes, 62, 66, 123–125, 136, 204, 208, 224
subjects, 196, 224, 227
subsystem diagram, 161, 233, 235
super-classes, 136
superior classes, 244
synchronous operation, 246
synchronous requests, 257

T

task diagram, 161, 235
task management component, 145
thread of control, 164, 184, 246
timed requests, 257

transaction analysis, 39, 231, 287
transform analysis, 39, 231, 287
transforming requirements, 8, 16–18, 23, 35, 307
   combined requirements, 55, 82
   data requirements, 21, 31
   process requirements, 19, 29
typing, 214, 228
   attribute types, 149
   data types, 150
   function types, 151
   operation types, 149
   strong typed language, 152
   weak typed language, 152

U

uses-for-implementation, 229
uses-for-interface, 229
utility classes, 145, 224, 227

V

validation, 14
verification, 14
vertical domain, 60
visibility, 70, 145, 213, 214, 250, 278
   examples of, 244

W

WOSA, 310